ALSO BY DAVID HALBERSTAM

The Noblest Roman

Making of a Quagmire

One Very Hot Day

The Unfinished Odyssey of Robert Kennedy

Ho

The Best and the Brightest

The Powers That Be

The Reckoning

The Breaks of the Game

The Amateurs

Summer of '49

The Next Century

The Fifties

October 1964

The Children

PLAYING

DAVID HALBERSTAM

FOR KEEPS

MICHAEL
JORDAN
AND THE
WORLD
HE MADE

BROADWAY BOOKS
NEW YORK

For Doug Stumpf

BROADWAY

A hardcover edition of this book was originally published in 1999 by Random House. It is reprinted here by arrangement with Random House.

PLAYING FOR KEEPS. Copyright © 1999, 2000 by The Amateurs Limited. All rights reserved. Printed in the United States of America. No part of this book may be reproduced or transmitted in any form or by any means, electronic or mechanical, including photocopying, recording, or by any information storage and retrieval system, without written permission from the publisher. For information, address: Random House, 201 East 50th Street, New York, NY 10022.

Broadway Books titles may be purchased for business or promotional use or for special sales. For information, please write to: Special Markets Department, Random House, Inc., 1540 Broadway, New York, NY 10036.

BROADWAY BOOKS and its logo, a letter B bisected on the diagonal, are trademarks of Broadway Books, a division of Random House, Inc.

First Broadway Books trade paperback edition published 2000.

Designed by Barbara M. Bachman

Library of Congress Cataloging-in-Publication Data
Halberstam, David.
    Playing for keeps: Michael Jordan and the world he made / by
David Halberstam. —1st Broadway Books trade paperback ed.
      p.   cm.
    Originally published: New York: Random House, © 1999.
    1. Jordan, Michael, 1963–   . 2. Basketball players—United States Biography.
    3. Chicago Bulls (Basketball team) 4. Basketball—United States History.
    I. Title. II. Title: Michael Jordan and the world he made.
    GV884.J67H35   2000
    796.323'092—dc21
    [B]   99–41931
                                         CIP

ISBN 0-7679-0444-3

10   24 23 22 21 20 19 18 17 16 15 14 13

CONTENTS

PLAYING FOR KEEPS

Paris, October 1997

IN THE FALL OF 1997, Michael Jeffrey Jordan, once of Wilmington, North Carolina, and now of Chicago, Illinois, arrived in Paris, France, with his team, the Chicago Bulls, to play a preseason tournament run by McDonald's, one of his principal corporate sponsors, as well as a very important corporate sponsor of the National Basketball Association. Even though it featured some of the better European teams, the tournament was not, in terms of the level of play, likely to be competitive for a top NBA team like the Bulls. Nor was it supposed to be: It was a part of the NBA's relentless and exceptionally successful attempt to showcase the game and its star players in parts of the world where basketball was gaining in popularity, particularly among the young. It was also done in no small part because it delighted the league's corporate sponsors by opening up and solidifying critical international markets. Not surprisingly, the American players did not take the competition very seriously. (Nor did their announcers. When the Celtics played in the tournament a few years earlier, their longtime announcer, Johnny Most, a man who did not always have an easy time with the names of *American* players, gave up completely, and fans back in Boston were treated to, "And so the short guy with the mustache throws it in to the tall guy with the beard. . . .")

The Bulls arrived to play for the hamburger championship of the world, as they often did these days, with all the fanfare of a great touring rock band. They were the Beatles of basketball, one writer had said years before, and in fact they flew over in the 747 normally used by the

Rolling Stones for their tours. There had been a time when Michael Jordan had regarded France as a kind of sanctuary, a place where he could vacation and escape the burden of his fame, sitting outdoors in front of a café and savoring the role of anonymous tourist. His appearance on the Olympic Dream Team five years earlier and his subsequent mounting international fame had ended that. His gross income had more than doubled, but he had lost Paris; he was as recognizable and as mobbed here as anywhere else. Huge crowds waited outside his hotel all day long hoping for the briefest glimpse of the man French journalists called the world's greatest *basketteur*. At the games themselves, the French ball boys seemed unwilling to serve their own team and wanted to work only with the Bulls. Some of the French players inked Michael's number, 23, on their sneakers as a means of commemorating their brush with greatness. At Bercy, the arena in which the games were played, copies of his uniform jersey sold for the equivalent of a mere eighty dollars.

JORDAN AWAITED LIKE A KING read the headline announcing his arrival in the sports daily *L'Equipe*. The games had been sold out for weeks, and the French press seemed ready to give Jordan head-of-state treatment and cut him some slack—when, during a press conference, he confused the Louvre, a great museum, with the luge, a dangerous winter sport, no one came down hard on him, though it was just the kind of mistake an American might make that normally the French would have seized on with great enthusiasm, to show the barbarity of the new world. MICHAEL HAS CAPTURED PARIS said another newspaper, and a writer added, "The young Parisians lucky enough to get into the Bercy must have dreamed beautiful dreams, for their hero had been everything they could have hoped for." Noting that Jordan was wearing his celebrated beret, journalist Thierry Marchand enthused, "We shall be able to call him Michel." *France-Soir* went even further: "Michael Jordan is in Paris," it said. "That's better than the Pope. It's God in person."

The games themselves were not, in fact, very good; if anything, they were just short of an embarrassment. The Bulls performed sluggishly but managed to beat Olympiakos Piraeus of Greece in the Final. Jordan's celebrated teammates Dennis Rodman and Scottie Pippen were not there, and Toni Kukoc, once the best player in all of Europe, scored five points. Jordan scored twenty-seven, but was not pleased to have to play without two critically important teammates. Staying home would have been more restful, as his toe was infected.

Jordan was well aware that the true triumph of Paris belonged less to him than to David Stern, the commissioner of the league. The tournament was not merely a reflection of the growing internationalization of the sport, which Stern helped engineer, but a celebration of the NBA's connection with McDonald's, one of America's blue-chip companies.

Stern, surrounded by most of the NBA executive staff and all sorts of McDonald's executives, had a wonderful time. Almost everybody in the basketball structure who was anybody had come. There was one notable exception, and that was the absence of Jerry Reinsdorf, the Bulls' owner, who rarely showed at things like this. Stern had pushed Reinsdorf to come and enjoy some *nachas,* a Yiddish word for pleasure, but that kind of *nachas* did not seem to appeal to the Bulls' owner, a man who seemed to prefer his privacy to the semidubious glitter and adulation that even an owner could be a part of at occasions like this. In addition, there had been a good deal of speculation at the last moment among the NBA people as to whether one other VIP, Dick Ebersol, the head of sports for NBC, would come. There was a powerful rumor sweeping Paris that even though the McDonald's championship coincided with the start of the World Series, Ebersol, whose heart was said to belong to basketball rather than baseball, would come to Paris instead of sitting in some highly visible box seat being seen by his own cameras at the Series.

Appropriately, given the symbiotic relationship between television and big-time sports, Stern and Ebersol were very close. Ebersol was wont to call Stern his boss, and Stern was wont to call Ebersol his. Stern was the most passionate and sophisticated of modern imagemakers, and it was Ebersol's company that determined which images went out to the nation. Stern understood, as not everyone in the world of sports did yet, that image was more important than reality in their business. He monitored the league's coverage of his sport *very* closely, and often seemed to take quite personally any departure on the part of the broadcasters and their cameras from what might be considered an image upgrade. In fact, when he had first ascended at the NBA, at a time when the league's image was still largely negative, he had been famous for calling network executives on Monday to complain about any image downgrade that might have taken place on Sunday.

Both Ebersol and Stern had a shared stake in the good name and the public image of basketball, especially in the public behavior of its best players, and the two men had worked closely in a collaboration that had seen a dramatic rise in the popularity of the sport, and in time in its network ratings as well. That the question even arose of whether Ebersol would bag the World Series for exhibition basketball games against weak opponents in a foreign land for a cup handed out by a hamburger company showed how much the fortunes of the two sports had changed in recent years. This World Series, between Cleveland and Florida, did not, as it was about to begin, seem to the average fan a particularly tantalizing one; it seemed to lack the sense of a traditional rivalry, or at the least, some degree of geographical animosity. It pitted a Miami team, one that few fans knew very much about, against a Cleveland team that was talented but not well known. Neither team, to the general sports public, had yet created any kind of persona. There was no rivalry, neither historic nor geographic, between the two teams. Eventually Ebersol had stayed in America to watch the Series. Stern had teased him about that—"Dick, if you want to stay back in the States and watch the lowest-rated World Series in history, feel free to," he had said. (Stern was wrong: It was not the lowest-rated World Series; the one in 1993, when for the first time the NBA Finals had been rated higher than the World Series, was.)

It had been a very happy couple of days for David Stern: Baseball was struggling with its image and its ratings, and Michael Jordan was bringing the NBA a full measure of fame in a city normally slow to grant homage to American celebrities. Then, on the night of the last game, a tall black man nearing middle age came over to the section where Stern and his wife, Dianne, were sitting. "I want to thank you for saving my life," Micheal Ray Richardson told Stern. Richardson had once been a great young star in the NBA, a high draft choice of the Knicks, but he had self-destructed on alcohol and drugs, and he was one of the first players severed from the league under its three-and-out policy. He was now playing for a team in Nice and lived there year-round. "If it hadn't been for you, I would have kept on using. Because of what you did, I stopped. I'm clean now." It was a poignant moment: Down on the floor, some of the best players in the game were taking their last warm-up shots, and here was someone who had once played at their level, forty-two years old now, a little heavy around the waist, who had virtually destroyed himself with drugs and who was still playing in a low-level league, most of his money surely gone, but grateful for the fact that he still had his life. Normally, David Stern was a man with a quick comeback, but on this occasion he was almost silent. He put his arm around Richardson and gave him a small hug.

At that moment, with the 1997–1998 season about to start, Michael Jordan stood at the very pinnacle of his fame. Not only was he the greatest basketball player in the world, but there was some debate as to whether he was the greatest basketball player of all time. A considerable body of expert opinion believed that he was. If anything, the question had gone beyond basketball: Was he the greatest team athlete of all time? Comparisons were made with the legendary Babe Ruth, a player who stood far above even the best of his peers. Of course, the comparisons were being made by young men mostly in their thirties, and Ruth himself had died forty-nine years earlier and played his last game in 1935.

The comparisons being made within the world of basketball were equally hard to calibrate. Jordan's Bulls had at that time won the championship the last five seasons in which he had played the entire season, but the Boston Celtics had won eleven championships in the thirteen years they had the great Bill Russell, a dominating big man of exceptional intelligence and equal quickness and power. That, of course, had been in a very different league, with far fewer teams, where the athletic level of most players was not as high as it was in the contemporary game; it was a league in which the talented Celtics general manager, Red Auerbach, had almost always been able to fleece his rivals and thus surround Russell with exceptional teammates. Therefore, the Jordan-Russell question remained unanswerable, although the noted basketball expert and filmmaker Spike Lee has come up with a devastating argument: Jordan was the best of all time, he said, because he was so complete a player—there was nothing he could not do on the court: shoot, pass, rebound, play defense. Therefore, Lee said, five Michael Jordans could beat five Bill Russells or five Wilt Chamberlains. It was a fascinating point, for it spoke to a certain kind of athletic completeness.

Whether he was the best or not, there was no doubt that he was the most compelling and most charismatic athlete in all of sports in the nineties. He was the athlete whom ordinary people throughout the world most wanted to see play, particularly in big games, because he seemed always to be able to rise to the occasion.

He was already rich, having made an estimated $78 million in salary and endorsements in the previous season, and the coming season seemed to promise as much or more. He was well on his way to becoming nothing less than a one-man corporate conglomerate, and he now spoke of the owners of the basketball team he played for as well as the heads of the sneaker company and hamburger company and soft-drink company he represented as "my partners." He was arguably the most famous American in the world, more famous in many distant parts of the globe than the President of the United States or any movie or rock star. American journalists and diplomats on assignment to the most rural parts of Asia and Africa were often stunned when they visited small villages to find young children wearing tattered replicas of Michael Jordan's Bulls jersey.

There was considerable statistical evidence of Jordan's value to the sport, of how much his own personal luster had added to its amazing success and profitability. Certainly the sport was already on something of a roll, as a result of the remarkable achievements of Magic Johnson and Larry Bird, when Jordan's career began to flower, but his arrival in the playoffs added greatly to the game's audience, bringing to the sport millions of people who were fans more of Michael Jordan than of professional basketball. The television ratings climbed fairly systematically in his earlier appearances in the Finals, reaching an unheard-of 17.9 in his third visit, against Phoenix, in 1993. That rating translated into an estimated 27.2 million Americans. But what was interesting about these numbers to Dick Ebersol was that so great a percentage was directly attributable to Jordan.

The network and the league learned the truth of this the hard way a year later when Jordan was on his baseball sabbatical and the Bulls did not make the Finals. The ratings of most of the other playoff games stayed about the same, but the Finals' ratings dropped dramatically to 12.4, or about 17.8 million Americans. That meant that roughly a third of the audience had been there essentially for Michael Jordan. Two years later, when he returned to basketball and brought the Bulls to two more championships, the ratings went back up to 16.7 in 1996 and 16.8 in 1997, or roughly 25 million people.

More and more the phrase "the best who ever laced up a pair of sneakers" was being used to describe him. "If Michael Jordan is not flawless in his craft," the *Chicago Tribune*'s Melissa Isaacson once wrote, "he is as close as we have to solid evidence that anything is possible." Again and again he was named the most valuable player in the league and in the playoff Finals, again and again he seemed able to lift a group of good but not always great teammates to a championship level. At the conclusion of each series, the MVP was duly awarded a new car, presented by David Stern himself; in recent years, Stern had taken to calling himself Jordan's car valet.

More and more frequently, the word *genius* was used to define Jordan. Harry Edwards, a black sociologist at the University of California, Berkeley, not a man lightly impressed by the achievements of contemporary athletes, wary that the self-evident achievements of black athletes cast an imposing shadow over many black youths and pull them away from careers in other fields, nonetheless talked about Jordan representing the highest level of human achievement, on the order of Gandhi, Einstein, or Michelangelo. If, he added, he were in charge of introducing an alien being "to the epitome of human potential, creativity, perseverance and spirit, I would introduce that alien life to Michael Jordan." Doug Collins, Jordan's third professional coach, once spoke of Jordan belonging to that rarest category of people who are so far above the norm, men like Einstein and Edison, that they were identifiable geniuses. Collins had never used that phrase before, certainly not about a player. Jordan's talented teammate B. J. Armstrong, frustrated in his early years with the Bulls by his failure to rise to Jordan's level and apparent expectations, and believing the game was so much easier for Jordan than it was for anyone else, had gone to the library and checked out a series of books on geniuses to see if there was anything he might learn about how to deal with or be like Jordan.

And when Jordan, after his third championship, decided to retire, he reluctantly went to tell his coach, Phil Jackson, what would surely be the worst of news for him. He outlined the likelihood of his retirement, but added that if Jackson chose to talk him out of it, he would not leave. He did it somewhat warily, fearing the ever-deft Jackson might indeed talk him out of it. But Jackson shrewdly answered that he would not try to change his mind, that Michael had to listen to and heed his own inner voices. But he reminded Jordan of the singular pleasure he would be denying millions of ordinary people when he left the game because his gifts were so special. His talent, Jackson said, was not merely that of a great athlete but transcended athleticism to become an art form. His gift was along the lines of a Michelangelo, Jackson said, and therefore Jordan at the least had to understand that it belonged not just to the artist but to all those millions who stood in awe of the art itself and derived, in a life otherwise filled with the mundane, such pleasure from what he did. "Michael," he added, "pure genius is something very, very rare and if you are blessed enough to possess it, you want to think a long time before you walk away from using it."

Jordan listened carefully. "I appreciate that," he said, "but I feel like it's something that's done—it's over." He heeded his inner voice and left the game, but the fact that Jackson had not at that moment advanced his own narrow interests cemented an already strong relationship and in some way helped create the process that would one day expedite his return.

What was special about him was his effect not so much on the fans as on his peers. "He's God's child," teammate Wes Matthews said in Jordan's first year, and there were a number of players more talented than

Matthews who agreed, albeit using slightly different wording. "Jesus in Nikes," in the words of Jayson Williams of the Nets.

Jerry West, acknowledged as one of the five or six greatest players of all time, who eventually became the general manager of the Lakers, also spoke of him as a genius, saying it was amazing how complete he was, not just as a basketball player but as a young man summoned, because of his talents, to become the public image of a once-troubled league. "It's like a generous God sprinkled a little more gold dust on Michael than he did on anyone else," he said.

After Jordan led the Bulls to their second title, Larry Bird said that there had never been an athlete quite like Jordan. "On the scale of one to ten, if all the other superstars are eight, he's a ten," Bird said.

"Michael Jordan," said author and Chicago resident Scott Turow, "plays basketball better than anyone else in the world does anything else."

In addition to his singular physical gifts, he had an unmatched will to excel, an inner competitive rage, a passion unmatched by anyone else in the game. That had become more and more clear over the years. Earlier in his career, observers dazzled by the artistry of his play had tried to explain his rise to a championship level solely in terms of his talent; now, late in his career, when he could no longer pull off all of the individual moves that had once set him apart, it had become increasingly obvious that what had distinguished him was his indomitable will, his refusal to let either opposing players or the passage of time affect his need to win. "He wants to cut your heart out," Doug Collins once said, "and then show it to you." "He's Hannibal Lecter," said Bob Ryan, *The Boston Globe*'s expert basketball writer, referring to the merciless antihero of *The Silence of the Lambs*. And his own teammate Luc Longley, asked by a television reporter for a one-word description of Jordan, said simply, "predator."

By the beginning of the new season, presumed by many people to be his last, Michael Jordan had so dominated not just the game itself but the psyche of American sports fans that all sorts of sportswriters were already beginning to write articles about who would become the Next Michael Jordan. One of the first of these, written by Mike Lupica for *Men's Journal*, had nominated as possibilities Grant Hill of the Detroit Pistons, a young man gifted both on the court and off it but perhaps not as charismatic as Jordan; Kobe Bryant, the teenage star of the Los Angeles Lakers, perhaps more exciting than Hill but possessor of a woefully incomplete floor game; and, of course, Shaquille O'Neal, the huge man-child of the Lakers, a young man of self-evident talent and power. All of this talk about the new Michael Jordan amused the old Michael

Jordan greatly. "I'm still here," he told his friend and trainer Tim Grover. "I'm not going anywhere. Not yet."

That there had been even one Michael Jordan seemed in retrospect something of a genetic fluke, and the idea that anyone would arrive in so short a span of time and do what he did both on and off the court seemed highly unlikely. For beyond the surpassing quality of his athletic skills, there were other qualities at work as well. He was dazzlingly good-looking, with a smile that seemed to bestow pleasure and comfort on all its recipients, and he inevitably became well aware of the benefits that derived from being that successful in his sport, and that good-looking as well—the uses of both fame and beauty. He was tall, but not too tall—six foot six—with a body that seemed eerily flawless, with wide shoulders, a slim waist, and only 4 percent body fat. (The average professional athlete is closer to 7 or 8 percent fat, and the average American male is somewhere between 15 and 20 percent.) He cared about clothes and wore them extraordinarily well; he was quite possibly the best dressed American male since Cary Grant, though the range of clothes he could look good in was vastly wider. He looked better in sweats, one member of the team that shot his Nike commercials noted, than most movie stars did in black tie. "Make me look good," Jordan would admonish Jim Riswold, the Portland advertising man who was in charge of the Nike commercials, before each shoot. Riswold once told him, "Michael, I could shoot you pushing little ladies into onrushing cars in the middle of downtown traffic or throwing puppies into boiling water and you'd still look good."

In the past, America's ideal of beauty had always been an essentially white one; American males had looked longingly in the mirror hoping to see Cary Grant or Gregory Peck or Robert Redford. Jordan, shaved head and all, had given America nothing less than a new definition of beauty for a new age.

What America and the rest of the world saw now was nothing less than a kind of New World seigneur, a young man whose manner seemed nothing less than princely. He was most assuredly not to the manner born—his paternal grandfather had been a tobacco sharecropper in North Carolina. His parents were simple and hardworking people, the first in their families to enjoy full rights of American citizenship, and they produced a young man who carried himself with remarkable natural grace. Because of the loving way he had been raised and because of the endless series of triumphs he had scored over the years, his personal comfort zone was dauntingly high: he had an inner confidence that was simply unshakable.

His manner with all kinds of people in even the briefest of meetings was usually graceful, particularly for someone subjected to so many pressures, and those upon whom he smiled seemed the grander for it. He had charm, was very much aware of it, and used it skillfully and naturally, rationing it out in just the proper doses, holding it back when it served his purpose. He was easy to like, and people seemed to vie to be liked by him. Veteran sportswriter Mark Heisler once noted in a magazine article that he had never wanted an athlete to like him so much as he did Michael Jordan. A vast variety of magazine editors longed to print articles about him because, as with Princess Diana of England, his photo on their covers greatly increased newsstand sales. All kinds of powerful, rich men competed to be his friend, to drop his name casually, and, of course, to play golf with him.

Because of all this, he had become a great salesman as well as a great basketball player. He sold the game of basketball to millions of people in different lands who had never seen it played before and to millions of others who had never seen it played *like this* before. He sold Nike sneakers if you wanted to jump high, Big Macs if you were hungry, first Coke and then Gatorade if you were thirsty, Wheaties if you needed an all-American cereal, and Hanes underwear if you needed shorts. He sold sunglasses, men's cologne, and hot dogs. Mostly he sold himself, and it was, year by year, as championship title was added to championship title, as one last-minute heroic replaced the previous one, an easy sell. There was already a statue commemorating his career outside Chicago's United Center, where he played, a building he hated but which had been built in no small part to accommodate the greater number of fans who would pay large sums of money to come and watch him. The statue showed him as Jump Man—Michael rising to dunk—but compared to the man it commemorated, it seemed oddly crude and heavy, art not so much imitating life as diminishing it.

Each year he seemed to add a new chapter to the legend in the making. As this new season was about to begin, probably the most remarkable chapter thus far had been written the previous June, when he woke up violently ill before Game Five of the NBA Finals against the Utah Jazz. Whether it was altitude sickness or food poisoning no one was ever sure. Later, it was reported that he had woken up with a fever of 103. That was not true: His temperature was high but not that high, not over 100, but he had been so ill during the night that it seemed impossible that he would play. At about 8 A.M., Jordan's bodyguards called Chip Schaefer, the team trainer, to tell him that Jordan was deathly ill. Schaefer rushed to Jordan's room and found him curled up in a fetal position, wrapped in blankets and pathetically weak. He had not slept at all. He had an intense headache and had suffered violent nausea throughout the night. The greatest player in the world looked like a frail, weak zombie. It was inconceivable that he might play that day.

Schaefer immediately hooked him onto an IV and tried to get as much fluid into him as possible. He also gave him some medication so he could rest that morning. More than most people, Schaefer understood the ferocity that drove Michael Jordan, the invincible spirit that allowed him to play in games when most high-level professionals were betrayed by their bodies and, however reluctantly, obeyed them. During the 1991 Finals against the Lakers, when Jordan badly injured his toe while hitting a crucial jump shot to tie a game, Schaefer struggled to create a shoe that would protect Jordan's foot in the next game. Jordan eventually rejected the shoe because it hindered his ability to start and stop and cut. "Give me the pain," he had told Schaefer.

Now, seeing him that sick in the Salt Lake City hotel room, Schaefer had a sense that Jordan might somehow manage to play, that Michael Jordan might, as he sometimes did in situations like this, use this illness as a motivational tool, one more challenge to overcome. He did make it to the locker room before the game, still frail and weak. Word circulated quickly among journalists that he had the flu and that his temperature was 102, and many assumed that he would not play. One member of the media who was not so sure about that verdict was James Worthy of the Fox network. He had played with Michael Jordan at North Carolina and watched him emerge as the best player in the NBA, and he knew how Michael drove himself. The fever meant nothing, Worthy told the other Fox reporters. He'll play, Worthy warned. He'll figure out what he can do, he'll conserve his strength in other areas, and he'll have a big game.

In the locker room, Jordan's teammates were appalled by what they saw. Michael's skin, normally quite dark, was an alarming color, somewhere between white and gray, Bill Wennington remembered, and his eyes, usually so vital, looked dead. As the game was about to begin, an NBC television crew showed pictures of a frail and haggard Jordan as he had arrived at the Delta Center, barely able to walk, but they also showed him trying to practice. It was one of those rare moments of unusual intimacy in sports, when the power of television allowed the viewer to see both Jordan's illness and his determination to play nonetheless. This was to be a unique participatory experience: When before had illness and exhaustion showed so clearly on the face of such an athlete so early in such a vital game? At first, it appeared that the Jazz would blow the very vulnerable Bulls out. At one point early in the second quarter, Utah led 36–20. But the Bulls hung in because Jordan managed to play at an exceptionally high level, scoring twenty-one points in the first half. At halftime his team was down only four points, 53–49. It was hard to understand how Jordan could play at all, much less be the best player on the floor. The unfolding drama of the event transcended basketball.

He could barely walk off the court at halftime. During the break, he told Phil Jackson not to use him much in the second half—just in spots. Then he came out and played almost the entire second half. He played a weak third quarter, scoring only two points, but Utah still could not put Chicago away. Late in the fourth quarter, when the camera closed on him as he ran downcourt after a basket, Jordan looked less like the world's greatest athlete than the worst runner in some small-time marathon, about to finish last on a brutally hot day. But what he looked like and what he was doing on the floor when it mattered were two separate things.

With forty-six seconds left and Utah leading by a point, Jordan was fouled going to the basket. "Look at the body language of Michael Jordan," the announcer Marv Albert said. "You have the idea that he has difficulty just standing up." He made his first foul shot, tying the score, then missed the second but somehow managed to grab the loose ball. Then, when the Jazz inexplicably left him open, he hit a three pointer with twenty-five seconds left, which gave Chicago an 88–85 lead and the key to a 90–88 win. He ended up with thirty-eight points, fifteen of them in the last quarter. It had been an indelible performance, an astonishing display of spiritual determination; he had done nothing less than give a clinic in what set him apart from everyone else in his profession. He was the most gifted athlete in the league, but unlike most other supremely gifted players, he had an additional quality rare among superb artists whose chosen work comes so easily: He was an overachiever as well.

Both supremely talented and singularly driven, he had not always been the most tolerant of teammates. But in the years after he had returned from his unsuccessful sojourn to professional baseball, he had often seemed to be a new and on occasion more mellow Michael Jordan. His teammates liked him more. He was a dramatically easier person to play with. Yes, he was still hard on Luc Longley and Toni Kukoc and could be caustic with both men on occasion. Much was expected from those two players and much was not always delivered. But the almost gratuitous, punitive quality of his tongue had softened. Obviously part of the reason for that change was that he had already climbed so many mountains, the three earlier championships not only confirming his greatness but ending the hateful argument, which had haunted him for so long, that he was a great individual player but a person who did not lift his team, and therefore not a winner. Another part of the change came from the fact that he had been away for almost two years from something he loved. Older and more mature, he was at a point in his career when he knew that time was working against him and he had to savor the sweetness of the game, and that part of the game itself was the friendship with teammates and the draining nature of a long and exhausting NBA season and how they all reacted to it. And part of it, of course, was the fact that when he had failed at baseball, he had for the first time realized what it was for a player struggling against his limits— for he had known no limits before, certainly no limits on his individual performance.

The flu-driven victory over Utah had helped cement the Bulls' fifth NBA championship, and with it a widely held conviction that they were one of the greatest teams of all time, if not *the* greatest. But it was not always easy to locate them on the pantheon of greatness. Yes, they had won five championships, and yes, during the 1995–1996 season, they had won a record seventy-two games. In the eyes of some basketball people, the question of their exact place in basketball history remained somewhat in doubt, in part because some of their own personnel seemed limited and in part because they had never been tested by another great team, as the Celtics and Lakers tested each other in the eighties. The Bulls beat some very good teams, but did they beat that many great teams? They were, some fans felt, an Ali without a Frazier.

That argument overlooked how hard their roads to the titles were. In the early stages of the championship run, they beat a very, very tough Detroit team that did not look that good on paper but was sheer murder to play against. It overlooked as well that early in the playoffs over a number of years they had disposed of a very good Cleveland team, which might have been of championship calibre if it had not run into Michael Jordan. The Bulls had a habit of beating teams that, until they had entered the Conference Finals or the Finals themselves against the Bulls, looked very imposing, and often looked better than the Bulls— until the Bulls actually played them and picked them apart. A key to their continued success was their remarkable defensive skill. Very good teams composed of very good players were, in a long series against the Bulls, made to look ordinary.

A good example of this was the Bulls' victory over the Orlando Magic in the 1996 Eastern Conference Finals. The Magic were, on paper at least, an awesome young team. They had gone to the Finals the previous year. They had all-star players at three critical positions, center, power forward, and point guard: Shaquille O'Neal, Horace Grant, and Penny Hardaway. If anything, Orlando seemed in position to become a dynasty. Yet the Bulls swept the Magic in four games, and Orlando was never the same again; soon thereafter, O'Neal went west, hoping to bring the next dynasty to California instead of Florida.

2.

Wilmington; Laney High, 1979-1981

I F MICHAEL JORDAN was some kind of a genius, there had been few signs of it when he was young. The Jordans of Wilmington, North Carolina, were solid people, a middle-class black family. ("Actually upper middle class," observed Michael Wilbon, a noted columnist for *The Washington Post* who was black, "but there's a tendency in the media to move black families down a notch in terms of class.") James Jordan and Deloris Peoples met after a basketball game in Wallace, North Carolina, in 1956. She was fifteen, and he was going off to the Air Force, but he told her he would be back some day to marry her. She eventually went off too, to the Tuskegee Institute in Alabama, but she returned home soon, homesick. Not long after her return, they were married.

James Jordan was very mechanically skilled; it was said that he could repair almost anything. When he retired from the Air Force, still quite young, he had moved his family back to North Carolina, and took a job at a General Electric factory. He started there as a mechanic and in time became a supervisor of three departments. His wife worked as a teller at a local bank. The Jordans enjoyed three incomes: his job, her job, and his not inconsiderable Air Force pension. North Carolina was now integrated after the great civil-rights struggles of the sixties, and the Jordans were eager to become a part of a newer, more modern, postfeudal South; more, they were catapulted forward in no small part by that great conduit of blacks into the middle class, the United States military. Both parents worked in essentially integrated jobs, and their five children attended integrated schools. Both parents were determined that their children be neither blinded nor burdened by race, and their children were under constant orders to treat everyone the same. The less they themselves factored in race as a determinant, they taught their children, the less it would be factored in against them. In order to be treated well, they were to treat others well. They were expected to, and in time did, have friends on both sides of the color line. When Michael was young and someone called him a nigger, it was more the painful exception than, as it had once been, the rule of life in North Carolina. His parents handled the moment deftly; it was a sign, they said, that the other child was ignorant, and Michael was not to lower himself to the level of ignorant people.

The senior Jordans, children of parents who had the most marginal economic and educational opportunities, and beneficiaries themselves of profound legal and social change, were determined that their children would rise to higher levels and finish college if at all possible. When, after Michael's third year in college, Dean Smith, his coach, thought that Michael had learned all he could at Chapel Hill and that it was time for him to turn pro, Deloris Jordan strenuously resisted the idea. She wanted her son to stay and graduate. "Mrs. Jordan," Smith finally said, "I am not suggesting that Michael give up his college degree. I am only suggesting that he give up his college *eligibility!*"

It was a very disciplined family, one with a good many rules, the first of which was that you were not to waste your talent and you were always to work hard. James Jordan, a military man with a strong sense of order, pushed his sons hard in athletics. But the real driving force, friends of the family thought, was Deloris Jordan. She was the parent who kept raising her expectations for her children, letting them know in different ways that the more that was given to them, then the more that was expected from them. They were not to be defeated by chance obstacles or momentary anxieties. In the back of her mind, she later said, was her own experience of having been allowed to come home from Tuskegee as a freshman, in tears, because she was homesick: "My mother should have put me right back on the train. I wanted to correct that error with my own kids," she once said. When Michael got in trouble in school one day for cutting classes, she took him to work with her at the bank, left him in her car, which was parked just outside a window where she could keep an eye on him, and made him study all day. Of the five children, Michael was by his own account the laziest, or at least the one most skilled at talking his way out of doing his share of household chores, shrewdly leveraging his allowance to buy his way out if possible. His father later joked that it was a good thing Michael found a place as a professional athlete because he was too lazy to hold any other kind of job.

Nor was Michael, like his father or his older brother Larry, very good at working with machines. This was a source of some frustration, since being mechanically skilled was considered important in that household. On occasion, James Jordan would tell Michael to "get in the house with the women." James Jordan, whom his son greatly admired, always worked with his tongue sticking out between his teeth, a habit he had picked up from *his* father; years later, Michael Jordan played basketball with *his* tongue sticking out through his teeth. In time, thousands of young kids played basketball with their tongues sticking out between their teeth, largely because James Jordan had repaired his car with his tongue sticking out.

The key to Michael Jordan's fierce competitiveness, friends from his junior high, high school, and college days thought, lay in his rivalry with his older brother Larry, a formidable athlete in his own right, though he was packaged in a wrong-sized body. Larry had great strength, athletic ability, and ambition but was simply too small to achieve in sports what his heart and his will and his talent normally would have earned him. "He was a stud athlete," Doug Collins once said. "I remember the first time I saw him—this rather short, incredibly muscled young man with a terrific body, about five seven, more a football body than a basketball body. The moment I saw him I understood where Michael's drive came from." Or as Clifton (Pop) Herring, who coached both at Laney High in Wilmington, once said, "Larry was so driven and so competitive an athlete that if he had been six two instead of five seven, I'm sure Michael would have been known as Larry's brother instead of Larry always being known as Michael's brother." And Michael himself once noted, "When you see me play, you see Larry play."

For a long time, even after Michael began to outgrow him, Larry could jump as high as his brother; in another time, in a school that had a more varied athletic program, said Ron Coley, one of Laney's assistant coaches, Larry would have been a gymnast—it would have been the perfect sport for him. (Eventually Larry Jordan would play for the Chicago team in the 6-4 and under professional basketball league, but eventually he became convinced that the team was just exploiting his connection with Michael and dropped out.)

Younger siblings often measure their places in the universe against the apparently unbreachable and permanent gap that separates them from their older, seemingly more talented and accomplished siblings. In this case, Michael was doing it against a brother who was fighting his own war against his physical size. As a result, every day the Jordan backyard saw some form of athletic combat: day after day the two of them banged against each other on the small court that James Jordan

had built. Larry was unbelievably strong, and for years he could dominate his brother; late in their high school years, however, Michael finally began to grow—much taller than anyone in his family. When that
happened, Michael believed his father tried to balance things out by
complimenting the shorter Larry more than he complimented Michael.

If anything, that drove Michael to work even harder on the court.
What was interesting, Michael's friends from those days thought, was
the combination of intense rivalry and powerful sibling affection that
Michael had for Larry. It was the most loving of protracted sibling
struggles. "Michael and Larry had obviously competed wildly as boys,
and Larry loomed very large in his life," said David Hart, a North Carolina team manager who was a roommate and a suitemate of Michael's
at Chapel Hill. "Michael really loved Larry and talked about him all the
time—really revered him. But if Michael had gone far beyond Larry as
an athlete, he never let it affect his feeling for his brother—his emotional connection and his respect for his brother were very strong.
When his brother was around, he dropped all his mounting fame and his
accomplishments and became nothing more than a loving, adoring
younger brother." But he could also tease him. Years later when Michael
was a star in the NBA, they played in a pick-up game. Michael looked
down at Larry's feet. "Just remember whose name is on your shoes," he
said. It was the ultimate triumph of the younger sibling.

The first signs of Michael's athletic excellence came in baseball: He
pitched several no-hitters for a very good Wilmington Little League
team. When he was twelve, he pitched for Wilmington in the eastern regional Little League championship game. The winner would go to the
Little League World Series. He pitched a two-hitter that day, but his
team lost 1–0. Basketball, a sport that also attracted him, seemed something of a distant dream, largely because he was only about five foot
eight and skinny. There was a brief time when, about to enter high
school and frustrated with his height, he started hanging from a chin-up
bar in order to stretch his body. His growth would come in time, but not
from do-it-yourself stretching exercises.

There were already signs that he had a good deal of talent. Harvest
Leroy Smith, a classmate and close friend who in those days played basketball with him practically every day, thought he was the best player on
their ninth-grade team—he was small, but he was very quick. "You'd
see him get a shot off, and you'd wonder how he did it, because he
wasn't that big," Smith said, "but it was the quickness. The only question was how big he was going to be—and how far up he would take his
skill level." If his skills were slightly less than those of some of the other
players, what lifted him up was his competitiveness. "He and I practiced

every day together and he *always* had to win. If it was a game of Horse and you beat him, you would have to play another game until he won," Smith said. "You didn't go home until he had won."

The summer after ninth grade, Jordan and Smith both went to Pop Herring's basketball camp. Herring, who was the varsity basketball coach at Laney, where they would enter in the fall, encouraged both of them to try out for the varsity as sophomores, Smith because he was six foot six, Jordan because he was so quick. Neither of them had yet come into his body, and almost all of the varsity players, two and sometimes three years older, seemed infinitely stronger at that moment when a year or two in physical development can make all the difference. In Smith's mind there was no doubt which of the two of them was the better player—it was Michael by far. But on the day the varsity cuts were announced—it was the big day of the year, for they had all known for weeks when the list would be posted—he and Roy Smith had gone to the Laney gym. Roy Smith's name was on it, Michael's was not.

It was the worst day of Jordan's young life. The list was alphabetical, so he focused on where the *J*s should be, and it wasn't there, and he kept reading and rereading the list, hoping somehow that he had missed it, or that the alphabetical listing had been done incorrectly. That day he went home by himself and went to his room and cried. Smith understood what was happening—Michael, he knew, never wanted you to see him when he was hurt or when you had gotten to him.

Years later, the Laney coaches realized that they had not handled the decision well, not cushioning it and letting Michael know that his time would come, and they had made it seem even worse when they had taken his close friend. Roy Smith thought the coaches were crazy—he might be taller, but he knew Michael was better than he was. "We knew Michael was good," Fred Lynch, the Laney assistant coach, said later, "but we wanted him to play more and we thought the jayvee was better for him." He easily became the best player on the jayvee that year. He simply dominated the play, and he did it not by size but with quickness. There were games in which he would score forty points. He was so good, in fact, that the jayvee games became quite popular. The entire varsity began to come early so they could watch him play in the jayvee games.

Leroy Smith noticed that while Jordan had been wildly competitive before he had been cut, after the cut he seemed even more competitive than ever, as if determined that it would never happen again. His coaches noticed it, too. "The first time I ever saw him, I had no idea who Michael Jordan was. I was helping to coach the Laney varsity," said Ron Coley. "We went over to Goldsboro, which was our big rival, and I entered the gym when the jayvee game was just ending up. There were nine players on the court just coasting, but there was one kid playing his heart out. The way he was playing I thought his team was down one point with two minutes to play. So I looked up at the clock and his team was down twenty points and there was only one minute to play. It was Michael, and I quickly learned he was always like that."

Between the time he was cut and the start of basketball in his junior year, Jordan grew about four inches. The speed had always been there, and now he was stronger, and he could dunk. His hands had gotten much bigger, Smith noticed. Suddenly Laney High had the beginning of a very good basketball team, and its rising star was Michael Jordan. He was as driven as ever, the hardest-working player on the team in practice. If he thought that his teammates were not working hard enough, he would get on them himself, and on occasion he pushed the coaches to get on them. If anything, the coaches thought he was not selfish enough in his days at Laney, and they pushed him to shoot more—in no small part because he could open up things for his teammates. But the more they pushed, the more he seemed to resist. Finally, the coaches went to James Jordan to enlist him in their cause. "I don't know," the senior Jordan said, "I've made it a policy to stay out of the coaching business—I don't want to intervene, I don't want to be one of these Little League dads. It doesn't seem proper for a father. But I guess I can if you ask me to." In Michael's junior year, Laney went 13–10, and in his senior year it was 19–4, and only a fluke defeat in a regional tournament kept the team from going to the state finals.

Chicago, November 1997

I N THE FALL OF 1997, as the Bulls returned to Chicago from Paris to start their run for a sixth title, there was trouble in paradise, if Chicago was paradise. Rarely had an organization with so many talented people been so rife with bad feeling. Whether this team would be able to return intact was a question that hung over everyone during the 1997 playoffs. The division between management and players and coach had grown more and more bitter over the years.

For a time after the fifth championship, it appeared unlikely that Jerry Reinsdorf would rehire Phil Jackson. In part because of the overall escalation of coaches' salaries—college coaches who had never won anything in the NBA were now being brought in to turn around dormant franchises at $4 million or more a year—Jackson's asking price had become very high. He had just finished up a one-year contract under which he had been paid $2.7 million, which made him, it was believed, the highest-paid coach who was not also a general manager. All in all, it was a goodly wage, especially for someone who only a decade earlier had been considered one of the leading figures of what counterculture there was in the NBA. There were other coaches out there, talented ones, who would be glad to work for a mere $1 million or $2 million a year, men properly eager to coach Jordan and Pippen (if not Rodman); why then, went the thinking of management, be caught in a bidding war for someone who in the end was only a coach and therefore seemingly the most replaceable of parts? But there was a strong reason, and it profoundly affected Jackson's asking price: Michael Jordan had sworn he would play only for Phil Jackson; otherwise, he would not return. It was blackmail of a sort that translated into massive public pressure to bring back Jackson in order to bring back the team and allow it to win or lose its title on the court.

This moment revealed something of the harder edged, meaner qualities of sports as their costs reached chillingly expensive levels in the late 1990s: the struggle for rightful (or unrightful) paydays and the covert and not so covert ego struggles that somehow always accompanied victory in a televised age. In a way, what was taking place in Chicago was a classic economic confrontation: It posed the question of what the true dollar value of talent was in an entertainment society that put a premium on great talent. Did traditional market realities extend to a fantasy world like this? It pitted on one side one of the smartest, toughest owners in sports, a man with a reputation of being a singularly shrewd negotiator, against the coach and players of the best team in sports, buoyed by an almost unprecedented championship run, one of the players being the most popular athlete in America. A fascinating, occasionally bitter, struggle between the dream world of sports and the cold world of business was taking place.

For a variety of reasons, tensions among the Bulls were far worse than normal, even at this championship level of professional athletics, where ego conflicts and frustrations over salaries and playing time were constants. Part of the reason for the unhappiness was the particular nature of the Chicago ownership. The managing partner, Jerry Reinsdorf, had made his millions in commercial real estate, an arena known for its tough negotiations, where the rigor of the negotiating process was part of the pleasure of the game and an end in itself to those skilled at it. Where basketball was the game his players played best and his coaches understood best, negotiating—tough, unsparing, often brutal, the person across the table treated momentarily as an adversary—was the owner's true game. Nor was the negotiating process made easier by the fact that Reinsdorf was represented in the difficult, often pyrrhic earlier rounds of the negotiations by Jerry Krause, whose skill with people was not considered a particular strength and who tended to personalize all conflicts. By the time agent and owner reached the climactic final rounds of negotiations, bad feelings often abounded.

Reinsdorf was considered to be an accomplished master at negotiating. Whether in fact he truly understood how the success of the Bulls—the many championships and the attendant unprecedented public interest—changed the nature of negotiations, taking them from the most private of arenas to the most public, was another question.

Reinsdorf was very smart and very tough, an immensely successful man with few illusions about the nature of his business. His net worth had gone up staggeringly over the last twenty years, in no small part because of his success with the Bulls. There was a simple equation at work here: The better Michael Jordan played, the richer and more influential Jerry Reinsdorf became. He had been a young tax lawyer in Chicago, working first for the IRS, then like many others who started that way, he had learned the tax codes and become a tax adviser to professional men in Chicago, teaching them how to incorporate. He learned in those years, he later said, "that if you try to be loved and respected, you'll end up neither." In time he set up his own company, Balcor, which, in the real estate boom of the late eighties, syndicated real estate deals. He did well with Balcor, selling it to American Express in 1982 for $53 million. He agreed to stay on for five years as CEO. He left in 1987. The real estate laws in the country changed quickly and dramatically, and soon there was a foul stench to Balcor. American Express eventually took a $200 million write-off for Balcor in one quarter. Later, not everyone at American Express thought kindly of Reinsdorf. He was a self-made man, having made his fortune on his own. Despite limited finances, he had taken control of two Chicago sports teams—the Bulls and baseball's White Sox—in a somewhat hostile environment and a somewhat alien city, while others—smoother, better pedigreed, and better credentialed—had stood by and mocked him. If there was a weakness to him, some people thought, it was that he was too used to winning, too used to getting his way, too accustomed to finding the weakness in his opponent. He had done so well after starting out with so little that he seemed to think that he was both smarter and tougher than anyone else, or failing that, at least smarter than those who were tougher and, most important, tougher than those who were smarter.

In dealing with his teams, he had at least one significant advantage over most owners: He retained a certain emotional distance from both the team and especially the players. Over the years, he had gotten on reasonably well with Michael Jordan. Their business meetings and occasional social interactions had generally been sufficiently pleasant and marked by mutual respect; Jordan, who greatly respected business success as an end in itself, seemed to admire a man who had made that much money on his own. But Reinsdorf seemed to have little need to be Jordan's buddy, and it was not a surprise that he had not made the trip to Paris to bask in the Bulls' glory. That kind of ego boost was not something he either needed or coveted.

Reinsdorf understood from the start that the more your ego needed a boost from a personal connection with your players, the more leverage you deeded over to them and their agents at the negotiating table. By contrast, many contemporary owners seemed to be wannabe high school or college athletes who had turned into passionate, committed fans now glorying in their association with these supreme jocks and in their ability to bring their friends into the locker room to meet the star players. For many owners, wealthy beyond comprehension, but often surprisingly anonymous in their principal businesses, the ego aspect of sports ownership was more important than the business side.

That was not true of Reinsdorf. He was a businessman, first and foremost. Though he was wont to talk of his boyhood in Brooklyn and his love for the old Dodger teams of the fifties and to show visitors to his office a seat from Ebbets Field, as an owner he was able to view sports ownership as a very Darwinian business. His view of the process was oddly detached, almost clinical.

When Reinsdorf bought the White Sox eighteen years earlier, he had noted, he was somewhere between the ages of the players and their fathers; now, near the turn of the century, he was older than their fathers and had even less desire to hang out with them. Sometimes he was on the committees that interviewed prospective baseball or basketball team owners, and he was surprised to hear them say in different ways that they wanted in because they did not get enough respect or acceptance in their local communities, particularly given their wealth. That kind of attention, he believed, was the worst thing about owning a sports team—it was a constant and unwanted invasion of privacy.

To people for whom negotiations were not a kind of life's blood, Reinsdorf's manner in negotiations could at critical moments seem like that of a bully. Reinsdorf was well aware of Jordan's special status, as well as the fact that Jordan played a critical role in making him a rich and powerful man. He knew the dangers inherent in any kind of public wrangle with America's foremost sports icon. No one who tangled with Jordan, on or off the court, ever came out the better for it. But his negotiations with Jordan (which nonetheless often dragged on and were exhausting) were very much the exception. Few other athletes he dealt with held Jordan's unique leverage at contract time. His reputation for toughness followed him in two sports. There were a goodly number of baseball people who, because of Reinsdorf's pivotal, hard-line position during the 1995 strike, absolutely despised him. They believed that he had conned the otherwise weaker small franchise owners into prolonging a labor dispute in support of salary restrictions and then, the moment the strike was over, betrayed their position by signing the ever-surly Albert Belle for a monstrous sum.

Reinsdorf even fought the NBA in court over the right to broadcast a certain number of Bulls games. No one sought a conflict with him lightly. To Todd Musburger, an entertainment agent who represented Phil Jackson and who struggled with him over a period of years in their ongoing contract negotiations, Reinsdorf represented the darker side of American capitalism; he had become accustomed to dealing with people who were in a weaker position than he, and doing it on his, not their, terms.

What was clear, however, was that some of the strengths that served him so well in the very private and semisecret world of big-time real estate did not serve him nearly as well in ever more public dealings with brilliant, creative, and talented but vulnerable young athletes who were constantly fearful of injury and whose playing careers were, to them at least, terrifyingly short. For Reinsdorf tended to zero in on the weaknesses of his adversaries and almost always found them, and he exploited them adroitly, perhaps in the long run too much so for his own good and the good of his organization. If there was one thing players feared, it was injury and the end of their careers; therefore, the one thing they were vulnerable to was the long-term contract—it was unusually seductive to them, yet in the long run it was often less costly for the team than a series of short contracts might be. Because of this, the two sides were always uneven when they negotiated: Businessmen had long careers, and the essential constancy of their money was a given; players had very short careers, and they often came to the table in the beginning with very little in the way of savings. Reinsdorf was very aware of this. He was also aware that agents, a powerful force in the new equation, liked long-term contracts, too, because they meant guaranteed money.

Reinsdorf understood early in Michael Jordan's career, for instance, that Jordan's one weakness in negotiations was a desire to protect his corporate image and his almost unique commercial value to the companies whose products he sold; therefore, Jordan was wary of holding out and looking like one more spoiled contemporary athlete. He knew as well that Scottie Pippen's vulnerability came not just from his childhood poverty but the fact that his father had suffered a stroke as a reasonably young man and had spent much of his abbreviated life in a wheelchair; therefore, Pippen desperately wanted some kind of long-term security and would tend to opt for a long-term contract. In almost all negotiations, however, Reinsdorf's short-term victories tended to create problems in the long run, dealing as he was with *talent*, men of unusual skills and artistic temperament who had comparatively short professional careers and who almost always ended up unhappy.

Over the years, because of constant contract squabbles, the public image of the Chicago Bulls management had become nothing less than a disaster, though this did not seem to bother Reinsdorf very much, as he fancied himself reasonably immune to public opinion. He seemed to take some measure of pride in his reputation for toughness; but that single-minded force as a negotiator that had served him so well in his first profession made him on occasion look unusually difficult and insensitive in his second. That his principal deputy, Jerry Krause, whatever his other professional talents, seemed to have an almost unique knack for offending many of the people whom he dealt with compounded the problem.

A number of agents had come to believe that dealing with the Chicago organization was simply much more difficult than dealing with most basketball organizations. Negotiations tended to follow a long and difficult pattern: The agent would start out dealing with Krause, Krause would set a relatively low figure from which he said he would not budge, then a long debilitating process would begin. Krause often seemed to be insulting about the skill of the player in these meetings. In the end, with both Krause and the agent exhausted and bleeding from mutually inflicted wounds and a stalemate seemingly in the offing, Reinsdorf would step in and the deal would be completed rather quickly. Reinsdorf, of course, would come out unscathed.

The one agent who eschewed this pattern was David Falk, Michael Jordan's agent who understood the dynamic and usually dealt directly with Reinsdorf. "I'm not going to get worn out by all that stuff," he told one friend in Chicago. "I'm not going to spend all that time dealing with a stalking horse who's taking all those bullets for the owner in the early rounds." Of course, the fact that Falk represented Jordan gave him special dispensation to go to Reinsdorf from the start.

But blame for the tensions on the Bulls was hardly the exclusive property of the team's owners. The other factor causing the unusually high degree of unhappiness was the remarkably volatile nature of player salaries. Some older, draconian labor laws, which had deeded all power to the owners, had collapsed virtually overnight, producing historic and rapid economic change in the last few years. As if overnight, power had passed from owners to players and their agents. Suddenly, an era in the NBA seemed to last only four or five years. A salary that had seemed like a dream deal for a player in one era might well come to be something of an embarrassment compared to what other, younger, less experienced players were making in the next era, perhaps only two or three years later and long before a contract was to run out. This dangerous and explosive phenomenon was also a source of embarrassment to the player's agent—no agent wanted to hear his player complain that a lesser player with smaller stats had gotten a larger contract from another team. The world of sports had become so volatile that a player's career could now span two or three financial eras, and a given contract could span two. Thus, Michael Jordan entered the league with a salary of $6.3 million over seven years, at the time the third highest salary ever given a rookie, which put him well above all but a small handful of veteran players, but now that entire amount was what he got for playing roughly one fifth of a season.

Jordan's contracts were in fact instructive about the explosive nature of sports finances and about contracts done under even the best conditions. The first one, very handsome indeed for a rookie who was only the third pick in the draft, had been signed before Reinsdorf took over the Bulls and was considered good at the time for an as-yet-untried young player, putting him well above many talented and experienced all-stars. Three years into it, based on Jordan's singular skills and his unique ability to draw fans both in Chicago and on the road (and to television sets at home), and given the fast-escalating nature of the NBA pay scale, it was obviously anachronistic.

That first contract was technically for five years, guaranteed, with options for two more years at $1.1 million and $1.3 million. Somewhere in the fourth year of it, Reinsdorf and Falk agreed to discuss redoing it. That brought together across the table two of the toughest negotiators in the world of basketball. If many agents thought that dealing with Reinsdorf (not to mention Krause) was more difficult than dealing with any other owner in basketball, there were owners who felt that dealing with Falk was a nightmare all its own, and there were several NBA general managers who would on occasion pass on prospective draft choices only because they were represented by Falk. "Dealing with David," Reinsdorf once said, "is never, never done without pain." But oddly enough, the two men got on reasonably well. Each man, aware of the other's power and how much was at stake, had dealt relatively skillfully with the other. In fact, there were people in the NBA who thought that in certain negotiating scenarios you could take Falk and make him the owner and make Reinsdorf the agent and there would be no difference at all in a transcript of their talks.

Falk believed he was the one to broach the idea of exploring a new contract. Reinsdorf asked whether, if he did *not* choose to redo the contract, Jordan would still play out the old one and play hard. Absolutely, Jordan answered. He had signed it and given his word, and he would fulfill it and always play hard. With that they proceeded to work out the new contract. Essentially it was between Reinsdorf and Falk, although Jerry Krause was present at all their meetings, not a great asset thought Falk, since he seemed determined to refer to Michael as a good, or very good player, but not one of the two or three best players in the game, and he seemed, either consciously or unconsciously, to denigrate Michael's role in making the Bulls an enormous financial success. Over a period of almost a year—with some fourteen long, exhausting sessions—they worked out a new contract that spanned eight years, from 1988 to 1996. The new contract averaged out to around $3 million a year, or a total of around $24 million. Falk liked to note that it took Jordan up from roughly $1 million to about $3 million a year; if it was judged only as a five-year extension on the old contract, it was close to $5 million a year, very high at that time. At the time, it was considered the largest salary ever given to an NBA player.

When Reinsdorf signed the new eight-year deal with Jordan, he told friends that he was scared—had he paid too much and for too long a period? What if Michael, who had missed most of his second year with a broken foot, now suffered a career-ending injury? What would other owners think? He remembered telling Jordan at the time that if he was a player he would have serious reservations about signing on for so many years. But Jordan seemed to want the contract, and he gave Reinsdorf his word that he would never come back and try and renegotiate, a promise he kept. But long the contract was, in an exploding business, and by the time the contract had run its course at the end of the 1996 season, Michael Jordan was woefully underpaid, one of the great bargains in professional sports. To some degree, Reinsdorf recognized that: He and Jordan had gone to dinner at the beginning of Jordan's baseball career, and Reinsdorf had told him, "Even I have to admit I had too good a deal," and suggested paying him in full for the year he was in baseball. (Later that day, Jordan called David Falk and told him, "I just made four million dollars.") In Reinsdorf's mind, it was something he owed Jordan. When the baseball adventure came to its end in March 1995, Falk called Reinsdorf to say that Jordan wanted to come back to the Bulls and asked Reinsdorf if he would pay for the whole season, even though much of it had already passed. Reinsdorf said yes, of course he would.

But by the end of the 1996 season, Reinsdorf had to renegotiate with Jordan in an era that bore no resemblance at all to the time in which he had signed his earlier two contracts. A number of forces that had been gathering for some time were now profoundly affecting all labor negotiations: the coming of virtually unrestricted free agency for veteran players; the coming of a salary cap for a team; the so-called Larry Bird exemption, which allowed a team to exceed salary-cap restrictions to keep its own marquee player; and, finally, an agreement with the Players' Association in the early nineties that prohibited a player from renegotiating an existing contract. When the Bird exception was instituted, salaries for a handful of star players rocketed out of control. What had once seemed a very large salary now suddenly seemed very small. In the summer of 1997, Kevin Garnett, a talented young player who had not attended college and had entered the league at the age of nineteen, rejected a seven-year offer from the Minnesota Timberwolves for some $103 million. Eventually, he signed for some $126 million for seven years, all of it guaranteed.

Whether or not Kevin Garnett was worth that much—he had yet to play in an all-star game when he signed—he and his agent knew that the very legitimacy of the ever-vulnerable Minnesota franchise itself was at stake. If Garnett, perhaps the most talented player in the short history of the team, departed after only two or three years, the franchise would have no credibility. Season-ticket sales would drop. Perhaps the franchise would have to be moved to some city in the Sunbelt where a rich new owner awaited his moment of fame. The general manager of the Timberwolves who had signed the deal with Garnett was Kevin McHale, son of a mine worker in the Minnesota iron range. Back when he played for the University of Minnesota in the late seventies, McHale thought that upon graduation from Minnesota he would coach and teach, making perhaps $15,000 a year. Instead he had been good enough to play in the NBA, and as the third player taken in the 1980 draft, he signed his first contract with Boston, three years for a total of $600,000. Now in a financial era that seemed light years away from his own entrance into the league, McHale was most unhappy with what he felt he had to do in the Garnett deal, even though he liked Kevin Garnett very much as a person. He hated the wild escalation of salaries in recent years and now suddenly here he was, a person forced by circumstances to set the newest level of the ever-escalating market. He himself, he noted, had become what up to then he had always condemned. For a time, appalled by what he was doing, he thought of leaving his job with the Timberwolves and going to work as a broadcaster for NBC, and he talked seriously with Dick Ebersol of NBC about coming aboard. In the end he stayed in Minneapolis. But Garnett's salary, roughly $18 million a season, thus became the benchmark, and that year general managers who had upcoming negotiations with their star players had a new phrase—they talked about whether their young players were worth "Kevin Garnett money." Though the baseline had, not surprisingly, been set by one of the league's weaker teams, desperate to keep its legitimacy and fan base, it immediately affected the salary structure of the entire league. Other, more experienced players on winning teams, represented by agents eager not to lose face to Garnett's agent, used Garnett's deal as a negotiating point.

The Garnett signing, like a number of other humongous new deals in the NBA, also cast its shadow over the Bulls. For most of the championship run, the Bulls management, by dint of shrewd negotiations and a number of long-term contracts, had gotten one of the great bargains in contemporary sports. Through the 1996 season, the Bulls' fourth championship, Jordan had been paid roughly $4 million a year; Pippen had been weighted down by a long-term contract which by then paid around $3 million; Rodman had come aboard in the 1995–1996 season for about $2.5 million. Toni Kukoc was making around $4 million. Phil Jackson was at the end of a three-year deal that paid him $800,000 a year, which made him a singular bargain. It had been in any real sense the last payroll of the old basketball order.

But most of the bargains were ending in the summer of 1996. That meant that the price of the 1996–1997 team was going to be significantly higher, most particularly for Jordan, who was a free agent and most of whose immense financial rewards until that moment had come from companies such as Nike, McDonald's, and Gatorade, not from the Bulls themselves. Negotiations thus might be a little difficult. In time, Reinsdorf met with Jordan, Falk, and Curtis Polk, a Falk associate, for dinner at the Ritz-Carlton in Chicago. Jordan was known for delighting in sticking his agent for very expensive bottles of wine, often around $500 a pop (this was known among those who knew them well as Jordan out-Falking Falk), and this night was no exception, Reinsdorf recalled. No offers were made at the dinner, and everyone proceeded quite tentatively, aware that a lot was at stake and wary of drawing lines that might later be hard to cross or might send Jordan to another city for more money in a snit. It had been a generally pleasant evening, a moment spent trying to establish some mutual goodwill for what might be tougher days to come. They talked about how many years Michael had played in Chicago and how well they had all dealt with each other in the past and how few problems they had had. It was the kind of evening with the owner to which other Bulls players were most decidedly not privy.

As they prepared for the negotiations to come, each side had its deterrents, although by this time Jordan's were considerably more powerful than those of Reinsdorf. Jordan knew all too well that he was the single greatest bargain in sports, that Reinsdorf and his partners had become very rich from his gifts, and that the value of the Bulls had gone from around $15 million to more than $250 million because of his deeds. It was a moment of maximum leverage for Jordan. He could easily leave Chicago and go to New York, the center of the world's media, a city in which he loved to play, and a locale that would not displease his corporate sponsors. If he went, he would more than likely take the championship with him. Certainly there were other talented free agents out there who would love nothing more than to play with him and his friends Patrick Ewing and Charles Oakley in New York. The threat posed by the idea of Jordan going to the hated, snobbish East Coast city and taking the title with him was not insignificant and would not increase the already marginal popularity of Reinsdorf or Krause in Chicago. Nor, for that matter, would it help the future sales of either Bulls or White Sox tickets. But Jordan was also wary of doing that. The Bulls were his team; he understood the historic value of playing for only one team and wearing only one logo. The players he admired most in sports, such as Larry Bird and Magic Johnson, had played for only one team, and he knew that the more championships the Chicago Bulls won led by Michael Jordan, the more it set him apart from the crowd and placed him in his proper slot in the record books. Johnson had won his five with the Lakers, Bird his three all with the Celtics, and those numbers were not wasted on Jordan, who took team loyalty seriously anyway.

A few weeks later they met again. Jordan at one point suggested that Reinsdorf put an offer on the table, and if it was in the right range he would say yes, and if it wasn't he would say no. Falk then added that if the offer was in the ballpark, they would work out a deal. But if it was inadequate, they would immediately go to another club, and if that club made a great offer, they would not come back to Chicago for another offer. That kind of goad had become standard operating procedure for agents in the modern era: Ownership got only one good chance, and if blown, the player might be gone. It was, Reinsdorf was aware, not unlike having a pistol pointed at you, but he was relatively confident that because of the Larry Bird exception it would be hard for anyone else to offer more to Jordan. Still, it was a considerable incentive not to waste too much time haggling and not to lowball Jordan.

Reinsdorf began by suggesting a two-year deal for $45 million, $20 million and $25 million respectively. Falk and Jordan came back and asked for $55 million over two years. Reinsdorf said that that scared him. Suppose Jordan was hurt? The size of the contract made him uneasy: It was the equivalent of an entire team payroll in what was virtually the same era. In the end, they settled on $30 million for only one year. The decision to make it for only one year reflected Reinsdorf's doubts about how long he wanted to pay that much money, championship or no. (As it turned out, the $55 million suggested by Falk was a bargain; Reinsdorf eventually paid $63 million for those two years.)

When Chicago beat Utah in 1997 for title number five, Jordan himself pleaded on national television during the victory celebration for management to bring the team back and thus give them the right to defend the title on the court. Jordan's demand reflected the growing belief on the part of the players that the ownership wanted to break up the team. It was said to have angered Reinsdorf, who felt that Jordan was forcing his hand by going public at that moment, which of course he was. Reinsdorf was not pleased by the way the most popular athlete in the world had used a public victory celebration, with millions and millions of people watching throughout the world, to begin a new round of negotiations. It was a true coup. Jordan had turned to a powerful force—the force of public opinion—to sustain a golden era of basketball in a city starved for victories.

There was a reason Jordan had struck at that moment: The coaches and players were aware that ownership did not necessarily want to go forward. During the 1997 Finals, Reinsdorf had taken Phil Jackson to lunch in Park City, Utah, where the team was staying. Over lunch, he suggested to Jackson that if the coming negotiations got too difficult, the Bulls would be willing to pay him a handsome sum—one or two million dollars—not to come back, in part because he would have lost his chance at other coaching jobs, but only if he left silently. It was the first sign that the ownership was battening down the hatches for a hard summer ahead. So in the weeks and months after the final victory over Utah, there were serious questions in the air of whether the team would return intact and whether Phil Jackson would return to coach. Locally, the question of Jackson's negotiations with the Bulls dominated the local media, becoming more important than issues of the city's schools or the local municipal budget. Jackson was not merely a coach, he was a critical domino, for Jordan, knowing that Krause wanted to bring in another coach, had already issued his de facto challenge that the only coach he would play for was Phil Jackson.

Just before the 1997 season had ended Jordan had joked with reporters that if he were in charge he would pay himself $50 million a year (a raise of some $20 million), Jackson $50 million, Pippen $75 million—a raise of some $72 million. Then he realized he had forgotten Rodman. "Dennis gets $25 million. He's probably worth more, but my budget is really tight," Jordan said.

Clearly winning the fifth championship had not lessened the tensions in the Chicago organization. There had been a significant increase in bad feeling between Jackson and Krause in the past year (if not between Jackson and Reinsdorf—that was always problematical), and Jackson seemed to go back and forth in his feelings about the owner and in addition between Pippen and Krause, and thus the organization.

If Jordan was to come back, and public pressure in Chicago and throughout the league virtually demanded it, he wanted the team brought back essentially intact, and that meant that a number of other dominoes had to be put in order first. One domino was Scottie Pippen, the player who allowed Jordan to be Jordan at this stage of his career, a player whose game meshed perfectly with Michael's.

Pippen, unlike Jackson, Jordan, and Rodman, was still under contract to the Bulls. As the 1997 season ended, he was now perhaps the single best bargain in the NBA and most unhappy about it. Chicago could trade him and get a reasonably handsome return in terms of other players, but if it traded him, both Jordan and Jackson might well pack it in. The team would be torn apart, and the blame placed largely on Reinsdorf and Krause. But if the owner waited a year, both Jackson and Jordan might be gone anyway, and Pippen, who made no secret of his dislike for the Chicago management, would almost surely opt for free agency, and they would get nothing in return. So the Pippen choice was a difficult one—it was about going for the short run and a chance to win a sixth title and thereby please the fans—by far the more popular choice—or taking the draconian step of trading him, alienating both Jackson and Jordan, and breaking up a team before its championship run was over.

Pippen's dislike of Krause and the organization was palpable. He was arguably the second-best player in the league, but at $3 million a year, he was the 122nd best paid. Part of that was his own fault, and Pippen realized that: He had opted for security earlier on and had signed a long-term contract back in an era when players could, if their value went up, still renegotiate their contracts. The rules had changed in the middle of that contract, prohibiting the right to renegotiate, and Pippen had been locked in. But even in circumstances like these, there were ways in which owners with some degree of subtlety could signal to players they admired and who had done well by them that in time their rightful payday would come. The Bulls management had given no such signal. Quite the reverse. Krause and Reinsdorf seemed particularly loath to give any public credit to Pippen's special role in the championship years: Though the Bulls had never won a championship without Michael Jordan, they had never won one without Scottie Pippen either.

If anything, they indicated that their interest in him had significant limits and that they believed that his body was breaking down. If they were giving any signal, thought Pippen's agent, it was that his big payday would have to come with another organization. Pippen had come perilously close to being traded for Shawn Kemp of Seattle a year earlier, and in June 1997 it was obvious that Chicago was still interested in moving Pippen. Krause was said to be eager to start building the new post-Jordan team; Reinsdorf, who would take the heat for it, was somewhat warier. But on draft day in the spring of 1997, Pippen was nearly traded once again. This time the projected deal would have sent him to Boston. It was a complicated deal. Luc Longley, the big center, was apparently part of it as well, and at one point the deal included Denver, which would turn over its top draft choice, potentially a player named Keith Van Horn, whom a number of general managers, including Krause, badly coveted. But at a certain point, New Jersey traded up and got Van Horn, and the deal fell through.

Reinsdorf later said that the decision not to trade Pippen and to go for the sixth championship had been his. He said he did it with mixed feelings: He had seen too many teams grow old overnight, he said, to be swayed by false sentiment. As Reinsdorf remembered it, he had asked Krause how good the young players they were going to get were going to be, whether they were going to be important pieces for a future championship, and Krause had not been confident enough. With that, Reinsdorf said, he decided to go for the sixth championship. He had no great sympathy for Pippen's feelings, he said. Trades were part of the business—players, even great players, were traded all the time. Jordan was not traded because Jordan was basketball's Babe Ruth. Scottie Pippen was not. It was a hard, cold world, and it was a business world. He had been blunt in letting Kyle Rote, Jr., one of Pippen's agents, know what he was doing at all times. What probably happened was a combination of things: the ideal trade for Pippen falling through and the awareness that Jordan and Jackson both wanted Pippen back, as did, of course, the fans. If the team was broken up now, one outside public relations consultant warned, the public reaction would cripple both sports franchises for a generation. That did not, of course, mean the Bulls might not yet trade Pippen, but he had not gone for draft choices. With that, the long and arduous process of bringing back the rest of the team began.

Jordan's statement greatly added to Jackson's leverage that summer. Normally coaches, even winning coaches, were expendable, the first to go in bad times, the easiest to hire for presumed good times. But Jordan's loyalty to his coach had changed the entire equation. "How lucky for Phil," one of the former Bulls coaches said at the time, only slightly enviously, "he's got great representation—a very good agent in Todd Musburger, and the greatest agent in the history of sports in Michael Jordan. Hard to beat that combination."

In recent years, the negotiations on Jackson's behalf between Todd Musburger (brother of the ABC broadcaster Brent) and the Chicago organization had grown increasingly tense. One reason was the extraordinary change in the going prices for coaches, a changed market value that was hard for the owner of a winning team to accept because it was being set primarily by teams that were notorious disaster areas. But a rising tide had in fact lifted all ships in the NBA. Because there were so many inflated payrolls and because so many players drawing huge salaries seemed to remain immune to any kind of motivation, the price for credentialed coaches who could motivate them—Chuck Daly, who had been a wizard in Detroit, Pat Riley, who had done so well in both Los Angeles and New York, plus the wunderkind college coaches—had risen accordingly. If coaches were not yet getting Kevin Garnett money, they were now getting what until only recently had been Michael Jordan money.

This was all quite new, and the idea of paying star-quality money to a coach was alien to the Chicago ownership. Back in 1992, when Jackson, on his way to his second championship, signed for $800,000 a year for three years, Musburger thought it well beneath Jackson's market value, perhaps half of what other coaches with comparable skills were making; he was sure that Jackson deserved far more. But Jackson was not, Musburger thought, an ideal client for wars like this: He was not sufficiently materialistic, and did not seem to care that much about the money. He wanted a fair return on his skills, but he was uncomfortable with the mounting hostility that the negotiations were producing. At that point, Jackson believed the Chicago organization had been very good to him, and $800,000 a year still seemed like a great deal of money. At one point, during what were increasingly unpleasant negotiations, Krause told Musburger, "No coach for the Bulls will ever make a million dollars. Write it down."

But Krause was wrong. Buoyed by championship number four and the rising expectations and pressures to keep winning in Chicago, the Bulls paid $2.7 million to Jackson for the 1996–1997 season. Musburger had at one point suggested a long-term contract, but there was no interest at the other end, a clear sign that by then the ownership saw a limited shelf life for this team and its coach and was already planning a new order with a coach more amenable to management's wishes. A year later, when the question of Jackson's salary for 1997–1998 came up, the negotiations became infinitely more bitter. Dealing with Krause and Reinsdorf, Musburger thought, was what dealing with the North Koreans must be like—they liked to pick obscure sites in which to meet, buildings that Reinsdorf owned, and they wanted to meet in secret, even though every sports fan in Chicago knew that re-signing the coach was a top priority and that the ability to keep Jordan and other key players flowed from that act.

By this time, the bad feeling between Krause and Jackson was affecting the upper levels of the organization. In the time since Jordan had returned from baseball, Krause had made little secret of his desire to break up the Jordan team. He had made that all too obvious in different statements, all of which seemed to say or imply the same thing, that his own idea of a dream team was a championship team in Chicago without Michael Jordan on it, a team where a great deal more credit would go to the organization—that is, Jerry Krause. At the time, he seemed to be involved in an intense professional romance with Iowa State coach Tim Floyd, and Jackson heard from friends that Krause had been sending videotapes of Bulls games to Floyd. A number of people close to the Bulls thought that Krause was in a private rage because Jackson, the man he had brought in from the cold to coach, a man who was in the technical sense under him in the hierarchy, had become infinitely better known and more popular in Chicago than he was. When Jackson was introduced at the championship celebrations, the fans cheered wildly, and when Krause's name was mentioned the booing was equally intense.

What surprised Musburger in the long and difficult negotiations with Krause was Krause's almost negative view of Jackson's place in this particular universe: It was very different from how most basketball people saw Jackson. Others saw how well he had done over a number of very hard years, working endless hours in preparation for games, particularly in the playoffs, coaching with great skill and holding together the complicated and often conflicting egos that can either make or break a great NBA team. But when Krause spoke about Jackson, Musburger thought, he talked about what Reinsdorf and Krause had done for *him*, taking him off the street when he was unemployed and giving him this plum of a job, and why therefore he should be grateful to them and, in effect, know his place. What was interesting about Krause when he spoke like this, Musburger thought, was that it was completely unconscious—he was incapable of seeing a complicated issue from any viewpoint save his own.

Those who dealt with both Reinsdorf and Krause thought there was a considerable difference in their attitudes in the negotiations. With Reinsdorf it was rarely about ego and almost always about money. With Krause it was quite different. Krause's resentment of Jackson seemed largely about who got the credit for these glorious championship years. Life was unfair: coaches were visible, always on camera; general managers were not. Jackson, by nature of his personality, got on very well with a wide variety of people both in the media and out; Krause, by the nature of his personality, tended to offend an equally wide variety of people, especially those in the media, people whom he by and large despised and whose mission in life—find out and tell as much as they could about the inner workings of the Chicago Bulls—seemed to him to be the work of enemy agents. The word he used in private to describe serious media representatives was "whores."

Krause's mantra, one that greatly irritated the players, particularly Michael Jordan, was the importance of the organization in the winning of these championships. The Bulls' 1997–1998 press book, in words approved by Krause, said that Krause was the architect of the five titles and was responsible for the acquisition of every player on the Bulls except for Jordan. One summer, broadcaster Billy Packer called Krause to get Jackson's home phone number, explaining that he was writing a book about exceptional coaches who had brought their teams to a championship level. Packer wanted to see if he could find any commonality in the ways the coaches went about their business and the ways they thought. "Why do you want to talk to him?" Krause asked. "*I'm* the one who put the team together—all *he* did was coach it." It was, thought Packer after he hung up, a revealing—and sad—conversation. "I knew he said things like that from time to time about organizations not players winning championships, but I hadn't realized he really believed it," Packer later said.

Negotiations with Jackson for the 1997–1998 season grew more and more bitter. Common cause had long ago been lost. It was clear that Reinsdorf hated dealing with a coach through his agent. After the season was over, the owner vowed he would never again hire a coach with an agent because coaches were part of management and should not have agents. Musburger, in turn, believed that Reinsdorf was unaccustomed to being challenged in business deals. Even powerful agents did not want to cross him for fear it might be hard on their future players. But Musburger primarily represented television people and had no fear of making a permanent enemy, if need be, of Reinsdorf.

The roots of the conflict were relatively deep. A year earlier, in what were also difficult negotiations, there had been a terrible confrontation between Reinsdorf and Musburger. At one particularly thorny impasse, Reinsdorf, whose original specialty was tax law, made a suggestion about putting money aside in a certain way that would allow Jackson to invest it without at first paying taxes. That way the money could be invested and accrue interest while remaining tax free for a number of years. It was something, he said, he had done in other business deals, including some with his baseball players. At that point, Musburger said something to the effect that Reinsdorf now wanted to be Jackson's stockbroker as well, and with that Reinsdorf blew. "You dumb bastard, you're going to fuck this up just like you fucked up your brother's contract at CBS. I talked to Neal Pilson [the head of CBS sports] about you, and he said he had no problem with Brent, but he couldn't stand dealing with you." That was a uniquely wounding reference for Musburger: He had pushed hard for a handsome new contract for his brother at CBS, but at a certain point CBS pulled back and let Brent go; he eventually ended up broadcasting for ABC. "I made a mistake when I said that," Reinsdorf later noted. "I was right in what I said, but I had no business saying it in front of his client." But it had been a terrible moment; Musburger was convinced that he had finally seen the real Jerry Reinsdorf, and he believed that after the blowup Reinsdorf was never able to deal with him.

At a certain point in the summer of 1997, the entire deal seemed stalemated. Reinsdorf made an offer of $4 million; Musburger had been asking for $7.5 million, which was close to what Rick Pitino was now making in Boston. Larry Bird, unproven as a coach, had signed for $5 million in Indiana, the same figure that Chuck Daly was now drawing in Orlando. In Miami, Pat Riley, Jackson's nemesis, had the best deal of all. He was in for $3 million, plus equity in the team. Jackson, Musburger thought, was not very well prepared for negotiations that became so confrontational; the harsher the words exchanged, the less taste he seemed to have for the combat of it. But at least, the agent thought, he wanted some fair value. If it was about anything with Phil, Musburger thought, it was about dignity.

Eventually Reinsdorf said he would no longer meet with Musburger, and he flew out on a private plane to Montana to meet with Jackson. Just to talk things over, he said. On arrival, he handed Jackson an offer sheet, calling for one year at $5 million, upping his previous offer by $1 million. Hearing that the owner was on his way to Montana, Musburger flew out to be with his client, even though he was not present at the negotiations. "That's all I've got," Reinsdorf told Jackson of the $5 million. At that point Musburger, pushed by Jackson to get this done, came down to $6 million. But there they stalled again. Reinsdorf flew off to Arizona. (Perhaps some of the vast differences between the two men could be measured by the fact that when Jackson suggested that the owner stay on a little longer so he could see some of the beauty of the land, Reinsdorf said that he had no need to: He had seen it while flying in.)

When they spoke again, Musburger said $6 million was the figure. "You don't understand, when I say that's what it is, that's what is," Reinsdorf replied.

"Well, maybe what we have here is an irresistible force meeting an immovable object and we can't get it done," Musburger then told Reinsdorf. But about nine hours later, Reinsdorf called to say that he could do it at $6 million. The pieces were beginning to fall into place. Pippen had not been traded, and Jackson had been signed, but with a clause that released him if the Bulls did not sign Jordan again.

The press conference announcing Jackson's re-signing was not the kind of joyous occasion normally seen when a team brings back a winning and immensely popular coach. Jerry Krause announced the signing in what was largely viewed by local reporters as the most mean-spirited way possible, emphasizing that it was for only one more year, no matter whether the Bulls won their sixth title or not. That eventually triggered another go-round between the coach and his boss, and Jackson said something to the effect that it had seemed as if Krause was rooting for the other side, not for his own team. At that point Krause exploded and said, "I don't care if it's eighty-two and oh this year, you're fucking gone."

Now that Jackson was signed, the way was cleared for Reinsdorf to go after Jordan. First, there was some residual tension to deal with. Reinsdorf heard that Jordan was angry at him. Was that true? Jordan said it was. Reinsdorf asked why, and Jordan mentioned that when they signed the previous contract, the one for $30 million, Reinsdorf had apparently said that he might live to regret it. Reinsdorf said he did not remember saying it, but if he did, he apologized. With that, the disagreement was in his mind over. It was not. About that same time, Jordan met with Henry Louis Gates, the distinguished Harvard historian and writer, and brought up the statement. After all those years of being underpaid but carrying the Bulls in the worst of times and then helping to carry them to five championships, he told Gates, a statement like the one Reinsdorf made was like a punch to his heart. Jordan's words were eventually printed in *The New Yorker*. A year later, in the text for a photo book on his life, Jordan brought the statement up again. Clearly, it still festered and it probably reflected something of a cultural divide: what Reinsdorf thought he must have said in a sardonic self-mocking way had been viewed very differently by a great and proud athlete who thought it showed a stunning lack of respect.

They started talking about the next contract. Reinsdorf began by offering to pay $25 million, saying that the previous contract for $30 million was a catch-up, a reimbursement for years of being underpaid. Soon he was up to $30 million again, but Jordan said that he thought he deserved a raise—after all, they had won the championship, and he had once again been the MVP of the Finals. A raise, he said, would reward him for doing his job that well. Jordan and Falk suggested a raise of 20 percent, to $36 million. Reinsdorf resisted, and finally Jordan suggested that they split the difference and he get a 10 percent raise, bringing his salary to an unheard-of $33 million. Reinsdorf immediately agreed that it was fair but was stunned at that moment to hear Falk now propose a two-year deal for $36 million and $40 million, respectively. "David, didn't your client agree to one year at $33 million?" Reinsdorf asked. "Isn't that right Michael?" Jordan said yes. So the deal was done, but it was clear that the tension that seemed to surround the entire organization was reaching even its greatest player.

So it was that the cost of being the best team in basketball and the highest profile team in sports had finally begun to reach a true market value. Jordan was in for his $33 million, Jackson for $6 million, Rodman, with various incentives, close to $10 million; that was $49 million right there. Ron Harper was in for $5 million, and Kukoc for $4 million. Pippen was in for $3 million. His long-delayed big payday was probably going to have to come somewhere else. Even without the bench, the cost of the head coach and probable starting lineup put the payroll over $60 million.

Now that the others had all been signed to newly lucrative deals, Scottie Pippen's anger only increased. The fact that he was almost traded again, even when his teammates and his coach were getting their handsome new rewards, enraged Pippen. It was not, his principal agent Jimmy Sexton thought, so much about money as about respect. As the season was about to start, the bitterness mounted on Pippen's part. Both sides came to this present impasse by way of a long and very unhappy history; by the summer of 1997, that history was so thick, so many things said and claimed and counterclaimed, that trying to find the truth was like trying to peel back the layers of skin on a giant onion in the dark. It was even uglier than expected because Jimmy Sexton had also represented Horace Grant, the onetime Bulls power forward who had opted for free agency and signed with Orlando after the 1994 season. Grant's departure had produced great bitterness: Reinsdorf felt he had done a handshake deal with Grant to stay on and that Sexton had subsequently talked Grant out of it. Worst of all, in Reinsdorf's mind, the Bulls had gotten nothing back in return. He did not want that to happen in Pippen's case.

Pippen felt there was a two-tier way of doing business in Chicago: Jordan on one tier and everyone else on the other. Pippen knew how accommodating management made itself in dealing with Jordan—the way Reinsdorf treated him like a peer—and while he had an acute sense of Jordan's ability, of all that Jordan could do that he himself could not, he felt he deserved some kind of special status as well, that he was not just a piece of expensive meat. He was not just a Dream Team member but a *star* on it, and one of the fifty greatest all-time NBA players. That special status, he felt, had always been denied him in Chicago.

During the 1997 Finals, Pippen's foot gave him a great deal of pain, but he managed to play anyway. And yet when the season was over, he did not bother to have an operation on it, and the summer had passed. Most players usually avoided appointments with surgeons, no matter how benign the potential operation was said to be, but in this case, Pippen did not trust the Bulls or their doctors. As the season approached, Pippen, feeling powerless and singularly disrespected, chose the one way he could get even: he did nothing about his foot. It was his way of sticking his finger in Krause's and Reinsdorf's eyes and a sign of how deep his anger was: He was willing to jeopardize both his health and his teammates' chances.

Bad feeling and deeply rooted—almost pathological—distrust begat more bad feeling and more distrust. That summer, Pippen played in a couple of charity games sponsored by other players in the league, though his foot had neither been operated on nor cleared by the Bulls' doctors. That produced an angry series of faxes from Krause telling him to cease and desist. These messages in turn enraged Pippen even more, for the Bulls seemed to be telling him that he was their property, that in effect they owned him. He complained bitterly to Jimmy Sexton that Krause's faxes were racist—though more likely they were, like a lot of things Jerry Krause did, just the clumsy work of an executive who had no reservoir of trust with a great and quite sensitive player.

Krause was exceptionally maladroit in almost all dealings with all kinds of people, his own emotional vulnerability so manifest that he had trouble handling a position of power with anything near the requisite grace needed in so charged an atmosphere. Krause was smart, he had a good eye, and he was unbelievably hardworking, and in every conceivable way he had beaten the odds in becoming a first-rank NBA executive. But any personal comfort zone, so critical for any executive in a management role, particularly one where so much of the job was dealing with other unusually volatile human beings, always seemed to elude him. In all negotiations, his own self-esteem seemed to be as much at issue as the value of the person he was dealing with. Adversarial statements, which were part of the normal give-and-take of big-money sports negotiations, that a cooler, more confident man could shrug off had a longer, more permanent shelf life with Krause. He was intelligent, decent, and immensely vulnerable. His job description was for a man who could deal with other people's problems. Instead he often seemed to create problems. All kinds of things that required a certain kind of coolness and distance in front-office dealings were with Krause intensely personal. His problem, as Reinsdorf once said of him, was that he fell in love with people and then was disappointed when it turned out that what had bound them together was a business relationship, not love. The fact that there was an explosive quality to much of what Krause did, did not seem to bother Reinsdorf at all; if anything, the owner might in his own contrarian way not be that unhappy that Krause left so much human wreckage behind—it meant that agents, players, and media people were almost always exhausted by the time Reinsdorf entered the battlefield.

Because of his foot, a very angry Pippen was not ready when the season started, and might miss as much as half of it, according to team doctors. And just rounding into shape was Dennis Rodman, the power forward/provocateur who had become something of a cultural icon (or con man) in contemporary American society, based on the fact that he dyed his hair differently for different occasions, his body was covered with tattoos, and he had multiple ornamental body piercings. Just exactly what Rodman was protesting—nondyed hair, unpierced bodies, untattooed skin—was not always easy to discern. He complained often and loudly about the injustice of the NBA, where this year, he might, if he fulfilled all the provisions of a contract loaded with incentives, make in the neighborhood of $10 million in addition to his endorsements. Rodman had joined the Bulls two years earlier for this second cycle of championship runs and had been a critical part of it.

Phil Jackson thought this was going to be an unusually difficult season. He had seen Pippen in foul moods before, but the anger this time exceeded anything he had witnessed previously and had turned into a kind of blinding hatred that threatened to impel Pippen to do things that were against his own best interest. The degree of alienation between players and ownership was almost unique in the annals of modern basketball, particularly for a championship team. In Los Angeles, Jerry Buss and Jerry West of the Lakers made their players feel like part of a family, and West was extremely shrewd about knowing how the changes in basketball's labor laws and collective-bargaining agreements affected many business aspects of the game, not least the human element in front office–player relations. Boston under the crusty Red Auerbach remained a family too through the mid-eighties, though it was a family from a very different generation, much more given to tough love than easy end-of-the-twentieth-century love. In Detroit, the combination of Bill Davidson, Jack McCloskey, and Chuck Daly had helped make for a strong and coherent franchise with generally admirable player-management relations back in the eighties.

The alienation of team from management was not without its potential upside for Jackson, a man both supple and subtle. Eventually, he was able to use the very isolation of the players from the front office—the belief on the part of many of the players that the front office was essentially hostile to their goals and did not want the team to win a sixth championship—as a unifying force. By the time the season was over, Reinsdorf felt that Jackson had bordered on disloyalty in the way he had taken the existing tensions and turned the players against the front office. Whether that was disloyalty or simple shrewdness, just making the best out of a bad hand, was impossible to determine.

Jackson was certain that the coming 1997–1998 season, win or lose, was going to be the last time around for this team—the Last Dance, he called it. Coming together for the Last Dance was, on the surface at least, an old team and a thin one. In a sport where players were supposed to hit their prime when they were about twenty-seven or twenty-eight, Jordan would be thirty-five in the coming season, Rodman thirty-seven, Pippen thirty-three. (When the Bulls won their first title Jordan was twenty-eight, Pippen and Horace Grant twenty-six.) Ron Harper would be thirty-four in January and was obviously coming to the end of his career: He was playing with two arthritic knees and was called Pegleg by his teammates. Toni Kukoc, in whom so much had been invested by Krause, both emotionally and financially, had yet to prove himself as a big-time NBA player who could play at a consistent high plateau with the requisite toughness. The players on the bench were smarter than they were gifted.

In addition, the players themselves were aware of how hard it was to win a third straight championship, even under the best of circumstances. The second year had been much harder than the first, because as expectations had heightened, so had the pressures around them. John Paxson, a key player on the team that had won the first cycle of three titles, and now a broadcaster, warned them that the third title was infinitely harder than the second, that it was much more difficult to sustain the proper level of motivation and concentration.

Still, Jackson thought the Bulls had a very good chance at winning another title. The four most senior players—Jordan, Pippen, Rodman and Harper—were all amazing athletes, stayed in great shape, and played young. More, all four were unusually smart players. Jackson knew his team had certain advantages: its intelligence, its experience, and above all its overall mental toughness, which was very important at playoff time. The Bulls knew how and when to focus and how to execute on the floor the things that the coaches talked about before the game—an advantage that set them apart from many other teams, even some with seemingly more talented players. These were not inconsiderable assets. And then, of course, there was an additional great asset, something not even quantifiable: the Michael Factor, the greatness of one player of indomitable willpower who consistently lifted his game and thus his teammates to impossible heights in very big games, especially at playoff time. Jackson thought his players were ideal for what they considered the real season—the playoffs. In fact, they would have been delighted to skip the regular eighty-two-game season and go to the playoffs right away.

Right before it started, Jackson talked to both Jordan and Pippen about the coming season. Each wanted to know if he thought that this would be the last hurrah, and Jackson answered yes, he thought they had been lucky to keep it together this long. They would have to assume that it would be over in June. His general view of the season was shared by Jordan. "We're really going to have to pace ourselves, aren't we?" Jordan said. Jackson agreed, but wondered how Jordan would be able to do that, particularly if Pippen was out. Jordan felt he was in reasonably good condition and pretty much where he wanted to be at this point. No one in professional sports took better care of his body than Michael Jordan, which was why he was still having peak years long after the point where his body and his skills should have begun their respective declines. Because the Bulls had been at a championship level for so long, every year the season stretched into the middle of June. With every year, Jordan felt the need to pace himself more keenly than ever.

Because Pippen was out, and because the bench seemed weaker than ever, there would be a greater burden on Jordan this year than ever before, and Jordan and his personal trainer, Tim Grover, decided to try and have him peak a little more slowly than in the past. They started their workouts much later in the summer than usual, and while Jordan was in good shape when he got to camp, Jackson, for the second season in a row, ran one-a-day practices rather than the normal two a day, to protect Michael and the other older athletes.

Jackson's own importance to this team was not to be underestimated. For a number of years he had failed to get the proper recognition from his coaching peers and from the media because it was assumed that it was easy to coach great players such as Jordan and Pippen. During the first three-championship run, he had not once been named coach of the year. That it was easy to win with these players was both true and untrue: While they were not only great players but unusually coachable ones, it was exceptionally difficult to integrate a superstar of Jordan's stature into a team game. There was the constant problem of getting the maximum from him, and not inhibiting his God-given instinct to take over the game, but at the same time preventing him from diminishing the instincts, abilities, and egos of his teammates. Jackson had to maximize Jordan's vast abilities, without letting him suck the oxygen away from his teammates, both on and off the court. Great players came with great egos: Winning, in the NBA and elsewhere, rarely made players control their egos. The more a team won, the more that egos, once suppressed for the good of the team, tended to come to the surface.

Jackson performed that most delicate bit of alchemy with great skill, and he did so for an unusually long time, almost a decade, which itself was amazing, given the pressures and the ego drives of the NBA, where great and passionate players quickly tired of great and passionate coaches, and vice versa. In the modern, star-driven NBA, it was extremely hard to sustain success for very long and even harder to sustain successful player-coach relationships for any period of time. Pat Riley, the most driven of men, someone who was clearly making up as coach for the limitations he had faced as a player, had been a brilliant coach for the Lakers, but in time he had overstayed his welcome; he had seemed, in the eyes of his players, always to be trying to ratchet up their level of commitment a notch or two too high, and there had been a virtual player rebellion against him at the end of his tour in Los Angeles. That it was Michael Jordan who fought to keep Jackson on as coach for the sixth championship run was the highest accolade a coach could gain in the modern NBA, far more important than winning the Coach of the Year award.

Over the years in Chicago, Jackson won the trust of most of his players. He was smart about them, he treated them as individuals, and he worked skillfully to keep them from becoming bored. Above all, he treated them with respect. Now, quite far into his tour as coach, most of them understood how adroitly he had managed to integrate Jordan into the system, something that had not been that apparent seven or eight years earlier when the process, awkward, difficult, and painful, had begun. He had gained and held Jordan's respect without looking like his pawn and thus losing the respect of the other eleven players. That was no small thing. His ability to convert Jordan into a believer in the triple-post offense, and thus into becoming a teammate who shared the ball more readily, was probably his greatest success.

Late in the second championship cycle, Steve Kerr, asked to describe the culture of the Bulls, answered that it was an unusual team in that so much of its culture and character came from the coach. It was not easy for other, more limited players to play with Michael Jordan, Kerr noted. For proud men like professional athletes, it was also not easy to deal with media hordes every day, knowing, even as you were answering their questions, that they had no interest in you, that all they really wanted to know about was Jordan or occasionally Pippen, Rodman, or Jackson. On a team with those superstars, it was easy for other egos to get crushed. Jackson, Kerr felt, was exceptionally gifted in keeping everyone involved and letting every player know he had a role. The role of reserves was extremely difficult here, for everyone knew that without Jordan nothing good happened to this team, but the players also knew that if they did not do their parts and were not ready at all times, nothing good would happen either.

4.

Los Angeles, 1997; Williston, North Dakota, 1962

THE BULLS STRUGGLED early in the 1997–1998 season. All the things that Jackson worried might go wrong early on in fact did. Their record was 6–5 when they arrived in Los Angeles to play the ever-troubled Los Angeles Clippers. If things were going poorly for the Bulls, they were going far worse for the Clippers, who were 1–10 under Phil Jackson's former college coach, Bill Fitch. The Clippers might well have been the worst franchise in the league. They played in a truly seedy arena, the old Los Angeles Sports Arena, and drew as few as two or three thousand fans to games against lesser teams. They only sold out when the Bulls or the Lakers showed up, whereupon their fans tended to cheer for the visiting team and only swung around to cheer for the Clippers very late in a game if they were still actually contesting it. The Clippers seemed to be a team with a curse on them: No matter how poorly they finished and how high they drafted, they never seemed to get better, and when they did draft young talented players, those players left as soon as they could.

On this night, though, the Clippers seemed destined to win. The Bulls were terrible, and had none of their aura of invincibility. This was their fifth road game, and they had yet to win one. Early in the second quarter, Los Angeles led 36–18. Jordan started out poorly, making only three of his first fourteen shots. Gradually, though, the Bulls mounted a comeback and began to grind down the Clippers. By the end of the evening, Jordan was eighteen of thirty-six, which meant that he made fifteen of his last twenty-two shots. Jordan had taken on himself the job of lifting his team, and the score was tied 92–92 at the end of regulation, with Jordan scoring the last seven Chicago points. In the first overtime, the Clippers led 102–98 with only thirty-nine seconds left, but Jordan hit a jump shot to make it 102–100. Then, with fifteen seconds left, he was fouled but missed his first foul shot. Jackson yelled for him to miss the second deliberately; he did and managed to get the rebound. With eight seconds left, he drove to the basket and scored for the tie.

In the second overtime, Jordan scored all nine points for Chicago, which meant he had scored twenty-two of his team's last twenty-six points. Los Angeles did not score at all in the second overtime. Though Jordan gave signs of his exhaustion, including three missed foul shots at the end, he scored the last thirteen points in the game. He had refused to let a vulnerable, struggling Bulls team lose a game on a night when they seemed unable to play up to expectations. He played fifty-two minutes and scored forty-nine points. An unimportant game became an important one; a likely defeat became a victory. It was the kind of thing that happened ten or twelve times during the season, the power of his will triumphing over the exhaustion of his body. Very few fans watching casually understood it—you had to be with the team day after day and see all the games, particularly the seemingly unimportant ones, to understand that he did it every night. That special willpower made a huge difference in the final won-loss standings, and it would mean that at the end of the season the Bulls had the home-court advantage in one crucial series, the Eastern Conference Finals.

When the Bulls played the Clippers that night it marked yet another crossing of paths for the two coaches and old friends, Phil Jackson and Bill Fitch. By now, they were a study in contrasts. Jackson, seeking his sixth title in nine years of head coaching, had the best winning percentage in the history of the game. Fitch, who thirty-five years earlier had recruited Jackson out of high school in Williston to come to the University of North Dakota—and had been then as now a workaholic of the first order—was now coaching what was arguably the worst team in the league and certainly working for the league's shakiest organization. Fitch had begun the season with the dubious distinction of having lost more games than any coach in NBA history; this was loss number 1,052. Fitch had had a profound effect on Jackson's career, and when Joe Jackson, Phil's older brother, spoke about his brother's professional career, he was quick to point out his good luck in having so talented and young a coach when he was a young and impressionable college student—a coach who could and did give him so much.

After the Clippers game, Jackson savored his first road victory and the near escape from the indignity of a defeat at the hands of the Clippers, even by the narrowest of margins. He thought with affection of Fitch—"He still gets eaten up by the game—he won't sleep tonight. He'll stay up most of the night watching film." Captain Video they had called Fitch back in Boston when he had coached the Celtics because of his penchant for sitting alone in his room studying film. The two men had known each other since Jackson's junior year in high school in 1962. Now Fitch was making $2 million a year, and Jackson, his onetime protégé, was making $6 million, not bad for either, although given the degree of difficulty in coaching their respective teams, the salaries probably should have been reversed.

An NBA game in Los Angeles in November 1997, even a Clippers game, felt a long way from Williston High School in the spring of 1962, when Fitch first met and started to recruit Jackson. Jackson was then a junior in high school and already a prominent schoolboy athlete: a football player, basketball player, baseball pitcher, and member of the track team, all at six foot five and probably 160 pounds. Jackson was growing at an accelerating rate—a year earlier he was six foot one and 140 pounds, which earned him the inevitable nickname of Bones. Fitch had just taken over as basketball coach at North Dakota. Another coach had been offered the job and accepted it, but his wife told him that if he went to Grand Forks he was going alone because it was simply too cold up there. So the job was Fitch's almost by default. He worked hard on his recruiting, trying to create almost overnight a basketball program at a school known for football and hockey. Fitch had coached both basketball and baseball earlier at Creighton, and he had done some scouting for the Atlanta Braves, in the course of which he became aware of a young kid named Phil Jackson. Jackson, whom he had heard about but never seen, was said to be a tall, skinny, string bean of a kid, six foot seven or eight. "Can't miss," his notes from his regional scouts had said.

Fitch, desperate to jump-start his program, drove down to Williston on a cold April day to see Jackson participate in a track meet. "He was throwing the discus," Fitch recalled, "and it was a very windy day, and he's built just like a pencil. The baseball scout's notes are right about that, anyway. No one in history was ever that skinny and yet strong enough to throw the discus. I think they probably needed to tie him down to keep him from blowing away. I fell in love with him from the very start. He's everything you're looking for when you're recruiting, a very good, respectful kid, everything is 'yes, sir, no, sir,' a great student, a kid passionate to excel—you could tell that from the start. Both parents preachers. I told him I wanted him for my program that very first day." At the urging of his high school coach, Jackson performed what he called the car trick for Fitch. He sat in the backseat of a car, any car, and, reaching out with his long arms, opened the doors on both sides of the car simultaneously.

A few months later, Fitch drove across the state to be the speaker at the annual high school sports banquet in Williston, his principal motivation being to sign Jackson up for North Dakota. "The single most dangerous thing I've ever done in my life," he remembered. "I've had open-heart surgery since, but the nearest I ever came to death was that recruiting trip. There was a major blizzard, more than twenty inches of snow, the worst storm in years. No one was getting through. All along the highway, cars were snowed under. In those days in North Dakota, one of the things you did when you took a major trip in the winter was take candles with you and put them in your glove compartment, so if you got stuck you could light the candle and maybe, just maybe, someone would find you. There were cars with candles all along the way that day, and I had a feeling I was the only person who got through. Three days later, they were still finding frozen bodies in cars along the way." Fitch somehow made it to the banquet, where he made a big hit with the local fans by calling the young Phil Jackson up to the podium, pulling out a pair of handcuffs and saying "I want you" as he handcuffed him.

Jackson liked Fitch immensely. He was young, only thirty-two at the time, and upbeat, and his warmth and enthusiasm contrasted sharply with the seeming coldness of the other coach who went after him, Johnny Kundla of the University of Minnesota. Perhaps because Kundla's was a far more powerful program, one accustomed to getting the regional kids it wanted, he seemed aloof and distant. He summoned Jackson and four other would-be freshmen to a recruiting meeting at the university in Minneapolis and told them that they were the five freshmen he wanted for next year's freshmen team (freshmen were not eligible for the varsity in those days). It was as if there was no decision to make: He wanted them, so they would come. "You're going to be next year's class," Kundla said. "We have a fine program here. You'll like the program, and you'll like the university, and if you have any questions, call me." And with that he walked out of the room. "That was recruiting Johnny Kundla style," Jackson said more than thirty years later, with no small amount of edge. He chose North Dakota instead.

He loved playing at North Dakota. When he was young, he had shown greater potential as a baseball pitcher and a number of professional teams had been interested in signing him, but in some way that he did not entirely understand himself, he was being pulled toward basketball. Paul Pederson, two years older than Jackson, was already a star on the team and an exceptional student as well, and Fitch deliberately had them room together so that Pederson could help guide Jackson through the first part of his college years. Pederson thought that Fitch always knew that he had something special with Jackson and was very careful with him. Acerbic and caustic with most of his players, he was surprisingly gentle with Jackson, aware of the stress he was going through as his body filled out and as he underwent a considerable amount of emotional stress because of the conflicts between the strict way in which he had been raised, in a fundamentalist household, and the relaxed, to some minds sinful, quality of college life.

Jackson was a good, hardworking athlete with unusual talents and certain vulnerabilities. Tall, a little awkward, but with fairly good foot speed, he had those long arms and a good left-handed hook shot that served him well as long as he was in college. The one thing Fitch worked on with him was his defense, particularly the press. Both because he wanted to increase Jackson's agility in college and because he was preparing him for a possible shot at the pro game, Fitch worked with Jackson constantly on something they called the hockey drill. It was a three-on-three drill, and Jackson's job was to lead the defensive press. Fitch always used him against their smallest, quickest player, their point guard. It was an unlikely test of dexterity that was to serve Jackson well.

His North Dakota teams did well while he was there. In his sophomore and junior years, they ended up third and fourth respectively in the NCAA's Division II tournament, losing both times to a Southern Illinois team led by a young player named Walt Frazier, whom Jackson had been assigned to guard, although with limited success. ("He was much quicker than I was," Jackson recalled. "He left me in the dust both times.") For a variety of ethnic reasons, North Dakota was not considered fertile basketball soil, and the general view of most professional basketball scouts was that it was likely to produce slow, heavy, obedient white kids. But two men did scout him. One was Jerry Krause, then a scout for the old Baltimore Bullets (who in time became the Washington Bullets, who in time became the Washington Wizards). Krause came up to see Jackson in the winter of 1966–1967, his senior year, liked him, and wanted to draft him for the Bullets.

Krause, who was eventually to play a large role in Jackson's life, had heard about a young, somewhat gawky player at North Dakota who had unusually long arms, and he drove through a snowstorm, which seemed to be a requisite part of the hazardous duty of any scout, to see Jackson play against Loyola. "Jerry, have you ever seen longer arms than this?" Bill Fitch had asked, and then he had Jackson perform the car trick, the same stunt sprung on Fitch four years earlier. That night, as Krause remembered, Jackson hit eighteen straight free throws. Krause hoped to get Jackson in the third round, but the New York Knicks were scouting him, too.

Red Holzman scouted Jackson for the Knicks and liked him very much. What impressed him the most was the way that Jackson led the team's press, that he was surprisingly lithe for someone who was not really an agile athlete. "How'd you get him to do that? How'd you get him to move so well?" Holzman asked Fitch after he saw him work the press. Fitch told him about the three-on-three press drill. The Knicks took him in the second round, two picks before Baltimore.

It was odd, Jackson sometimes thought, to be at the center of all this contemporary basketball hysteria, to be coaching the most famous athlete in the world, to be flying every day in plush charter jets, and to need security men to escape the crowds after games, and to be making as a coach about $60,000 a game, including playoff games. That figure was roughly double the sum of his first Knicks contract, which was for two full years. His professional career, which marked thirty years in 1997, had spanned much of the modern NBA. Television was so new in the Great Plains where he grew up that he had seen very few NBA games, and none before he went to college; to the degree that sports events had been broadcast during his boyhood and that he had been allowed to see them—not in his own home, of course—they had been World Series games. In college, he managed to see a few NBA games. He had never seen the New York Knicks play.

A competing team in the American Basketball Association (ABA), the Minnesota Pipers, drafted him as well, and they offered a two-year guaranteed contract for $25,000. The Knicks matched that, coming up with $26,000 for two years—$12,500 and $13,500—plus a $5,000 signing bonus. It seemed like a vast amount of money at the time, and Jackson gladly signed. He was sure of his future: He would play for a few years, take graduate courses in the summer, eventually get a graduate degree in psychology, and then go into some kind of work where he could use that interest. He was sure his life was set. He flew to New York in early May 1967. It was an eye-opening experience. Red Holzman, not yet the coach, still the player-personnel man, met him at the airport. They drove toward Manhattan, and as they went through an underpass in Queens, some kid dropped a rock down on Holzman's window with perfect timing, and the glass shattered. Holzman, absolutely furious, cursed under his breath. He finally controlled his anger and turned to Jackson and said, "Well, that's part of what you have to take if you're going to live in New York."

Jackson met briefly with Eddie Donovan, the general manager, who had never seen him play. Donovan asked him what he knew about the professional game, and Jackson answered that he had seen a handful of playoff games while he was in college. That pretty much exhausted their mutual topics of conversation. He had never seen anything quite like New York. It was the height of the Vietnam years, and there was a protest that day. He expected that because New York was a liberal city, the protest would be an antiwar one, but on this spring day it was a prowar protest by union men, hard hats, and it turned quite ugly. That had both surprised Jackson and frightened him slightly. He went off by himself walking the city, and at one point stopped at a small cafeteria where two waitresses were screaming at each other over a tip. He continued his serendipitous tour, finding in other parts of the city people standing on soapboxes and criticizing the war. It was, he decided, going to be a fascinating place in which to play. His searching, it would turn out, had finally begun.

"Phil always amazes me," Bill Fitch said years later. "When I first met him, the last thing I thought he would be was a pro player—I didn't think he'd be a minister either, I thought he wanted to grow away from that. By the time he got to college, I figured he'd be a college professor some day. Then he got better and a few years later, he was playing for the Knicks, so he *did* become a pro player and a good one. I remember visiting him in New York in those days. I think we spent all our time together in Greenwich Village, and he had hair down to his shoulders, not just a hippie but a superhippie. So I left him that night and the last thing I ever thought he'd be was a coach."

Chapel Hill, 1980

I N THE SUMMER OF 1980, Michael Jordan got a chance to go to Dean Smith's basketball camp, which was a big thing in North Carolina, because it was believed that only the best players were invited. His pal Leroy Smith went with him, and they were paired as suitemates with two white players from the western part of the state, Buzz Peterson and his teammate Randy Shepherd. Buzz was already a celebrated figure in regional high school athletics, a candidate for Mister Basketball in North Carolina, an honor that went to the outstanding high school player of the year. That made him one of the blue-chip players at the camp, along with Lynwood Robinson, who had been the point guard on the state championship high school team and was already being talked about as the next Phil Ford, a player who had not only been a great star at Carolina, but one of the most skilled and feared point guards in the NBA before injuries ravaged his game.

Years later, because Smith and the other coaches had done such a skillful job of playing down how impressed they were when they got their first look at him, it would become part of the myth of Michael Jordan that he had been something of an afterthought as a recruit to Carolina, someone whom they had stumbled on by chance at the camp and to whom they had eventually decided to offer their last scholarship. That version had him as something of a late bloomer, with the Carolina coaching staff as surprised by the steady blossoming of his skills as opposing teams were.

That was not exactly true. Michael Jordan was a late bloomer, but he was not *that* late a bloomer. The North Carolina coaching staff knew from the first day he showed up in the summer of 1980 that he was immensely talented. By the end of that week, though the coaches badly wanted both Peterson and Robinson, the number-one recruit as far as they were concerned was Michael Jordan of Wilmington Laney. They had first become aware of him earlier that year when Michael Brown, the athletic director in the New Hanover (Wilmington) County school system, called Roy Williams, a young assistant on Dean Smith's staff, and said that he had a player who was quite possibly the best young athlete Brown had ever seen. The call came early in Jordan's junior year, right after his first great surge of growth. At first, Williams was assigned to scout him, but at the last minute the scouting assignments were switched, and the job fell to Bill Guthridge, who was Smith's top assistant. When Williams, whose interest had been piqued by Brown's phone call, asked Guthridge what he thought of the Jordan kid, Guthridge answered that it was hard to tell. All he had done that night was shoot a lot of jump shots, Guthridge said. "But he does have an extra gear," he added, meaning that at the very·least he had an extra bit of athletic ability that would allow him to run and jump better than most kids. What Bill Guthridge told Dean Smith was that Mike Jordan was probably good enough to compete in the Atlantic Coast Conference (ACC), athletically quite gifted, with underdeveloped skills. That was the only time they scouted him in his junior year.

One of Roy Williams's jobs was to make sure that the best players in the state came to Smith's camp, and in addition to lining up both Buzz Peterson and Lynwood Robinson, he had called Jordan's high school coach, Pop Herring, and arranged for Jordan and Leroy Smith to come. About four hundred high school kids had shown up that week, players of all different sizes and ages and abilities. A handful were players that North Carolina was interested in, but most of them were kids of more limited talent who hoped that with a boost from this camp they might make their high school or junior high school teams. It was brutally hot on that first day. Roy Williams was in charge of all the kids, and he made sure that they all got to play for a little while in Carmichael Gym, which was where the Tar Heels played their home games. That way, when they went home, they could all tell their friends that yes, they had played in the storied gym. Because of that, Williams had to run them in and out of Carmichael rather quickly, and he organized it as best he could, big kids playing against big kids, little kids against little kids. He did it in groups of thirty, which meant that they could have three full-court games going at a time.

He also kept his eye out for this young player from Wilmington, Mike Jordan, and in time he introduced himself to a rather skinny young kid. When Jordan's group was finished, Williams separated him from the others and suggested he stay on for a second session. Afterward, Jordan left the gym with the others, but he somehow managed to sneak back to the gym for a third session. That impressed Williams, who loved any sign of a true gym rat, but he was impressed even more by what he saw in Jordan, the raw athletic ability that separated him from every other kid there and made him the kind of young player that coaches always dream of finding. When the workouts were finished, Williams walked back to the office of Eddie Fogler, another Smith assistant and a close friend, and said, "I think I've just looked at the best six-foot-four high school player that I've ever seen."

"Who's that?" Fogler asked.

"Mike Jordan—the kid from Wilmington," Williams answered. Williams, who would go on to become one of the nation's most successful coaches at Kansas, had been simply stunned by his overall athletic ability, his quickness, his jumping ability, his defensive intensity—the kids whom Jordan guarded simply could not breathe. In addition, Jordan seemed to have what coaches called, for lack of a better phrase, a nose for the ball. Somehow, no matter what happened—a loose ball off the boards, a ball up for grabs in the backcourt—Jordan seemed to get to the ball a little more quickly than anyone else. Thus was the first big-time sighting of Michael Jordan made.

Buzz Peterson, Randy Shepherd, Michael Jordan, and Roy Smith made an easy connection through basketball. The former pair might be middle-class white boys from Asheville, in the Appalachian part of the state, and the latter were two black kids from the coastal city of Wilmington, but more than anything else they were four passionate gym rats. It turned out that Shepherd and Jordan were in the same group and played with each other every day, while Peterson and Smith were in another group. That meant that each day Shepherd reported back to his friend on what had happened, and each day the report was about Jordan. Daily it seemed to escalate. "Hey, that guy Mike in the connecting room, he's a really good athlete, he can really jump," Shepherd reported the first day. The next day it was, "He's a *great* athlete," and the third day it was, "Buzz, you can't believe what it's like to play with him—you just throw him the alley-oop [a pass lofted very high over the rim, so a teammate can catch it in the air and dunk], and it's gone. He doesn't like to play outside much, but inside he's a killer, because he's so quick and because he's such a great jumper." By the fourth day, he told Buzz, "Buzz, you and I have never seen anything like him. I think this guy can play in the NBA." Jordan was skinny and wiry, Shepherd thought, but you could already see the beginning of moves, moments when he would take the ball, drive under the basket, and then reverse himself and score. Not many high school kids could do that.

By the middle of the week, Randy Shepherd, who thought of himself less as a blue-chip player than a blue-collar one—a player of limited natural ability who worked diligently to maximize every part of his game and who gave his body up every chance he could—was dreaming of a basketball future at a higher level. He had arrived at the camp thinking that a scholarship to Chapel Hill, which was virtually a sure thing for his friend Buzz, would be beyond his reach, that he would have to settle for a smaller, less prestigious school. But now, because this Michael Jordan was making him look so good, he was beginning to think Carolina. By the end of the week, there was talk from some of the Carolina coaches of Shepherd attending Carolina as a walk-on. He did not, choosing to play at North Carolina–Asheville instead, but he always suspected that Michael Jordan had elevated his status as a prospect.

It was absolutely fascinating, Shepherd thought. There they were, four Carolina kids, two of them black, two of them white, so much at ease with each other, hanging out all the time now. Though he and Buzz were best friends in high school who played in Buzz's backyard every night and had snuck into the high school gym when it was supposed to be closed, he could also sense the separation that was beginning to take place because of basketball, both between him and Buzz and between Roy and Mike. For Randy Shepherd had a shrewd sense of what was taking place around him, and a critical part of that was that Roy Williams and the other Carolina coaches were never taking their eyes off of Buzz Peterson and Mike Jordan. It was never stated, but it was clear that while Randy and Roy were going to play some college ball at some smaller school, they were not going to do it at the level of their two friends. Buzz and Mike were going to be very heavily recruited; they were going to end up at a major program—Carolina, Duke, or Kentucky—they were probably going to star there as well, and they both might play professionally.

There was an unofficial acknowledgment of this among the four of them, with the coming of a new friendship between Jordan and Peterson based on their higher level of skill. "Roy and I were a notch or two down, and we understood this," Shepherd said years later. "Michael and Buzz were just beginning to emerge, and the future was clearly theirs.

They saw their destinies being very similar, and it pulled them towards each other." The separation was not quite the same as that between two high school friends, one going to go on to college, the other staying behind in the small town facing a life as a blue-collar worker, but it was not without its parallels.

Buzz Peterson was taken with his new friend's ebullience. Jordan seemed almost innately joyous. His pleasure seemed to come from playing basketball, and he generated the most natural kind of self-confidence. He was already beginning to talk a big game, but it was done with such childlike innocence that the net effect was not of arrogance, but more of a certain sweetness. Years later, as Peterson matured and became a college coach himself, he understood better the process Jordan was undergoing, the explosion of talent and emotional confidence. The thing Michael loved most in the world was basketball, and after all those years of fighting the limits of his size, he was just beginning, now that he had suddenly spurted to six foot four, to realize how good he was going to be. He was pushing himself to his outer limits and finding that at this particular moment, because of his God-given abilities, there *were* no real limits on him. "He knew that he was going to get better, and for the first time he had a sense of what the future might bring for him—and he was in love with it," Buzz said.

The Dean Smith camp was very controlled; it emphasized fundamentals, so there was not that much opportunity for Jordan to show his pure athletic ability. Perhaps the occasional dunk on an alley-oop, but players were not encouraged to drive to the basket and dunk. Through the fourth day, Buzz Peterson had yet to see Jordan play because he was in a different division, but one day he was coming back from a workout and he saw a pickup game taking place on one of the outdoor courts. Some of the recent Carolina players like Mike O'Koren, Al Wood, and Dudley Bradley were hanging around, and they had drafted Jordan and a few others in the camp to play with them. The game was very intense and physical. On one play, O'Koren drove to the basket and in the process he gave Roy Smith a shot to the chest so hard that Smith thought his chest was being turned inside out. But there was a freedom on the playground that was not allowed during the camp's more controlled play, and Michael Jordan seemed to be enjoying it. Everything that Shepherd had been saying, Peterson decided, was true, and perhaps more. What struck him watching his new friend was how easy it all seemed to him; he could not only make great athletic moves but also make them seem effortless. Seeing him, Peterson thought, was not only seeing someone with a potential for greatness but, for the first time in his own career, seeing the limits that existed on his own game, comprehending what he would never be able to do, no matter how hard he worked.

The best high school juniors were not just beginning to receive letters from colleges interested in recruiting them but also beginning to be selected for the various all-star camps where the best high school players auditioned for the best college coaches. Buzz Peterson had already been invited to the B/C All-Star Basketball Camp, named after its proprietor Bill Cronauer, in Milledgeville, Georgia. Jordan, with only one season as a varsity player behind him, had attracted less attention at that point in his career and had not been invited to any camps. A player who wanted to go to Cronauer's camp apparently had to have letters from three college coaches expressing their interest, and Jordan did not have them. He questioned Peterson very closely about it, and years later Buzz could see this as part of his competitive instinct: In effect he was wondering, How come you have it and I don't? The competitive juices, he decided, were always flowing in Michael. (Years later, when Jordan, about to sign a sneaker contract with Nike, met for the first time with Sonny Vaccaro, Nike's top basketball talent scout, the first thing he did was tease Vaccaro, who ran the Dapper Dan, a high school all-American camp, for not selecting him for his camp.)

From the moment Roy Williams, then the most junior member of the coaching staff, spread the word on Jordan, the other Carolina basketball coaches paid attention, and they all saw the same thing that Williams had seen. It was clear early on that there were three players at the camp whom Carolina wanted—Buzz Peterson, Lynwood Robinson, and Michael Jordan—and they wanted Jordan most of all. Dean Smith, wary of creating false hopes in players he was not that interested in, cautious in all expressions of emotion, somewhat apart from all but the tiny handful of players he badly sought, had two meals with him. "By the end of the week, we had decided that if we had been allowed only one recruit in the country," Roy Williams remembered, "that player was going to be Michael Jordan. We worked hard to conceal it because he was not yet well known and we wanted to keep it that way, but it was also clear that he was the best player there, and we knew he was going to grow into that body and that he was going to get better—how much better, of course, we did not know."

What few realized was that the word on Jordan was already beginning to spill out into not just the college world but the professional world of basketball as well, through the tightly knit Carolina basketball alumni network. Doug Moe, who was then the Denver Nuggets assistant coach, came back for a visit that summer, as Carolina alumni were wont to do. One day he called his pal Donnie Walsh, like him a member of the Carolina inner club, and his boss at Denver.

"How's Worthy?" Walsh immediately asked, because James Worthy, who had just completed his freshman year, was already known as a superstar in waiting, a player of remarkable speed and agility.

"Forget Worthy," Moe said. "There's someone here who's going to be a great, great player."

"Who's that?" Walsh asked.

"A kid named Jordan. Mike Jordan."

"He's that good?"

"Donnie, I'm not talking good. I'm talking great. I'm talking Jerry West and Oscar Robertson," Moe said, which impressed Walsh because Moe was a tough grader, a coach who did not think that anyone who came after him could really play. The word was beginning to get out, at least within the somewhat closed world of the Carolina people.

It was at this point that Roy Williams helped arrange for Jordan to go on that same summer to Howard Garfinkel's Five-Star Camp, near Pittsburgh. It not only attracted the very best players, but it was less of a meat market than many comparable institutions. The coaching there, Williams thought, was simply superb, with many of the best high school and college coaches in the country participating. Williams called Garfinkel to tell him about Jordan and to ask if there was a place at the camp for him. More, he suggested that they put Jordan in with the top players at Five-Star.

Williams thought he was doing the right thing: He was sure that Jordan was going to end up at a camp somewhere—a player this good was not going to remain a secret very much longer—and he was going to help a local coach by making sure his best player went to a very good camp and got good coaching. One day, he hoped, that good deed would be paid back. In addition, Williams talked to Tom Konchalski, a Garfinkel sidekick, about Jordan. Later, both Konchalski and Garfinkel were under the impression that the Carolina coaches had looked at Jordan and liked him but were unsure how good he really was because of the limited competition at Smith's camp, and thus wanted him to go to Five-Star to see him play against the best. Garfinkel was pleased to oblige.

Dean Smith was not so sure about the whole thing and more than a little irritated with Williams for going ahead and placing him in a camp. "Why'd you do that?" he asked, and Williams wondered later if he had gone too far. Clearly, Smith saw no particular advantage in letting other coaches view this young man in a showcase setting. At Five-Star, the top players' names were put in a pool, and the coaches—some of them from college, some of them from high schools—drafted players for their teams, which then competed against each other all week. Brendan Malone, then an assistant coach at Syracuse and later an assistant coach for both the Detroit Pistons and the New York Knicks, and briefly the head coach for the Toronto Raptors, was supposed to draft a team, but his wife had been in a minor moped accident, so he asked Konchalski to draft for him. He gave Konchalski very specific instructions: He wanted him to draft Greg Dreiling as a big man and Aubrey Sherrod, a highly touted shooting guard from Wichita, as his two, or shooting guard. On several occasions in the past, Malone had drafted players who had thereupon never shown up, so he was more than a little sensitive about the entire process. When he arrived a day after the draft, he asked Konchalski if he had taken Sherrod. No, said Konchalski, I drafted a kid from North Carolina named Mike Jordan. Malone was furious. "Who the hell is Mike Jordan?" he asked. "Brendan," Konchalski answered, "I don't think you're going to be disappointed. In fact I think you're going to be very happy."

Michael Jordan, of course, was thrilled to be at Five-Star. He flew up to Pittsburgh with Leroy Smith, and they were both exhilarated and terrified. It was one thing to go to Dean Smith's camp in Chapel Hill, where they were among the relatively few accomplished high school stars and where their own high school coach already had some connections; it was another thing to go to a place where all the best players in America were going to be, the kind of players who were already being written about in the basketball magazines. They heard that there were *seventeen* high school All-Americans at the camp. Some of these All-Americans were said to have received fifty, sixty, even one hundred letters from interested colleges and to be keeping their letters stacked up in shoe boxes. So far, both Jordan and Smith had received very few letters, perhaps North Carolina–Wilmington, East Carolina, Appalachian State at Boone, and not much more. This was the make-or-break moment for them, the moment when they could perhaps go higher and be recruited by one of the better schools and live their dreams or fall and perhaps not even get a college scholarship. Leroy Smith's father was a welder for the Navy, and his mother a seamstress; if he did well it would take a great deal of financial pressure off them in terms of paying for a college education. Besides, they felt they were representing Wilmington, and it was important to make a good impression and not to seem like country hicks who didn't belong there.

The Five-Star camp was a throwback to the age of basketball past. There was nothing fancy about it. Garfinkel's camp was a place where not just young players arrived full of hope, thinking that if they played well they would not only go on a faster and better track to college, and perhaps the pros, but where a great many young coaches showed up sharing comparable hopes, in their cases of becoming college assistants, and then college coaches, and then one day, perhaps, professional coaches. In a way, Garfinkel was like a tout in the world of horse racing except that instead of horseflesh he touted young teenage males who played basketball. His great skill and contribution was to be able to pick up on a young player when he was still undiscovered and tout him to the world, so that people would later say that he was discovered at Five-Star. Garfinkel himself talked like a figure out of Damon Runyon, and his de facto office in New York, fittingly enough, was a back table at the Carnegie Delicatessen.

Later, Garfinkel identified that week as the moment a star was born. He remembered the moment the draft was about to start. Everyone expected Konchalski to select Aubrey Sherrod, and he picked Michael Jordan instead. Determined to see what this kid from North Carolina was like, Garfinkel arranged his schedule so he could watch Jordan's first game. All he needed, he later said, was to watch three possessions. "Actually," he added, "I only needed one possession." Jordan was playing defense, and he stripped the offensive player of the ball and drove down the court. He did not dunk, because dunks were not allowed at Five-Star. So Jordan raced ahead, with as explosive a burst of speed as Garfinkel had ever seen, and then as he approached the basket he slowed up slightly and softly laid the ball in with a gentle finger roll.

This was a teaching camp, and there was a certain wariness about dunking, a fear that a kid might get hurt going for a dunk and, even more important, a feeling if the kids were allowed to dunk, that was all they would do; they would believe that dunking was their ticket to the next level. But even without dunking, the Five-Star game was significantly more open than the Dean Smith camp, and it offered Jordan far greater opportunity to show off his physical ability.

Garfinkel watched a few more possessions and was amazed: Michael Jordan was the most explosive young player he had ever seen. He was quicker than anyone else, he had great jumping ability, and yet, amazingly, he played with an exceptional degree of poise and control. That was the surprising part. Most young kids with that kind of athleticism, Garfinkel thought, tended to play out of control, as if they thought that athletic talent was an end in itself. But this young kid had a degree of polish to his game that belied his years and the level of coaching he had already received.

Even as Jordan was playing, Garfinkel went to the phone and called his friend Dave Krider, who was also in the touting business. Krider was in charge of the high school All-American selections for *Street and Smith*, a kind of bible for colleges looking for quality players. Garfinkel's stock-in-trade was his reputation as someone who could spot greatness before anyone else, and now he was moving as quickly as he could to tout a player to another tout. Even as he made the call, Garfinkel was watching the game. Jordan was playing with nine other talented young players, almost all of whom had received more coaching than he had and several of whom were already prospective blue-chip college players, and he was completely taking over the game. In the brief time that Garfinkel watched, Jordan blocked three shots and made two steals. "Dave, I'm watching something extraordinary. I've got a great young player here. His name is Mike Jordan. He's amazing. Do you have him listed?" Thirty seconds later, Krider came back and said that he had never heard of him. "Well he's one of the top ten players in the country. You've got to get him on one of your two or three All-American teams. If you don't, everyone's going to make fun of you."

Krider called back later to say that his listings were all locked up and it was probably too late to change them, but he would talk to his editor. (Krider was in fact furious over what had happened—he later decided that the man in North Carolina who did the spotting for him, who had strong UNC connections, had deliberately left Jordan off his list of the top twenty players in the state because he wanted to keep other colleges off his trail.) A few hours later, Krider called Garfinkel back and said it was too late to change. "Tell your boss even if it costs $100 to make the change, it's worth it because the kid's going to be a great star, and they'll make fun of you if you don't have him," Garfinkel said. But it was all too late. Later that day, Garfinkel told Jordan that he had tried to get him onto Krider's listings.

Garfinkel had taken Jordan for two weeks. The first week seemed almost miraculous. He was MVP of the league and MVP of the all-star game. He was beginning to make his name. Brendan Malone fell in love with him, not just because of his ability but because he was so receptive to coaching. Nothing would be better than to bring him to Syracuse, Malone thought, but as he watched Jordan go to the various instructional stations each morning, he noticed that wherever he went there was a shadow; the shadow was a big one because it was cast by Roy Williams or some other Carolina coach. Someone from Carolina was always there.

Buzz Peterson went to the Five-Star Camp as well, although he arrived a week after Jordan. By the time he arrived, the only person anyone at the camp was talking about was Jordan. Once again they were able to spend a good deal of time together. They had now both moved to the elite of high school stars about to enter their senior year. Peterson had already played at the B/C Camp, where he had done unusually well and had greatly enhanced his own reputation by outplaying Aubrey Sherrod. It had been one of those days when he had been in a zone and almost everything he threw up went in. Years later he could remember what he had shot on that critical day: twelve of fifteen. After the game, Eddie Fogler came over to him and let him know that North Carolina wanted him. "A lot of other people are going to come after you," Fogler said, "but we want you to know that we want you very badly. We want you to know that we think this is the right place for you." Peterson's own future now seemed assured.

He and Jordan grew closer during their week at the Five-Star. They played against each other in the one-on-one championship, and Jordan won in a close game. They liked each other, and that week Jordan suggested that they go to North Carolina and room together. "We could win a national championship together there," Jordan said, and with the innocence and enthusiasm of youth, Peterson immediately agreed. They would go to Carolina together, and room together, and win the national championship together. They exchanged telephone numbers and decided to keep in touch that year.

The recruiting was heavy that year for both of them, but Carolina had the inside track. When he was younger, Michael Jordan had been interested in North Carolina State because David Thompson, a dazzling young player from the same state who had played above the rim, had gone there, but after Jordan went to the Dean Smith camp and Smith himself showed such a personal interest, Carolina was his first choice. (Years later, after he met many important and powerful people, including President Bush, Michael Jordan was asked if he had been nervous about meeting the president. No, he answered, the only person he had ever been nervous about meeting was Dean Smith.) Of course, there were other possibilities. Virginia was interested, and they not only had Ralph Sampson, a big man who could get you the ball and help win championships, but its players wore Adidas sneakers, which Jordan greatly preferred to Converse, the Carolina sneaker. South Carolina made a stab at him, too, and he was at one point brought in to meet the governor, a sign of the state's obvious concern with his education. And there was a brief moment when Dean Smith was a little worried about Duke because Deloris Jordan seemed to think Gene Banks of Duke was an exceptional player. But in the end, given the awesome hold Dean Smith and the Carolina program had on the state, it was extremely difficult to steal a great high school player from North Carolina. Not many in-state players whom Dean Smith really wanted were weaned away from Carolina. At one point, Brendan Malone called to ask if he would like to visit Syracuse.

"Coach, I really liked playing for you," Jordan answered, "but I've already made a decision to go somewhere else."

"I think I know where it is," Malone said. "Good luck anyway, Michael."

He went to Carolina, and Leroy Smith went to North Carolina–Charlotte, where he did well, becoming the school's second-leading rebounder behind Cedric Maxwell.

Carolina was the signature school in the state; Jordan had already visited Chapel Hill earlier on as a part of a high school civics program for minority students; a close friend from high school, Adolph Shivers, was already there; and his sister, Roslyn, intended to go there as well. In addition, the Jordan family liked Dean Smith, and both Jordan parents were particularly fond of Roy Williams, who had made the first connection with Michael and who kept in touch with them. In those days, Williams was the lowliest of the low on the Carolina staff, a graduate assistant. He did all the scut work, and he was paid the most marginal of salaries—$2,700 for the first year and $5,000 by the time Michael Jordan arrived. In years to come, one of the reasons Michael Jordan remained so intensely loyal to the Carolina program was because of the sacrifices that men such as Williams had made when he was there, working bone-crushing hours as assistant coaches and making tiny salaries. Their sacrifices, he believed, had gone into making him and his closest friends better, and he honored that gift and felt he owed them something in return.

That sense of indebtedness was shared by Michael's father. James Jordan enjoyed the company of Roy Williams immensely, and his wife later told the coach, "Ray [her private name for him] really likes you because he thinks you work so hard for your money and that always appeals to him. It's the way he sees his own life." During Michael's senior year in high school, Williams spoke to the senior Jordan about how he liked to chop wood, both for the exercise and for the fuel, and how he needed to get a woodstove for his house because he wanted to cut back on his heating bills. James Jordan asked for the measurements of his fireplace and said he thought he could take care of his woodstove problem. A few weeks later, Jordan drove up with a woodstove he had made himself. It gave him great pleasure to do this—he loved working with his hands and he liked making stoves for friends; this was the thirteenth one he had made, he said. Roy Williams tried to pay him something for the stove, and Jordan became irritated. "Coach," he said, "I'm really tired from finishing it and hauling it up here and bringing it in the house. If I have to carry it back out and take it all the way back to Wilmington I'm going to be very angry." Though the NCAA had somewhat draconian rules about players accepting gifts from coaches, it had none about assistant coaches accepting homemade woodstoves from parents, and the stove stayed, one more part of the glue that connected Michael Jordan to Chapel Hill. When Williams moved to a better house as he rose upward in the Carolina coaching hierarchy, James Jordan made him a woodstove for that house as well. When Williams eventually took the Kansas job and put his house on the market, the buyer asked what kind of woodstove it was. "Is it a Fisher?" he asked, mentioning a prominent brand of woodstove. "No," Williams answered, "it's a Jordan."

Somewhere in the middle of Michael Jordan's senior year there was a brief crisis. Kentucky, a big-time basketball power, made a run at Buzz Peterson. For a moment, Peterson fell in love with the basketball in Lexington. Basketball was obviously king there, the football program being significantly weaker than it was at Carolina, and he was awed by the Wildcat Lounge, where the basketball players resided. Kentucky seemed to treat its players like gods, and to his teenage eye the chance to cut such a wide swath on campus so quickly seemed wonderful. For a moment he more than wavered, and one Sunday he told the Kentucky people he was going there. The next day, his phone rang, and it was his high school coach, Rodney Johnson, who had heard from Randy Shepherd of his change in plans. Is it true about Kentucky? he asked. Yes, Peterson answered. It was at that point that Carolina turned on the pressure.

The tentacles of the Carolina program were not to be underestimated. Rodney Johnson was a Carolina loyalist, and he and Roy Williams were old and close friends; they had played with and against each other when they were young, and Johnson worked regularly at the Dean Smith camp. He was not about to let his prize player go to a powerful rival program. On Monday morning, Johnson spent two and a half hours with Buzz, talking him through his decision and subtly and not so subtly outlining the advantages of Chapel Hill. That night, there was a phone call from of all people Michael Jordan, and Peterson was sure that the Carolina people had put his friend up to it. "I hear you're thinking about Kentucky," Jordan said. Buzz said yes, that was true, that he had loved the program in Lexington, and he thought he would go there. "I thought we were going to go to college together and room together and win a national championship together," Jordan said, and Peterson could hear the disappointment—indeed, the hurt—in his voice.

The next day Dean Smith himself had shown up at the Peterson home. That was the coup de grâce. With his prestige in the state it was awesome, far more impressive than having a governor or a senator show up; if Dean Smith had driven all the way across the state to recruit him and say he wanted him, who was he not to go to Carolina? By the end of the week he was back on track for Carolina. His senior year in high school had been a great year for Buzz Peterson: He was Mister Basketball in North Carolina, and he had won an award that the Hertz company gave for being the top athlete in the state. When he finally announced which college he would attend, it was a huge statewide media event, and the Peterson home was crowded with television and print reporters. Peterson's father, Robert, was furious with all the commotion, feeling it was all too much, too much fame applied too soon to too young a person, something that would, he was sure, inevitably create too much pressure and too many expectations. He thought they were all in danger of stealing part of his son's childhood from him, and he barked at the media people that day to back off and give the boy some peace—to let him be a boy.

That fall, Michael Jordan showed up at Chapel Hill during the big recruiting weekend. All the people involved were supposed to be on their best behavior, both the chosen high school seniors who wanted to make a good impression at Carolina and the Carolina underclassmen whose job it was to be advertisements for Dean Smith and his program. All the doors to all the rooms were open so that the recruits could see how the players lived. James Worthy, by then a sophomore and already ticketed as a coming All-American, was in his room when he heard a voice in the hallway. The voice preceded the owner, and it was more than a little boastful. The voice was saying things like "this is going to be my hall," and "I'm going to be a star here." Worthy wondered what brash young man belonged to this cocky voice, and he looked out in the hall and saw a slim, almost skinny kid. Worthy thought to himself, If we get this kid here, then we're going to have to teach him some manners and some modesty. Even if he can back it up, Worthy remembered thinking, we don't talk like that around here, for modesty was a very conscious part of the Carolina program. That was his first introduction to Michael Jordan.

There were to be several more important sightings of Michael Jordan before he began his college career at Chapel Hill. He and Buzz Peterson kept their friendship up that summer, and they played together in a couple of all-star games: the Capital Classic in Washington, where Michael played against Patrick Ewing, then presumed to be the best high school player in the country, and then the McDonald's All-American Game in Wichita. In the process, the Peterson and Jordan families grew close as well. At the McDonald's game, the two young men started in the same backcourt, and Peterson, who scored ten points that day, could sense that Jordan was about to take off, that he had gone to a higher level. Adrian Branch, a highly recruited player already ticketed for Maryland, was also on the team and he played very well, but Michael was brilliant, scoring thirty points on thirteen of nineteen shooting (seventeen years later, his point total remains the highest for the game) and getting two rebounds. Branch got twenty-four points and eight rebounds. After the game, the judges who voted for the MVP—John Wooden, Sonny Hill, and Morgan Wooten—chose Branch, a decision that appeared slightly tainted on the surface, since Wooten was Branch's high school coach. For that reason, however, Wooten had excused himself from the judging. Branch won, the two other judges later explained, because he had hit his baskets at more decisive moments in the game.

The decision surprised some people in the crowd and some of the other players, because Jordan seemed the more dominant player. At one point after the decision was announced, Buzz Peterson looked behind the bench and spotted his own mother and Deloris Jordan coming down from their seats, headed straight for the judges' seats. They both seemed to be very angry, and he thought that a terrible confrontation was ahead and that Morgan Wooten might be in serious physical danger. Even as he saw their approach, he noticed Bill Guthridge, the Carolina assistant, trying to head them off, which he finally did. You could, thought Peterson, see where some of Michael's drive and competitiveness came from.

After the game, Billy Packer, who had covered the game for CBS, was leaving the floor with Bob Geoghan, one of the game's sponsors, when a still somewhat irate Deloris Jordan caught up with him and questioned the MVP decision. "I wouldn't worry that much about it, Mrs. Jordan," Packer had said. "It's only an all-star game, and there are going to be a lot of those in Michael's future—I think your son has a great career ahead of him."

If that decision to make Branch the MVP was a mistake, then it was Lefty Driesell, the coach of Maryland, who would eventually pay for it. Some three years later, as Jordan was finishing his junior year, Carolina played Maryland at Maryland's Cole Field House. With the game fairly well wrapped up at the end, Jordan, led by a brilliant pass from Sam Perkins, drove to the basket and unleashed one of the most thunderous dunks of his career. It was, thought Roy Williams, as if his whole body was above the rim. The dunk eventually came to have a name, Michael's rock-a-bye dunk, and it would make a number of the highlight videos of Jordan's greatest moments. "The most vicious thing I'd ever seen a college player do," remembered Michael Wilbon, who then covered the

ACC as a young sportswriter for *The Washington Post* and had not known of Jordan's history with Branch. "It was a truly angry act—a kind of super-in-your-face move." One player watching the game that night thought he understood the root and cause of it. Buzz Peterson knew that Jordan always liked to pay back anyone who slighted him, and this, he was sure, was nothing less than the payback for Branch, who had made the mistake, however involuntary, of being the recipient of the MVP award at the McDonald's game.

There was one more important sighting that summer. Both Peterson and Jordan were named to a team playing in the National Sports Festival. It was a pre-Olympic program held in Syracuse, New York, and forty-eight young players were working out there. The teams were selected by region: East versus West, North versus South. Tim Knight, the son of Indiana coach Bob Knight, was a manager there. Tim Knight was only eighteen years old, but having spent much of his childhood in his father's gym, he had a good eye for talent, and when he got home he told his father that he had seen a young man who was going to be the best college player in the country. Who's that? his father asked. "A kid named Michael Jordan who's already signed with North Carolina," he said.

So a few days later, Bobby Knight, in the way that coaches do, always checking up on things, called Dean Smith ostensibly about other things and then mentioned very casually that he had heard that Smith had a great young player coming in. Years later, Knight remembered something of a quick feint on Smith's part, possibly a reference to Buzz Peterson, who had been the more publicized player, but Knight countered quickly. No, a young kid named Michael Jordan. He sensed Smith becoming a little cautious at the other end, and Smith asked why he was asking about Jordan. "Because my son Tim saw him in Syracuse and says he's going to be the best player in the whole country," Knight said.

"Well, I hope so," Smith said, already working hard to limit the fuss and media attention about Jordan. "You know he wasn't that highly recruited. He's from around here, Wilmington—he's just a regional pick."

"Well, Tim thinks you have a great one," Knight said.

A few years later, Smith and Bob Knight were on a committee screening players for the Olympic team, and they were trying to decide about two kids no one seemed to know much about. Tim Knight, then attending school at Stanford, had seen them both play, and Bobby Knight looked at Tim's notes, which said that both players were quite limited.

"Well," said Dean Smith, "I don't know if you know Tim Knight, but if he says they can't play, they can't play."

Chapel Hill, 1981

I N 1981, when Michael Jordan arrived on campus as a freshman, Dean Smith was at the apex of his power and reputation, and his program was considered the best single basketball program in the country, even if Smith had yet to win his first national championship. Bob Ryan, the doyen of NBA writers, once noted that Smith did not so much recruit his choice players as he selected them. Ryan meant that Smith's program was so rich, the dynamic of it so powerful, that he, unlike other coaches, had the luxury of choice, of taking the players he wanted and who would fit readily into the program, rather than players of talent who might not adapt to the program and its uniquely rigorous demands. It was not an unflattering statement and it contained a considerable grain of truth but it irritated Dean Smith anyway.

Visiting coaches and players who were accorded the considerable honor of being allowed into the Carolina practices were always struck by a number of things. The first was how quiet it was, almost silent except for the noise made by a bouncing basketball, or the occasional yell of "Freshman!" when a ball went out of bounds, or the quick blast of a whistle that signified the end of one drill and the beginning of another, or the loud grunt of a player as he drove himself across the finish line in one of the endless running drills that Smith demanded in order to keep his players in top condition. The next thing was how brilliantly and carefully organized it was, with a schedule posted each day that outlined how each minute of practice would be used. Rick Carlisle, who had played against Carolina in his years at Virginia, was later let in when he worked as an assistant coach in the pro game, and he thought watching the Tar Heels practice was a revelation. Not only was practice mapped to the very second, but there was always a manager standing alongside the court holding up his fingers to show how many minutes to go in each drill. No wonder the Tar Heels had always seemed so calm and collected when he had played against them, no matter the frenzy in the gym, Carlisle thought. The answer was right here in this gym, where they repeatedly practiced each potential game situation: how they would play, for example, when they were six points behind with four minutes left. Nothing was ever to surprise them, and nothing, Carlisle thought ruefully, ever did.

No one was to be late for practice, for they were never to be behind schedule. Lateness hurt the team, and nothing was to be done that damaged or slowed down the team. When they went on the road, everything was to be done the right way: The players were to be well dressed, and they were not to be late; all the players set their watches to what they called GST, which was Guthridge Standard Time, in honor of Smith's top assistant, Bill Guthridge, who more often than not traveled with them. In Jordan's freshman year, the team bus was leaving Carmichael for the ACC championship at the appointed minute when a car began to pull up. The car contained James Worthy, the team's star, and because of a red light it was unable to cross the street to reach the bus. The bus pulled out exactly on schedule, and Worthy had to follow it in his car, knowing that he was in for some tough disciplinary words. On another occasion, three of the starters were three minutes late to a pregame meal because they had gone to get a haircut and been delayed by a slow barber. That meant they did not start and came into the game three minutes into the first half.

Dean Smith liked to be in charge of everything, and he did not relish surprises; thus, everything at Carolina was very carefully controlled. His was an extremely hierarchical system, where everyone was supposed to wait his turn. The coach, for example, made his crucial decisions about what the team would do—where it would stay on the road and at what restaurant the players would eat—in consultation with seniors. Freshmen were at the absolute bottom of the hierarchy, below even the team managers. In practice, when a loose ball came off heading toward the sidelines, someone would shout "Freshman!" and a freshman player, not a manager, would go racing over to get it. If the coach called for a water break, it was done by class: There might be a three-minute break with the seniors called first, and thirty seconds later the juniors called, and then a minute later the sophomores, and then with a minute left a coach would say, as if he had almost forgotten, oh yes, freshmen.

Everything was built around the concept of team and against the idea of individuality and the danger of individual ego. At the heart of it was a very disciplined system. Close observers of Dean Smith thought that over the years he was willing to lose certain games that he might otherwise have won by opening up the game completely and giving his players greater freedom, because in the long run he believed that you went further by working as a team and by sacrificing individuality to team effort. He also thought that the kind of discipline and selflessness he demanded would eventually serve his players better later in their lives. Expressions of a certain kind of emotion were frowned on. If a player drew a technical foul during a game, then at the next practice he was forced to sit comfortably on the sidelines, drinking a Coke while his teammates ran extra sprints to atone for his sin. Over the years, not many Carolina players drew technical fouls. Everything in the Carolina program had a multiple purpose: respect for team, respect for authority, respect for the game, respect for opponents. Smith's players were never to do anything that would diminish an opponent. Once when Carolina was playing a weak Georgia Tech team and was ahead by seventeen points, Jimmy Black and James Worthy combined on a showboat play in which Black flipped Worthy a behind-the-back pass and Worthy dunked. Smith was furious, and he immediately yanked both players from the game. "You don't do that," he said, truly angry. "You don't show people up! How would you like it if you were down seventeen points and someone did that to you!"

Out of all this came an ethic, a system, and, finally, a community, which if not unique was certainly special in high-powered contemporary American athletics. By the late seventies, Carolina had replaced UCLA as the premier basketball program in the country. Alcindor/Jabbar, Walton, and their amazing teammates (some of them more easily recruited once the big man was already signed up) and in time John Wooden himself were gone, freshmen were eligible, and the glue that had held UCLA together cracked. A series of coaches came hoping to restore UCLA's past glory and departed more quickly than they intended. By the eighties, when the past had come to haunt UCLA, it had been adroitly used to strengthen Carolina.

Dean Smith was the perfect man for a high-quality program at a quality school in the particular era in which he coached. That was an era in which the authority of the coach still had not been eroded by the growing material pressure from the outside world, pressure that allowed young talented players to enter college with too much leverage, and to remain there ever so briefly, more often than not on their own terms, and to depart all too soon for the pro game, more and more using what was now their first three-year pro contract as a surrogate for their college years. Certainly by the time Smith retired, those pressures were affecting Carolina as well, and the blue-chip players of his last years, young men like Rasheed Wallace and Jerry Stackhouse stayed a briefer time and seemed to go out into the professional world less well prepared than their predecessors, players like Worthy, Jordan, and Sam Perkins. Dean Smith was quiet and somewhat introverted, in direct contrast to the gregarious Frank McGuire, who had preceded him and who had the particular talents and charm of the best of the Irish-American politicians of his generation. Smith was acutely aware of the inherent natural limits of his own personal charisma. Other coaches were emotional, he was not. He always seemed to be on the same emotional plane, and if anything colleagues sometimes criticized him privately for his lack of pregame emotional fire, for treating an early-season game with Davidson and a Final Four game with the same coolness. It was probably one of the things his players liked about him—his consistency and the fact that he never played with their emotions.

Smith's early years at Carolina had been hard. At first, he was an alien in the land, a transplant from Kansas, a man without any local roots in a region where that mattered greatly, a man modest and somewhat uncomfortable with the easy, blustery collegiality that was the sportsworld norm. He was also, in his own way, very ambitious and driven, someone who left as little as possible to chance, and he possessed a strong sense of right and wrong that went far beyond basketball. His basketball world was, if anything, an extension of his own religiosity.

At first, he had trouble recruiting because of the violations committed by McGuire before him. His early teams were not that successful, and Billy Cunningham, one of his first great players—a man who had once rushed out of the team bus to cut down an effigy of Smith that was being hung on campus—always wondered whether Smith would have been successful twenty-five years later, in a subsequent era. The question was not about his talent as a coach, Cunningham thought, but whether with the increased pressure to win and win immediately Smith would have had a chance to install a system and create the kind of winning dynamic that eventually served himself and the university so well. If there was a glue to the Carolina system, it was that once you had arrived, as far as the coaching staff was concerned, there were no stars.

The twelfth man on the bench was treated as well as the team's best player, and Dean Smith would fight as hard trying to help find a bench player a job upon graduation as he would for the most gifted player on the team, and he would treat him as well off the court.

Cunningham, an All-American at Carolina and a high first-round draft choice, believed that if anything Smith had been harder on him than on other, less gifted players—withering in his sarcasm if Cunningham took too many shots or shot too early in a possession or did not set a proper screen. The lessons were clear: There were no favorites, and exceptional ability did not entitle a player to any favoritism from the coach. Rather, Smith clearly believed that from those to whom much more had been given, much more was expected. As the other players saw the inherent fairness of the program, the lack of favoritism to the favored, and as they learned that the coach's loyalty to them had nothing to do with their point-per-game production, almost all of them bought in, the great ones as well as the lesser ones, knowing deep inside that it was better for them to be pushed than to be catered to.

As his program became more and more successful and Dean Smith became, like it or not, far more famous than anyone else in the university, his friends thought he became uncomfortable with that fame, as if there was something wrong when a coach could become more famous and more powerful than a gifted professor or the chancellor of a great university. (He was not pleased that when UNC built a new basketball arena, it named it after him. The Dean E. Smith Center, it was called, the Dean Dome in the vernacular. He went along with it only because he thought the university needed it, and the people behind the drive assured him that the drive might fail unless they used his name.) Smith was also very much aware of the uses of his position. He became in his own way a very good recruiter because he remained true to himself. He could not be like Lefty Driesell, who was considered a brilliant recruiter. Driesell was hotter in style, and there was nothing understated about him or his pitch; he was a joyous, old-fashioned huckster. By contrast, Smith was involuntarily cool and understated, the well-regarded local minister who happened by chance to be as committed to the concept of winning basketball as he was to the idea of living a good, virtuous, religious life. (Smith's religious beliefs were a serious part of his life: For a long time he smoked, but seemed to be embarrassed about it, and he tended to sneak his cigarette breaks, not unlike a teenage kid trying to fool his parents, and he liked an occasional drink, but also did it somewhat covertly.) If anything, because of the almost formal nature of his personality, he was often better with the parents than he was with the kids. With parents, his very lack of charisma was often an asset; he was skilled at reassuring them that he knew what was good for their sons in the long run and that his values were an extension of theirs.

His great strength was not, in the end, in his words but in his life. His program was his own truth, and the longer he ran it, the more powerful year by year the magnetic force of it became. In the end, what he had done, and what kinds of lives his players went on to lead and their reverence for him spoke more than anything else for who he was. This had its own benefits—it allowed him to make his recruiting pitch in a lower, softer key than many competitors. Dean Smith was particularly good with old-fashioned God-fearing people, such as the Worthys and the Jordans, who had raised their children under a strict value system, who valued hard work, and who were properly distrusting of any recruiter who seemed to promise too easy a route to success.

Dean Smith never promised anything. Other programs were passing money, offering cars, and above all promising playing time—saying that a player would be in the starting lineup as a freshman. Sometimes high school seniors would arrive on a campus as recruits to find that a photo had been created of them standing there in the school's uniform as part of the starting five. Smith's pitch was the reverse: We will not promise you minutes, but we think you can play here, we think we can make you a better player, we know you'll get a wonderful education, and we think you'll like the people in our program, particularly the other players. The premise was that the better the kids, the more likely Carolina was to get them; meanwhile the kids they did not get were the ones who were going to cause problems in the long run. That particular soft pitch worked very well in most homes. Mitch Kupchak had been warned by his high school coach to be wary of college coaches bearing promises—"if they're promising you something, try and imagine what they're promising other kids just like you." So when Kupchak went to one college for his interview he found himself waiting outside the coach's office along with two other tall young men. He was the last to be called in and the coach promised that he could be the starting center as a freshman. When he returned home Kupchak found himself wondering what the same coach had promised the other two young men.

As the stakes in the world of basketball mounted in the sixties and seventies and eighties, and as the rewards for those successful heads of powerful programs became ever greater, Smith remained remarkably true to himself. A great many of the younger coaches who were considered great recruiters were selling first and foremost themselves rather than their programs; Dean Smith never made that mistake—what he was selling was the program and the university, a great basketball program at a great American university, where even if there was not a pro career later in life, a young man would be well prepared to deal with his professional future and would have a variety of options to choose from. He used the talented young men already enrolled at Carolina as an additional instrument of his recruiting. They were the proof of his program's excellence, and they were exceptionally effective recruiters, their names already well known to the high school players who were now hoping to follow in their footsteps. *We are a very special club, we are each other's friends,* they seemed to say. *Come here and join us and be part of something unique. You'll like it, and we'll like you.*

The tradition was important. At Chapel Hill, the past not only lived and was enshrined but was skillfully used to open the door to the future. The sense of the past, of all those great teams and all those great players who had starred at Chapel Hill and gone on to professional fame, was an important part of the mystique, hallowed and very much alive. It was not an abstract part of the recruiting; it was critical. At Carolina, the best recruiters were the players already in the program and the ones who had recently graduated and had gone on to professional careers. For a prospective blue-chip prospect, they were always ready to pick up the phone and use the authority that went with their success to say how much they had loved playing at Carolina. So it was that a trembling high school junior or senior would put down the phone one night in his home and mention the next day to his friends that James Worthy or Michael Jordan had called and pushed for Carolina. But even more than the alumni, it was the friendliness and the enthusiasm of the current players and the camaraderie built into the program that was so effective. And of course, the current players peppered their conversation with references to the informal games that took place during the summer, when the alumni great—Phil Ford, Walter Davis, Mitch Kupchak, Mike O'Koren, and, in time, James Worthy, Sam Perkins, and Michael Jordan— came back and played with them every day. It was heady stuff.

More, it stood in sharp contrast to many other colleges where the principal pitch came entirely from the coaches and the assistant coaches and where the authorities seemed more than a little wary of having the current players interact with recruits when there was no one else around. For at many schools where corners were being cut, and where the ethical slopes were significantly more slippery, the programs were more cynical. In such programs, coaches did not lightly turn their backs for fear that the current players would talk to the recruits about promises made at the height of the recruiting lovesong but broken once the player arrived on campus. At some schools where coaches ran exceptionally successful programs in football or basketball, powerful feelings of loyalty were generated among the alumni and the student body; at Carolina the most powerful feelings came from the players themselves.

No school worked its connection to the past as skillfully as Carolina. Mitch Kupchak had finished his rookie year with the Washington Bullets and returned to Chapel Hill one summer when he was introduced to a young gangly boy, whom he learned was only fifteen years old. "Mitch come over here—I'd like you to meet James Worthy," Roy Williams had said that day. "We're all hoping that James will be a great star here." And Kupchak could also remember a few years later when he flew from Los Angeles to New Orleans to watch Carolina in the championship game against Georgetown. It was Michael Jordan's freshman year, and Kupchak was standing around in the lobby when Bill Guthridge brought over a slim young man and said, "Michael, I'd like you to meet one of our great players from the past, Mitch Kupchak."

Because there were a lot of rules at Chapel Hill and because the program demanded sacrifice and patience, it was critical for the kids to buy in. In time, almost all of them did. The disappointed kid who transferred out was extremely rare. The players bought in because the purpose of it all became obvious: The rules existed to make you a better player and a better person, not to make Dean Smith more famous or richer or to get him a job coaching in the NBA. Much of the program was driven by peer pressure, by the fact that the upperclassmen and the existing stars had endorsed it and had waited their turn. Who was some freshman hotshot to say that the rules did not apply to him when the best players on the team were spokesmen for the system?

It was as if it were a university within a university, with its own exceptional set of lessons, lessons that were more about life than about basketball. Behind it was a series of old-fashioned, almost Calvinist values more and more at risk in the increasingly material culture of American sports, driven by the ever more predatory force of a new entertainment culture, in which money is presumed to buy anything, first and foremost loyalty. At Carolina, the ethic seemed to come from another time: The more you sacrificed for a goal—the higher the price you paid in personal terms—the more it would one day mean to you. That which came too easily would never be valued. There was a second corollary, and it was simply that team was more important than self, no matter how exalted and talented and highly promoted the self. What you did on the court you did in concert with and for your teammates. The more you thought about them and the less you thought about yourself the better.

When they were about to leave Carolina, the players felt an enormous connection to the distant, often gruff man who had at times seemed so unreachable but who had played so important a part in their and their closest friends' lives. As they were about to depart, the veil around him dropped, and he reached out to them as a friend, not just as an authority figure. What was essential to their feelings was their elemental belief that he had cared more for them as men than as basketball players and worked harder to prepare them for life than for the NBA. "It was," James Worthy said years later, "as if there was a long list of things that Dean Smith could teach you and that basketball was at the bottom of the list, and preparing you for life was far more important than anything else. He taught us how to be patient, how to wait our turn, how to be courteous to people, how to respect teammates and the game."

What strengthened the tissue, of course, was that Smith seemed to pay more attention to them once they graduated, guiding, if at all possible, their careers, putting more energy into the players whose talent was more limited than those whose skills were such that they had no problems upon graduation. Within the professional ranks, general managers learned to be extremely wary of players whom Dean Smith pushed exceptionally hard—it was often unconscious, but it was considered his way of paying back some of his less talented players for their years of loyalty to the program. Sometimes it seemed as if his real commitment to them began only after their eligibility was completed.

Right after American players began playing in Europe, some Italian executives had come to see him about the possibility of signing Billy Cunningham, a player who was about to be a major star in the NBA. Smith directed them instead toward one of his other players. "The man you really want is Doug Moe," he said. "He'd be perfect for you." Doug Moe signed with them, and he played in Italy for two happy years. When he returned to the States he seemed to be floundering, selling insurance, still short of his college degree. Dean Smith pushed Moe to go back to school, but Moe had not listened. One day Moe got a phone call from Smith. "You've got an interview at Elon College [a small college near Burlington, North Carolina] at two o'clock today. Wear a coat and tie." There he worked as an assistant coach, in time finished his studies, and got a degree.

Dean Smith's boys were to go to class, and their attendance there was monitored closely. They were also to attend church unless they had a note from their parents saying that they did not go to church at home. There were all kinds of lessons that had nothing to do with basketball.

Lessons on how to talk to the media, how to look reporters in the eye when you spoke to them, and how to know before you started to talk what you wanted to say. They were taught how to deal with people who wanted to talk with them, how to dress and order in a restaurant, and how to stand up when a woman approached their table.

The loyalties that this program created—to the school, to the man, and above all to each other—in the end were remarkable and quite possibly unmatched in contemporary college athletics. Dean Smith was forever Coach to them. Grown men in their thirties and forties still checked in with him when they made critical career decisions. When professional basketball teams fighting for crucial playoff berths met in decisive games, before the game Carolina players now on rival teams would be on the sideline talking about Coach. One year, George Karl, Carolina '73, coach of the Seattle SuperSonics, talked with Mitch Kupchak, Carolina '76, assistant general manager of the Lakers, bitter rivals in the West, about whether, on their way to the all-star game in New York, they would go through Chapel Hill to see Coach and watch a Carolina-Duke game. They did. When a terrible tragedy took place in the family of Scott Williams, a former Carolina player, it was a *Carolina* tragedy. His father killed his mother and then took his own life. At the funeral of Williams's mother in Los Angeles, one NBA executive noticed that in addition to Dean Smith, both Mitch Kupchak and James Worthy were there, players who had been at Chapel Hill long before Williams. "I didn't know you knew him," the man said to Kupchak.

"He was one of ours," Kupchak answered.

If anything, Donnie Walsh, part of the Carolina mafia and in 1998 the head of the Indiana Pacers, felt there was a certain professional contradiction if you were a Carolina man trying to run your own professional program. The danger, Walsh had come to realize, was that Dean Smith was so powerful a figure in your life that you were accustomed to listening to him and taking his word as gospel, but you could no longer do that if you were doing player personnel because his interest and yours were not necessarily compatible. Smith's primary consideration was advancing his latest kids; your primary consideration was improving your program. The two were not necessarily the same. Larry Brown, another member of the Carolina group, still listened a bit too much, it was said, and took some of Smith's kids, which pleased Smith at first, but then when they were cut, Smith would become furious, because cutting one of his boys was like cutting him.

"The Dean Smith thing at North Carolina is like a cult," said Chuck Daly, the former Penn and Detroit Pistons and Dream Team coach. Daly was one of the few outsiders allowed to attend a Carolina golfing reunion held under Smith's supervision at Pinehurst each summer. "Most cults are bad, but this is the rare good cult. But it's a cult nonetheless." Or as former NBA coach Kevin Loughery, a man who had spent more than his proper share of time coaching weak teams, and who had also been granted dispensation for the Pinehurst golf game, added, "I never rooted for Carolina. I always root for the underdog. I know all too well what it's like to have the less talented team. But after I met Dean Smith I found that if I could not root for him because his teams were so loaded with talent, at least I couldn't root against him. Because I'm struck by the loyalty, the reverence of so many truly accomplished men for him, the sense that their feeling about him is absolutely genuine."

Not everyone outside the program, particularly those who competed with Dean Smith, admired him as much. Some were put off by what seemed a surface piety in a man whose competitive instincts were so fierce. Others resented a sense he sometimes seemed to project that he always had the moral high ground and that what he did was a little purer and less materialistic than what they did: that coaching basketball was nobler than being a lawyer or an agent; that coaching college ball was purer than coaching professional ball; and, finally, that coaching at Carolina was purer than coaching anywhere else. Some thought him less pure than his image, and others were bothered by the way he tried to manipulate the press, constantly seeking, despite the depth of his teams, the role of underdog. Dean Smith was the only man in history who had won seven hundred games and been the underdog in every single one of them, said Lefty Driesell. Mike Krzyzewski, the coach of Duke, who ran a rival program of comparable strength and integrity and who battled him over the years for victory and for the same high-quality blue-chip kids, once said that if he ever became president of the United States, the job he would hold out for Dean Smith was the head of the CIA, "because he's the sneakiest guy I know."

There was one additional very important thing about Dean Smith that most white sports fans did not realize: He was, as Michael Wilbon has noted, a bigger hero and a bigger god in black America than in white America. Black Americans were acutely aware of his history at Carolina, that Smith had been far ahead of the curve on race.

Parts of black America faced something of a dilemma in March 1982, Wilbon pointed out, when Georgetown, coached by John Thompson, who is black, played Carolina in the NCAA championship game. Thompson, as Wilbon said, was considered one of ours by black people, but Dean Smith was looked on with good favor as well, as a kind of fellow traveler. He had integrated his program far earlier than other southern schools had, never under duress but with grace and skill and even tenderness. He had also helped integrate a popular downtown Chapel Hill restaurant early in his career, at a time when his own job often seemed on the line and when integration was hardly fashionable.

As early as 1961, Smith had tried to recruit Lou Hudson, a great player who had been unable to meet Carolina's academic requirements and had gone to Minnesota and on to an exceptional pro career. Smith continued trying and eventually broke the barrier by successfully recruiting Charlie Scott in 1966. Smith dealt with Scott during his years there with great sensitivity, in a region that was not yet entirely prepared for so earth-shattering a sight as that of a black Carolina basketball player. Smith made Scott a member of the Carolina family from the start, taking him to church on his first visit—a white church, not a black one, as Scott had anticipated. When a fan at the University of South Carolina yelled cruel racial epithets at Scott, two Carolina assistants had to stop Smith from going into the stands. Unlike many coaches in those days who integrated their programs but not their hearts, Smith went the full distance; years later, Scott named his second son after his college coach. The effect on black players who followed was not inconsiderable. "My father," James Worthy once said, "admired Dean Smith very much even before he stepped foot in our house. My father never went beyond the eighth grade, but he read the papers and he watched Walter Cronkite on television, and he was a man who knew about things, and he knew what Dean Smith had done in Chapel Hill, and how he had dealt with Charlie Scott, not just playing him, but being there for him, and that was the kind of man he wanted me to play for. That was a good deal more important to him than the money that some other schools were offering."

The ideal career trajectory for a highly recruited Carolina player would find him sitting for almost his entire freshman year, taking his solace and reward from practicing against the varsity each day and from the camaraderie of his peers. He might make a few cameo appearances, as much for psychological effect as anything else. As a sophomore, showing that he had been worthy of being a recruit, he might play between seven and eight minutes a game. By his junior year, he would be in the rotation and he might play twenty-five minutes a game. As a senior, he would be virtually a lord of the realm, making decisions in alliance with the coach.

Above all at Chapel Hill the system, the concept of team, absolutely overshadowed individual ability. There was a great belief in the professional ranks that the Carolina system suppressed individualism, but James Worthy, a brilliant athlete and a classic examplar of the Carolina system, phrased it differently: The system was designed not so much to reduce athleticism and individualism as it was designed to reduce risk. The ball was always to be shared. The purpose was to create good shots for everyone. That meant that a superlative athlete who at any other school might get twenty-five shots a game would get only twelve or fifteen at Carolina. In his last year at Carolina, on his way to being a consensus All-American and the number-one pick in the NBA draft, Worthy averaged only ten shots and 14.5 points a game; Michael Jordan, who would ring up seven seasons in a row as a pro where he averaged 30 or more points a game, averaged only 17.5 points a game in his last season at Carolina.

It was sometimes hard for pro scouts to tell how good Carolina players were because the program at once made certain players look better than they really were—they became the beneficiary of the system, their strengths magnified, their flaws hidden, or at least partially hidden—and at the same time it often suppressed the talents of great individual stars who might average ten or fifteen points a game more in another system. By the late 1980s, as the salaries of pro basketball players escalated ever higher, more and more talented young players started racing through their college years, staying only one or two years before coming out and signing lucrative contracts. As a result, when they chose their colleges they often chose programs that would showcase their individual abilities. They listened to the siren songs of coaches who promised them that from day one they would be the main man and the offense would be built around them.

That meant that the value system that Dean Smith had orchestrated so carefully over more than two decades at Carolina was in danger of becoming something of an anachronism in the fall of 1981 when Michael Jordan showed up at Chapel Hill. Here was the arrival of a remarkably gifted young man, one who by dint of his superlative athletic ability could readily have represented a challenge to the existing ethos. For try to suppress the news of Jordan's talents as Smith and his staff might, talent was talent. Even though Jordan played happily within the Smith system, there were constant sightings within the ACC of just how brilliant this young man was, quick flashes in an ordinary game where there would be a burst of speed on offense and an exceptional move to the basket or a dazzling defensive play. By the middle of his freshman year, even though nowhere near as many games were being seen on television as would be seen a few years later, there was a back-channel word among ACC aficionados that there was a brilliant young kid at Carolina, a kid who was being talked about as the next Julius Erving.

What Dean Smith did with Michael Jordan, therefore, was nothing less than brilliant. He brought him along slowly—much more quickly than he probably wanted to and might have done in another age, but this was a new era—but he never bent his program or his rules for him. He made Jordan work his way to stardom through the program. Michael Jordan would have to play by the Carolina rules; he would have to earn everything. He would have to be willing to excel at all the hard, gritty work of practice drills. As a result, he became an infinitely more finished and more complete player and, perhaps even more important, a player who, for all his wondrous natural talent, respected authority and was unusually easy for a series of coaches to reach once he turned pro.

Yet even before the season began, there had been a sense of his raw talent and his great cockiness. Barely enrolled in school, he was telling upperclassmen in team pickup games that he was going to dunk on them, players such as James Worthy, Sam Perkins, Jimmy Black, and Matt Doherty, members of a team that had gone to the NCAA Semifinals the year before. At first there was a certain irritation with his brashness, but gradually that began to disappear, first because the boasting was of a sweet kind, more joyous and ebullient than arrogant and mean-spirited, the talk of a bubbly kid rather than an ugly, conceited one; second because he could almost always back up his words with his play. His boasting, Buzz Peterson decided, was part of his game. He used it as a motivational tool to push himself, for if he talked big then he had to deliver big. And even in these first preseason practices, he was delivering big.

He wanted to be on the starting team that first year. In his hunger and enthusiasm for basketball, in his growing sense of how good he was, the future was now. But there were two people to beat out: Jimmy Braddock, a veteran player entering his third year whose asset was his experience, and Buzz Peterson, his roommate and best friend, who hoped to start as well. The competition between the two roommates was particularly intriguing. Peterson was not like a lot of white high school basketball players who were wonderful pure shooters but who hit their peak at about eighteen. He was in fact a very good all-around athlete, and his high school coaches in Asheville had thought, in the years before he decided to concentrate on basketball, that he might even be an NFL quarterback one day. He had speed and moves and quickness, as well as an exceptional outside shot.

The NBA player his peers eventually compared him to was Rex Chapman, a quick, talented, almost reckless guard from Kentucky. More, the two or shooting-guard slot was open when he and Jordan arrived, which was one reason Peterson had decided in the end to opt for Chapel Hill instead of Kentucky. Beating out Peterson posed a significant challenge for Michael. Peterson had genuine speed: in the forty-yard sprints they ran on the first day, Peterson came in second, behind James Worthy but ahead of Jordan, much to Michael's chagrin.

At first, the competition between them seemed relatively even. If Jordan had more pure athletic ability, then Peterson was probably a little more experienced as an overall player. He had had better coaching in high school and had a better overall sense of the game, was a better pure shooter, and probably had better defensive fundamentals. But Peterson knew that because Jordan was so superior an athlete, it would only be a matter of time before he was on a considerably higher plateau. Michael was not only a better jumper and was quicker (the sprints notwithstanding), he had those long arms and giant hands that made him deadly when he drove to the basket. Besides, with that great quickness he was also a very tough defender. The other thing Peterson could sense was his roommate's hunger—he was desperate to excel, and he seemed to soak up every bit of coaching.

What Buzz Peterson did not know at first about Michael Jordan, however, something that few knew and most would learn the hard way, was his competitive rage, his driving desire to be the best, and his almost unique ability to motivate himself and to use slights, real or imagined or self-invented, to drive him forward. Eventually, that particular ability was to become well known, and NBA players and coaches learned to censor what they said about Michael Jordan, lest the most innocent words come back to haunt them. But this was early in his career, and no one else knew of Jordan's ability to push himself to a higher level. In this particular case, he used the fact that Peterson had been more highly heralded as a high school player, had won more awards, including Mister Basketball of North Carolina and the Hertz Award, and had gotten more recruiting letters earlier on. Even worse, there were some people on the playgrounds of Wilmington who taunted Jordan after he won his North Carolina scholarship, told him that he would never play there, that he was going to sit behind Peterson because Peterson was a far bigger star: *Michael, you're going to sit behind Buzz Peterson, he's player of the year and you ain't big at nothin' but Laney High. Man, you ain't leavin' that bench!* With most athletes, words like that quickly fell away, but Jordan had learned early on their uses, just as he had learned from being cut in his sophomore year of high school. They became a weapon he could use to push himself to his outer limits.

Jordan, it turned out, did start his freshman year. He was not only beating out Peterson, his roommate, when the latter was injured, but equally important, he was winning a tight competition with Jimmy Braddock, a veteran player. The coaches thought Braddock was more complete offensively, and it was Jordan's defensive skills that catapulted him forward.

Dean Smith hated to start freshmen. Starting freshmen, allowing them big minutes and chances to gain fame precipitously (as well as chances to make costly mistakes in big games), went against the very purpose of his carefully constructed hierarchy. Smith had a rule against freshmen talking to the media before their first conference game. Smith was extremely wary of what the media could do to his team. Reporters caused swelled heads and tended to emphasize individual rather than team accomplishments. In particular, he did not like the media's focus on his freshmen, who had not yet been formed by the culture of the program, with all its little disciplines. But at Carolina everything was supposed to be earned, and the truth was that as the season was about to start, Michael Jordan had earned a place as a starter. Only three other freshmen had started in Carolina history: Phil Ford, against whom all potential point guards were to be measured; James Worthy, who had begun to attend Smith's camp as a freshman in high school and about whom Smith had once said, using the phrase that the pros used about college stars, that he hoped that Worthy would come out of high school as a hardship case in the tenth grade because they were so eager to have him; and Mike O'Koren.

But if he had earned the right to start, he had not earned the right to have a big head. Quite the reverse: Because he was so innately cocky, because he was always talking to teammates about how he was going to dunk on them, he had been elected—as a sign of both affection and the need to keep him in his place—to one of the more onerous freshman jobs: carrying the film projector that they took with them on all trips to visiting schools. The projector, in those prevideotape days, was heavy and bulky, and there was no way a person, even one as strong and graceful as Michael Jordan, could walk through an airport and look good while carrying it. That also made him the target for a considerable amount of good-natured teasing.

If anything, some thought, Dean Smith was a little harder on Jordan every day in practice than he was on other young players, as if accepting his greater possibilities and his own limitless ambition and holding him to it, setting higher standards for him than for the others. Roy Williams was also always pushing Jordan to work harder in practice. "I'm working as hard as everyone else," Jordan answered.

"But Michael, you told me you wanted to be the best," Williams once reminded him. "And if you want to be the best, then you have to work harder than everyone else." There was, Williams thought, a long pause, while Jordan pondered that.

Finally he said, "Coach, I understand. You'll see. Watch."

He had certain strengths that could not be coached, which were simply physiological gifts. There was the speed, which was critical at Chapel Hill. Everyone was supposed to run, and everyone was supposed to be in great condition. Jordan obviously had unusual speed, even if he had come in third in the first day's sprints. The players from then on ran in different groups according to size and position. The C group was for the big men, who were supposed to be slower; the B group was for off guards and small forwards, the medium-sized players, who might be fast but not that fast; and the A group was for the point guards, the quickest players on the team, and the occasional slightly taller superspeedster like the great Walter Davis. Technically, Michael Jordan should have been with the B group, but from the start Dean Smith put him with the A group as a means of putting more pressure on him.

The other players learned to accept him. Michael talked big and then played big. He was, decided Worthy, like a friendly little gnat who was always buzzing around boasting of what he was going to do. You'd swat him away, Worthy thought, and then he'd come buzzing right back at you, boasting a little more. Tenacious as hell, Worthy decided. Every day in practice there was a moment when they saw a quick flash of his amazing talent.

Once, when he was playing against the varsity in an early practice, he had amazed everyone with one of his moves, not the least because he had done it against two bigger men, both of them future All-Americans, Worthy and Sam Perkins. It was a move James Worthy was to remember for a long time, a sign of what was to come over the next two decades. Jordan drove down the lane, and Perkins came out to stop him. Jordan moved the ball to his left hand to get away from Perkins, but that gave Worthy, who was just behind Perkins, an excellent shot at him. But even as Worthy moved toward Jordan as Jordan went by Perkins, Michael twisted his body in a way to cut off Worthy's angle on the ball, and he shot the ball from an impossible angle, using his body as a kind of umbrella to protect the ball, ending the move with his body essentially turned away from the basket. The ball, of course, went in.

Practice did not stop, because practice never stopped at Chapel Hill, but it was a breathtaking moment nonetheless, and later everyone was talking about it. Worthy had never seen anything like it. No one had: the body control, the ability to adjust. But what he remembered most about it was that it had all been pure instinct, that Jordan had been able to make up his mind and have his body obey his mind even in the microseconds after he left the ground. It was a combination of athletic ability, pure basketball instinct, and instantaneous athletic intelligence the like of which Worthy had never seen before. Years later, Worthy thought of it as the first real glimpse of what was to come. Michael was eighteen at the time.

Carolina was an ideal situation for him. He was playing with experienced, talented, demanding teammates in a disciplined program where everything had been carefully thought out long ago. He did not have to carry a team, and he could learn without being at the center of the program. Not many supremely talented young men, still growing into their bodies—for he was still growing that year—work out in a program that has coaches as skilled as Dean Smith, Bill Guthridge, Eddie Fogler, and Roy Williams. This meant he could come of age at something of his own pace.

Jordan had earned the right to start, but he was going to do it under certain restrictions. That year, *Sports Illustrated*, knowing that Carolina was loaded—the unanimous preseason pick for number one in the country—asked Dean Smith to let them put the starting team on the cover of its annual preseason college-basketball issue. Smith agreed somewhat reluctantly, but with one caveat: They could have four of his starters but not the fifth, the young freshman from Wilmington. The *SI* people pleaded with him, for they had already begun to hear a good deal about Jordan, but Smith was adamant. He would make the other players available and he would make himself available, but not his freshman.

"Michael," he later explained to the freshman, "you haven't done anything to deserve the cover of a magazine. Not yet. But the others have. So that's why I don't think you should be in the photo." So it was that *SI* featured Sam Perkins, James Worthy, Matt Doherty, and Jimmy Black, ready, it appeared, to play a new kind of NCAA basketball, four on four. Later, after that team won the championship, an artist's sketch was made of the same cover for a poster, only this time the likeness of Michael Jordan had been added. Dean Smith had handled the situation brilliantly, Roy Williams decided; he had not so much denied a talented young player an honor of the most fleeting kind as he had issued a challenge to a young man who more than anything else loved to respond to challenges. (That year, Billy Packer and Al McGuire went on national television to pick their candidates for the coming national championship. McGuire picked Wichita. Packer picked Carolina. "I hear Carolina's going to start a freshman," McGuire, the former Marquette coach, said, "And I know you can't win a national championship with a freshman.")

There was a kind of underground quality to the early sightings of Jordan, not unlike the early sightings of the young Julius Erving when he was just starting out in the old ABA. Because few ABA games were on television, the early legend of Dr. J was largely created by word of mouth, by an awed description of a spectacular move by someone who had not seen it but had heard of it from a friend he trusted as he passed the sighting on to yet another basketball junkie. When Michael arrived at Carolina, ESPN was in only its second year, and relatively few games were on television. That, plus the particular understated nature of the Carolina offense, meant that the moments when the basketball elite actually saw Michael Jordan make a great move were relatively few. Mostly it was stories passed along among the junkies, the scouts, the assistant coaches, the hard-core basketball journalists, the people always looking to spot the next soaring superstar. That season, Michael Wilbon was already hearing a great deal about this wildly talented kid at Chapel Hill. It was. mostly word of mouth, people claiming to have seen a move; more often than not, it would turn out that they had heard of the move from someone whom they knew and trusted. Some of these moves were made in games, but most of them took place in practice. Sometimes the sighting might take place at a pickup game somewhere in the region: This young phenom named Michael Jordan who played at Carolina suddenly appeared as if out of the mist, it was said, got out of a car at a playground in Raleigh, laced up his sneakers, and proceeded to amaze everyone there for an hour before racing back to his car and disappearing as mysteriously as he had appeared. The reports had a wonderful ghost-as-legend quality to them: He was only six foot one but he outjumped men five inches taller, someone said. He was six foot eight and handled the ball like Magic Johnson, far better than smaller men at the point, someone else said. Some stories had the tantalizing quality of sounding at once true and exaggerated. On one dunk, he had hung in the air forever, longer than Julius Erving ever had, or he had driven to the basket, gone into the air, and switched the ball to his left hand at the last moment. Some of the professional scouts who claimed to have been allowed into Dean Smith's practices were reported to have said that Jordan in practice occasionally made moves that even Perkins and Worthy could not match. He was still a freshman at the time, almost no one in the world of basketball had seen him play, and yet Wilbon remembered that a ferocious debate had already started over whether Dean Smith was holding him back.

The truth was that the coaches were generally quite pleased with his progress. He was not only a hard worker, he was a quick learner, with exceptional powers of concentration. He had been taught in high school to defend the backdoor play one way, and Carolina defended it the opposite way, but in just one coaching session Dean Smith managed to teach him the Carolina style. It was, the coach later reflected, an early sign of Jordan's willingness and desire to improve and push himself to a higher level. His freshman year was not always smooth. He was not that good a shooter, and veteran opponents wanting to stop Worthy and Perkins often played a zone and conceded him shots. In one early season game against Kentucky, he kept shooting and missing. Watching that game on television were the former Tar Heel great Phil Ford and his professional teammate, Otis Birdsong. "What's that kid Jordan got on Coach Smith?" Birdsong asked Ford.

The road to the Final Four was difficult in 1981–1982. There were some people who thought that Virginia, with the towering Ralph Sampson, might be the best team in the country. The two schools split their regular-season games. Then, in the ACC tournament, in the days when there was no shot clock in college basketball, Carolina won a boring game in which Sampson simply hung around the basket and Carolina, with six minutes to play, went into its slow-down four-corner offense, refusing to take any shots. The score had been 44–43 in favor of Carolina when they went to the slow-down, and five and a half minutes later, when Virginia finally came out to challenge them, it was still 44–43. In the NCAA semifinal game, Carolina defeated Houston 68–63, beating a team that had two future NBA stars, Akeem (later Hakeem) Olajuwon and Clyde Drexler, in its lineup.

That victory set up the perfect ending for the final, Carolina against Georgetown, one of those dream matchups where arguably the two best teams in the country, quite different in style and temperament, would meet for the championship. Some white fans, made uneasy by their belief that John Thompson and his teams exuded a new kind of athletic black nationalism, wanted to see this game as white hats versus black hats, and there was no doubt who was wearing the white hats. Actually Smith and Thompson were close friends, both ran strong programs, and both insisted that their kids attend class and graduate, although Thompson tended to deal with inner-city kids who had already traveled a longer journey just to get to college and who had an even longer journey still ahead of them than most of the kids who enrolled at Chapel Hill.

These days, because Patrick Ewing has had a fine but slightly limited professional career—in part because of his own limitations, those imperfect hands and a significant weakness in passing out of a double team, in part because he played for too many coaches and for too long with too many marginal teammates—it is hard to remember him as the dominating force he seemed to be as a young Georgetown player. As a freshman, he was big, muscular, and quick. He ran the floor far better than most young big men, and he seemed to be the prototype of a new kind of a big man, combining unusual size with equal athletic ability. He seemed to stand above the field, intimidating to his opponents in all ways. To younger, less muscled college players just coming into their bodies he was nothing less than awesome. Yet Carolina was hardly intimidated. If Georgetown was physically more powerful, James Worthy said years later, Carolina was confident that it had a better, deeper all-around team and that it was very well prepared for the game. For if Georgetown seemed to project amazing physical power, particularly in its center, Patrick Ewing, North Carolina had almost as much physical ability, but it seemed to be of a different kind, a combination of power, speed, and finesse exemplified by the play of James Worthy.

It was one of those rare games that was every bit as good as it was supposed to be. Georgetown's defense was simply overwhelming—five physically gifted players putting enormous pressure on the ball for forty minutes. Only a team as well coached and poised as North Carolina, an excellent passing team on which everyone seemed to know exactly what his role was, could have withstood the assault from the relentless Georgetown press. Most other teams would have unraveled early on. Ewing had been intimidating at the beginning, perhaps too intimidating for his own good. He seemed to want to block everything the Carolina players put up, and in fact he was called for goaltending on five of the first nine shots. "I'll say one thing for Ewing," Brent Musburger, calling the game for CBS, noted on the air after Ewing's third goaltend in the first half, "he's not timid." At one point, Georgetown led 12–8, and all four Tar Heel baskets were on goaltending calls against Ewing. (A few months later, after Ewing and Jordan had been chosen for the *Playboy* All-American team and were in Chicago together, Jordan asked Ewing why he had gotten so many goaltending calls so early. Ewing answered, "Coach told me not to let anything go in.")

That game was nothing less than college basketball at its best. Worthy was on a roll—he ended up hitting thirteen of seventeen shots for a total of twenty-eight points. He was strong, he was amazingly quick, both with the ball and without it, and he could get his shot off quickly in traffic. Almost anyone with any sense of the game could look at him and know that his professional career was going to be even better than his college one. Jordan was another matter. He was young, and he did not yet have superior ballhandling skills. Only a veteran scout with the ability to project could see what he might be. But there were two tip-offs.

First there was his rebounding. He was the leading rebounder in the game with nine, but it was more than the sheer numbers, it was the nature of the rebounds he got—many of them seemingly outside his reach—and the fact that someone his size had the quickness and the jumping ability to get to so many balls. The other thing that some scouts picked up on was a drive he made against Ewing, the most intimidating player in college basketball. With about three minutes left and Carolina leading 59–58, North Carolina was in its slow-down offense, running down the clock. Suddenly, Jordan saw the faintest glimmer of a lane and took the ball to the basket, angling his body as best he could away from where the defense would come from. As Michael neared the basket, Ewing, with exceptional quickness, jumped out to make the block. Jordan, already in the air and seemingly vulnerable to Ewing's awesome force, moved the ball from his right to his left hand and flipped it up and just over Ewing's outstretched hand. The ball floated up ever so softly and so high that for a moment it seemed that it might go over the glass. "He put that ball up twelve feet," said Billy Packer, one of the announcers. On the bench, Roy Williams was sure that Jordan had laid it up too high and that it would go over the backboard. Instead, it hit the very top of the glass, fell gently off it, and dropped down softly through the net. It was nothing less than the play of a champion.

That basket made it 61–58, but Georgetown fought back. Two baskets later, the Hoyas had a 62–61 lead, and Carolina had the ball. With thirty-two seconds left, Carolina called time. Smith knew John Thompson well and knew he was a huge James Worthy fan. Thompson would not want Worthy to beat him. The next option would be Perkins, but they would be looking for him as well. In big games in the final seconds, coaches like Thompson make their opponents beat them with their lesser players, not their pressure players. That meant the player most likely to be free would be the talented freshman, Michael Jordan, and Smith called for the ball to go to Jordan. "Knock it in, Michael," Smith said. When his teammates in time swung the ball around to him, he was, as Smith had suspected, wide open. There were seventeen seconds left on the clock and he was seventeen feet away from the basket. It was a shot that any coach drawing up a diagram for a talented player for the final seconds of a big game would die for. He knocked it in as requested, his defensive man arriving even as he was releasing the ball at the top of his jump. Georgetown turned the ball over on the following possession, and Dean Smith had his first national title. It was also the first big notch in the legend of Michael Jordan. A good many professional basketball men, many of whom paid relatively little attention to the college game, saw that game, and they saw a freshman take the big pressure shot (and an experienced, very conservative coach who had enough faith in a freshman to give him the shot). Lenny Wilkens, who in the future would coach against Michael Jordan in many big games, remembered watching that game on television and knowing later that it was the first time someone named Michael Jordan had appeared on his radar screen. *Oh,* Wilkens had thought, *that kid is going to be something very special.* The kid from Carolina, Wilkens thought, had stepped up in a way that few freshmen could have.

After the game, amid all the celebration, Billy Packer ran into Deloris Jordan again, for the first time since the previous year's McDonald's All-American game, when he had told her not to worry about the choice of Adrian Branch as MVP. "See Mrs. Jordan," he said, "the decision about the McDonald's MVP doesn't seem so bad now, does it?"

7.

Chapel Hill, 1982–1984

H E WAS DIFFERENT AFTER THAT, his friends and coaches thought. There had always been a certain cockiness to him, but before his sophomore season, there was a new confidence, almost a certain quiet swagger. It was as if he had begun to realize that all the things he had been saying about how good he was might in fact be true. His dream and his life were becoming one and the same. It was, thought Buzz Peterson, who was with him every day in that period, as if for the first time Michael Jordan understood that he could be not just good but great.

That he had gone to a different level was obvious to everyone in September, in that four-week period when everyone—last year's players, the incoming freshmen, and alumni now in the NBA—played against each other every day at Carmichael, waiting for practice to open officially. James Worthy was there, getting ready for his first Lakers' camp, as were Sam Perkins, Mike O'Koren, Al Wood, and Walter Davis. For the first few days, Jordan seemed to be just one of a number of very good players on the court, and then suddenly, after about a week, he took off. Despite playing against seasoned NBA pros, there seemed to be a remarkable jump in his confidence, and he became the dominant player on the court, scoring on them when he wanted to.

His confidence now matched his physical talent. No one could stop him. For Matt Doherty, one of his teammates, those preseason pickup games were the first real clue to how good Jordan might be. Here he was, just about to enter his sophomore year in school, playing against established NBA players and showing that he was as good as they were.

It meant there might not be a ceiling on his talent—or at least not any ceiling they were likely to see for a while. Another teammate, Steve Hale, saw the same thing. Hale noticed another thing about Jordan: Even in pickup games, he had become unusually purposeful. There was a tendency in games like this, when there were no coaches around, for players to resort to what they did best, to reinforce their strengths and avoid going to any part of their game that was essentially weak. But Jordan, Hale believed, was constantly working on the weaker part of his game, trying to bring it up. It was, Hale thought, one more sign of his desire to be the best.

He returned to college bigger and stronger and faster. To the pleasant surprise of the coaches, he was still growing. On October 15, 1982, the first day of practice of his sophomore year, the moment each season when the coaches collected what Dean Smith liked to call objective data, they noted the changes. Roy Williams had measured him at six foot four and a half as a freshman, and now, a year later, he was six foot six. More, his body was filling out and becoming stronger and faster. The previous year, he had run the forty-yard sprint in 4.55, which was very good. The coaches who were clocking him this year compared their watches: Williams had it as 4.39; one coach had it a tad slower, others had it a tad faster. They decided to log it as 4.39, aware that it might even be faster. That was the kind of speed only the fastest athletes in the world—Olympic-class sprinters and NFL cornerbacks—could match. Here was a young man who could do all the other things he could do on a basketball court, whose anticipatory instincts about the flow of a game were so pure, who also had that rarest kind of speed. The two axioms of all basketball coaches were that you could not coach speed, nor could you coach height; they were God-given. Here they had a player who had both speed *and* height, as well as talent and passion, and who was immensely coachable—who seemed, as James Worthy once said, to be like a sponge soaking up everything around him.

Dean Smith noticed with pleasure the growth in height and the even greater growth in confidence. Jordan, he saw, was becoming a dominating player in practice. He almost always won the varying one-on-one drills they competed on in practice, and when they went to five-on-five games, Smith noticed, Jordan's team always managed to win.

Dean Smith and the other coaches were also dealing with him with great skill. After his freshman year, Smith took him aside and showed him a film, much of which showed Jordan being a little lax on defense. Then Smith asked him, "Michael, do you realize how good you can really be defensively?" He added that if he worked hard on his defense, he could be the complete player, both in college and in the professional game, and Smith reminded him of one of the most elemental coaching axioms: In the end, it was defense that won games. On certain nights, your offensive skills desert you, but because defense was a product of hard work, it would always be there. Jordan's teammates could see that idea begin to take hold in his second year, as it became increasingly obvious that on certain nights he was more interested in his defense than his offense and was concentrating on shutting down his man. The other thing Smith did in practice, some thought, was stack the sides against Jordan, so that he would have the challenge of trying to carry weaker teammates against their more talented peers.

The improvement in him in just one year, from the slight and somewhat uncertain freshman to this new, more powerful, more confident sophomore, was obvious. Billy Cunningham, one of Dean Smith's first great players and by 1982 the coach of the Philadelphia 76ers, dropped by his alma mater and watched a practice; afterward, he turned to Smith and said of Jordan, "Coach, he's going to be the greatest player ever to play at Carolina."

Smith, eager to protect Jordan from just that kind of speculation and the concurrent expectations that might be so damaging to so young a man, and wary as well of damaging the egalitarian base of his program—everyone is equal and no one is more equal than others, particularly the best player in the country—almost snapped back at Cunningham. "No! We've had a lot of great players here! Michael is just one of them!" But what he had said was true, Cunningham thought—Jordan *was* better than all the others. There he was, barely twenty years old and doing things that could not be taught, and that only a handful of professional players could do.

What was interesting about the intensity of Jordan's practice habits, thought Steve Hale, was that they were rare for a player so naturally gifted. Hale was aware of his own physical and athletic limitations, and he understood from the start that he would only be able to play at Carolina if he pushed himself to the highest level and became something of a kamikaze, constantly diving for loose balls and leaving some of his skin behind in every game. Yet Jordan, who so obviously had the highest level of physical gifts, was there every day, practicing as if he too were somewhat limited athletically. That was a powerful combination.

Jordan's ascending level of skill and fame did not diminish his cockiness. He talked more trash than ever, but in an almost boyish way. One of the drills that Dean Smith favored was the explode drill, a one-on-one routine in which the offensive player was given the ball about fifteen feet from the basket and the defensive player was supposed to stop him. Most of the Carolina players loved that part of the practice, watching the emergence of one of the greatest one-on-one players in the history of the game, the young man who was surfacing as a lineal descendant of the great Julius Erving. Here he was, in their gym, in the process of perfecting his craft. Those who had to go against Jordan were not so enamored of the drill. How did you stop him? his friend Buzz Peterson wondered. He had those long arms and great hands—he could hold the ball with one hand better than most players could with two—and he had an unmatchable, explosive first step. None of the defensive men assigned to him—Steve Hale, Buzz Peterson, or Jimmy Braddock—liked going against him in this practice, particularly because afterward he went to the locker-room blackboard and wrote down their names and, in Roman numerals, how many times he had dunked on each during practice: I, II, III, or IV.

The other thing his teammates came to realize was that he was driven by an almost unparalleled desire—or need—to win. The ghost of losing to his brother Larry in backyard contests still lived. All top athletes are driven, and no one made the Carolina roster unless he had been by far the hardest-working kid in his neighborhood, his high school, and finally his high school conference, but Jordan was self-evidently the most driven of all. He simply hated to lose, on the court in big games, on the court in little games, in practice, in Monopoly games with his friends (if he fell far behind late in a game, he was capable of sending his opponents' hotels and houses crashing to the floor with one great sweep of his arm). In card games and pool games, his passion to win was obvious—in fact, he often seemed to change the rules to ensure his victory. A pool shot that he missed did not count because someone spoke just as he was about to shoot. Once when Carolina was playing Virginia at Charlottesville, he and his teammates were hanging around a game room, and Jordan issued a challenge to play anyone in pool. Matt Doherty took it up, they played, and to Jordan's surprise Doherty won. Jordan threw down his stick, studied the table carefully, announced, "This table's not regulation size," and stomped out.

He simply hated to lose at anything, and this would be a trademark for the rest of his life. Every competition had a quality of life-or-death struggle. If he lost in a card game, he would want to keep playing until he won. In his sophomore year, the Tar Heels went to Atlanta for a game against Georgia Tech. Roy Williams was in charge of doing the bed checks. He knew the players were in the hotel's game room. There was Jordan, drilling everyone in pool and having a wonderful time, lording it over all the people he had just vanquished. Williams was pleased by the ambience, seeing his players all so comfortable with each other, and he had joined in the laughter, at which point Michael then challenged him as well: "You're laughing, Coach—well I can handle you too. Come on, take a stick."

They played three games, and Williams, a very good pool player, won every one. At the end, when it was over, Jordan did not speak to Williams, did not thank him or say good night as the group broke up, nor did he speak to him at the bed check or the next morning at breakfast. An hour later, when Jordan boarded the team bus as they got ready to drive to practice, Williams was on one side of the aisle and Eddie Fogler, the other assistant coach was on the other. Williams had not mentioned the previous night's pool game to anyone. Michael got on the bus, and went right past both coaches, obviously shorn of his normal ebullience. Fogler, sensing the coldness and even a kind of anger there, said, "Hey Michael, what's the matter—Coach Williams beat you in pool last night?"

Jordan, quite irritated, turned to Williams and said, "You told everyone!"

"Michael," Fogler said, "Roy didn't tell anything to anyone. I could tell from looking at you what happened. The defeat is on your face."

Then there was golf. That was the year he was learning to play golf, and his competitiveness was now surfacing on the golf course. One day that spring, he played with three of his friends in a match: he and David Hart, the manager and his roommate for this season, teamed against Peterson and Doherty. It was a close game, with a lot of woofing, and when they came to the final hole it was winners take all—losers to buy the Cokes and endure the taunting of the others. All four of them drove to the hole, an elevated one. Three of them made it onto the green, but Michael's shot went over the edge, back down behind the hole. Everything now depended on his shot to the green, and he, a novice, needed nothing less than a miracle chip shot. He thereupon hit an almost perfect shot to win. When they got back to their room, Hart congratulated him on the shot and asked how in the world he had managed to hit it. Michael looked around as if to be sure that no one else was there. "I didn't hit it," he said, "I just threw it up on the green."

For Jordan's sophomore year, Smith had moved him to the three, or small forward, slot, with Buzz Peterson playing at the two guard. Though James Worthy had turned pro after his junior year, it was still a good team, but it was a significantly younger one and somewhat untested. But of Jordan's blossoming brilliance there was no doubt.

There were, in that sophomore year, numerous examples of his exceptional defensive ability, his instinct for the game, and the speed with which he could break down talented opposing players. One came in a game against Virginia. Because of the presence of Ralph Sampson, the

Cavaliers were a powerhouse in those years, and on this occasion they were ranked number one in the country. Carolina won their first game in Charlottesville, and now, on February 10, they were playing at Carmichael. It was a memorable game in a number of ways. Just before the half, Buzz Peterson tore up his knee; sadly, it was an injury from which he would never completely recover. With Peterson out, the Carolina outside threat was greatly diminished, and Virginia, with the advantage of a dominating big man, took complete control of the game, leading by sixteen points at one time.

But then, slowly, Carolina started chipping away. With 4:12 on the clock, Virginia still led by ten, 63–53. The Carolina defense tightened, and the Cavaliers did not score for the rest of the game. The Tar Heels kept coming on. The Virginia lead was 63–60 with 1:20 left when Sampson missed the front end of a one-and-one foul-shooting opportunity. Then Carolina's Jimmy Braddock missed a three-point shot, but Jordan grabbed the rebound and scored, making it 63–62 with 1:07 left to play. Rick Carlisle, a talented Cavalier guard, took the inbound pass for Virginia. He saw the Carolina double-team coming. One of the defenders was Michael Jordan, but Carlisle was confident he could split the double-team because he had done it before. As the trap tightened, he started to put the ball on the floor, as he had done so often in practice and in games, sure he had the opening, sure there was going to be a clear court ahead for him. Then, something terrible happened. The ball did not come back to him off the floor, and he turned to see one of the worst sights of his entire life: Michael Jordan, with what had been his ball, driving to the basket for a one-handed dunk, going up so high, his arm cocked so violently, that for one brief instant Carlisle thought he might miss it. That was a sentiment shared by Dean Smith, who after the game asked, "Michael, why didn't you just lay it up? You might have missed the dunk." Jordan looked at him with a small smile and answered, "Coach, I wasn't planning on missing."

Virginia had the ball with fifty-one seconds left. The Cavaliers brought it up the court, and Carlisle took a last-second shot and missed. Ralph Sampson, all seven foot four of him, went up for the rebound with two hands and somehow Michael Jordan reached out with one hand and snatched the ball away. That gave Carolina the victory. It was a signature play, taking the ball away from Big Ralph. It was the Tar Heels' eighteenth win in a row, but they were to prove a different team with Peterson out for the season.

The injury to Peterson and injuries to other important players (center Brad Daugherty had played near the end of the season with a stress fracture in his foot) limited the team, however, and the Tar Heels were upset in the Eastern regional final by a somewhat unheralded Georgia team, 82–77. The last defeat was a bitter one for a team that sensed that it was better than it had played. Carolina teams, after all, expected to upset other teams in big games; they did not intend to be upset by lesser players from lesser programs. It was an abrupt and bitter end to a frustrating season.

That game was played in Syracuse on a Sunday, and afterward most of the coaches went off on recruiting trips. Roy Williams had been detailed by Dean Smith to go back to Chapel Hill with the players that night. Smith's message to them was a simple one: They were not to relax academically, because there were only five weeks left in the school year, and he wanted everyone to do well. On the flight back to Chapel Hill Sunday night Williams passed that message on to the players. On Monday afternoon, Jordan came in to see Williams.

"Coach," Michael said, almost apologetically, "I think I need to rest. I think I'm tired. I've been playing basketball steadily, even in the summer, for two years, and the truth is, I haven't had any time off in a long time. I think I need to take a break."

Williams said he thought that sounded right on the money, and he encouraged Jordan to take some time off, lest he begin to face a basketball burnout. Later that day, Williams went out for a run, still angry over the defeat by Georgia, still needing to burn off his own frustrations, and when he came back he encountered Michael in his practice sweats, with a ball at his side.

"I thought you were going to take some time off," Williams said.

"I can't afford to, Coach," he answered. "We didn't win—I've got to work on my game. I've got to get better." It was, thought Williams, the surest sign yet that nothing was going to stop him from being a champion. Here he was, a player who had just completed a brilliant season in which he had delivered on the promise of his freshman year and earned all kinds of honors, including All-Conference, All-American and soon the *Sporting News*'s National Player of the Year. He would be a champion, Williams thought, because it was not just where his talent and intelligence would take him but where his heart would take him as well.

There were other glimpses of his inner toughness, his refusal to back down no matter what the size and strength of the opponent. There was a game against Maryland in which Ben Coleman, a big, physical Maryland player, was running down the court side by side with Matt Doherty, and Coleman gave Doherty a quick slap to the face. Michael Jordan bided his time. Late in the game, Jordan had the ball with Carolina safely ahead and playing in its four-corner offense. Coleman was positioned near the basket. Jordan took off for the basket and dunked right over Coleman, put his finger right in his face, and said, as icily as imaginable, "Don't you *ever* slap one of our players again!" It was such a violent moment, so much the conqueror dealing with the conquered, even though Coleman was the bigger and stronger man, that to Roy Williams it conjured up the image of Ali standing over a sprawled Liston.

Maryland missed its next shot, and Carolina came up the court with the ball. Jordan stood on the perimeter, just holding the ball, with no defensive pressure on him. Maryland's Adrian Branch yelled out to Herman Veal, one of his teammates, to pick him up. "You want his ass?" Veal yelled back to Branch. "You pick him up yourself!"

On the Carolina bench, Dean Smith, who prided himself on never swearing, turned to Roy Williams and asked excitedly, "What did he say? What did he say?"

"He said," Williams answered, "exactly what you thought he said."

Jordan's third year at Carolina was rich in some ways but ended in bitter disappointment. Buzz Peterson was his roommate again (they had been suitemates in their second year because the coaches wanted Jordan to room with Brad Daugherty). Buzz Peterson had never come back completely from his knee injury, and he was going through a difficult time. His minutes were disappearing, and he was losing playing time to others like Steve Hale, who played with an intensity that bordered on the violent. (Years later, when Michael Jordan was asked who defended him well in the NBA, he often mentioned that Steve Hale back at Chapel Hill had been as tough on him in practice as anyone in the professional game.) Peterson thought he was playing as hard as ever, but Jordan did not think so. He thought his closest friend had run into some kind of post-injury mental block. Jordan, who accepted nothing but the most intense level of competition, thought his roommate had become tentative. "You're missing something," Jordan told Peterson, "I feel like I can take my fist and hit where your heart is and my hand will come out the other side." At the time, Peterson thought Jordan was wrong, but later, when he looked back, he decided that in fact there was a tentative quality to his game, an almost unconscious fear of being hurt again. Michael, because of the intensity of his personality and his instinct to hone in on the weaknesses of other players, had been the first to pick up on it.

It was a painful year for Peterson. A certain kind of dream of who he might be and what his ceiling would be was dying in front of him, and for one brief moment he walked away from the game, went home on his own, which was something that was not done. When he returned, he found that the person who wanted him back the most was Jordan.

Michael's personal offering to him—a kind of special welcome-back gesture—was to put all of Peterson's clothes in perfect order, hanging all his pants on hangers and carefully folding all his sweaters and other clothes. It was his way of reaching out to someone he cared about who was going through a hard time.

In Jordan's junior year, which would be his last at Chapel Hill, he played with Sam Perkins, Brad Daugherty, and Kenny Smith, who became the fifth Carolina player ever to start as a freshman. There were four players who were to be drafted in the first round of the NBA starting on the team, three of them—Jordan, Perkins, and Daugherty—drafted among the top five. Before the season, there was an awareness among the players, with the blossoming of Brad Daugherty, arguably the most talented pure center to play at Carolina in the Dean Smith era, of how good they might be. There was talk not merely of winning the NCAA championship but of being known as one of the five or six best college teams of all time. "We had a feeling," Steve Hale said years later, "that if we played any other team in the country ten times, we'd win nine of them." At one point this Carolina team won twenty-one straight, but then it lost to a seemingly undistinguished Indiana team in the Eastern Semifinals of the NCAA tournament.

It was widely assumed in basketball circles that Bobby Knight flat outcoached Dean Smith that particular night. He assigned Dan Dakich, a modestly gifted player, to guard Jordan, and Knight's marching orders to Dakich were simple: "You've got to keep him from back cuts and going to the basket for easy points, and you've got to keep him off the boards. Don't let him have anything easy. Give him the jumpers if need be." In both Knight and Dakich's retelling, the moment Knight explained to Dakich that he was to guard Jordan, Dakich went to the bathroom and threw up. (A few months later, when Knight had Jordan on the 1984 Olympic team, he teased him by threatening to add Dakich to the roster as a defensive specialist to hold Jordan down.) But the strategy worked. Indiana played with exceptional skill and discipline, executing its offense with singular precision. Jordan picked up two quick fouls, which limited his play, and Indiana went on to win.

It was a defeat that burned among the players. Years later, Steve Hale, who had become a doctor, still found the subject of the game painful, not something he could easily talk about. He had never, he noted, been able to watch a replay of the game. He did remember, though, that the next day he had seen Michael Jordan in the gym alone, working on his game, determined to get better.

Dean Smith was the one who thought it was time for Jordan to turn pro. One of Smith's great strengths, his players believed, was that he always did what was best for the players, and the best thing for Michael Jordan was to get on with his career. He had been college player of the year again, and he had won the Naismith Award, and he was again an All-American. But the truth was that the defenses were keying on him now, throwing zones and double-teams at him, and Smith sensed that Jordan's senior year would be even more difficult. To the degree that he could be coached at the college level, the job had been done. Now it was time for him to adjust to a different, faster game and greater individual challenges. The danger if he stayed in college was that he might sustain an injury that would seriously affect his professional price, which was likely to be very high.

Smith had, of course, started checking around to find out where Jordan could go in the draft, and the word was that he was going to go very high. Billy Cunningham, the coach of the Philadelphia 76ers and a Tar Heel true and blue, wanted him badly. The 76ers were to pick fifth, and as the draft approached Cunningham was trying desperately to move up, willing, other general managers believed, to trade the talented Andrew Toney to get a higher pick. "But it never came to how much we would give up," Cunningham said years later, "because Rod [Thorn, the Chicago general manager] knew exactly what he had in Michael." Soon it became apparent that Jordan would be picked no lower than third, the pick held by Chicago. The beginning salary would probably be at least $700,000 a year, perhaps more, and it would be for at least three or four years.

Dean Smith decided to explain what he thought was the right move to the Jordan family. There were two people who questioned his wisdom. One of them was Deloris Jordan, who badly wanted Michael to finish college with his class and who had always had a particular dream, one that had validated much of the sacrifice in her and her husband's own lives, of two of her children, Michael and his sister Roslyn, graduating from Chapel Hill on the same day. Only gradually did she come around to the idea that he would get his degree a year or two later. The other person who was wary of turning pro was Michael himself. He loved Carolina—the program, the coaches, the friendships—and as far as he was concerned, given the defeat by Indiana, there was still some unfinished business to attend to, one more national championship to win.

The decision was his, but in any real sense it had been made for him by his coach. The night before Michael Jordan acceded to that decision and held his press conference, he went out for dinner with Buzz Peterson, still uncertain what the right course was. Jordan went off for the press conference early the next morning, and Peterson stayed in bed. When Jordan returned, Peterson asked him what he was going to do.

"You don't want to know," he answered.

"I thought you'd stay," Peterson said, slightly wounded at losing a friend and seeing something of his own dream torn apart. "I thought we'd come together, and room together, and graduate together." But Jordan just shook his head, and Peterson understood that the decision was not really his, that Jordan as always had deferred to those with authority, in this case Dean Smith. The decision had been made for him.

The greatest testimonial to Dean Smith and the skilled way he handled so talented a young player was not just that he helped make Jordan into an unusually complete and disciplined athlete, with significant skills as a defender, but that Jordan left Chapel Hill for the pros reluctantly and that he remained passionately committed to his old school and his old coach. As a pro, he not only wore Carolina shorts under his regular uniform, but he checked in with Smith regularly and thought of him, many of their friends thought, as a kind of second father. Rarely had a college program worked so effectively with so gifted a young player.

The hold that Dean Smith had on him, the degree of his respect, was immense, and if anything it continued to grow over the years. He had taken away from Carolina not just great discipline to go with his natural ability but something more, a sense of right and wrong and of how you were supposed to behave on a basketball court and away from it as well. He continued to clear many important decisions with his former coach, and certainly Dean Smith remained a living presence with him. Several years after Jordan left Carolina, he returned there for a preseason exhibition game. He and his friend Fred Whitfield drove up to Carmichael (soon to be replaced by the Dean Smith Center) a little late. The parking lot was absolutely filled, and he had to park far from the entrance. Whitfield spotted a space near the door for handicapped people and suggested that Jordan, already in something of a rush, take it. "Oh no, I couldn't do that," he answered. "If Coach Smith ever knew I had parked in a handicapped zone he'd make me feel terrible—I wouldn't be able to face him."

Chicago, 1984

IN 1984, the Chicago Bulls were a weak organization struggling in a city where basketball seemed to be something of a minor-league sport, running a bad second in the winter to hockey's beloved Black Hawks. Chicago was first and foremost a football city, where the fate of the Bears seemed to reflect the city's self-image. The Bears were a tough physical team playing a tough physical sport in a tough physical city, the city of the big shoulders, as Carl Sandburg called it. In the summer, the north side of the city belonged to the Cubs, the south side to the White Sox. In 1984, professional basketball existed on the margin. In a city as sports mad as Chicago, this said more about the Bulls ownership than about the city.

In the days just before Jerry Reinsdorf and his group bought in, the most important member of the ownership group was Arthur Wirtz, a major and somewhat feared real-estate figure in Chicago. Wirtz was as different from the smooth new modern sports owners of the nineties as it was possible to be. He was a formidable figure in the tightly held power structure of the Chicago of his day, an old-fashioned power baron when Chicago still had a few barons who knew how to exercise power. He was an enormous man, perhaps six foot four and nearly three hundred pounds, very much resembling, one of his partners said, Sydney Greenstreet, and he tended to build large, somewhat grim slab buildings that looked like architectural extensions of himself. He was an old-time wheeler-dealer and fixer, and he had very little interest in sports, particularly basketball. But he did own Chicago Stadium, and what he did like were tenants, and an NBA team was good for forty-one dates a year, even without the playoffs.

He was not a man for frills or promotions or marketing, the key ingredients in the emerging fantasy world of modern sports. When Brian McIntyre, later head of media relations for the NBA, worked for the Bulls in the late seventies, he discovered to his horror that there was only one person working the ticket office. Incredibly, no one on the Bulls front-office staff was assigned exclusively to selling season tickets, the lifeblood of professional sports franchises. Only about two thousand season tickets had been sold in 1984 when Michael Jordan was drafted. The standing joke in those days, McIntyre said, was that there was a break-in at the front office in the middle of the night: Thieves had returned a vast number of season tickets.

McIntyre suggested that the Bulls employ a bunch of college students part-time and have them sell season tickets, and that their pay would be a 10 percent commission. But Wirtz wanted no part of his suggestion— he didn't think they would sell that many tickets, and equally important, if they did sell he hated the idea of giving away 10 percent of the price. When McIntyre got there, he remembered, the local radio contract was for about twenty games at $5,000 each. Eventually, the price went up, although to a station with a weaker signal so that much of the city could not hear the games. What McIntyre remembered best was an incident one year when the Bulls did make the playoffs. He was late to work, so he was driving too fast, and he was picked up by a cop for speeding. McIntyre tried to talk himself out of a ticket by explaining who he was and offering playoff tickets to the cop. "I hate basketball," the cop said. "Do you have any hockey tickets?" The cop, McIntyre decided, could have been speaking for the entire city of Chicago.

In the past season, Reggie Theus, the team's star player, had feuded with his coaches and had held out for a while before the start of the season. Kevin Loughery, the coach, irritated by this and by Theus's apparent belief that every offensive possession should end with him shooting, had put him on the bench. That annoyed Theus and the Chicago fans, to whom he was the team's one bright, shining light. On occasion, Theus waved a towel over his head to incite the crowd to take his side, and once he apparently ordered pizza from the bench during a game.

Not even the coin flip for the right to draft the best college player in the country had gone right for the Chicago Bulls in the pre-Jordan days. Five years earlier, based on their appalling play and their last-place finish, the Bulls had been in a coin flip with Los Angeles, the prize being a young man from East Lansing, Michigan, named Magic Johnson, an obviously talented, joyous player who was well known in the region because he had played in the Big Ten. The possibility of drafting Magic Johnson had created a considerable stir locally, and the Bulls management had tried to exploit it by having the fans vote on whether to call heads or tails in the coin flip.

That was a mistake, thought Johnny Kerr, first the team's coach and since 1975 its broadcaster. Kerr had done a brief stint as a coach of the Phoenix Suns when a similar situation had arisen, on the occasion of the then Lew Alcindor's entrance into the league. The Phoenix fans had been polled on which way to call the flip, the Suns management had duly listened, had miscalled it, and Milwaukee had won Alcindor's draft rights. The Suns, for their trouble, had gotten Neal Walk, a drop-off of cataclysmic proportions. "Listen to the fans," Kerr cautioned after that, "and you'll end up sitting with them."

Nevertheless, when the rights to Magic Johnson were being decided, Rod Thorn called heads, as demanded by the fans. Tails it was. Instead of Johnson, the Bulls got David Greenwood, a decent player, but finally a journeyman; they had not even drafted Sidney Moncrief, who went to Milwaukee, where he was to become one of the league's best offensive and defensive players for a decade. Beforehand, Jonathan Kovler, the Bulls managing partner, said rather casually that it was a $25 million coin toss. "Actually I was wrong," he noted years later. "It turned out to be a $200 million toss."

All of Chicago's recent draft choices had in fact been dismal. Sometimes the problem was that they picked high in a year of limited talent, and sometimes when they picked high they just flat out picked wrong. In 1980, picking relatively high, they drafted Ronnie Lester, whose career was destroyed by a bad knee, while later in the same draft the 76ers got the talented Andrew Toney. In 1981, the Bulls drafted Orlando Woolridge, who arrived significantly out of shape and whose statistics were always better than his overall game; Larry Nance and Tom Chambers were picked after him. In 1982, they picked Quintin Dailey, who struggled with a serious drug problem; Ricky Pierce and Paul Pressey were subsequent picks. When team trainer Mark Pfeil pressed Dailey about his off-court habits, threatening him that if he did not get his life in order he would end up on the street, Dailey responded, "I'm going to end up on the street? I've already been on the street. I *survive* on the street. I can make more money on the street than I can in basketball. You can't threaten me with that." Then in 1983, picking fifth in a weak year, Chicago picked Sidney Green, a big man of modest abilities. The turnover in personnel was constant, and because of that the turnover in head coaches was comparable. In a brief period starting in 1978–1979 and ending with the arrival of Doug Collins for the 1986–1987 season, head coaches included Scotty Robertson, Jerry Sloan, Rod Thorn (briefly after he fired Sloan), Paul Westhead, Kevin Loughery, Stan Albeck, and finally Collins.

In the 1983–1984 season, they won only twenty-seven games, losing fifty-five, which gave them the third pick in the 1984 draft behind Houston and Portland. Everyone in the NBA in those days, it seemed, wanted a big man. This was in the age before Michael Jordan and players of his height changed the general philosophy of drafting. Self-evidently the best big man available was the University of Houston's Akeem Olajuwon. Virtually everyone in the draft coveted Olajuwon. He was big, he was athletic, he had a very good work ethic, and he was relatively new to the game, so there was reason to believe that he would get better year after year, which in fact he did. After that, a lot of basketball people thought Michael Jordan was the obvious choice. But he was a shooting guard, not a center, not a power forward, and not a point guard. Could a mere shooting guard turn around a franchise? The NBA mythology at that point was that shooting guards could not lift a poor team. A great shooting guard was thought of as the final piece that completed a championship team, not the centerpiece of one.

The number-two big man was apparently Sam Bowie, who had played at Kentucky. Bowie was tall and intelligent, but there was a down side to him: He had suffered a serious leg injury as a college player (more were to come in the NBA), and there was a more covert question of whether he actually enjoyed the game and whether he had the requisite passion to raise himself and his team to the highest level. The Bulls were wary of him. They had only recently drafted Ronnie Lester, who had arrived as medically damaged goods. But Portland, picking second, clearly wanted to go big. Some people thought that was because the Trail Blazers' one transcending moment had come when they had built a championship team around a gifted big man, Bill Walton (though self-evidently Bowie was no Walton); others thought that it was because they already had a player of Jordan's size and type in Clyde Drexler, who had undergone a difficult rookie season in the highly disciplined offense of Coach Jack Ramsay. To the delight of the Chicago scouts, Portland would go big. Not everyone thought it was a great move. Bobby Knight, who had coached against Jordan in college and coached him in the early days of training for the 1984 Olympics, had fallen in love with him and had pushed his close friend Stu Inman, the Portland player personnel man, to draft Jordan instead.

"But we need a center," Inman had said.

"Stu, draft him and play him at center," Knight had answered.

The operating partner for the Bulls in those days was Kovler, a wealthy young man who was an heir to the Jim Beam liquor fortune and something of a basketball junkie. He was the front man for an unusually unwieldy ownership, with numerous other partners. On occasion, an excellent trade was offered Chicago but slipped away before Kovler was able to round up his partners and pull the trigger. The principal scout, working just under Thorn, was a young man named Mike Thibault. Thibault was a classic NBA lifer, a man born—or doomed—to be around the game all his life as an assistant coach or a scout, knowing the game, loving it, never making that much money, finding himself on endless puddle-jumping planes to tiny towns to watch seemingly unimportant games between undistinguished teams. But he was caught up in the unique allure of basketball scouting, the search for the undiscovered great player, the hope of getting several average players who would together, with the special synergy of the sport, make a whole larger than its pieces.

The third draft choice was like gold. Because of expansion, there were more and more teams in the league, which meant that a chance at a high draft pick was rarer and rarer. Mistakes, because of rising salaries, were ever more costly. Thibault had scouted Michael Jordan perhaps a dozen times that year, and Rod Thorn had seen him several times as well. Thibault and Thorn decided that though it was hard to tell because of the particular nature of the Carolina program, Michael Jordan was likely to be a very very good professional player. He might well be a great one. He was obviously a rare thing: an absolutely complete basketball player.

Until he began to watch Jordan, Thibault had thought that Magic Johnson was the most competitive college player he had ever seen. Now, zeroing in on this young man, he began to think that there was a fire to Jordan that exceeded even Johnson's. Thibault saw Jordan completely take games over, and the word Thibault kept hearing from the Carolina assistant coaches was that Jordan was even more spectacular in practice. Thibault decided early on that he wanted Jordan, and he only hoped that Portland stayed with Sam Bowie.

Rod Thorn agreed. Thorn was wary of Bowie's physical condition, particularly after the disaster with Lester, and of his love of the game, and he was equally high on Jordan. He had not seen as many games as Thibault, but he had become something of a pal of Dean Smith and had been allowed to sit in the Chapel Hill film room and look at films of ACC games. That was a significant courtesy, and it helped in scouting not just the Carolina players but their opponents as well. There were a number of things that Thorn liked about Jordan. He was clearly improving year by year, adding things to his game, particularly his defense, but above all it was the athleticism, the quick flashes in a game where he would come from nowhere with a sudden burst of speed to make a play that no other college player could have made. Sitting there by himself, Thorn would see one of Jordan's plays and he would have to stop the film in disbelief and rewind it to watch it again and again, dazzled. Some of Jordan's moves on offense, some of his instincts on defense, simply could not be taught. I am, Thorn decided, watching a different kind of player than anything I've seen before. As the season wore on and he spoke to his people back in Chicago, his voice became more and more confident. They were about to draft a great player, he said.

Dean Smith was high on him, but then Smith tended to be high on all his players. But the fact that Billy Cunningham coveted Jordan confirmed to Thorn and Thibault that they were on to something. They were still a little unsure about Kovler. Thibault feared that Kovler was still thinking of drafting a big man, and he told Thorn it was their job on draft day, if Kovler hesitated on Jordan, to tackle him and make the pick themselves. But Kovler was with them, and on June 19, 1984, the Chicago Bulls drafted Michael Jordan of North Carolina as the number-three pick in the country.

There was one other player whom Thibault liked very much that year, a small white kid named John Stockton playing for Gonzaga, a small school in Spokane. Thibault thought Stockton was very tough, with very big hands and great court vision. For a time, Chicago tried switching players and picks in order to get a shot at Stockton as well, but Frank Layden of Utah had seen the same thing as Thibault, and the Jazz took him with their first-round pick. But it always intrigued Thibault— the idea of Jordan and Stockton playing in the same backcourt from day one.

The day of the draft, Ron Coley, who had worked for a time as a volunteer assistant at Laney High School back in Wilmington, called James Jordan. "Move over Oscar Robertson and Jerry West," Coley had told Michael's father, invoking the names of the two best guards from his era, "because the greatest guard in basketball history has just been drafted."

9.

New York City; Bristol, Connecticut, 1979-1984

PROFESSIONAL BASKETBALL WAS in the midst of something of a pleasant renaissance in the year in which Michael Jordan was drafted, thanks largely to the emergence of the Magic Johnson–Larry Bird, Lakers-Celtics rivalry. Five years earlier, in their rookie year, the league had been commercially at an absolute low point. Madison Avenue scorned it, and therefore so did network television. The final game of the 1980 Finals—seemingly an ideal matchup for a network, pitting the ascending Lakers led by the youthful Johnson against the Philadelphia 76ers led by the charismatic Julius Erving—had been shown to most of the nation late at night on a tape delay by CBS.

The college game by contrast was in good shape. The nation seemed to love the skillfully promoted Final Four, and indeed one of the favorable bounces that the NBA had taken into the eighties had come from the fact that the Bird-Johnson rivalry had its roots in the 1979 NCAA championship game. That had been a high point for the college game, an almost perfect matchup of two great teams: a big-time powerhouse, Michigan State, against unheralded little Indiana State, and a black star, Johnson, against a white star, Bird.

When the two men entered the NBA, the professional game was in bad odor. In the particular schizophrenia of American society, the professional game was considered to be badly tainted. It was seen as far too black, and the majority of its players, it was somehow believed, were on drugs and willing to play hard only in the last two minutes of the game. In addition, it was believed that the players were seriously overpaid, although in those days the cumulative annual salary for many starting teams was probably around a million dollars.

By the winter of 1982, despite the professional advent of Bird and Johnson, CBS was broadcasting few games, and it was a struggle even to get the seven-game finals on prime time. The NBA put as skillful a spin on this network disinterest as it could—less is more, they said—as if by broadcasting too many games they would be giving away too much of a prized product. But it was the winter of their discontent. When the owners met at the all-star game that season, there was talk of closing down two or three of the league's weakest franchises and per-haps combining the two franchises in the Rocky Mountain area, Utah and Denver. The Cleveland ownership was so dreadful—a man named Ted Stepien seemed to have an irresistible impulse to trade away wildly valuable high picks for good but not great players who had reached the tail ends of their careers—that in order to bring in a solid new local owner, a man named Gordon Gund, the league gave the team two high bonus picks to undo some of the damage. There was additional talk about splitting the season into two sections in order to heighten fan in-terest and, to counter the claim that the players did not play hard for forty-eight minutes, of awarding a point in the standings to a team every time it won a quarter.

That year, the all-star game was held in New Jersey, home of a perennially troubled franchise, the Nets. The Nets were quite possibly doomed to extinction, located as they were in an odd kind of suburban void, with ownership that seemed even more transitory than the team's player roster. On the eve of their entrance into the NBA from the ABA, the Nets had managed to give away the rights to Julius Erving, a player so magnetic that he was one of the principal reasons the merger had gone through in the first place. The response for tickets to the all-star game was so pathetic—there were some five thousand tickets unsold as the game day approached—that it became the responsibility of every NBA employee to give out as many tickets as possible to friends, lest the network cameras sweep the arena and show thousands of empty seats at the game that was supposed to be one of the high points of the season.

At about that time, there were already a number of larger forces at work that would change not just the viability of the league as a profes-sional entity but the larger perceptions of it among the corporate lead-ers of America and the people who did their bidding on Madison Avenue. One of the forces was the league's own leadership: David Stern, a young man with a passionate love of the game and its players and an increasingly subtle sense of contemporary public relations, was not yet commissioner, but he was becoming the dominant force within the league.

The commissioner himself, Larry O'Brien, seemed surprisingly passive about his job (other than being present for televised ceremonies on the occasion of title games). O'Brien was a skilled politician who came out of the upper levels of the Kennedy organization, an old-fashioned vote counter who worked well with other professional political workers back in the days when such people still existed. He was close to John Kennedy, and, as with a number of others who had been close to the president, a large part of him died on November 22, 1963. It was probably true that because of the rise of television and the emergence of modern media politics (that is, the use of television spots and the ascent of pollsters) his importance as a vote counter and political contact man had already crested. He made a lateral move for a time to Lyndon Johnson's administration, becoming postmaster general, but Johnson never really trusted him because of his Kennedy roots, and many of his oldest friends, pure Kennedy loyalists, felt he had gone over to the enemy.

O'Brien had come over to the NBA in April 1975 as commissioner with one principal assignment: to bring a merger with the rival ABA, and he had done that with considerable dispatch and skill. From then on he had seemed to have little passion for the game or, equally important, its great players. There was one exception to that, and that was when he went to the Boston Garden. The Celtics had some good teams in his years, and he still loved going back to the Garden, where almost everyone in the crowd seemed to know him and treat him as a returning hero. For those blissful moments, his two worlds, basketball and politics, merged, and he was young and optimistic again. Other than that, he seemed an oddly disengaged commissioner, a man more than a little disappointed in the way his life had turned out, as if somehow the bright promise all those young men had sensed in early 1961 had never quite been fulfilled. He generally did what his staff pushed him to do during the late seventies and early eighties, but he did it without passion or real interest.

First and foremost, David Stern was determined to turn around the league's image. Stern believed that the league's financial and psychological stability depended upon its corporate connections. He saw and envied the tight, almost symbiotic connection between the National Football League and corporate America, so skillfully engineered by Pete Rozelle. He desperately wanted some of the same corporate endorsements to give his shakier league some badly needed legitimacy. He wanted the best of America's heartland companies as his sponsors, nothing less; he wanted companies such as Coke and McDonald's, signature companies of the postwar nation. If they came aboard, so would everyone else. And so he set out, very early on, to try and bring those companies in.

But when he visited the offices of the nation's great advertising firms, the gatekeepers to the great name-brand companies whose sponsorships he coveted, he found a stone wall of resistance, though many of these companies were enthusiastic sponsors of college basketball. One Madison Avenue agency representing an auto company was particularly blunt about it—the ad man said he had been instructed by the head of the auto company to sponsor college ball because the pro game was too black. The answer came back, yes, we know your surveys, but the head of the company—my boss—thinks you're too black. When Stern tried to show them the demographic studies that the league had put together, studies that showed that the audience for the professional game was not that different from the college game and that blessedly the viewers were *young*, he received the blankest of stares. Perception, Stern realized, was everything, and the general perception of blue-chip American companies was that the game was tarnished, too much a reflection not of sports but of something most Americans wanted to know as little as possible about: black America.

As Stern rose to power within the organization, one of his first hires was Rick Welts, a bright young man who had worked for the SuperSonics in Seattle and done very well in a comparable situation. Welts's marching orders were very clear: He was to be a kind of advance man for Stern, working Madison Avenue, pushing the league with potential major corporate clients. But he had no more success than Stern had, and for the same reason. The game had gotten blacker, and there were clearly problems in getting the nation's commercial tastemakers to accept a sport where so disproportionate a number of the great players were from a minority race. "We were," Welts later said, "regarded as being somewhere between mud wrestling and tractor pulling."

What was frustrating for both Welts and Stern was that the college game—particularly the highly heralded Final Four—was a very popular corporate sale. The college game was almost as black, but perceptions were important, and the college game was perceived, perhaps unconsciously, as still operating within a white hierarchy, under powerful white supervision, a world where no matter who the foot soldiers were, the generals were still white. (That was at least part of the reason why many people in the world of sports did not like John Thompson and his Georgetown team, a sense that the white hierarchy did not include or control his particular team. Not only was Thompson himself black, but despite Thompson's insistence that all his players go to class

and graduate, the team projected a sense of nascent black consciousness.)

As a result, the college game was still perceived as an extension of
mainstream America, as the professional basketball game was not, since
no one could control these athletes now that they had no-cut contracts.
It was clear that with the changes in the labor laws of sports, players
were becoming more powerful than their coaches. The players were
often perceived as being lazy, which was an amazing misconception
considering how hard they competed during a very demanding season.
Worse, because of the race issue, any story about player drug abuse
seemed to define the sport, although people knowledgeable about both
the NBA and Wall Street, both highly pressurized places where almost
everyone was probably overpaid, thought the use of cocaine by young
men in both places was about the same. But there was little consolation
in that bit of knowledge. Welts had come to New York eager to perform
his new job, but several months into it, he sat alone at night in his hotel,
sure that he was failing. He ended one day wanting to cry but telling
himself he was too old.

If there was one saving aspect to Welts's job, it was David Stern.
Somehow, no matter how long and hard Stern's own day, he managed to
check in with Welts every night, just to let him know he cared. Whatever else, Welts thought he had in Stern an ideal boss: he was young, he
was enthusiastic, he was incredibly bright, and he not only loved the
game but believed in it, as Welts himself did.

Stern, like Welts, was absolutely convinced that the core of the resistance was about race. He believed that if the NBA could show some discipline and could limit the worst, or at least the most noticeable, of the
current excesses, then people would be able to see the truly compelling
parts of the game: the unmatched athletic ability of the players and the
fire with which they competed.

Still, it was a struggle in those days. The NBA's beer sponsor at the
time clearly wanted to cut back, reducing the game to what was called a
specialty market, a polite term for a segmented (and segregated) part of
the population, in this case black people. Rather than going all out with
television commercials, cutting back meant promoting the NBA impri-
matur somewhat covertly in bars and stores in predominantly black
neighborhoods, and doing promotions there as if the black constituency
were a separate and effectively second-class market. In time, working
with an executive named Tom Shropshire, Stern signed up Miller as his
new beer company.

If perception was more powerful than reality, then Stern set out, with
others in the league and with the help of the Players' Association, to

change perceptions. In the early eighties, largely under Stern's leadership, two landmark agreements were reached with the Players' Association; one of these was an agreement on drug testing and the other was one on a team salary cap. Both were extremely important in changing the image held not just by ordinary Americans but by corporate America. The word now spread that the NBA was putting its own house in order, that the players were showing unusual maturity, particularly for rich young men—maybe they weren't so spoiled after all. Nothing thrilled the leaders of American business quite so much as the idea that their employees held the same vision of the future as they did, and here was living proof in which union members—well, they were wealthy union members to be sure—had signed on to a management vision of corporate sanity. They were being *responsible*.

With the drug-testing rule, the league in effect admitted that it had a problem and was now moving to correct it, in conjunction with the players themselves. If a player came forward voluntarily, he would retain his salary and receive treatment. If he came forward a second time, he would get treatment but no salary. The third time, the player would be gone for life. This agreement appeared both to deal with the problem and to protect the civil rights of the players. The Players' Association, Stern thought, had been a very valuable partner. He was particularly grateful to Bob Lanier, the former Detroit center who hated the prevailing stereotype that if you were tall, black, well dressed, and a basketball player or former basketball player, you were hooked on drugs.

Under the salary cap, the owners and players effectively became partners, the players getting 53 percent of all revenues. This was a time when salaries in all sports were rising in astronomical increments, and one advantage that basketball players had was the fact that it was obvious to serious fans that they played very hard. It was a skill game, but they also ran hard up and down the court, and it was an adrenaline game as well. Baseball, by contrast, was not an adrenaline game, and baseball players in general were about to become significantly less popular than basketball players. All too often television cameras cut to a shot of a new multimillionaire baseball player who did not seem to be running very hard.

Within the NBA itself, Stern was given much of the credit for bringing off both of those agreements, and it solidified his position as the in-house candidate to succeed Larry O'Brien, whose seven-year contract was about to expire in 1984. Years later, Kevin Loughery, a former player and coach, said that five people saved the NBA at its lowest point: "Julius Erving, Magic Johnson, Larry Bird, Michael Jordan, and of course, David Stern." Stern was too shrewd a man to accept credit for that large a role; his capacity for self-deprecation was just one of his many strengths. He was very good at never trying to make people think he was throwing his weight around (especially when he was) or that he was taking credit for things he had not in fact accomplished—or, for that matter, for things he *had*.

Stern was the first to point out that all kinds of forces in the larger society were also working in his favor: Larry Bird and Magic Johnson had arrived just before he became commissioner, and Michael Jordan arrived in the same season in which he became commissioner. In addition, he was smart enough to focus on the importance of other forces, particularly the coming of cable television, for Johnson and Bird had arrived in the fall of 1979, which was exactly when a small and seemingly dinky little round-the-clock sports network called ESPN started broadcasting. It was part of David Stern's innate wisdom that in the long run if you did the right thing and did not try to take credit for too much of what you did, then people would give you not only the right amount of credit but perhaps even more. In addition, if they felt that any settlement during difficult negotiations was at least equitable, they were more likely to want to deal with you again.

That was something he had learned as a boy. He was the son of a delicatessen owner in the Chelsea section of Manhattan, and even though he had led a reasonably privileged life, going to Rutgers and Columbia Law School, his roots were very simple, and he had worked in the deli all the way through school. The store, located on Eighth Avenue between Twenty-second and Twenty-third, was not far from Madison Square Garden. It had succeeded despite the harsh competition of the much larger surrounding supermarkets by dint of being open longer hours—9 A.M. until 1 A.M. six days a week and 9 A.M. until 2 A.M. on Sunday. It closed two days a year, on the Jewish High Holidays. It was the classic American story, one generation working endlessly hard and sacrificing greatly so that the next generation would have access to a better education and therefore greater freedom of choice.

There was no better way to prepare yourself for a job that demanded a good deal of skill with the public, David Stern thought, than working behind the counter in a deli. Stern's friend Dick Ebersol, the head of NBC sports, thought that no one he had ever met had a wider circle of friends, and no one was as comfortable talking to as many different people, from Michael Eisner to Tiger Woods to custodial employees, as David Stern. Ebersol was sure that the roots of that skill and innate ease were in the Stern delicatessen.

The key to the success of the Stern deli was a fierce work ethic blended with a certain kind of self-effacement and rare high courtesy in its management. William Stern, his father, had grown up in an orphan-age, and he was driven by the idea of protecting his own family from so painful a life. He was a relentlessly hardworking man, and he never threw his weight around. It would have been hard for any customer to know that he was the owner. He knew the importance of elemental courtesy, of offering people, in addition to the things they purchased, some sense of dignity and self-importance. He treated everyone who came in well, and his son learned to do that as well, and he learned that all too often in comparable stores the owners and staff tended to re-spond to the customers based on a quick reading of their clothes and what those clothes seemingly revealed about a person's status.

The Stern deli did not judge people on their clothing, and it had been a very useful lesson for him as he began to move from the simplest part of American society to a place where almost everyone was significantly more privileged, and where he dealt with titans of business and industry every day. David Stern was never more aware of that than when he at-tended Columbia Law School, auditioning for what seemed like the upper tier of American life, while working every day after school in what was clearly the lower tier. Some people who worked in stores, he learned, were nice, others were not nice but pretended to be nice based on their judgment of a customer's success, and others were simply not nice to anyone. That his father was good and courteous and spiritually generous with everyone who walked in the store was, he was sure, a key to the store's unusual success.

David Stern was extremely sensitive to the slights storekeepers—and others—could so readily and casually inflict on customers. Soon after he left law school, he and his wife, Dianne, both quite casually dressed, went looking for a new car. The salesman on the lot treated them from the start with overt rudeness, fending off serious questions about the ac-tual price of the car, as if somehow people dressed as they were could never have the money for so elegant an auto. Increasingly irritated with the veteran salesman, Stern demanded a different salesman and got a young man who had just been promoted. "You're about to make the eas-iest sale of your life," he told the young man, and thereupon bought the car in a matter of minutes.

Stern was a sports nut as a kid, a Giant fan, although sometimes a beer salesman would drop off some free tickets to a Yankee game and he would go anyway. The great issue of his childhood, he sometimes thought, was the question of who was the best of the three New York centerfielders: Willie Mays, Mickey Mantle, or Duke Snider. In the win-ter, he was a Knicks fan, and he could often get into a game with his school card for fifty cents and tip an usher for a better seat once inside.

He loved the game, and he loved the Knicks, which was not always easy to do. Those were not, regrettably, great Knicks teams, and a devoted young fan was doomed to a kind of annual disappointment. "I had my heart broken every year," he once said. "My favorite player was Harry Gallatin, Harry the Horse, because he worked so hard and he would play against [Bill] Russell and the Celtics every year, and Russell would always kill him."

In reality, Gallatin overlapped only two years with Russell, who was three inches taller and light-years ahead of him athletically, but Russell probably would have killed him every year had they competed. After he became commissioner, Stern sometimes ran into Bill Russell, and he always told the former Celtic that Gallatin had been a better player. Russell would answer with a deep, joyful cackle, as if to say that it was a shame that he had not been able to play against Harry the Horse every game of every season. In 1990, Stern was in Springfield, Massachusetts, when Gallatin was inducted into the Basketball Hall of Fame, and he raced over to introduce himself to his hero. "I'm thrilled to meet you— you're my hero," Stern told him.

Gallatin looked at him in utter disbelief. "Come on," Gallatin said, "I can't even believe you know who I am."

"Of course I know who you are—you're Harry the Horse and you were my hero when I was a kid, which means you'll always be my hero," Stern answered.

After graduation from law school in 1966, Stern went to work with Proskauer, Rose, Goetz, and Mendelsohn, one of the top Jewish law firms in New York in an era when law firms were still quite segmented ethnically. Very early on he learned that the firm was defending the NBA in the Connie Hawkins lawsuit, a suit on behalf of a talented schoolboy player who had his NBA career wiped out in an earlier and less tolerant era because a local district attorney told the commissioner that Hawkins had been contaminated by association with gamblers who were fixing games. It was a case in which the league was self-evidently in the wrong, and no one knew this better than Stern. He also knew that on occasion it was the responsibility of corporate lawyers to take on cases in which they were on the wrong side. What he needed was a settlement, for a miscarriage of justice had taken place years earlier because of the D.A.

What he loved about this case was taking the depositions, which brought him in contact hour after hour with the league's founders: Eddie Gottlieb, Red Auerbach, Maurice Podoloff, and Fred Schaus. It was more like doing an early oral history of the game itself. Later, when he did the depositions in the Oscar Robertson case, where the Players'

Association had challenged the right of teams to control the players' freedom of choice and movement, he found himself interviewing players such as Robertson, Lenny Wilkens, Bill Bradley, and Dave DeBusschere. He was enormously impressed by their intelligence and essential decency and goodness. Great athletic stars, who could readily have been arrogant, seemed instead to have an abiding degree of common sense, modesty, and inner toughness. If there was one lesson he was learning, it was that the league was its players, nothing more, nothing less, and that the best of these players, white and black, were uncommon men. More often than not, they were self-made, some of them the first generation in their families ever to be a success. They were men who had often lifted themselves up by the hardest work to reach their lofty positions. In time, when Stern eventually became commissioner, that simple perception served him well. Because most commissioners in professional sports are chosen by the owners, they are to all intents and purposes little more than the owners' man, but Stern was different. He came in with such a love of the sport that even though he was very good with the owners and performed admirably for them, there was a large part of his soul that was always committed to the game itself—which meant it was committed to the players.

Stern thought he was one of the luckiest people in the world: He was being paid to do what he would have done for free. He was always busy: Society was becoming more litigious all the time, and professional sports, because of the archaic nature of its labor laws, was a perfect target for much of that litigation. From the time he joined the Proskauer firm in 1966 to when he went to work for the league itself as counsel in 1978, he spent almost all of his time on NBA work.

Once he became the NBA's counsel, he soon became known as Larry O'Brien's consigliere. The league was struggling with its image problems, but things were changing. In some ways it was the illuminating spotlight itself that was changing, Stern thought. Television was casting a larger, brighter light that lasted a longer time on the sport, and it was revealing its beauty to more and more people.

If there was one moment that seemed to separate the old tradition-bound NBA from the new, more modern NBA that was about to surface, pushing and celebrating its star players, it was the all-star game in Denver in late January 1984. Until then, the all-star weekend had been something of a marginal event: there was the game itself and a traditional, rather boring banquet the night before. Baseball, by contrast, seemed to be able to do a great deal more celebrating of past glories. Stern had always wanted the league to be more in touch with its past, and now he and some of the young people around him pushed for a larger all-star celebration. In the end, they came up with a two-pronged idea: In addition to the regular game on Sunday, on Saturday they would have an old-timers' game, and they would resurrect the old ABA slam-dunk contest, still familiar from the famous footage of the young Julius Erving taking off from the foul line for a thunderous contest-winning dunk in 1976. The younger people pushed Stern for it, and he loved the idea. O'Brien, however, clearly wanted no part of it. Stern pushed and finally O'Brien assented. "All right," he said, with notable lack of enthusiasm, "as long as it doesn't embarrass me and as long as it doesn't cost us a nickel." So sponsorship was duly found, American Airlines to fly the players in, Schick to underwrite part of it, and this new fledgling television network called ESPN to tape it and show it a week later.

Until then, the NBA had needed only about 250 hotel rooms for its all-star weekend, but now, as if overnight, the number suddenly doubled. The Denver Nuggets sold tickets to the Saturday events for two dollars a seat and did a brilliant job promoting it. The place was packed. That weekend, for the first time, there was a sense of the NBA past and present blending, of Larry Bird and Magic Johnson mingling with Oscar Robertson, Elgin Baylor, Jerry West, and all the other great players from the past. Julius Erving, then approaching his thirty-fourth birthday, graciously agreed to be a part of the slam-dunk contest, going up against young Larry Nance. On his final dunk, as somehow everyone knew he would, Erving went to the far end of the court and started his run. When he reached the foul line, he took off (there were those perfectionists who thought he might have gone a bit beyond it), and the crowd seemed to rise as one. It was a huge success. No one was embarrassed, David Stern soon replaced Larry O'Brien, and a year later a young man named Michael Jordan came into the league, ready to win the slam-dunk contest, if he so chose.

That only a few years later the NBA was a hot sport, particularly among the young, whom Madison Avenue so coveted, was amazing. What was even more remarkable was that this phenomenon was taking place not just in the United States but worldwide; therefore, corporate sponsors saw this sport, more than baseball or football, as an opening to a world youth market. Stern himself was very careful about taking too much credit for the change. The real forces, he was quick to say, were completely outside his control and driven more than anything else by technological change, most particularly the blossoming of cable television. Suddenly, there were hour-long news shows devoted solely to the day's events in the nation of sports. "We were, without knowing it," he said, "entering a new golden era for sports, particularly basketball, fueled by the enormous growth of television, particularly cable." That, he pointed out, led to a quantum leap in how many games were broadcast, not just nationally but regionally, and a comparable quantum leap in marketing possibilities.

That golden era hardly began in a golden manner. ESPN started broadcasting on September 7, 1979, a date that roughly coincided with the entry of both Larry Bird and Magic Johnson into the NBA. Cable television, driven by technological breakthroughs derived from the space program, was just beginning to come into existence at that point. ESPN hardly seemed a sure thing. It started in a bargain-basement manner, and all of 1.4 million potential subscribers had the option of getting the service. It was the brainchild of a man named Bill Rasmussen, who was hardly a powerhouse in the world of American sports. He was then forty-six years old, and his most recent full-time job had been as sports-information officer for the New England Whalers in the old World Hockey Association, a job from which he had been somewhat unceremoniously fired because the team had not made the playoffs for the first time in several years. "They did what teams always do in situations like that—they fire someone who can't skate, like the PR man," he later noted.

Though his idea eventually wrought a giant explosion of the sports world in America and an even greater one in the internationalization of sports, Rasmussen's original vision had been neither national nor global. He had first envisioned something along the lines of a local or regional network to highlight Connecticut schoolboy athletics, principally the University of Connecticut's basketball games, as well as the games of Yale, Wesleyan, Fairfield, and other colleges. He had no earthly idea what it would take technologically to do this, but he was sure there was an audience for it.

Rasmussen had once created an informal regional network of radio stations to broadcast the football games of the University of Massachusetts, so he had some connections in the world of college sports and a sense of what it might take—some kind of mobile unit visiting various campuses. He and John Toner, the director of athletics at UConn, talked about the idea, and Toner encouraged him. Then, in June 1978, Rasmussen met with a few friends to get their reactions. One of them mentioned that there was a new thing called satellite reception that was just opening up in the world of cable television that might be the key to some form of very cheap broadcasting. That afternoon, Rasmussen called the offices of RCA. He spoke to a man named Al Parinello, who was in charge of selling channel space on a communications satellite. The demand for slots on the satellite was so small that Parinello asked him where his offices were and said he would be there the next day.

Parinello explained what the satellite would do, and he came equipped with his rate card. For normal cable use—five hours a day—they would have to pay $1,250 per day, he said. There was another rate, he noted, but no one had ever used it before. What was it? Rasmussen asked. Well, for twenty-four-hour-a-day service it was $34,167 a month. One of the people at the meeting was Rasmussen's twenty-two-year-old son Scott, who did some instant math and realized that the full service would come to only $1,139 a day. The decision was easy: They wanted it all day long.

The next question was what to put on the channel all day. Scott Rasmussen suggested college football games. Bill Rasmussen knew from his own experience at UMass that the NCAA permitted taped replay. Even if the big networks had the biggest college football games tied up, only a tiny handful of the NCAA's games were being broadcast. What about all the college games that were never aired? Could they do them live or on replay? What about reairing old games? What about all the other intercollegiate sports that were not televised at all? Was college hockey televised? College wrestling? Women's championships? The regional conference basketball championships that paved the way to the NCAA Finals and that fans found so enthralling? Helped by his friendship with Toner, Rasmussen talked to people on the NCAA television committee and found them intrigued and supportive—televising more games, and particularly televising the games of minor sports, was something they thought would be good for everyone involved, particularly the kids playing otherwise ignored minor sports.

The Rasmussens rented a bare-bones office in Plainville, Connecticut. The tables, Rasmussen liked to recall, were made by nailing wooden legs on old doors. Early in September 1978, Parinello called Rasmussen and urged him, if he was still interested, to get his application in to the FCC, which screened all applications for channels, as quickly as possible. Rasmussen did. A few days later, *The Wall Street Journal* had a front-page story detailing what the satellite breakthrough might mean in terms of cable programming. Suddenly, RCA was besieged by applications for transponder slots by all the broadcasting giants. But the FCC operated on a first-come, first-served basis, and Rasmussen was in line ahead of the big boys. He had stumbled into something that was almost literally priceless. When in late September the channels were awarded, Entertainment Sports Programming Network (or on occasion E.S.P. Network) of Plainville was the only unknown company with a channel.

Within two hours of the announcement, Rasmussen remembered, the phone rang in his office. It was a New York City investment company representing a media company that wanted Rasmussen's transponder slot. "Mr. Rasmussen," a voice said, "I work for an important Wall Street brokerage house and we have a very powerful client interested in that slot, and we can make you a very wealthy man by the end of this day." All that call did, Rasmussen recalled, was teach them that they were on to something quite valuable. Later, he thought he might have been able to swap his ticket for at least $5 million. Meanwhile, the Rasmussen family members all started kicking in to try and put together some start-up money. Rasmussen's credit cards were stretched to their rather narrow limits. An investment company in Pennsylvania, sensing something of value in the works, put up $250,000 and promised to look for additional funding. Soon, Getty Oil came in with $10 million, which was good for 85 percent of the company stock. That was the real seed money and it meant they were in business.

Years later, effectively squeezed out of the company that emerged out of his original idea but a very rich man nonetheless, Rasmussen thought what had happened was testimonial to the American entrepreneurial system. He was amused by the fact that he, a complete outsider with no wealth, no access to wealth, and no experience in network television, had come up with an idea of such singular originality and importance when all the top executives from all the great media companies—many of whose assignments were to deal exclusively with sports—had not thought of it.

In February 1979, Rasmussen made a deal with the NCAA for a large package of different sports, including football. Then Anheuser-Busch made a $1.4 million advertising commitment, the largest advertising buy thus far for any cable company. A logo was created. It was supposed to be called ESPN-TV, but it came back from the printer as ESPN, and they left it that way. The company located its headquarters in Bristol, Connecticut, largely because it was cheap. Not everyone welcomed them. A former Bristol mayor, running for reelection, looked at the company's two giant satellite dishes and predicted that they would kill lots of birds and inflict radiation on anyone living nearby. In September 1979, ESPN began broadcasting.

Thus did a technological revolution orchestrate the beginning of a profound cultural change. Without anyone entirely realizing it, the future of sports had arrived. The attention that America focused on its athletes, which had grown with the coming of radio earlier in the century (a technological breakthrough that greatly enhanced baseball's popularity), then had grown again in the late fifties with the coming of network television (which had greatly helped professional football, taking it from minor-league to true major-league status), was about to take another huge jump, one that this time would enhance all sports, but basketball in particular. That same year, Michael Jordan grew a great deal taller in a very short time, made the Laney High School varsity for the first time and became its star player, and Michael Brown called Roy Williams to say that he had a very talented high school player whom Carolina should look at.

ESPN's growth pains were not inconsiderable. Within a year of the start-up, the Getty people decided that Rasmussen was not big-time enough to handle his own company, and they moved him out. For a few years, the fledgling network seemed to symbolize potential rather than actual profit. Early on, before there was true commercial recognition of its potential, it simply hemorrhaged money, losing, it was said, $30 million in the first year alone and $40 million by 1982. The Getty executives were underwhelmed by the entire operation. At one point they wanted to get out but decided that the network was not yet worth enough and that they had to stay the course a little longer. But then, gradually, the network took hold—more than anything else because of the passion of its viewers, those great American sports junkies, who were committed even before the network made money. Desperate to turn the corner, ESPN decided to ask local cable companies for a fee of five cents a subscriber. The cable companies were not delighted with the idea, but under pressure from their constituents, the fans, they came around. Starting in 1983, subscribers had to pay, however indirectly.

Things were heating up. Texaco bought Getty and put ESPN up for sale. In April 1984, ABC bought it, not so much because the people there wanted it but because they did not want Ted Turner, architect of CNN and thus a rising power in cable, to have it. The ESPN ticket had already grown exponentially—the cost to ABC was $237 million. The Rasmussens still owned 12½ percent of the company, which meant they got about $30 million from the deal. ABC's arrival changed everything: It brought high-powered television skills to ESPN. By 1984, ESPN was entrenched: It already reached thirty-four million homes and had become a part of the fabric of life for the nation's sports fans. If anything the fans were somewhat ahead of the television decision makers. They knew what they wanted, virtually a sports fix each night, and this odd little network, with its occasionally erratic and occasionally brilliant programming, could supply it.

The year ESPN truly came of age, 1984, was also the year David Stern became the commissioner of the NBA, and the year Michael Jordan left the University of North Carolina to play for the Chicago Bulls.

Two years earlier, ESPN had broadcast its first NBA game, as part of a two-year contract. More important, the network had been broadcasting college games from the start in 1979, making the players bigger stars by the time they got to the NBA, more familiar to the fans watching at home. Basketball's reach was becoming larger, first in the United States and soon around the world. The game traveled far more easily across national boundaries than its two homegrown rivals, football and baseball, in part because its rules were self-explanatory. In the new commercial and technological world being wired together by satellite, the United States was the home team. It was the richest country in the world, its broadcast possibilities greater by far than those of any other country because of the vast broadcasting apparatus that already existed. It had a language that was internationally accepted, and it was on the cutting edge of popular culture, a force that appealed to the young throughout the world, always anxious to break away from the dogma and restrictions of an older generation. All of this worked in favor of David Stern and the NBA.

For better or worse, by the eighties America exported not its machine products or its cars but its culture: its fast foods, Cokes, and Big Macs; its more relaxed and informal dress codes; its popular music, movies, and television shows. And its sports. The ascending new sport in the world, one that was winning ever greater popularity with the young, was not soccer, though that reigned supreme in many parts of the world, but basketball. Soccer was viewed in the United States as too slow and as a sport in which less talented defensive players could too readily neutralize the skills of more talented offensive players, a mistake the NBA was careful to avoid. Traditionalists in other countries might bemoan a new American cultural imperialism, might see this Americanization—or democratization—of their culture as a kind of new barbarism, but its pull upon the young (and in time the not so young) was undeniable. More, the explosion of modern technology was changing the pace of life throughout the developed world, speeding it up all the time. Basketball was a sport of speed: The action was quick, goals were frequent, the score changed quickly.

If America was the home team in the new international culture, then it was inevitable that sooner or later some American athlete would become a signature commercial figure, the perfect salesman for a vast variety of goods exported by companies from this rich, culturally and commercially dominating superpower. This figure would have to be a surpassing athlete in a sport readily understood worldwide but also popular in America. Pele, the great Brazilian soccer player, might have been a possibility—his charm and talent were self-evident, and he had an awesome smile that flashed its way past old, historically rigid national barriers. But his great years came before the true internationalization of the economy, and soccer was, of course, of limited appeal in the United States. Muhammad Ali might have been a possibility, for he was beautiful and charming and funny, but his great years had come early on, in the sixties and seventies, he performed in a sport that had an innate brutality, and he was anathema to the gods of Madison Avenue, for he had made two fatal mistakes by their standards: taking a Muslim name and opposing an unwinnable war in Asia. Madison Avenue never came running to Ali's door, though late in his career he got a commercial for D-Con roach killer.

In retrospect, it was inevitable, therefore, that the player catapulted forward as the signature commercial representative of this great new athletic-cultural-commercial empire would be an American and a basketball player. The other dominant Americans sports were eliminated because of the nature of their footwear. There were no international commercial battles to be fought over football cleats or baseball spikes like those waged in the eighties for the right to be the sneaker king of the world. Nike and Converse and Adidas were at war with each other, and the NBA was the beneficiary. Hamburger and soft-drink companies followed. The NBA players, as Nike commercials were soon to prove, were highly marketable and attractive, particularly with younger customers who were not as burdened by the concept of race as were their elders—the people who up until then had made the decisions on Madison Avenue.

More, basketball was aided by all kinds of improvements in technology, not just the satellites. The technology had also improved at both ends of the viewing process—cameras on location were better and television sets were bigger and better. Because the pictures were clearer, basketball players projected a sense of physical and emotional intimacy. In minimal uniforms, they played a sport that demanded acrobatic movement, and they played both offense and defense, so their athletic ability and their emotions were both evident. This in contrast to football players, who were more heavily clad, and baseball players, who were by tradition less emotionally self-revealing. Basketball players projected a sense of physical and emotional intimacy. And a superstar in basketball, one truly surpassing player with only four other men on the court with him, playing both offense and defense, could dominate the play and fire the imagination of the public as one baseball player among nine or more or one football player among twenty-two never could. Suddenly, with the gifts of the best advertising image makers available to them, the charms of Michael Jordan, Charles Barkley, and Magic Johnson became obvious.

As Nike and other companies featured individual players such as Michael Jordan as *stars*, and as the league and the network became co-conspirators in the promotion of stars, a major new direction, barely understood at the time, was being charted for the league. It was part of a larger new phenomenon taking place in sports, and in society in general, but most nakedly and obviously in basketball. The game and its top people made a fateful choice: They would go this modern way or their league would perish as a big-time sport. Individual players were now being promoted rather than teams. Something that would have been anathema to owners, coaches, and many athletes in the past, the cult of personality, was now, however unconsciously, becoming mandatory as the sport sought to broaden its fan base. Its advocates, owners, and sponsors no longer saw themselves competing against rival teams, or even rival sports. Now they were competing in a far larger and more cutthroat arena—against rock stars, movies, and all kinds of other forms of modern entertainment—for a slice of the entertainment dollar. The arenas would have to be new and modern and feature luxury boxes, and there would have to be constant entertainment provided: gymnasts and dancing girls on the floor, and rock music booming out. Jumbotron screens would have to appear above the floor so that the fans could watch not merely the action, but in time, with perhaps even greater pleasure, themselves. Silence or dead time in the arena was to be abhorred above all.

Purists who loved the game as an end in itself and were wary of the culture of stardom in this sport were appalled. The managers of the Bulls, like many of the old guard in the league, were not at first entirely sure they liked this new direction. When Michael Jordan's first big sneaker commercial for Nike was screened, Bulls' general manager Rod Thorn was quite uneasy. "What are you trying to do to my player," Thorn asked David Falk after viewing the spot, "turn him into a tennis player?"

"As a matter of fact," said Falk, "that's exactly what I want to do."

The nature of the audience began to change from diehard fans, often less affluent, to wealthier people able to afford luxury boxes, whose interest in a team was more casual and whose commitment was less rooted. That Michael Jordan was unusually well prepared to play his assigned role as a new all-purpose entertainment superstar and yet remain absolutely pure as a basketball player made him very much the excep-

tion. Other teams, drafting other talented young men, were not always
to find themselves so lucky.

So it was that when Michael Jordan came in the league, a vast number
of changes were already beginning to take place in terms both of technology and of international economics that would affect his future and
of which he was to become a principal beneficiary. David Stern himself
later noted that he had barely noticed Jordan's arrival because he was so
caught up in the mundane legal and commercial issues that dominated
the daily calendar of a commissioner. In fact, what he remembered most
about the draft that year was fining Portland for tampering with Akeem
Olajuwon. Still, the arrival of Jordan in the very prime of Stern's career
was to be one of the great determining factors in the commissioner's
singular success. If Stern had sought not just success but a new kind of
respectability for his league, then the arrival of Michael Jordan was like
the answer to a dream.

Nothing revealed the changes being wrought by cable coverage, and
the growing affluence of the league, more than the television deal NBC
offered for the rights to the NBA in 1989. CBS had had the rights for the
previous seventeen years, and by 1989 it was doing a very respectable
job. With one year still left on the existing contract, the rights were up
for bid. CBS was coming off a four-year, $188 million contract, or $47
million a year, and it had the right to match the bid of any competitor.
NBC's Dick Ebersol badly wanted the sport. He was sure the sport was
on the rise. If Bird and Magic were coming to the end of their run, the
Pistons were a very good draw, and it was clear that not only was
Michael Jordan coming to the height of his powers, but that his team
was improving as well. He made a bid of $600 million for four years.
David Stern, always on the alert for new constituencies and younger
customers, also asked for a morning show for kids as part of the package; NBC was willing to do it, CBS was not. (The show was eventually
called *NBA Inside Stuff.*) CBS thought NBC overbid, particularly with
Larry Bird and Magic Johnson on the way out, and passed. Neil Pilson,
the head of CBS sports, was heard to tell his staff that it was all right because the Finals were probably going to be Utah and Cleveland anyway.

Pilson was wrong, and so was CBS. NBC's first year covering the Finals was 1991, the first year the Bulls made it, and the increase in ratings
was impressive. It would continue. The first Bird-Johnson Finals game
took place in 1984 and drew a rating of only 7.6. Three years later, for
their final face-off, it averaged almost 16. By comparison, the last game
of the 1998 Finals had a rating unheard of in basketball only a few years
earlier: 22.3. ·

As much as anything else, the new NBC contract symbolized that David Stern had achieved a critical part of his original goal of respectability. It was a huge victory for him. That day, Ebersol asked Stern what he was going to do to celebrate. "I'm going home and have dinner with Dianne," he said.

"But who's going to tell the owners?" Ebersol asked, knowing that on a victory like this there was a special pleasure for a commissioner to make the calls letting the varying owners—his bosses—know, and thereby take credit for the deal. Oh, he said, Russ Granik and Garry Bettman, his two deputies, would make the calls. In a way, that was the most impressive part of the entire negotiating process, Ebersol later thought, a boss who was so secure that he let his deputies make the celebratory calls to the owners.

10.

Chapel Hill; Chicago; Portland, 1984

WHEN ONE OF his players was about to turn pro, Dean Smith tended to oversee and orchestrate the entire operation, bringing in only agents he approved of, making sure that none of his boys were fleeced by fly-by-night hucksters. In those days two men who worked together, Donald Dell and Frank Craighill, had the inside track at Carolina. Dell had been a tennis star and had gotten into the agent business by representing other tennis stars; Craighill was a financial guy who had gone to Chapel Hill and had been a Morehead scholar, which was something Dean Smith liked. Smith seemed to like both Dell and Craighill, and soon they were part of the fabric of the North Carolina program. At the time, Dell's primary focus and love was tennis, and basketball was on the periphery of his affections. The Dell-Craighill organization had done well by Smith's players, getting a very good contract for Tom LaGarde, a big, somewhat awkward center with an already banged-up knee who had been drafted ninth in the country in 1977, a contract said to be better than the one received by Walter Davis, who was the fifth pick that same season. Smith had liked that, the ability to do well for a player of less than surpassing skills. With that, the pair began to get other North Carolina players, including Phil Ford, Dudley Bradley, and James Worthy.

When Dean Smith made the decision for Michael Jordan to come out after his junior year, David Falk was Dell's rather junior partner. There was an element of chance in how Dell and Falk came to represent Jordan. That year, the Dell-Craighill office split up, with Dell and Falk staying together and Craighill and another member of the firm, Lee Fentress, opening a competing office. The split presented Dean Smith with something of a dilemma. He was connected to both groups, and therefore unsure about which way his boys should go.

When one of his players was about to come out early, as Jordan now was, Smith liked to recon the issue, to be sure that the dollar value for the player was worth his giving up the year of eligibility. In this instance, he had let Dell and Falk do the recon, so their feet were slightly in the door. Smith finally let them take Jordan, while Sam Perkins went to Craighill and Fentress.

In those days, the pattern was that Dell would do the original contract, and then Falk, quite junior to Dell but far more of a basketball maven, would follow up, handling subsequent dealings with the player, including the sneaker contracts, then considered the peripheral money. By the time Jordan came out in 1984, the Carolina alumni in the pros were beginning to talk a great deal more about David Falk than they did about Donald Dell, because Falk was the one who was the hands-on representative with whom they dealt, the man who kept up with them and handled all the side business deals, which with the rise of a new level of celebrity for NBA players were not quite so peripheral anymore. As Falk later noted, "Dean Smith still saw me as the kid and he saw Dell as the man, but his players were beginning to see me as the man, the person they really dealt with."

From the moment that he went with the Dell agency, given the way the peripheral money grew, Michael Jordan was essentially going with David Falk, choosing him, he liked to say later, because Falk had the same haircut as Jordan's father—that is, he was virtually bald. Few benefited from the changes then taking place in basketball and in American sports more than Falk. In a brief period of time—a decade, really—he went from being a bright young guy hustling relentlessly at the entry level of the sport, who seemed to be enthralled by Dell's prestige and sophistication and who tried to dress like him and talk like him, to a power-broking millionaire whose leverage at times seemed to rival that of the commissioner himself and to be greater than that of many owners. Two things contributed to that rise: first, the dramatic change in labor laws during which power passed almost completely from owners to players and thus their agents; second, the brilliant job Falk did handling the representation of Michael Jordan. A new era was starting, and he was present at the creation. In an age of free agency and seemingly limitless salaries, his stable of athletes came to include not merely Michael Jordan but about twenty of the league's top players—among others, Patrick Ewing, Allen Iverson, Juwan Howard, Alonzo Mourning, Dikembe Mutombo, Keith Van Horn, and Antoine Walker—some of whom had signed up hoping that Falk would do for them what he had done for Jordan: make them a cultural icon who transcended the boundaries of basketball or, failing that, at least get them contracts worth $20 million a year, which by 1998 was a figure in the arena.

David Falk did not always wear his new power lightly. He was not averse to letting those he perceived to be beneath him know their more limited place in the hierarchy in which they both operated. It was not the job of good agents to be nice, it was the job of agents to take good care of their clients, and if need be to make enemies in the process. There was by consensus a feeling that no one did better by most of his clients than David Falk, and therefore not surprisingly no one had more enemies. Within the world of professional basketball, there was always a question about whether or not it was a good idea to be a lesser player on Falk's roster—would an owner take out his anger on a lesser Falk player that he couldn't on a Falk frontliner? Or would a minor Falk player catch a bit of extra slack from owners hoping to curry favor from Falk when it was time to deal with a superstar?

That his agent was often privately despised by many of the most powerful people in basketball did not bother Michael Jordan in the least. He was quite pleased that he emerged in his career with seemingly limitless popularity himself, but he was in no rush to have his agent be chummy with anyone in the power structure. As Jordan once said of Falk, mentioning in the same breath one of the league's most feared players, "He's a lot like Rick Mahorn—no one likes him unless he's on your team." If you want a dog to guard your house, John Thompson—both a Falk client and a Falk friend—once said, you don't want a poodle.

David Falk's rise to a position of power in the world of sports was hardly preordained. He was a middle-class kid from Long Island who had nothing particular going for him in his earlier years other than a passion for sports and a desire to be a lawyer. His father ran two butcher shops. He attended Syracuse as an undergraduate, a sign that he had fallen somewhat short of the elite world of the Ivy League, and he was hardly among the chosen people of his generation as he moved on to law school, hardly a first-round draft choice. "I was," he said, "a marginal person on the scale of bright young stars in the world of law, and I had to realize that no one was going to come running after me."

He was admitted to George Washington Law School in Washington, D.C., and while there he tried to gain a connection to the world of sports as an apprentice in a sports agent's office. He tried for a connection with Bob Woolf in Boston and Larry Fleisher in New York, but they were essentially lone operators who didn't have staffs. But then someone suggested Donald Dell. Falk called Dell repeatedly and could not get through, until one day, enraged by Dell's inaccessibility, he kept calling until Dell took the call, which he did, by Falk's reckoning, on the seventeenth try. They set up an appointment, and according to Falk, Dell kept him waiting three hours, but in the end he started working as an apprentice, sometimes going to school at night or in the summer and working for Dell during the day. He was assigned the donkeywork on Arthur Ashe, and he went at it with a rare intensity, checking, as few agents did, every time figures on Ashe's financial statements came in and making himself invaluable to Ashe, a man he greatly admired.

Even in those early years, he was nothing if not passionate and committed to his clients. One year, he represented a young basketball player named Rod Griffith, who had been drafted by Denver. That fall, Griffith's limits as a player had become obvious to the Nuggets management, and he was on the bubble, about to be cut. Falk called Donnie Walsh, the Denver general manager, every day to push his man, and in fact on the day the Nuggets intended to cut Griffith, Falk happened—a connection with the occult? Walsh wondered—to show up in the Denver camp. "It struck me since there were no commercial flights from Washington to the Air Force Academy, where we were practicing, that he probably figured out how to get on Air Force One and fly out," Walsh mused, "but you had to be impressed by that degree of commitment, and it worked at least for a little while because we didn't cut him that day."

Falk often seemed wired. It was as if he had a hyperactive mind: He thought quickly, saw things quickly, and felt compelled to speak quickly. Words and thoughts seemed to explode out of him, as if he were in a rush to hear what he said before anyone else did, perhaps for fear that if he did not speak quickly enough someone else might utter the exact same thought and get credit for it. As he became more and more powerful, he left less and less doubt that his time was extremely valuable, certainly more valuable than yours, and quite possibly more valuable than anyone's except perhaps that of Michael Jordan himself. Negotiating with Falk, one NBA general manager thought, was like wrestling with a brilliant octopus: There were so many moves and such resilience. "He'll threaten, he'll promise, he'll shout—if you don't do what he wants it's all over, you're finished with him, your team will never win another game, and you'll be fired for your lack of foresight. On the other hand if you do what he wants, you might well be first in line for the next Michael Jordan."

His players were always on the right side in any conflict, and there were inevitably a lot of conflicts associated with David Falk. Anyone else was on the wrong side. His people *always* wore the white hats. A reference to a book about Jordan by Sam Smith, a good deal of it apparently based on interviews with Horace Grant, might bring a prolonged and impassioned series of verbal assaults upon Grant, most of it aimed at his presumed lack of intelligence. Someone who stood in Falk's way in a lawsuit might, he once suggested to writer Rick Telander, be crushed.

A great many owners and general managers disliked him intensely but concealed that dislike as best they could and worked extremely hard to accommodate him lest their new superstar center, unhappy with a contract that paid a mere $18 million a year and around whom a $3 billion arena (named, of course, for an airline) had just been built, might decide that he wanted to opt for a different and of course happier clime, and a newer arena, named in honor of a rival airline.

What, general managers sometimes wondered, were the limits of Falk's power—and what was the nature of his whim? When a star player seemed unhappy about something, was it the star who was unhappy, or was it Falk who was unhappy? Did Falk long for a winter tan and prefer to visit Miami in January and February instead of Minneapolis or Vancouver? Might he steal their star player and move him to another team in another city where Falk had an existing but older star player who was badly in need of some additional supporting talent? There was one thing that was a constant about David Falk, and that was that, as he went from arena to arena to visit with and hold the hands of his various players, he always got *very* good seats.

Michael Jordan and David Falk helped make each other, and each profited to a remarkable degree from their special collaboration. It is true that Michael Jordan was the person who in the end actually did the deeds, went on the court and hit the final jump shot again and again, but it is also true that David Falk helped revolutionize the process of representing a basketball player, going into a team sport and creating the idea of the individual player as a commercial superstar, an iconographic act that was considered breathtaking at the time. Before Falk made the first great deal for Michael Jordan, the big sneaker money favored tennis players: Arthur Ashe or Jimmy Connors or John McEnroe might be making millions, while basketball players got a tiny fraction of that. The deal with Jordan changed that—a basketball player, a member of a team, could also be a star.

From the start, Falk sensed that Michael Jordan was special, that he might be able to transcend the narrow boundaries of his sport, that he had a charismatic quality that ordinary people would understand and respond to, qualities that placed him in a special elite of athletes like Pele, Muhammad Ali, and Arthur Ashe, whose fame and celebrity were greater outside the United States than inside it.

What David Falk helped to do with Michael Jordan changed the nature of sports representation. It is true that the timing was absolutely right, that a number of things tumbled at the same time, most obviously the technological changes in the world of communications. It is also true that he had the perfect athlete for the age, a virtuoso of a sport whose unique artistry was nakedly apparent even to neophytes and who was a strikingly handsome and articulate young man at that. Dean Smith, representing the other part of Michael Jordan's world, was not entirely pleased with the limitless commercial bonanza that Jordan's success had produced (or at least with the idea of an agent who was more powerful than a coach), and he was heard to say that his daughter could have represented Michael Jordan just as well as Falk. It is also true that though Falk did, by any kind of measurement, a better job for Jordan than any agent in history did for any other athlete, David Falk never got another Carolina player after Jordan.

What is true and to Falk's credit is that he saw the future before anyone else. Why, after all, had what happened with Jordan not happened slightly earlier with the coming of Magic Johnson? He had arrived in 1979 with an NCAA championship under his belt, and he went on to lead the Lakers to an NBA championship in his rookie year, playing brilliantly in the championship game against Philadelphia. Los Angeles was certainly a far better media city than Chicago from which to promote a sports icon who might be able to cross traditional cultural and social boundaries in the society. Like Jordan, Johnson had a wonderful, engaging smile. If anything, it was quite possible that the young Magic Johnson had an even more ebullient personality than the young Michael Jordan. Unlike Jordan, he even had a marvelous nickname, Magic. Some of it was timing: Johnson had arrived on the eve of the explosion of the newer, more bountiful sports culture, and Jordan arrived after the pioneers had opened the way. Clearly, Jordan reaped what Johnson and Bird had sown. But it was also true that Johnson was, in contrast to Jordan, poorly represented by people who saw him only as a basketball player. In no small part due to the money Jordan was making, Johnson eventually changed his own representation.

At the time Jordan came out in 1984, sneaker money was just beginning to go up exponentially. In those days, the big companies were Converse and Adidas. Nike was relatively small, hardly a big player in the world of basketball shoes, even as the overall stakes were becoming bigger and bigger. At the start of the eighties, it was believed that only Kareem Abdul-Jabbar had a six-figure sneaker contract—for $100,000. Bird and Johnson were said to be in the $70,000 range. Just a few years earlier, in 1977, Nike had signed Marques Johnson, the third player taken in the draft, for only $6,000. Then a year later, Phil Ford came out and got $12,000. In 1981, when Mark Aguirre was the first pick in the entire draft, he got a $65,000 contract. A year later, James Worthy, represented by Dell (and Falk), had been number one in the nation, and he had signed a long-term contract with New Balance, eight years for $1.2 million—roughly $150,000 a year. That, thought Falk, represented the breakthrough.

When Jordan came out, Falk liked to say later, the realm of commercial endorsements for basketball players was like the world before Columbus, when many people still presumed that the earth was flat. Baseball was still America's most deeply rooted sport and football its most exciting one. The endorsements most team athletes got were quite limited, save for the rare exception like Joe Namath; the endorsements black athletes got were even more marginal. The young Willie Mays had been a charismatic player in the nation's most celebrated sport, his ebullience impossible to fake, imitate, or hide, but the consensus on Madison Avenue had been, of course, that the country was not ready for a black man endorsing products for a predominantly white nation. Mays starred in the fifties, when the perception was that the country was not ready; now, some thirty years later, Madison Avenue still seemed to believe that the country was not quite ready.

Falk, however, thought it was time to get beyond the color line in sports advertising; the country had changed, the demographics were different. Moreover, because he had been around tennis, Falk understood that pure athletic ability was only a part of the package, that some players had personal qualities that made them unusually attractive commercial salesmen. He sensed that Michael Jordan was different from most other team athletes, that there was an attractiveness, a charm, a certain grace about him. Jordan was very well spoken, he made an excellent impression on a wide variety of people, and he had a decidedly winning smile.

Falk decided from the first that when he met with the sneaker companies he would issue what he called the Kennedy challenge: What can you do for us? What would they do in terms of marketing? How big would the television advertising budget be? Would they give Jordan his own shoe line? His own apparel line? Falk knew he was going into virgin territory. Magic Johnson, already a proven champion, an extroverted *winner*—what could be better?—had not received anything like that, nor had Julius Erving. Falk understood that the odds were against him. Not only was there the enduring prejudice about what blacks could do as salesmen, but there were the facts that Jordan was not even the first pick in the draft and Chicago, unlike Los Angeles or New York, was not considered a great media center. Besides, Jordan was not a big man, and in those days big men got the big money.

The Converse people were appalled by the audacity—indeed the arrogance—of Falk in demanding so much for someone who did not register on their seismograph. We have, Joe Dean, one of their representatives, said, sixty-three people who work for our company who are over six foot six, meaning that the company specialized in hiring former basketball players, and basketball formed the company culture. We do it the right way. We'll treat you the way we treat Magic Johnson, Larry Bird, and Dr. J. They did not even know what they were saying, Falk thought: What they were really saying was, we're the big time, we have all the best players, we don't need to be creative, we don't need to try and think, and, finally, we don't really need you. Falk was not the only person in the negotiations who was bothered by their response. Michael's father, James, was very much a part of the negotiations, and, watching him, Falk quickly decided that the senior Jordan was a very shrewd businessman. At one point during the Converse negotiations James Jordan looked up and said, "Don't you have any new, creative ideas?"

By chance, Nike's needs matched Falk's. At the time, it was coming off a flat period. It had been an upstart running-shoe company that had caught the early wave of the jogging craze in the seventies and prospered as if overnight, but then the company seemed to hit a wall. Nike was a very small player in the world of basketball. All the best professionals wore Converse: Bird, Johnson, Isiah Thomas. "If you had gone to a playground and asked kids what sneakers they wanted, they would have said Converse," Peter Moore, one of Nike's executives, noted years later.

Nike's strategy in the past had been to sign up a large number of good but not great players for a relatively limited amount of money—the average contract seemed to be about $8,000 a player, but in no way did it compete with Converse and Adidas. If it had fielded a team against the Converse all-stars, the game would have been a rout, like Angola taking on the Dream Team nearly a decade later. But that policy was about to change, driven by budget pressures, among other forces. Nike's Phil Knight wanted to cut back on the basketball budget in general—too much money being spent on too many players, without much commercial benefit.

The Nike executive charged with making a new policy work was Rob Strasser, the top Nike person dealing with talent. Strasser was not a cautious corporate man. Rather, he was a man driven by impulse and faith in his own instincts, and his instinct when he had an idea was to go for it. Just do it, as someone might have said. The new policy was that Nike would direct its energies onto one player, making him Nike's signature athlete, funneling all of Nike's advertising resources into him, and making him, if the policy succeeded, more than a basketball player. Because all of the great players who had come out before were already signed up, they would need a rookie. The question, as the draft neared, was which one.

If professional basketball teams had their talent scouts, so did sneaker companies. Nike's scout was a ubiquitous figure named Sonny Vaccaro, who seemed to know a good deal about the world of East Coast basketball and was well connected at certain schools. He was a close friend of John Thompson at Georgetown, Bill Foster at Duke, and Jim Valvano at North Carolina State. Running the Dapper Dan game, one of the early high school all-American games, put him in an enviable position with high school coaches who wanted to promote their kids and college coaches who wanted to recruit them. Vaccaro moved in and out of playgrounds, high schools, and colleges, a skilled connector and tout in a world where it was the nature of the business for everyone to be looking for a better connection than the one he already had. The most natural thing in the world for Sonny Vaccaro was to venture out to some seedy playground, hoping to find one more diamond in the rough there.

Sonny Vaccaro did not know Michael Jordan personally, but he had been watching him closely since his freshman year, and he had decided very early on that Jordan was something special. Nothing had impressed him more than Jordan's deciding basket in the 1982 NCAA title game. That was something big, a kid willing to take the ultimate big shot under supreme pressure and hitting it as if he were Mr. Cool.

Vaccaro had no doubt about which player they should sign. It was Michael Jordan. At a strategy meeting held in the early winter of 1984, he pushed Jordan as hard as he could. Akeem Olajuwon might come out slightly higher in the draft, but he was Nigerian, new at the game, and still working on his English. The only other player with some degree of charisma was a chubby young player from Auburn named Charles Barkley. At one point, Vaccaro was asked, because this was a critical corporate decision, whether he was willing to bet his entire career with Nike on the choice of Jordan. Absolutely, he answered. And if he had a choice of signing ten guys at $50,000 each or one guy at $500,000, would he still go with only one player? Absolutely, he said, if the player was Michael Jordan. With that, the Nike people decided to go after Jordan.

Nike, however, represented something of a problem for Michael Jordan, because in truth Jordan did not particularly like Nike shoes. He had worn Converse in Carolina's games because that was the shoe Dean Smith had linked up with, but the shoe he preferred and the company he wanted was Adidas. Unfortunately, the Adidas people did not seem to reciprocate his feelings. But Falk and Nike had similar interests, and that summer, as the Olympics were going on, Rob Strasser and Peter Moore went to Washington to meet with Falk. Falk was full of ideas, Moore thought, not all of them inspired. Perhaps, Falk suggested, Nike could create a commercial showing Jordan dunking, and the dunk would be in the arc of the Nike Swoosh. Or Nike could do a commercial showing Jordan playing pool and hitting a shot in which the cue ball traveled like the Swoosh. Falk wanted Jordan to have his own line of shoes, and they agreed to do that, as it was in their mutual interest. The one idea which Falk proposed that they both liked was the line's name, Air Jordan. Moore sketched out a simple design, the center of which was a badge with wings lifting a basketball. Moore was a designer of considerable skill—he eventually gave the world the Jump Man logo of Michael soaring in the air, about to dunk. By the end of the meeting, everyone seemed pleased by the direction they were all going.

Still, even as it became increasingly clear that Nike not only was very interested in Jordan but also would give him most of what he wanted, Jordan's lack of interest in Nike was a problem. Falk and Jordan's parents had a hard time even getting him on the plane to Portland. Like most other players coming out in those days, he thought a sneaker deal was a sneaker deal: You chose the shoe you liked best, took some money for endorsing it, and then got a lot of free shoes that you could give to your friends. That a sneaker deal was part of something larger, the selling of himself as a player, that he might make more money from commercial endorsements than from his basic salary, was something he did not entirely comprehend yet, because no one really comprehended it yet, not even the Nike people or Falk. Finally, Deloris Jordan told her son that she and his father were going to be on that plane to Portland, and he had better be on it, too.

Nike made a special presentation for him. Though by the standards of what was soon to come in the business it was relatively modest, at the time it was way ahead of the curve. The Nike people had created a video of the best clips of his college days and his Olympic games, and they had it ready for him. At the key moment, however, when Strasser hit the VCR's PLAY button, the machine did not work. Eventually, it did, and the video, accompanied by the music from the Pointer Sisters hit "Jump," was played for the Jordan family. Peter Moore had also sketched out a design of sneakers, which were colored, not just white. They had also made sketches of jumpsuits and all kinds of other sporting apparel. In one of the sketches, the shoes were colored red and black. "I can't wear that shoe," Jordan said. "Those are the Devil's colors."

"Michael," Strasser said, "unless you can get the Chicago Bulls to change their colors to Carolina blue, those are going to be your colors."

It was, thought Peter Moore, like recruiting a great high school player for a college. They all went from the first meeting to the giant Nike store, which seemed like the greatest toy store in the world for athletic gear: Just go in and help yourself, take all you can and throw it in your cart. Jordan emerged with six huge bags of stuff. Then there was the car. Sonny Vaccaro suggested that they give Jordan something tangible. At that point, Rob Strasser said that he knew that Jordan loved cars and they were going to give him one. He brought out a toy Porsche. It was something of a joke, but Phil Knight was not in on it, and he turned ashen when Strasser spoke, sure that his money was being thrown away on an untested player whom they had not even signed yet. Michael, Strasser quickly added, with the kind of money you're going to make, you can buy all the cars you want.

James and Deloris Jordan were beginning to come Nike's way, thought Peter Moore. They were obviously impressed by Strasser's raw enthusiasm, by the fact that the company saw Michael as special, and by the amount of energy that had gone into the presentation. About Michael's own feelings there was no telling. He sat there with Falk and his parents during the meeting, not showing any emotion at all, absolutely stone-faced. Falk, who did not know his client that well at the time, was surprised. Here was a company making every gesture—human and financial—that it could, and this young man appeared almost completely immune to its seductive powers. As they came out of the crucial meeting, Jordan turned to Falk and said, "Let's make the deal."

"But you never cracked a smile, or showed any enthusiasm," Falk said to him.

"I had my business face on," Jordan answered, and with that Falk had a quick sense that he was dealing with more than just another bright, talented athlete, that there were dimensions to this young man that he was still to learn.

That night they all went out to dinner. The Jordan family got in the limo and there again, playing on the limo VCR, was the video of

Michael's college highlights set to music. The Nike people had chosen a popular downtown restaurant, and as the party of Nike executives and the Jordan family descended down the stairs to the lower-level dining room, they passed a large number of people who seemed to recognize Michael Jordan. Moore noticed immediately that he was witnessing something different. Jordan made his way down the stairs, tall, handsome, innately graceful, a kind of young American prince, immensely comfortable within himself, and people there began to turn and stare at him.

As they did, Michael sensed their recognition and smiled back at them in the most natural way imaginable. It was clear that the power of his smile was formidable. These were upper-middle-class citizens of Portland, all of them white. The scene was nothing less than an epiphany for Peter Moore, for the voltage of the young man's smile was unique. As Jordan smiled, race simply fell away. Michael was no longer a black man, he was just someone you wanted to be with, someone you wanted as your friend. The smile was truly charismatic, Moore reflected in later years: It belonged to a man completely comfortable with himself and therefore comfortable with others. It seemed to say that only good things would now happen. More, it had a lift to it, a lift that carried ordinary people past their own normal prejudices. If Michael Jordan, he of the brilliant smile, was not burdened by the idea of race, why should you be burdened by it either?

Later that night, as the Nike people dispatched the Jordan family in the limo once again to the sound of the Pointer Sisters, Rob Strasser turned to Peter Moore and asked if he thought they could get Jordan. "I think we can," Moore answered. "They all seem pretty comfortable with us." Then he added, "If we do get him, I think we're getting something special—there's a personality there the like of which I've never seen before with any athlete." If he's any good as a basketball player, Moore thought, we really have something great.

Indeed, they could get him. But it would cost them. Falk was asking for certain advertising guarantees, and when the deal was done it signaled a commercial breakthrough in the new sports-entertainment world, for it guaranteed Jordan roughly $1 million a year for five years. Little did the Nike people—or the Bulls' management for that matter—know they were getting one of the great bargains of the time.

When he returned to Chapel Hill, Jordan told Buzz Peterson that Nike was going to name a sneaker after him. It's all getting to him, Peterson thought, all these awards and trophies, the Naismith and all the other awards. No, insisted Jordan, they're really going to name a sneaker line after me. "Michael," Peterson argued, "they haven't named a sneaker line after Larry Bird or Magic Johnson, and they're NBA stars. You're not even the first player taken in the draft." Later, after the Air Jordan line came out, Jordan mentioned to some of his friends that if they had any money it might not be a bad idea to buy some Nike stock because he thought the whole thing was really going to take off. Well, thought Peterson, Coach kept him in line a long time, but he's got the big head now.

11

Los Angeles; Chicago, 1984, 1985

S O HE WAS on his way to Chicago as a Nike man. But first there were the Olympic games. He was clearly ready for the pros. The Olympic games and pre-Olympic workouts against NBA players were a singular advertisement for how good he was going to be.

That summer, in Los Angeles, Jordan had been the best player on a star-studded American Olympic team. At first, coach Bobby Knight was a little uncertain about him: He was immensely talented, Knight told Billy Packer early in the Olympic camp, but he was a poor shooter, especially for someone who was supposed to be a shooting guard. But Knight soon became one of Jordan's foremost advocates. The coach, one of the most demanding in the game, was impressed by the intensity of his defensive presence, how coachable he was, and how competitive he was—all in all a natural leader.

Knight took him aside early on and said that he might come down hard on Jordan as a means of motivating some of the other, less passionate players, and Michael said that was fine with him. He soon emerged as the team spokesman. On the day of the final game, when they were to play Spain for the gold medal, Knight prepared his greatest pep talk ever—to the effect that the next forty minutes were likely to be the most important forty minutes of their lives, and that they would remember this day long after everything else in their careers was long forgotten. When he came in to his office that day, Knight found a piece of yellow paper on his chair. On it was written this simple message: "Coach—

Don't worry. We've put up with too much shit to lose now." Signed: "The Team." It was obviously the work of Michael Jordan, Knight decided, for no one else would have had the courage to do it. So Knight kept his mouth shut and simply told them, "Let's go out and win."

At halftime, with the United States ahead by only twenty-seven points, Knight decided to get on Jordan just a little, so there would be no second-half letdown. "Goddamn it Michael," he yelled, "when are you going to start setting some screens—all you do is rebound and score!"

Jordan gave him a big smile. "Coach," he said, "didn't I read some place where you said I was the quickest player you ever coached?"

"Yes," said Knight, "but what's that got to do with it?"

"Coach, I set those screens faster than you could see them," he answered.

Later, reporters, hoping to draw a contrast between the volatile Knight and seemingly more controlled Dean Smith, asked Jordan what it was like to play for both men. He had answered that they were very similar, but that Smith employed the four-corner offense, and Knight employed four-letter words.

He was obviously the best player on the American team. After the Americans destroyed Spain, reporters asked one of the Spanish players, Fernando Martin, about him. "Michael Jordan?" he answered, "Jump jump jump. Very quick. Very fast. Very very good. Jump jump jump."

The Olympics had added greatly to his contract leverage with the Bulls. By the time he played his first professional game, Michael Jordan was already a very rich young man. Donald Dell handled the main contract. Chicago was boxed in—here was this talented young player who had obviously been the best player on the Olympic team, and Chicago was a weak franchise with its credibility very much on the line. He signed for seven years for a total of $6.3 million, said to be the third-largest contract for a rookie in league history, ranking behind those of Olajuwon and Ralph Sampson, both of them big men. "It took some give and take," Jonathan Kovler said at the time. "We gave and they took." In addition, there was the million-dollar Nike contract. He was going to be well paid, and the Chicago ownership was pleased. "Here Comes Mr. Jordan," ran the first promotional ads for the man the ownership hoped would be the city's newest athletic star.

Jordan did very well at his first press conference in Chicago. David Falk wrote out a few things for him to say, but it turned out that he had little need of help; he had a natural talent for dealing with the press. Someone asked him about his teammates in Chicago, and he answered, Well, he did not think the Bulls would go undefeated. Falk did not bother prepping Michael for the press anymore.

He had taken over the team at the very first day of camp. Rod Thorn and Kevin Loughery thought they had made the right pick from the start, and everything they had seen that summer during the Olympic Games confirmed that judgment. It was not just the athletic ability, but the focus: Unlike a lot of gifted players with exceptional athletic ability, Jordan, so well coached and so intelligent, could and did use his gifts with rare purpose. Day in and day out, he could use that superior speed, jumping ability, and strength to create his shot. The ability to create shots was one of the gifts that divided pro players and college ones. Pro defenses were so much tougher that many players with fine shooting eyes who had seemed invincible in college quickly faded. They lacked the physical strength or quickness to create their own shot at this level, and they were dependent upon their teammates for picks to get free. From the start, it was obvious that Jordan was uniquely qualified to create a shot, perhaps better than anyone in the league.

From the first day of practice, Jordan had absolutely dominated the camp. No one could stop him in the one-on-one drills. Soon, the other players were beginning to stand around and watch him. At one point in an early scrimmage, Jordan rebounded the ball high off the backboard, drove the length of the court to the foul line, and took off for a resounding dunk. "I don't think we have to scrimmage any more," Loughery told one of his assistants. Later, he told Rod Thorn, "I think we've hit the jackpot."

Few realized how strong he was because he looked so wiry. Bobby Knight had picked up on it, and he told everyone he met about Jordan's secret strength, which was a source of so much of his special ability. "You don't see the strength because he's not that powerful looking, not one of those brute bodies, but it's there and when he backs in on you and you're the defender and he seems to put his hand lightly on your knee— it's like you're locked in an iron vise," Knight said. And his body was as yet untouched by any high-level fitness program.

The other thing Loughery saw and absolutely loved from the start was the size of Jordan's hands. They were simply huge. Loughery himself had been an excellent pure shooter in another age, but he did not have particularly big hands. In fact, he had often covered them in stickum when he played to give him better control of the ball. All the great players Loughery had dealt with except for Moses Malone had huge hands. Julius Erving had huge hands. Larry Bird had huge hands. Magic Johnson had huge hands. Michael Jordan had huge hands. It's almost unfair, Loughery thought, it's as if guys like that are playing with a softball, not a basketball, and they can control the ball so much more readily. It made the game so much easier for them—they could go up in the air and still do things with the ball while up there that players with ordinary hands could not.

From the start, Jordan was much better than anyone expected. Everyone thought he was good, but no one thought he would be this good, this fast, that he would be an immediate superstar. He entered the league with a jump shot that was, by NBA standards, a B–, Loughery thought, better than anyone expected and probably better than the scouts had suggested. The mechanics were quite good, but the trajectory was a little flat. If anything, it didn't seem quite as good as it actually was because every other aspect of his game was a straight A, Loughery thought. But he was eager to improve, and he and Loughery worked on his jump shot every day, sometimes for an hour before practice, sometimes for an additional hour after practice, always working on technique and trajectory. Even here he was competitive: They bet on their games of Horse, and in the early rounds Loughery always won, but Jordan forced him to keep playing until gradually Loughery wore down a little and Jordan might win. Jordan didn't like to leave any game until he won.

He was the first player at every practice and the last to leave, the hardest-working NBA practice player any of them had ever seen. The only problem was the degree to which he dominated everyone else. Early on, Rod Thorn called over to the Bulls' practice facility, Angel Guardian, to talk to Loughery, only to find that everyone had already gone home. Why was practice over so early?, he asked the next day. "I had to let them off early," Loughery said, "Michael was wearing them all out."

In those days in practice, they played five-on-fives until one team reached ten baskets, and the losing team had to run laps, ten of them to be exact. Jordan did not like to run laps, so he was very tough in those games. Once, with his team up 8–0, Loughery switched him to the weaker team. Michael was furious about it, and for the first time started to argue with Loughery. Life was unfair enough playing in this grim gym after the luxury of Carolina, but to be switched to another team after you had built up a safe lead seemed a particularly cruel cut. Loughery held his ground. "Same score, Michael—your team is losing." Jordan played in a fury, of course, which was what Loughery wanted, and his new team came back to win, 10–8. Afterward, he glared at Loughery, said, "I got your losing—right here," and strode to the locker room. (A few years later, with Loughery coaching in Washington, the Bullets were playing in Chicago and took an eight-point lead late into the fourth quarter. Then Jordan went on one of his patented runs. When he hit the basket that put the Bulls ahead, he ran back down the court past Loughery and said, "Just like Angel Guardian, right, Coach?")

He was going to be a great player, Loughery thought, not just because of the talent and the uncommon physical assets but because he loved the game. That love could not be coached or faked, and it was something he always had. He was joyous about practices, joyous about games, as if he could not wait for either. Not many players had that kind of love. All too many modern players, Loughery believed, loved the money instead of the game. But Jordan's love of what he did was real, and it was a huge advantage.

Because of that, and because he seemed to have a unique metabolism—one which would one day allow him to play fifty-four holes of golf on the day before a key playoff game and not be tired out—he never seemed to wear down. His energy level was unique. It was traditional for players coming out of college, accustomed to playing only about twenty-four games a season, to wear down during their rookie seasons, playing the exhausting eighty-two-game NBA season with its harsh traveling schedule. Mark Pfeil, the team trainer, warned Jordan of the fatigue factor, that he had to pace himself carefully because there were so many games and the travel was so hard. Jordan seemed if anything amused by Pfeil's concerns. "Are you tired? Do you want fewer minutes?" Pfeil would ask.

Jordan would just smile and say, "Watch me."

Jordan made his mark in the league almost from the start of the season. In his second game, played at Milwaukee, Mike Dunleavy watched Jordan take off from near the foul line for a long dunk attempt, a move that only Julius Erving had ever been able to pull off. Dunleavy tapped Kevin Grevey, sitting next to him, and said, "There's his first big mistake." And then Dunleavy watched Jordan soar to the basket, and he realized that it was *his* first mistake, not Jordan's.

There were also some clear early signs of his toughness and indomitable will. Very early on, the Bulls played Washington, which in those days had both Jeff Ruland and Rick Mahorn, two very physical players, known as McFilthy and McNasty. Ruland knocked Jordan down hard after a drive, and he hit the floor with a sharp crack. He got up, made his free throws, and came back and drove as hard as he could right at Ruland again. In another game, against Milwaukee, a very good team in those days coached by Don Nelson, he went against Sidney Moncrief, one of the two or three premier defensive guards in the league. Moncrief was utterly unable to stop him, and soon it was as if Nelson had altered his entire defense so that everyone was guarding Jordan. To no avail: Chicago won. It was, reporter Ron Rapoport thought, as if one man were running a picket line of five defenders, none of whom could stop him. Rookies did not do things like this.

From the start, the crowds began to turn out, both at home and on the road. The home attendance at Chicago Stadium almost doubled, from 6,365 a game to 12,763 in the first couple of months of his first season. Sales of season tickets, a virtual dead item before he came aboard (the Bulls sold only 2,047 the year before he joined the team), increased five-fold in his first three years there, to 11,000. Whenever Bulls games were broadcast locally, the ratings showed that some 30,000 more homes were tuned in to watch him.

Still, the Michaelmania, the true craziness, had not yet started. The crowds were bigger wherever he went, but there was no madness to it yet. Tim Hallam, then the Bulls' press officer, remembered early glimpses of the cult in a preseason game in Gary, Indiana, in which Jordan scored about forty points. After the game, Hallam remembered, there was a small parade of little kids following Jordan through the halls of the gym. That fall, the *Sporting News* asked him to pose wearing a surgeon's togs for a cover headlined THE NEXT DR. J. He went along with it, though Hallam could tell he didn't really like doing it because he thought the cover was gimmicky. The ball they supplied was not the ball Jordan was endorsing, and Hallam noticed that he placed his hand over the logo of the ball—he wasn't going to advertise another company's product. Even then he was very careful about his corporate sponsorships.

Jordan was particularly good with the beat reporters in those early years, always accessible and friendly. Part of it was the way he had been raised, part his understanding that this was an important part of his job, part his natural confidence, and part his innate shrewdness. He realized that he could learn a great deal about the league and about other teams—including which players were having trouble with their teammates and their coaches—by talking to reporters informally. He soaked up information readily and traded tidbits of his own, learning, as good politicians learn, that to get information you have to give information. He seemed to have a sixth sense for which of the younger reporters were the comers, the ones who soon would be stars and have their own columns—Mike Lupica, Michael Wilbon, David Remnick, Jan Hubbard—and were worth taking a little extra time with. He was, even then, an astute judge of quality.

Even though the media fascination with him was, by the standards of what was to come, relatively minor, it was immense for a Bulls player in that era, and Hallam was soon bombarded by requests for interviews. He would duly make a note of each request on a little pink slip and hand it to Jordan, who dutifully returned every call until about midseason when he came to understand that he was the only player on the team doing this, that everyone else let it fly. The great unwritten rule of the NBA was that if a reporter wanted to talk to a player, he had to nab him in the locker room. In time, Jordan and Hallam worked out a deal: When Hallam had an interview he felt was important, Jordan would do it, but he could also order a steak and charge it to Hallam (even though Jordan was already collecting a handsome per diem).

In those early days, they could still go through airports with relative ease. Occasionally when he was spotted, there would be a brief commotion, and when it happened he was unusually graceful. Once, when the Bulls were having breakfast in the Dallas airport at about 7 A.M., Jordan was standing in line with his tray like everyone else when a fan came up and asked for his autograph. Jordan answered very politely that he would be glad to oblige but he wanted to finish his breakfast first. The man exploded: "You goddamn athletes are all alike—you're all too spoiled." In time, the Michael fever got worse and worse, and the Bulls management decided to take the earliest flights out of each city in order to minimize airport mob scenes; they learned to smuggle him on and off planes as best they could, sometimes hiding him in an airline's lounge until the last minute. By the early nineties, they were flying charter.

His rookie year was a hard adjustment for him in many ways. It was not that there were four times as many games—he loved basketball, and he seemed to have boundless energy. What was hard was entering so weak a program from one so strong. In Chapel Hill, everything had been first-class. The program had been carefully thought out and brilliantly organized. There was a depth in the coaching staff—assistant coaches who were recognized as being better than most head coaches— that was almost unique. There were a great many very good players (lest someone get a swelled head and think he was bigger than the program), and they were all absolutely committed. Players always put out as much in practice as they did in games. The facilities were first-rate, surely better than those of almost every other team they played. Most of all, the sense of purpose was clear and constant.

That was far from true at Chicago. Kevin Loughery was a good coach, but his overall staff was nothing like Carolina's. The facilities were terrible. Worse, the players themselves were disappointing. Not only were they limited in talent, not only did a number of them have substance-abuse problems that limited their nightly performances, but there was no clear passion to win, no sense of purpose. One day early in Jordan's rookie year, when the Bulls were on the road, he was told of a party in a player's room. He dropped by the party to find a number of his teammates doing drugs—some smoking marijuana, some using co-caine—and he got out of there as quickly as he could. Nothing could be farther from Carolina.

Everything about the organization seemed a little worn down. Paul Westhead, who had arrived for a brief tour as coach from the plush habitat of the Lakers, was stunned to find out how meager the Bulls' resources were in terms of scouting, videotaping, and practice facilities. Angel Guardian, a converted orphanage, was a dank place with concrete floors, windows that had been painted over (adding to a sense of constant gloom), and a constant unpleasant stench. The journey from that practice center to the Bulls' later, handsome, multimillion-dollar suburban facility in Deerfield exemplified Jordan's effect: Angel Guardian was the NBA past; the Berto Center, with its security provisions to keep fans out and reporters at a distance (there was a pleasant enough press room with a Plexiglas window that overlooked the floor, but with the push of a button a curtain would quickly descend and cut off the view), was the NBA future.

There were two particularly prophetic judgments about Jordan that first year. The first was from Larry Bird, when the mighty Celtics played in Chicago. After the game, Bird singled out Jordan's play. The fascinating thing, thought Dan Shaughnessy, the Celtics beat writer at the time, was that it was not a case of the writers pushing the great star to talk about what he thought about the new kid on the block. Bird volunteered it, quietly, almost matter-of-factly, but above all admiringly. He had never, he said, seen one player turn a team around like Jordan had. "Even at this stage of his career he's doing more than I ever did. I couldn't do what he does as a rookie. Hell, there was one drive tonight: He had the ball up in his right hand, then he took it down, then he brought it back up. I got a hand on it, fouled him, and he still scored. All the while he's in the air." Pretty soon, Bird predicted, Chicago Stadium would be packed every night because of him.

The other judgment was from the other nonpareil of the NBA, Jerry West—so brilliant as a player that the NBA logo was designed from his silhouette, and now the general manager of the Lakers—considered the best judge of talent in the league. West had seen Jordan early that year and turned to Josh Rosenfeld and said, "He's the only player I've seen who reminds me of me."

It was not a bad season. Jordan was the rookie of the year, and though he was playing with unusually weak teammates, the Bulls improved their record, winning ten more games than in the year before. He was young and handsome and rich and living in Chicago in a small condo where he seemed to do much of the housecleaning himself. Nike had assigned a young man named Howard White, a former ballplayer at Maryland and a close friend of Moses Malone, to be its ambassador to Jordan, to help guide him through the predatory world that surrounds the NBA, a world filled with people willing to exploit the fame of the players. It had been a shrewd move on Nike's part, out of which a true friendship blossomed. The older, wiser White helped steer Jordan through the potentially difficult first season and helped him to avoid many of the pitfalls that await most rookies. Jordan seemed to be handling his fame quite well. David Stern remembered that when Jordan was named rookie of the year, the Schick Razor Rookie of the Year to be sure, the NBA had to spend almost all of its limited promotional budget to get a charter plane to fly him back and forth from Chapel Hill, where he was back studying to get his degree, to San Francisco, where the owners were meeting.

The Air Jordans were an immediate, stunning success, grossing $130 million. There was some resentment in the league about his overnight commercial success, a feeling that he had not yet earned it, that his team had not won anything. Some of that resentment showed at the all-star game because he came wearing the livery of Nike. At that game, some of the veteran players, led by Isiah Thomas and Magic Johnson, conspired to freeze him out. These players all seemed to be connected to Dr. Charles Tucker, who did some sports representation. After the game, Dr. Tucker had made the mistake of boasting in front of reporters of what they had done. There were some weak denials on the part of Thomas and Johnson about what had happened. (Johnson, at least, was on the opposing team so his role in it was smaller.) Two days after the all-star game, the Bulls played Thomas's Pistons, and Jordan scored forty-nine points. For a time, the incident colored Jordan's relationship with Johnson, but over the years Johnson worked to heal the breach. That was not necessarily true of Jordan's relationship with Thomas.

As the season wore on, Jordan, to the amazement of Mark Pfeil and others, was becoming stronger. He surprised even his own teammates. When he had first come in and started dominating practice, noted teammate Sidney Green, everyone said he would slow down by mid-season. "And then at mid-season he was still doing it," Green noted, "so we said 'by the three-quarter mark his legs will give out,' except at the three-quarter mark he was still going strong, maybe stronger." Green paused and made a comment that would be oft repeated: "Michael Jordan is the truth, the whole truth, and nothing but the truth, so help us God."

12

Boston, April 1986

I T SEEMED AT FIRST a minor playoff game, the lowly Chicago Bulls against the powerful Boston Celtics. But it was, said Dick Stockton, who broadcast it for CBS, Michael Jordan's coming-out party, his true debut as a professional basketball player in front of a still somewhat unsuspecting sports nation. In retrospect, what he did on the afternoon of April 20, 1986, was entirely predictable, given his instinct for the dramatic. And predict it Jordan did: He played golf on a Boston course the day before with Danny Ainge, one of the Boston guards, and two sportswriters. When the game was over, Jordan turned to Ainge and said, "You're in for a surprise tomorrow."

"I'm not in for a surprise," Ainge said. "D.J.'s guarding you." D.J. was Dennis Johnson, the big Boston guard.

"Well, tell D.J. that I may have a surprise for him tomorrow," Jordan warned Ainge. "Tell him to get his sleep tonight."

It was the perfect setting: a playoff game in the hallowed Boston Garden against the best team in the league, broadcast on national television. It was Jordan's second season in the league, and he hungered to play at this level. He had missed virtually the entire year after breaking his foot in the third game of the season.

That year's Celtics team was considered by many basketball people, including a number of the Celtics players themselves, to be the best of the Larry Bird era. It had lost only one of its forty-one home games. Twelve years later, Kevin McHale, one of its great stars and by then the head of basketball operations for the Minnesota Timberwolves, reflected on that special year: "If a merciful God ever reached out and said, 'OK, McHale, you've been a pretty good citizen, so you can go back and play one more season of basketball, just because you loved playing so much, the year I would pick was '85–'86.'"

So it was the ideal challenge, playing the Celtics on national television on a Sunday afternoon, and, even better, playing against Dennis Johnson. The Celtics had traded for D.J. because he was big and talented, and they desperately needed someone who could shut down Andrew Toney, the great Philadelphia shooting guard, whose pre-D.J. success against the Celtics had earned him the nickname the Boston Strangler. D.J. was arguably the best defensive big guard in the league.

If the requisite for being a sports dynasty was total dominance of one's league, then the Larry Bird–era Celtics were not a genuine dynasty, for they had to share a dynastic cycle with Magic Johnson's Lakers. Together, they were certainly a dynasty: During one stretch of nine years, Los Angeles won five titles and Boston won three, with Julius Erving's Sixers the only outsiders to reach the top. On the occasion of the first Celtics championship in the Bird years, Red Auerbach, ever gracious and charming in victory, held up the trophy and said, "Whatever happened to that Laker dynasty I've been hearing so much about?"

In 1985–1986, the Celtics had a great team: To some purists, particularly purists who liked big men, they were simply the best team of the modern era, featuring a magnificent front line of Bird, McHale, and Robert Parish—who among them had twenty-six appearances in all-star games—and a backcourt of Johnson and Ainge. The Big Three, Bird, Parish, and McHale were called. And they had added that year an almost perfect extra piece, the legendary Bill Walton, who at his best had been one of the two or three greatest big men in the game. Though by 1985 his skills had been reduced significantly by a series of cruel injuries to his feet, he remained, in limited minutes, an almost magical player in his ability to play defense and pass the ball on offense.

That season, Walton, in the twilight of his career after a series of draconian foot operations, used his own money to buy his way out of a handsome contract with the Los Angeles Clippers. That allowed him to go from a kind of basketball purgatory to what was for him a kind of basketball heaven, even if for dramatically less money. (It cost him roughly $800,000 to buy out his Clipper contract and leave.) He tried the Lakers first, calling Jerry West, an old friend, but West said, "Bill, I know you, and I love your game, but I've seen the X-rays [of your feet] and I just can't go that way." With that, Walton picked up the phone to call Red Auerbach, the architect of all those Celtic championships. "This is Bill Walton of the Los Angeles Clippers," he announced. "I would like to come and play for your team. I think I can help you." Larry Bird happened to be in Auerbach's office when Walton made his call, and Bird immediately told Auerbach to get him, with no questions asked about his feet—if Walton thought he could play that was good enough for Bird.

Because Walton's reputation as a superstar who might demand special clubhouse attention preceded him, the Celtics decided to bring him down to earth. On his first day there, Walton turned to the clubhouse attendant and asked him to bring him a cup of coffee. The next day in the locker room there was a large hand-drawn sign that said simply, "Get Your Own Fucking Coffee, Bill." No one was allowed to think that he was better than anyone else on this team, although, of course, everyone knew that it was Larry Bird's team. When Walton made a critical comment about Rick Carlisle in practice one day, Bird said, "Hey, Rick, tell him to shut the fuck up—you've only been here one year but you've probably played more games than he has in his entire career."

Thrilled to be out of basketball Siberia, thrilled this late in his career to be with a team whose players exuded passion for the game, and thrilled as well to be an ordinary player, someone who did not have to carry a team, Walton called this year one of the happiest of his life. He even loved the fact that he had replaced Danny Ainge as the main target of his teammates' wit. On this team that meant something. They were good, and because they were good, they were also cocky. They played the practical jokes of winners on each other. At one game in Los Angeles, during the pregame shoot-around, McHale and Carlisle were practicing alone. Carlisle, who was extremely boyish looking, was wearing simple, old-fashioned gray sweats with no Celtics markings on them. They were shooting at opposite ends of the court. McHale went and found a security guard: "Who is that guy?" he asked, pointing to Carlisle. "Is he a new Laker player?" The security guard said he thought that Carlisle was a Celtic. "Never seen him before in my life," McHale said. "Listen, Coach [K. C.] Jones isn't going to like this—he might just be a Laker spy." So the security men came and started taking Carlisle away. The young player kept yelling, "I'm with him," pointing at McHale, but McHale just kept shaking his head.

There was the game in Portland before which Bird decided basketball was too easy, so on that night he would shoot only with his left hand. He hit his first four baskets, and McHale yelled out to Jerome Kersey, the player covering Bird, "Hey, Jerome, wait 'til he starts shooting right-handed." Some evenings, just before the tip-off, McHale would wander down to the other end of the court and tell an opposing player how D.J. or Ainge had said before the game he was going to kick his ass that night. McHale had earned the right to do that, because on the occasion of the first NBA game he ever started, against the Washington Bullets, Bird, who had arrived one season earlier, had walked over to Elvin Hayes, the great Washington star, and said, "Elvin, I just want you to know that our rookie, McHale, says he's going to eat your lunch tonight."

Their confidence grew out of the presence of one truly great player, Larry Bird. The team was driven by the sheer force of his will. His greatness and toughness set him apart, and it was contagious. His teammates dared not disappoint him. The one thing they never wanted was for Bird to think poorly of them as basketball players, because in their eyes, he was the best they had ever seen, and therefore he had the right to judge what took place in their small, intense, closed-off universe.

No one on that team was allowed to let him down. Nor were the referees. In a game that year against the Hawks in Atlanta, they played badly in the first half, going down by twenty-two. Worse, the Hawks did a lot of trash talking as they increased their lead, most of it by players whom the Celtics did not regard as immortals. K. C. Jones was so disgusted with his team that he did not say a single word during the intermission. When it was time to start the second half, Bird, unusually grim faced, walked over to the referees and said, "We're not quitting, and don't you quit either," a clear warning that he intended to make a game of it. Then he went on a run, scoring seventeen points in the third quarter. By the end of the quarter, the Celtics were down by only eight, and they won the game in overtime. Bird's teammates thrilled to that kind of toughness, and they came to expect it every night.

It showed every day, not just in games but in practice, too. Once, the Green Team (second team) caught the White Team (the starters) on a bad day and ran up a huge lead. Everyone was talking trash, and even K. C. Jones, disappointed with the play of his starters, joined in. That got Bird going, and suddenly he started taking three-point shots, hitting all of them. Each shot was launched quite deliberately from farther out, first twenty feet and then twenty-two, then twenty-four, then twenty-six, and then thirty-two feet. He hit every one. The practice was winding down, the score was close, and with time for only one more play Bird took the ball upcourt. As he reached the half-court line, the entire Green Team rushed at him, leaving Parish, McHale, Ainge, and D.J. completely unguarded. Bird launched the ball from just inside the frontcourt, and it went in. With that, the White Team won, and Bird pranced around the floor, his arms up in a victory celebration.

He led more by example than by talking, although he was capable of stinging his teammates with his words if he thought they were giving less than they should. His teammates knew that no one played or practiced in greater pain. When he came into the NBA, everyone knew he was a great shooter and a gifted passer—he had huge hands and great peripheral vision—but the fact that a player with so limited a body by NBA standards was also a first-rate rebounder surprised everyone. He was a very good rebounder because he worked at it, and he was exceptionally skilled at picking up the tiniest fault line among the players jammed around the basket and somehow muscling his imperfect, flawed body through that seam to get the position he wanted. If the ball came down anywhere near him, it was his: He had those huge but wonderfully soft hands attached to great, thick wrists. If there was a key to Bird's game, which few people saw, thought Jimmy Rodgers, an assistant in Boston for several years, it was those wrists. He was in many ways a wrist shooter—just a little flick of the wrist and he had his shot.

The other thing he had, which Magic Johnson and Michael Jordan had as well, was a great sense of where everyone was on the court all the time. Bill Fitch, Bird's first professional coach, had pushed his young players to take pictures, as he called it, to use their eyes as cameras. Bird was the best cameraman in the business, Rodgers decided. One quick glance on each play and he knew where all the other nine players and the referees were. That meant that his blind passes weren't so blind, because he *knew* where the other players were, where their vectors were taking them, and how long it would take them to get there. His sense of anticipation extended to taking into account the mind-sets of other players going into games, including his own teammates.

Once, early in the championship season, Parish was out and Walton was due to start. Walton got there early and was virtually alone on the court, doing his stretching exercises when Bird, always early himself, showed up. "I know what you're thinking," Bird told him. "You're thinking you're going to get Robert's shots tonight, and you're going to get twenty points. Well, forget it. Those extra shots are mine. Your job is to take care of the rebounds on the weak side." The amazing thing, Walton said later, was that Bird was right, it was *exactly* what he had been thinking.

He forced his teammates to be tougher. He played in pain, indeed in great pain, and he expected them to do nothing less. There had been one season when Cedric Maxwell had come back after signing a big contract—four years, it was said, at $800,000 a year—and he did not return, it was decided by some of his teammates, full of great enthusiasm for the grunt work in the pit. One day after practice, Maxwell was sitting in the locker room talking about how now that he had the big contract he might just fake a knee injury and go into semiretirement. Bird, irritated by it all, said, with no laughter in his voice, "You want a knee injury? You don't want to play? Just put your knee out and I'll take care of it for you right now." It was a very clear warning that the contract was to have nothing to do with the level of energy expended in practice and games. They were all to play hard. They were lucky to be here, lucky to be doing something they loved and making big money. And career-ending injuries were not jokes—they were something to be feared like the plague.

Because Bird exuded mental toughness, a hatred of losing and a willingness to play at the highest possible level, his teammates gradually took on the same attitudes, as if absorbing his qualities by osmosis. "I saw that close up," Danny Ainge once noted. "None of us wanted to let him down. All of us wanted to be worthy of him. The great thing about Larry was his effect on his teammates. Everyone on that team rose with him, not just to his expectations of them, which were high enough, but to his expectations of *himself*, which were even higher." McHale had been known as a talented but not particularly tough player in college, and Parish was thought to be soft when he first entered the league, but they were not soft when they played alongside Bird. He would not permit it. In the locker room before a big game, Bird, who did not usually talk big, would say something like, "I'm going to add another chapter to my book tonight—this is going to be another big Celtic win," and his teammates believed in him, believed that he was going to rise to the occasion and carry them with him.

Though his and McHale's names were linked endlessly in the descriptions of that singular front line, there was a certain unspoken undertow of tension between them because of their very different personalities. McHale was by most standards hardworking and committed, but he might not have been as dedicated as Bird. That was a source of some irritation for Bird. He believed that if McHale, with his amazingly long arms and great low-post moves, became just a bit more serious, no one could ever stop him, and he could get fifty points—fifty *easy* points—a night, every night.

And so there were some nights when Bird would decide that McHale was not working quite hard enough to get free and he would not pass to him, even if by normal standards he was free. McHale, on the other hand, the most gregarious of men, a man who with his love of talk could have been a great pol or the most charming saloon keeper around, a man who came to work each day not only to play basketball at a high level but to luxuriate in the social pleasures of being with his teammates, seemed to think that Bird was too monodimensional, that he had no life other than basketball. There was some truth in that. Years later, Bill

Walton would say of Bird that there had only been three moments in his life when he was truly happy, and they were the three occasions when the Celtics won the NBA championship. It was quite possible that both Bird and McHale were right. People who studied Bird noted that when he spoke of the best player he ever played with, he named Dennis Johnson instead of McHale, and their assumption was that it was his way of saying that he thought that Kevin McHale never reached his true greatness.

There was a certain purity to Bird. His life was basketball, nothing more, nothing less. In an age of new arenas that cost nearly a billion dollars to build and were ringed with luxury boxes, he spoke of where his team played as "the gym." His value system was simple and unvarnished. He neither knew nor was much interested in any other universe. He measured others only on how they behaved on the court: Were they good, team-oriented winning players or were they statistic-hungry punks? He was uneasy with the growing hype and hoopla that his very arrival in the league and his rivalry with Magic Johnson had helped create. Others, such as Magic, loved the new fame and celebrity that the change in the culture was bringing; Bird was uneasy with it and sensed that it was something that might distract from the very essence of his life, which was playing team-oriented winning basketball. He did not need the up side of it and he was extremely wary of the down side.

The rest of popular culture, which was a powerful draw on his peers—since they too were stars of the popular culture and increasingly there was a crossover, basketball players hanging out with rock stars and movie stars, and being welcomed on dopey talk shows—interested him not at all. Once when the Celtics were playing in Dallas and had a night off, he was sitting with a few friends in a hotel lobby crowded with young people. Suddenly, around 7 P.M., as if on a signal, the young people all left the hotel lobby, clearly going some place. That was puzzling, since the Celtics did not play until the next night. Where were they all going? he asked his friend Shaughnessy, the *Globe* writer. They were going to a Bruce Springsteen concert nearby, Shaughnessy answered. "Who's Bruce Springsteen?" Bird asked, and Shaughnessy, thinking of the parallels between the two stars, their blue collar roots and their lack of pretense, and their similar constituencies, had answered, "Larry, he's the you of rock 'n roll." That had intrigued Bird just enough to make him go to the concert, and though he did not particularly like the music, he did like how hard Springsteen worked, and the fact that he sweated so much. That much he understood.

Knowing that his physical skills were limited, knowing he could never let his body slip even a little, every summer Bird went back home to Indiana and worked out diligently, trying, not only to stay in the best of shape with a strict regimen, but to improve his game by adding shots. One year it was an up-and-under shot coming off a fake. Another year it was a shot designed to add a degree of separation for a player who was not getting any younger: a faked drive forward followed by a quick backward step as he released the ball. One year it was improvement in his left hand; he had come into the league with a good left-handed shot, but as his career progressed, he sensed the need for that additional option and refined it. On the first days of Celtics' preseason camps, the other players liked to see what Bird had added to his game over the summer.

Bird expected his teammates to care as much as he did and to show the same loyalty that he showed. In the 1986–1987 season, he had one of his great nights, matched against a declining Julius Erving, who was in his last year. He blistered the once-great star, talking a lot of trash and counting out his points and Erving's to the Doctor, 42–6. Erving suddenly snapped, and there was a quick, vicious fight, stunning everyone because these two great players were supposed to be above it and were known for their mutual respect. The next day, Bird came in, slightly subdued, and watched a tape of the fight. There had been Julius going after him, getting in several quick punches. What the video revealed appalled him: He saw Moses Malone and Charles Barkley come over to help Erving out and in the process holding Bird; he saw Robert Parish stand by and do nothing. *Do absolutely nothing to help his teammate.* Bird ran the tape again just to be sure: Yes, Parish had stood there and let a teammate be pummeled. Bird was furious, and he stomped out of practice. His closest friends were never sure that most of his teammates even knew what happened, what had set him off, but he did tell one teammate in disbelief, "Did you see Robert during that fight? Did you see that?"

In the 1985–1986 season, Boston was a team without a weakness. Isiah Thomas, who studied the Celtics, trying to learn their special secret so his Pistons could be more like them, remembered one particular quote from K. C. Jones that season that seemed to sum up their special arrogance. The Celtics were about to go on a four-game road trip and someone asked Jones how many victories he wanted. "I'd settle for four," he answered.

For the young Michael Jordan, new in the league, desperate to play at a championship level, the Celtics were self-evidently the standard of excellence. They were the North Carolina of the professional game: They had tradition, loyalty, mental toughness, a sense of purpose, and a great deal of depth.

While the Celtics had been making short work of the league that year, Jordan had suffered through the most miserable season of his life. The Bulls had beaten Cleveland in overtime in the first game of the season, and Jordan took a vicious hit from Bill Laimbeer in the second game but rose to lead his team to its second victory. But then, three nights later, in a game against Golden State, he broke his left foot. It was the one serious injury of his entire career. He had gone up high for the ball and come down off balance, and he had jammed his foot hard. Though the early X rays had shown nothing, he had had trouble stopping and starting, and he had not been able to play for the final two games of the road trip.

Finally, back in Chicago, they spotted the fracture, in the navicular tarsal bone. Even with a CAT scan, it was hard to pick up the particular angle of the break. No one knew how serious the injury would be or how quickly the foot might heal. Early on, there was talk of six to eight weeks, but that optimism faded quickly. Suddenly Michael Jordan was being forced to sit out virtually an entire season as he rehabilitated his foot. The loss was singularly frustrating, for playing was his principal source of joy, and it gave him his sense of identity; Michael Jordan was one of the rare basketball players who had a love-of-the-game clause in his contract that allowed him to stop by any playground in America, put on a pair of sneakers, and play in a pickup game, something he quite often did. Such a clause might strike fear in the heart of any sensible management, wary of injuries, fearful of losing its most gifted player in some pickup game where a macho player might try and nail its superstar. But it was something he had insisted on, and it reflected his pure, childlike pleasure in the game.

The injury was devastating. It was his second season and he was suddenly separated from the thing he cherished the most, and he was living in a small apartment in a city that was still somewhat alien. A Chicago winter without basketball proved very hard. He asked for permission to go back to Chapel Hill to rehab. He owned a condo there and had a lot of friends, including the entire North Carolina coaching staff. Permission was granted, and he spent the time in typical Michael Jordan fashion. Limited for a while in his ability to run and jump, he practiced his shooting for several hours a day. Eventually, without the Chicago authorities knowing it, he began playing in five-on-five games. Nonetheless, it was a difficult time for him; he had never before understood how much he loved the sport.

Monitoring the healing process with CAT scans was still new, and Michael's foot was used as a kind of study project. Yet because the machinery *was* so new, the doctors were somewhat limited in calibrating the progress they were making, because there was little in the way of precedent. Sometimes, team physician Dr. John Hefferon thought, the process felt like watching grass grow. The slowness of the process gradually came to enrage Jordan, who was desperate to play again. As his foot began to heal, and the pain began to disappear, he became increasingly convinced that he was ready to play. He would show up at Hefferon's office sure that each visit was the last, that the cast was finally going to come off. In February and March, more restless than ever, he arrived at Hefferon's office with a sneaker for his bad foot, hoping that he would be able to walk out without his cast. Again and again he told Hefferon he was ready to play, and Hefferon told him he was not sure, so Jordan would end up autographing the sneaker and leaving it with Hefferon's secretary as a gift. One day, Hefferon told him that they were going to recast the foot, and Jordan simply refused. It took all of Hefferon's persuasive powers to get him to change his mind. The argument that Jordan made at this and other critical moments was a simple one: No one knows my body better than I do, and I know I'm ready to play. Hefferon, more than anyone else who was participating in the decision, took whatever Michael Jordan said seriously. He had learned in his brief two years working with him that he was not only unusually gifted as an athlete and intelligent as a man, but that he was uncommonly articulate in describing any symptom of pain or illness. He was, Hefferon thought, unusually body-aware and well worth listening to.

Hefferon, wary of making a decision like this on his own, began to consult with other orthopedists, but none of them was absolutely sure what Jordan's status was. They were clearly in a world without guarantees, dealing with the most passionate kind of young man who was desperate to get his life back. The physical risk of clearing him precipitously was obvious. But as the tensions grew, it also became clear to Hefferon that the physical risk that everyone feared might be matched by another risk, that of the growing alienation of the team's most talented, most joyous, and charismatic young player from the organization itself. When Hefferon next talked to Jerry Krause, the team's general manager, Krause wanted to know what the risk of reinjury was. Hefferon said there was no telling, but he would put it at roughly 10 percent. But, Hefferon said, they were dealing with an extremely passionate player who was cut off from the principal source of his pleasure, and who was desperate to play, and that if they did not listen to Jordan, there was going to be trouble down the road. Unless they let Jordan play, he would probably never forgive them. Because of that, Hefferon said, the 10 percent physical risk seemed like a small one.

Back and forth it went between player, doctors, and management. Somewhere in this time, Krause made the first of what were to be two fateful mistakes in dealing with Jordan—mistakes that created a fault line, at first rather marginal but later far more important. In a conversation with Jordan, he rebuffed one of Jordan's pleas to play and said that he and Jerry Reinsdorf would make the decision because Jordan was their *property*. It was a colossally stupid thing to say about any player, particularly a black one, and it was a statement that Michael Jordan never forgot and never forgave. It was the beginning of a split between star player and the head of the organization that became over the years increasingly bitter, and that never healed.

The second mistake was a more subtle one. Jordan came to believe—and most people who followed the team thought he was almost certainly right—that the Bulls' management had another reason for keeping him out. The Bulls had won their first three games with him. Without him, they had lost eight of their next nine, and by the time he was finally allowed to play, with severe limits on his minutes, they had a record of 24–43. Krause and Reinsdorf were, Jordan and others believed, content to keep him out not just to protect his foot but to secure a place in the lottery where the seven NBA teams with the worst season records had a chance to draft the best college players available that year. With the lottery, the Bulls might get a chance, however slim, at picking Brad Daugherty or Len Bias, the two best players coming out that year. To someone as competitive as Michael Jordan, the idea was simply sinful; it meant that the people who employed him were not as committed to winning as he was, that they accepted the idea of defeat as he did not, and that they were willing to bag the current season and any chance at the playoffs in order to improve their roster for the future. Even on a bad team with marginal players like the early Bulls, the remarkable thing about Michael Jordan was that he never accepted the idea of defeat. He believed that as long as he played, the Bulls could still make the playoffs, and that if they got there, he could carry them on to victory.

In time, as the decision about when he could play became ever more contested, a conference call was arranged in which all of the Bulls' principals participated: Reinsdorf, Krause, Lester Crown (a wealthy Chicago businessman who was probably the largest shareholder in the team), Stan Albeck (the coach who had replaced Kevin Loughery), Hefferon, two other doctors, and Jordan himself. Again Jordan made the case for himself—no one, he said emphatically, knows my body like I do. I tell you I'm 100 percent. But no one accepted that. A compromise decision was reached: Jordan could play, but only six minutes a half. Just to make sure that Albeck knew his limits, he received a letter from

Reinsdorf to that effect. That meant that Albeck was now caught between Jordan, who wanted more and more minutes, and Reinsdorf and Krause, who wanted strict observance of the time limits. In one game, Albeck allowed him to play five seconds too long, and those five seconds by NBA rules counted as a full minute. The next day, Krause called Albeck and told him he had an angry owner because Jordan had played seven minutes. Soon, Tim Hallam was detailed to sit at the scorer's table with a stopwatch to make sure that Jordan did not exceed the limits. Jordan was restless with the limits, of course. He wanted the playoffs and a chance to play against the Celtics.

The Bulls were still behind Cleveland in the race for the last playoff spot, but with Jordan back they began to close on the Cavaliers. They had gone into Indiana for their seventy-seventh game. But Indiana took a quick lead, and the Bulls were down by fifteen at the half. Albeck started Jordan in the second half. "Just get us back in the ball game," he told him, and Jordan did exactly that: In fewer than four minutes, the score was tied. The game remained close, but with twenty-eight seconds left, Chicago was down one point. Jordan's time, however, had run out. Albeck had to take him out of the game, and Jordan threw a fit: He started screaming at Albeck, "You can't do this! We've got to make the playoffs!" But Albeck replaced him with Kyle Macy. With the clock running down, Chicago guard John Paxson threw up a long shot, really nothing but a prayer in Albeck's eyes, but the prayer was answered, and the Bulls won.

After the game, the Chicago writers pushed Albeck hard. "How can you do this to Michael?" they asked, something he wondered himself. The next day, a beat writer called Reinsdorf to ask him what happened, and Reinsdorf said that Albeck was a poor mathematician. With that, Albeck knew that he was going to be fired at the end of the season. But even with Jordan playing limited minutes, he took over these final games: The Bulls won five of their last six games and Jordan averaged 29.6 points. That took them out of the lottery and into the playoffs against the Celtics.

In the first game at Boston Garden, Jordan played well. The Celtics had not deigned to put two men on him, and he scored forty-nine points. It was a very good performance by a talented player, but it was not *that* extraordinary; the Bulls ran their offense specifically for him, giving him the ball and clearing out for him. Boston had won easily, 123–104. But the Sunday game was special. It was a brilliant game, the day he captured the attention of the basketball world. In a way, much of the quantum new increase in his fame came from that game. No one was really prepared for what happened. The great thing about sports, thought Dick Stockton, the CBS announcer, was that each time that you went to the ballpark or an arena like the Boston Garden you never knew when you were going to witness something well beyond the ordinary, perhaps nothing less than a bit of history. As a boy, Stockton had seen Willie Mays's famous catch of Vic Wertz's tremendous drive to center field in the 1954 World Series. As a grown man, he had broadcast the famed 1975 World Series game in which Carlton Fisk hit a dramatic home run in the twelfth inning to give the Red Sox a 7–6 victory over the Cincinnati Reds in a game widely considered one of the greatest World Series games of all time. Now, as he broadcast this game, he had a sense that he was once again watching history.

The Celtics were so heavily favored that they treated the Bulls as something of an expansion team and did not pay much attention to them. The haughtiness of the team, Stockton thought, was mirrored by the Boston crowd. Clearly, it was not up for this game as it might have been for a game against the 76ers, then the Celtics' principal Eastern Conference rivals. For a time, the crowd watched more quietly than usual as Jordan performed his heroics, waiting for him to run out his string and for the Celtics to take their rightful command of the game. But gradually, as the game progressed and as Jordan seemed to be holding off the entire Celtics team, Stockton could sense a change in the crowd noise, a rising murmur of disbelief, apprehension, and, finally, in some way, admiration. It was as if the crowd was no longer sure of its role: Should it cheer for this virtuoso performance or signal its growing anxiety over the failure of its beloved Celtics to dispatch the uppity Bulls?

The Michael Jordan who played that day looks on video like the younger brother of the Michael Jordan who played in the nineties. He was slimmer, distinctively less muscled. He played at around 185 or 190 pounds in those days, twenty-five to thirty pounds less than the 215 pounds that his much stronger body carried some seven years later. He still had some hair; the shaven head, which became his trademark and in time the trademark for a generation of young black players in the NBA, was yet to come. He still wore short shorts, not the longer ones he later wore and which therefore also became part of the fashion in the NBA.

What stood out in that game was his timing, his ability to see the entire court and to know down to the millisecond how much time he had on each possession to make a decision, pass or shoot. Few players had it. Stan Albeck asked him once what he thought when defending teams threw a double-team at him. The matter-of-fact quality of the answer stunned the coach: "I think I have about a half second to a second to make my decision—to put the ball on the floor and beat or split the double-team, or to shoot before the second defender gets there. And if I split the double then I can go right to the basket. But you want to know what happens next?" Yes, Albeck said. "There's a seven footer waiting to challenge me, but I'm going to dunk on him anyway."

Bill Walton and Dennis Johnson, both of them defensive greats, fouled out that day, and Parish and Ainge finished the game with five fouls each; Walton fouled Jordan four times, Johnson did so three times, and Ainge, Parish, and McHale fouled him once each. He drew a total of ten fouls from men who were considered among the best defensive players in the league. Again and again, Jordan had been able to drive past the guards to get near the basket, and his agility had forced Walton to lunge at him at the last second. For Walton, it had been a thrilling if painful performance. Generally, if you were a big man playing defense, it was possible to gauge the great offensive players coming at you, to know their moves and to understand the angles they were coming from and the limits of their reaches. Yet here was this young player who seemed to defy those normal limits, who came on a drive, after escaping the outer defense line thrown up by great defending guards, and who—when the normal drive or float time seemed over, his body's ability to drive finally expended, and you were ready to make the block—managed to extend his drive, floating by you as if with an extra gear. You thought you had his trajectory mapped out, and then he extended it. Or you thought you had his plan of attack charted, and then once in the air he switched the ball from one hand to another. It was a dazzling display.

The Celtics knew Jordan was good, but they never thought of him or his team as a threat to them. But that day he simply took over the game. What amazed Bob Ryan of *The Boston Globe* was that Jordan worked through the regular Chicago offense; it was not as if they were clearing out for him and trying to go to him. It was simply that in the regular execution of the Bulls' offense, he could not be stopped, could not be guarded, because he was too quick. As the game progressed, the Celtics players began to relish it. Most of them were aware of what they were watching. It was, thought Chris Ford, a Celtics assistant coach, just pure pleasure watching him that afternoon. He was seeing a player go to a playoff level that no one had ever witnessed before, and against the best team in the league.

In the middle of the third quarter, when Dennis Johnson had a number of fouls on him, Danny Ainge came in to replace him. Johnson had a little more size, but Ainge had a little more quickness; no one, however, was going to stop Jordan today. Ainge decided that at least he would make Jordan work on defense. (Ainge went on to score twenty-four points.) It was, thought Ainge, a wonderful day of basketball: "The danger was that he was so good you were tempted to stop playing and just watch. It was not just what he did, but the way he did it. We knew when we had gone into the game that he was very good, but none of us knew yet that he was going to be the best player who ever laced up sneakers, but we were in the process of learning it, and that afternoon was a good beginning."

At the end of the first overtime, Jordan missed a simple jumper that would have won the game. The Celtics won in the second overtime 135–131. In the end, he simply wore out. The game lasted 58 minutes, and Jordan played 53 of them, the last 39 without a break. "I thought," K. C. Jones said later, "he had played 78 minutes. It certainly seemed that way."

Michael Jordan scored sixty-three points, a playoff record. Not everyone had realized how remarkable his game had been. Kevin McHale was taking a shower after the game when they brought him the stat sheet, and he said something about Jordan having a big game and then he looked down and saw *63 points* and he was amazed. Jordan himself was not very pleased. After the game, he told reporters, "I'd give all the points back if we could have won the game. I wanted to win so badly." Years later, when people brought the game up, expecting him to go on about it with some degree of nostalgia, he quickly changed the subject. "It's not one of my favorite games," he would say, and then quickly add, "Because we lost. That fact never changes."

No one had been more impressed than Larry Bird. "That was God disguised as Michael Jordan," he told the assembled sportswriters after the game.

The sportswriters loved Bird's line about God, an immortal line for an immortal performance, and they loved the game as well, one David taking on so many Goliaths—and they loved the fact that it had been played early in the afternoon so they had plenty of time to work on their stories and try to immortalize what had happened that day. "He painted his own masterpiece on the ceiling of basketball's Sistine Chapel, and he didn't need a scaffold to lift him there," wrote Ray Sons in the *Chicago Sun-Times*. "Michael can fly."

He had hit twenty-two of forty-one shots from the field and nineteen of twenty-one free throws. Of his baskets, thirteen were jump shots, and seven came on drives, one was a dunk and one came because of a goal tend.

Bird, with his wonderful eye and his instinct to welcome any great talent, had seen it first, and now the others saw it as well: This was the prototype of a new, super player. There had been great jumpers before, such as Julius Erving and David Thompson, but their games had been incomplete: Erving had great physical ability, and no one drove to the basket as dramatically and emphatically as he did, and David Thompson was a great jumper, but neither of them was considered to have a great jump shot. Now here was this young player who seemed to have no identifiable weakness: He could jump, he could put the ball on the floor and drive, he could shoot, and he could pass.

Chris Ford, who coached Bird and coached against Jordan, came in the end to think that despite the vast differences in their games and their styles and their bodies, the similarities between them were greater than the differences. There was the hunger for excellence, the singular need for a championship, the effect they had in lifting their teammates, the sense they gave off that they were invincible men. They had one other thing in common, Ford thought, that set them apart from so many supremely talented young players now entering the league, who arrived at weak franchises by dint of the whim of the draft, and could not wait until the three years of their first contract were up, so that they could go to a better team. They both shared the same sense of obligation. "If you were drafted by a team which was at the bottom, then part of the responsibility which went with your contract was to turn that team around and make it a winner—in fact, make it a champion. That was an obligation and it was deeply felt. It was about not just being a player, but in a larger sense a citizen, and they both shared that feeling. Larry thought he owed Boston a winner, and Michael felt he owed Chicago a winner. That was part of their job, part of their contract," Ford said. "I'm afraid not a lot of people feel that way today."

After that hard-won victory, the Celtics changed their strategy for Game Three. Talking the next day at practice, someone commented that some of the other players on the Bulls were Dave Corzine, Jawann Oldham, Sidney Green, Kyle Macy, and Gene Banks—none of them a significant threat to the Celtics. The strategy would change: They would double Jordan and double him early, in order to keep the ball away from him. It worked. They went to Chicago for the third and—if necessary—fourth game two days later. Kevin McHale got on the plane with no suitcase, only an extra pair of sneakers and a dop kit for his shaving gear. Someone asked him where his suitcase was. "I don't need one," he said, "we're only going to be there one night." They were. Under the new Stop Michael defensive pattern, Jordan had a much harder time getting the ball, and Boston won easily, 122–104.

The memories of that series lingered long after it was over. During the 1998 Conference Finals against the Indiana Pacers, a reporter asked

Larry Bird, by then the Pacers' coach, about the game. Bird, eager to shake the idea that Jordan was an invincible man, said, "The only thing I remember is that we won the game." At almost the same time, Bill Walton, then a broadcaster with NBC, made his way into the Bulls' locker room to interview Michael Jordan, only to be reminded that Jordan had managed to foul him out of the game twelve years earlier.

New York City; Portland, 1986

NOT LONG AFTER THAT GAME, two basketball junkies connected with each other to create a series of commercials that greatly enhanced Michael Jordan's fame and helped take it far beyond the bounds of sport. Jim Riswold was a young and irreverent writer for a very small Portland, Oregon, advertising agency called Wieden and Kennedy, and Shelton Jackson (Spike) Lee was a struggling filmmaker in Brooklyn, and just beginning his career.

Riswold was originally from Seattle, where he had gone to the University of Washington; uncertain of exactly who and what he wanted to be, he took seven years to get through college, in the course of which he earned three separate degrees in philosophy, history, and communications. Because he loved basketball, he worked part time for the Seattle SuperSonics, doing some promotion and local advertising. That drew him into the world of advertising, and since there seemed to be no ads in the local help-wanted columns for companies demanding in-house philosophers, he decided that advertising might be a place where his talents, whatever they might be, could finally blossom. In 1984, the year Michael Jordan entered the league, Riswold left Seattle and went to work for Wieden and Kennedy.

Portland was essentially Nike's home. At that time, however, Nike gave almost all of its major advertising business to Chiat/Day, one of the big New York powerhouses, well known for the talent of its people. To the degree that Wieden and Kennedy had a share of the Nike account early on, it was relatively small and somewhat mundane in nature.

It was known at the time as Nike's other agency, a less than desirable designation. About the time Riswold joined them, however, Wieden and Kennedy got the contract for a Honda motor scooter commercial. With Riswold as the talent on the shoot, they came up with something quite original, an offbeat, grainy commercial showing Lou Reed on his Honda, cut to his song "Walk on the Wild Side." It was tough to say whether it was shot by the most skilled professional or the rankest amateur, but it was hip and oddly compelling, in part because the scooter message was pitched only at the last minute.

There were more Honda commercials to come, all of them equally interesting. This series of commercials turned out to be a very good signature line for this little firm so far from the center of the action in New York, and it helped Wieden and Kennedy get the contract from Nike for the Michael Jordan commercials. And when Jim Riswold heard that his firm was going to do commercials with Michael Jordan, he was so sure he was the right man for the assignment that he went to see his superiors and literally begged for it.

The previous commercials done for Jordan by Chiat/Day had been quite conventional. They showed his sheer athletic brilliance, as well as the beauty of his body. Who he was—what kind of man he was, whether he was someone you wanted to watch play and then have dinner with or just someone you wanted to watch play, and finally whether there was some great inner mystery to him—had not yet been explored. But Riswold had other ideas. He had once read that Bill Russell thought that Michael Jordan was a very good human being and had once congratulated Mr. and Mrs. Jordan for raising not just a great basketball player but a fine son as well. That intrigued Riswold, for like anyone who had ever been around Russell, he knew that Russell did not lightly compliment contemporary players, even former Celtics. In fact, his tour as general manager of the SuperSonics had not ended happily for many people, in no small part because a number of the team's younger players, originally thrilled by the idea of playing for the great Bill Russell, soon felt only his scorn and his open contempt.

But if Jordan was so exemplary a human being that he earned the praise of the lofty Russell, then he posed an intriguing challenge for an advertising man: how to reveal this special quality in a movie that lasted all of thirty seconds. So far, the only given had been how brilliant an athlete he was, which had made millions of young American teenagers who wanted to jump a good deal higher buy the shoes, but there was a ceiling on that kind of message. If the Nike people could show that he was a likable human being as well, if they could reveal the innate charm that so many people, including Riswold himself, felt soon after meeting

Jordan, then they would have a *main character*, whom they could begin to unveil through a story line. About that time, in 1986 Riswold and Bill Davenport, his executive producer, were in Los Angeles shooting another commercial, and they went to the movies. The movie they saw, *About Last Night*, was highly forgettable, but there was a trailer for another movie that intrigued Riswold greatly. It was for a movie called *She's Gotta Have It*. It showed the director and putative star of the movie, a slim young black man named Spike Lee, hawking his own film and selling tube socks, two for five dollars, and saying that unless people went to see his movie, he would be selling socks on the street for the rest of his life. Tube socks, two for five dollars, he said, as the trailer faded out.

Riswold had been weaned on *Mad* magazine and Monty Python as well as Jack Sikma and Gus Williams, and the trailer hooked him immediately. So he went to see Spike Lee's first movie, which was very low budget, shot for about $175,000. It was, Riswold thought, funny and almost sweetly innocent. Years later, Spike Lee reflected that Riswold and Davenport had liked the movie because of a certain funky style, which was not too slick because he could not afford slick in those days; it was what he came to call involuntary *pauvre*. To save money, Lee not only played the lead himself but shot the movie in his own apartment.

The great surprise of the movie for Riswold was that it featured a kind of Jordan cult—indeed, an Air Jordan cult. The lead character of the movie, Mars Blackmon, was a messenger in New York City and deeply in love with the beautiful Nola Darling. The only thing he loved more than Nola Darling were his Air Jordan shoes, and when it was time for him to make love with Nola, he refused to take them off. This was manna for Riswold: a movie with a commercial already built into it. ("The only thing Nike ever gave me for the film," Lee said with some irritation years later, "was the poster of Michael which hung in Mars's apartment. I had to buy two pairs of Air Jordans out of my own pocket—part of the budget.")

Spike Lee, talented and innately hip, was hardly a ghetto kid. He was a third-generation Morehouse College man, which marked him as part of a black elite. Lee had a profound sense of the richness of black culture and talent, as well as the degree to which larger white society had in general either suppressed it or ignored it. His father was a jazz musician, a purist who refused to use electrified instruments, and his mother taught English and black history at Saint Ann's, an exceptional private school in Brooklyn. Lee was a lifelong Knicks fan, and one of the great crises in his childhood had come when his father was giving a jazz recital at the same time as the New York Knicks were playing the Los Angeles

Lakers in the NBA Finals at Madison Square Garden. He went to the Garden, of course.

Lee's Mars Blackmon character was, like Lee himself, a devoted Knicks fan and a man who had a hard time choosing between his love of the sport and his love of a woman. In Spike's real life, for example, in the spring of 1985, his relationship with his girlfriend was steadily disintegrating, and she wanted to talk seriously about their future. He, however, was too excited by the fact that the Knicks had just drafted Patrick Ewing to focus on her. The relationship with the girlfriend quickly came to an end, but the one with the Knicks intensified greatly—Lee rushed down to the Garden the day after the draft to buy season tickets, tickets he could ill afford. He started with poor tickets up in the nosebleed section, but in time, as his role as Michael Jordan's Sancho Panza increased his fame and his leverage (the Knicks used a video clip Lee made to help lure Allan Houston from Detroit a decade later), his seats got steadily better. Eventually, he had the best seats in the house, better even than those of another basketball-crazed film director, Woody Allen. To Lee, the game was nothing less than an art form, and he saw Michael Jordan not so much as an athlete but as an artist, one in a pantheon of black geniuses whose skills transcended not just the circumstances of their birth but the category seemingly allotted to them in life—men such as Duke Ellington, Miles Davis, John Coltrane, and Louis Armstrong.

When Lee wrote *She's Gotta Have It,* it was tough for him not to make his alter ego's hero a Knick, and for a time he favored the Knicks' Bernard King. In the end, though, Lee knew that Michael Jordan was unique, the next great superstar, and so the fateful choice was made.

Of the three young black men pursuing the rather promiscuous Nola Darling in the film, Mars seems at first the least attractive—a little goofy, a little hyper, hardly the gentleman of choice. Her odds-on-favorite, Jamie Overstreet, is light skinned and handsome, if a little too smooth, but he is also—and with Lee basketball is always a metaphor for something larger—a Larry Bird fan. Lee has Mars say at one point, "Bird is the ugliest motherfucker in the league." In some way, Mars is the most likable person in the film, or at least the most endearing; he talks a certain impassioned, juiced-up, pleading street language.

Riswold loved the movie and sensed that the immensely talented Lee could be the person, the Jordan idolater, who might help them solve the equation of how to shoot commercials that would show Michael Jordan's remarkable qualities without turning him into something he was not, an actor.

Michael, age twelve: Dixie Youth Player of the Year and MVP of Wilmington's state championship Little League team.

Michael's boyhood home in Wilmington, North Carolina.

The Jordans of Wilmington (left to right): brother Ronnie; father, James; Michael; sister, Roslyn; mother, Deloris; and brother Larry.

Nike-shod and trademark tongue out, number 23 soars above everyone else in the Laney High School gym.

© Wilmington Morning Star

The Shot, March 29, 1982: With UNC down by 1 and 17 seconds left in the game, freshman Michael Jordan launches the winning 17-footer. The Tar Heels claim their first national championship.

© UPI/Corbis-Bettmann

Jordan wins his first All-Star Slam-Dunk contest with this stunning effort; taking off from the free-throw line, Jordan soars above the competition.

© Andrew D. Bernstein/NBA Photos

Basketball player as icon: "It's gotta be the shoes," says Mars Blackmon, Spike Lee's alter ego, as he plays one-on-one with Jordan in these short black-and-white fantasies. © Nike

The passing of the torch:
Michael and Magic
embrace after Game 6
of the 1991 NBA Finals.

© Andrew D. Bernstein/
NBA Photos

Seven years after
entering the NBA,
an emotional
Jordan weeps as he
holds his—and the
Chicago Bulls'—
first championship
trophy. His father
holds him.

© Andrew D. Bernstein/
NBA Photos

James Jordan congratulates his son, the guest of honor at a 1991 ceremony dedicating a section of Interstate 40 in North Carolina to Michael Jordan.

© Todd Sumlin

Michael and his wife, Juanita, with Dean Smith at the Interstate 40 dedication ceremony.

© Todd Sumlin

Flying above the crowd.

© Andrew D. Bernstein/NBA photos

The Dream Team star on the Olympic podium with Scottie Pippen and Clyde Drexler. To avoid controversy with Nike, Jordan carefully draped the American flag to cover the Reebok logo on his uniform.

© UPI/Corbis-Bettmann

October 6, 1993: Michael Jordan announces his retirement from basketball. Behind him are his teammates. Seated with him (from left) are David Falk, Jerry Krause, Phil Jackson, and Jerry Reinsdorf.

© Lou Capozzola/NBA Photos

Jordan batting for the White Sox in a spring exhibition game against the Chicago Cubs, 1994. His father had thought baseball was his best sport. The curves and sliders proved otherwise.

© UPI/Corbis-Bettmann

Jordan and Rodman stop traffic: This billboard for a Chicago men's clothing store caused jams for weeks after it was painted.

© AP/Wide World Photos

The differences between Phil Jackson, the coach (left), and Jerry Krause, his boss—the man who hired him— went far beyond body contour and grew ever more bitter during the season. © Bill Smith

The Last Shot at the Last Dance. The ball has not yet cleared the net, but Jordan's follow-through is exceptional and the Utah fans know it.

© *Fernando Medina/NBA Photos*

Riswold called Lee the next day. He found his director-to-be a little wary at first, suspicious that this might be a prank call from a film-school classmate. ("Spike still answered his own phone in those days," Riswold noted with some amusement.) Riswold liked Lee over the phone immediately. He told him that he was hoping they could put him in the commercial, as Mars Blackmon, and that in fact he hoped that Lee would direct it as well. For Lee, only recently out of film school, it was the call he had long hoped for. In his innocence, having won a prize in film school for his class's most exceptional film, called *Joe's Bed-Stuy Barbershop: We Cut Heads,* he had expected all kinds of phone calls from people like Steven Spielberg and George Lucas. Those phone calls, of course, never came. "Do I get to work with Michael Jordan?" Riswold remembered him asking. Yes, of course he would. Lee was then very receptive to the idea of directing a commercial, a field that had been largely closed to black directors in the past. Besides, he would make some $50,000 for his efforts. After getting Lee aboard, Riswold and Davenport went to Jordan, who gave his approval.

Years later, Riswold reflected that being in a small, offbeat agency in Oregon, so far from the advertising capital of the world, had been a great boon for all of them. There were fewer obstacles in their way: fewer inhibitions, fewer rules, much less tradition. There was no one going around telling Riswold what he couldn't do and why he couldn't do it—usually because it had never been done before. There was no one telling him that he dare not use Nike's money and Wieden and Kennedy's reputation to take a chance on a young black film director whose name no one knew. And race was not a factor in Portland. Portland was a Northwest city without, by the standards of the Northeast, a classic ghetto, and it seemed far less burdened by racial consciousness than other places. Many of the black players who played for the Trail Blazers stayed on after their careers were over because it was so comfortable a place to live and raise families. Indeed, the first time the Kennedy family lost a primary was in 1968 in Oregon, when Robert Kennedy lost to Gene McCarthy and the Kennedy people complained bitterly afterward of the lack of a ghetto that probably would have helped create the standard Kennedy coalition.

The commercials worked for a number of reasons, Riswold thought. The first was that both he and Lee were demented fans, and they brought to their work the same wonder that any fan would have. Race, he thought, did not factor in. He did not think of Jordan as black. He had always loved the game, and the game was black, and he had the assumption, like many young men of his generation, that if others could only see what he saw in the game—the artistry and the beauty—they would love it as much or more than other sports then seemingly more popular. And of course, the more they enjoyed it, the less they would see race as a factor. And here was this young man who was not just a great player but simply beautiful.

Michael Jordan tested Spike Lee, as was his way. In their first meeting, Jordan, already famous, had looked Lee over carefully and said only, "Spike Lee," but he said it as a challenge, as if, Lee remembered, he was saying, Show me what you can do. But they got on well. The courage in the Nike commercials, Lee later thought, was that Nike let him direct them as well as act with Jordan. It took no courage to portray Jordan as the hero—he was already a star, and he was beautiful. You could do things with him that you could never do with Larry Bird. But here he was paired with a scrawny, nerdy guy who was black and a little hyper. Most of America was not necessarily prepared to accept Spike Lee as partner to an icon.

But it worked from the start. Jordan was a little stiff and tentative in his early shoots—he grew more confident through the years—but he was ready to be a wonderful straight man. The first commercials were shot with Mars doing the talking as a kind of Every Fan. The first one they shot had Lee standing on Jordan's shoulders, holding on to the rim and wearing a giant gold "MARS" chain. In the middle of it, Jordan, the coolest smile imaginable on his face, mischievously left Lee hanging there and dunked right through him and the hoop.

From the start, Jordan impressed everyone with his innate charm and wit, and his obvious confidence. He knew who he was and *liked* who he was. There was nothing threatening about him. He was judgmental—you had to win his respect, and he was clearly shrewd about how he was used—but there was an innate coolness and elegance about him as a man. If this was yet expressed in anything he said, it was self-evident in the smile, in the deft facial gestures, in the ability to roll his eyebrows at just the right moment. He was beautiful, he was likable, he had that luminescent smile, and he might well be the greatest basketball player in the world.

The commercials were the perfect counterpart for his other incarnation, Jordan the total predator, the warrior who went out three or four nights a week and simply destroyed enemy teams. Opposing teams got the killer, and the fans watching the Nike commercials got the charmer, a man of humor and intelligence, someone everyone seemed to like. "We broke it open, and we did it not by brilliance, but by sensing what felt right, and showing him as a human being," Riswold said years later. "The rest just followed."

"What Phil [Knight] and Nike have done," Jordan himself said several years into the campaign, "is to turn me into a dream."

The Nike commercials were so good, of course, that they fed on themselves, and inspired other companies, such as McDonald's, Coke, Hanes, and, in time, Gatorade, to do comparable commercials. This in turn made the dynamic more powerful and allowed David Falk to go to other companies and tell them that a good deal of their national advertising had already been done for them. Or as Falk once said, "Air Jordan paved the way for all the other deals. Nike spent more than $5 million on advertising, so now we can walk into a designer like Guy Laroche . . . and say 'You don't have to spend that much because Nike and McDonald's and Coke are constantly putting him on television for you.' " It was what was called the ruboff effect. Phil Knight hated it, but that did not matter.

So it was that an American icon was born. In the modern entertainment culture, in a society obsessed with celebrity, deeds performed on celluloid often seemed to become substitutes for reality, and an ever more careless audience took more and more of its reality off a television screen. Men whose heroism was completely artificial and was limited to acting upon Hollywood sets were increasingly perceived as heroes, and their deeds, however synthetic, had a resonance that lasted and formed its own reality. That had been true in the past: A grateful if slightly deluded Congress had struck a medal for John Wayne as an American hero even though as a young man he had taken a pass on World War Two in order to advance his embryonic film career. Later a young man named Sylvester Stallone, who had not deigned to fight in Vietnam and had spent part of those war years teaching at a girls' school in Switzerland, had made a career for himself by playing an embittered, wronged superhero of the Vietnam War. But now, given the growing power of the popular culture, the line between the authentic and the inauthentic was blurred more than ever.

That made Michael Jordan almost unique as a cultural icon. For there he was on the court, night after night, his athletic supremacy on display, again and again winning big games in the last minute, again and again rising above the level of the world's very best players. That gave him a powerful hold on Americans who loved sports, even those whose interest in basketball had once been relatively minor but were drawn more and more to the sport because of word of mouth about the ascent of this superstar. And then there was his other incarnation, which because of the creative force—and frequency with which the Nike commercials were viewed—gave him nothing less than the power of a film star. The commercials were brief, but there were so many of them and they were done with such talent and charm that they formed an ongoing story. Their cumulative effect was to create a figure who had the power and force and charisma of a major movie star. Yet unlike so many people whom the Hollywood fantasy machine projected into theaters and homes who were beautiful but whose deeds were artificial, his deeds were real. Jordan, aware of the stakes, was extremely careful about his off-court behavior, among other reasons lest he cause any damage to the cumulative image now crystallizing and turning out to be so financially rewarding.

Thus did he gradually go beyond the boundaries of sport, carried by his great ability, his looks, and his charm more deeply into the psyche of the American public than any sports star had ever gone before. Success built on success. It was a dynamic that fed on itself: Those who did not know or love basketball were often piqued by the commercials and the beauty of the man in them, and they started to watch the occasional game if he was playing. When they did, he almost always did something exceptional, which meant that in varying degrees, they too were hooked. He was becoming better on the court and more famous off it. In a world where so many stars and heroes were inauthentic, he remained remarkably authentic.

14

Chicago, 1986–1987

STAN ALBECK LASTED one year. In that year, Michael Jordan missed sixty-four regular-season games. But Jerry Krause was dissatisfied with Albeck, and whether he had been given a fair chance was immaterial; his job had effectively ended the night Jordan hurt his foot in Oakland. His successor was Doug Collins. Collins was thirty-five at the time, one of the youngest men ever to become a head coach in the NBA. He was passionate, extremely driven, and very bright. No one understood the flow of a game better than Collins. Sometimes it seemed to his players that he was almost too smart. "If you could call thirty time-outs a game," his longtime assistant Johnny Bach, who admired him greatly, once said, "he'd win every game."

Collins had been a great player himself in college at Illinois State. He was six foot six, rail thin, and very quick, the rare white guard who seemed to have the speed of the black players around him. In his best years as a pro he averaged nearly twenty points a game, but his career was ended prematurely by injuries before his thirtieth birthday. He was thrilled by the new job and the prospect of coaching the best young player in the league, and he thought he and Jordan would have something in common. He was sure he understood the pressures of the modern game as many of the older coaches, some of whom had never played, did not. In addition, he knew all too well what it was like to suffer a shattering foot injury. At his first meeting with Michael Jordan in June 1986, he talked with his star about his injury and about the problem of the blood supply to that particular area. It was, he said, a hard injury to deal with and a hard one to come back from. And so, he suggested that Jordan take it easy that summer, that he not push his workouts or his foot. Collins added that he had had the same injury, implying that they shared this bond and that Collins did not want what had happened to him to happen to Jordan.

Jordan gave Collins a very cool look and said, in a voice that was very distant and that did not encourage collegiality, "That was your foot, this is mine."

It was not an ideal first meeting, and later Collins realized that Jordan had misread his attempt to be solicitous. It had been seen not as the gentle attempt of a young coach to cushion the reentry of a young player after so devastating an injury but as one more attempt by management to manipulate him.

That summer there was going to be a charity game in Las Vegas, UNLV alumni against Carolina alumni, and Collins did not particularly want Jordan to play in it. He suggested that Jordan show up at the game but not play and blame it on Collins. "I'll be the heavy for you," he said. Jordan, of course, went, played, and dominated the game, becoming the high scorer. After the game, the two men went out to dinner.

"I know you're not happy about my playing," Jordan said, "but I want you to know something. I just went through the worst year of my life because of an injury, and too many people who didn't know anything about me or my body were telling me what to do. They were all telling me what was good for me, but the truth is what they were really thinking about was what was good for them. I never want to go through that again."

Collins answered that he could understand that. "I'm not management on this issue. I'm just someone who loved to play, and I lost a lot of my own career because of the same injury, and I don't want what happened to me to happen to you."

With that, they began to connect. Later that summer, Jordan visited Collins at his home in Arizona, a visit that was both professional and social, aimed above all at getting the two men better acquainted. It was to be a brief stopover: They would play golf in the morning, and Jordan would fly back to Chicago later in the day. Collins played regularly with two friends who were very good golfers. He and Jordan split up, each playing with one of Collins's friends. Collins's team won, and so Jordan, ever competitive, hating to show up for one day and lose, decided to stay over one more day to avenge the defeat. He and his partner won the second game, and he was able to fly off happily.

The Bulls opened that year against the Knicks in New York. The Knicks had a strong team, Collins thought, with Patrick Ewing and Bill

Cartwright and Gerald Wilkins, among others. Chicago had very little—Michael Jordan, and an unusually large number of backup centers,
it sometimes seemed. But Michael Jordan was absolutely pumped that
night, glad to be back playing again and thrilled to be doing it in Madison Square Garden. His energy was palpable, and Collins thought there
was a danger that he might try and do too much. He had sixteen points
at the half, and Collins sensed the hunger in him—the need to take over
the game. "Michael," Collins told him at halftime, "take it easy, you
don't have to do it all. Wait and let the game come to you."

Collins was tense and sweating heavily, and by the second half his
shirt was soaked through. He was also chewing gum and, because he
was superstitious, he would not change it. He had ground it down to
powder, and some of the powder had gotten on his face. With about two
minutes to go, during a time-out, Jordan came over to Collins with a
glass of water. "Hey Coach," he said, "have a drink of water and wipe
that crap off your face." Then he smiled. "I'm not going to let you lose
your first game." He didn't. The Bulls won, 108–103. Michael Jordan
scored fifty points, including the Bulls' last eleven points, and twenty-
one of their last thirty-one. He was flying that night—sometimes, he
told reporters afterward, he went so high on his dunks that his wrists hit
the rim, but on this evening he was so juiced he was close to hitting it
with his elbows. "I almost overdunked the whole rim," he said. When
the game was over, he told his father he had been excited by the huge,
noisy Madison Square Garden crowd. "So you were playing on the
crowd, not on the floor?" James Jordan asked him. "I always play on the
crowd," his son answered.

15.

Albany; Chicago, 1984–1988

ECAUSE THE RISE of Michael Jordan within the world of basketball was not in the beginning without its generational overtones— younger fans were drawn to him first, thrilled by the sheer beauty and originality of his moves, while many older fans wondered if he was a player who could lift a team—it was not surprising that the first person to pick up on Jordan's ability in the home of Phil and June Jackson was their son Ben, all of five when Michael played his last college game in 1984. Ben had begun watching Jordan when he was still playing in the ACC, and he started pushing his father to pay more attention to him, particularly after Jordan became the star of the 1984 Olympic team. "Daddy, you've just got to check him out," Ben kept saying. In time, there appeared in the Jackson home, as in many other American homes, a photo of the very young Ben Jackson in a Chicago Bulls jersey, number 23, his tongue sticking out in the approved Jordan position.

Phil Jackson, then a coach in the minor-league Continental Basketball Association (CBA), *did* check out Michael Jordan, and in Jordan's rookie year Jackson went from Albany, where he was coaching the Patroons, to Glens Falls, New York, to watch a Bulls' exhibition game. He sat in the balcony, which overhung the floor, making it a poor vantage from which to examine a basketball player. He could not tell that much on this first viewing, except that Jordan seemed to want to drive each time he got the ball. After the game, Jackson went to the locker room and talked to Kevin Loughery, for whom he had once played. Loughery told him that Jordan was the real thing and was going to be a great, great star. But the world of Michael Jordan, then entering a brilliant career and about to be made rookie of the year and inundated with staggeringly handsome commercial endorsements, and the world of Phil Jackson, then struggling in the CBA for a marginal salary, could not have been more different. Jackson was also coaching in the summer in the Puerto Rican League, because it augmented his salary and because the coaching purists he knew, like Red Holzman, had told him it was the ultimate test of whether or not you liked coaching, which in fact it probably was.

He was making about $35,000 a year at the time in the CBA, plus about $12,000 more from his summer gig. He was struggling to get back in the NBA and finding that he was something of a pariah in the rather conservative world of professional basketball. When he went to events such as a tryout camp for marginally scouted but talented college seniors, none of the basketball men seemed interested in talking to him.

Jackson's body had begun to break down in the late seventies after a successful if not glittering career as a backup forward-center on two championship New York Knick teams. He was an immensely popular player in New York, giving many of that city's basketball fans a sense that he was a hip, irreverent kindred spirit. He lived right in Manhattan, he walked to the Garden from his apartment on the West Side, and he got around the city on a bike. So recently transplanted from rural North Dakota, he was not just a hungry student of the game but a searcher in the city, and he was exceptionally accessible in a place that knew and loved basketball and had fallen in love with that Knick team. He had not, as most pro athletes were wont to do, sealed himself off from the city around him but seemed to thrive on the rich but edgy quality of New York life. "He was different from most professional athletes," journalist and lifelong friend Charley Rosen said. "He thought that what you did and what you thought were as important as what he did and thought. He was as curious about you as you were about him. He did not put a wall up around himself."

That he had a professional career at all was a tribute to his intelligence, his personal dedication, and his capacity to retool himself to the needs of his coach and teammates. The offensive skills that had served him so well back in North Dakota were perilously close to useless in the pros. In college, he had been tall with a good hook shot, but in the pros he was no longer considered tall, and the hook shot was of little use against tall, athletic defenders who could readily block it. What saved him was his passion for the game, those long arms, and his willingness to give himself up on defense. He played a very physical game, and opposing teams learned early on to respect the unpredictable but always dangerous arcs of his elbows. "I had to play against him every day in practice and it was murderous," his teammate Bill Bradley once said. "He would bang you and bang you and bang you all the time—not dirty, just very physical—and he had those long arms. It was like being guarded by a giant spider. After practicing against him, playing in games against other defenders was a vast relief."

He was a perfect piece for that team. It was something of a connoisseur's team, and it was a great place to learn the game. Sometimes it seemed as if New York had a gifted coach on the sidelines, Red Holzman, and five other coaches on the floor. The players were, even by the standards of the time, surprisingly small—the starting team was really four guards and a forward—but everyone could shoot, everyone could pass, and everyone played smart, team-oriented defense. The ball moved quickly from player to player, everyone working to create mismatches and open shots.

When the more gifted big men on that team—Willis Reed, Dave DeBusschere, and Jerry Lucas, all of them better shooters than he—began to retire, Jackson was forced to become a starter. Then the real weaknesses in his game—the lack of a dependable jump shot and a certain inherent vulnerability when he put the ball on the floor—were revealed, and the end of his career was hastened. He was a player who gave a very good team a smart, intense eighteen or twenty minutes—just the right amount of time so the starters could rest. His presence on the floor helped guarantee that there would be no defensive letup and no drop-off in on-court intelligence. But if a team needed thirty-five minutes and a good deal of offense, he was not the right man. No team playing the Knicks in the latter part of his career agonized in its pregame strategy sessions about how to stop Phil Jackson's jumper.

He was in a kind of exile in 1984, coaching in the CBA, fighting a reputation that he was somewhat different, too much a free spirit. The people who knew him well knew how smart he was, but the people at the top in the world of basketball were bothered by his reputation as a hippie, someone who had rebelled against the midwestern fundamentalism of his youth semipublicly in New York, letting his hair grow long, growing a beard, and becoming one of professional basketball's ambassadors to the burgeoning counterculture. He and a black teammate Eddie Mast both grew beards in honor of the changing times, and Red Holzman was not bothered by it at all. He called them the Smith Brothers, in reference to the two bearded men depicted on the package of the cough-drop medicine. Jackson was, Holzman said years later, an absolutely fascinating young man, "always trying to balance off his rebellion with his religion."

Jackson protested the war in Vietnam, and in general he seemed more political than basketball players were supposed to be. In those days, it was quite all right for athletes to talk of their political beliefs so long as those beliefs were the conventional ones. In the late sixties and early seventies, Jackson was on something of a fascinating personal journey of discovery—political, philosophical, and sexual. If his protest in the end turned out to be more personal than political, that was lost on most basketball executives.

He had not helped things by writing a book with Charley Rosen called *Maverick*, which was published with the fully bearded Jackson's photo on the cover. Worse than the cover was what was inside the book, for a couple of minor passages detailed, among other things, his experimentation with drugs, including mind-enhancing ones such as LSD. At hiring time, that was what the powers that be in basketball remembered about him, not his intelligence or self-evident love of the game.

Thus, in the fall of 1984, Jackson was coaching in his second full season in the CBA and beginning to wonder whether he would ever get a shot at an assistant's job in the NBA. It was not that he disliked coaching in the CBA and in Puerto Rico. If you loved basketball, you loved coaching in both places because it was all so raw. Players came and went in the CBA, most of them hoping that one day the lightning would strike, and they would be called to the NBA. If your players were any good, Jackson knew, they were snatched away from you just as you entered the playoffs—which was the way it should be.

Still, there was something earthy and funky about coaching in the CBA. A team got a point for every quarter it won in each game and three points for winning the game itself; the Patroons' coach was rewarded with a $25 bonus for each point. That meant if the Patroons won the game and won every quarter, Jackson might get a bonus of $175. Not surprisingly, the fans at the home games sometimes heard the somewhat lonely sound of June Jackson cheering far more enthusiastically than anyone else for a Patroon buzzer beater at the end of the quarter. "Yes! Grocery money!" she would shout.

In the CBA, you paid your dues. The level of play was erratic. Relations between players and coaches were often strained: Once a CBA player, irate about his lack of playing time, ducked his coach's head in a toilet bowl. There had been times when certain teams folded with payrolls unmet. One coach was paid with silverware. Once, the Patroons coveted a big man on the Casper, Wyoming, Wildcats named Brad

Wright—six foot eleven, out of UCLA. Casper steadfastly refused to trade him. At the time, the Casper owners had a promotional gimmick in which they brought a new car out on the court, opened the sunroof, and encouraged their fans to turn their programs into paper airplanes and try to sail them down through the sunroof. If an airplane went inside the car, the fan who threw it won the car. Unfortunately, the team did not own the car. Given the distance of the car from the seats and the limits of most paper airplanes, it always seemed a fairly safe promotion. But one accomplished fan made a splendid paper plane, and its trajectory carried it right into the car. Needing the money to pay for the car it had just given away, the Wildcats traded Wright to Albany.

It was not a world of charter flights or even very much coach commercial travel. Despite the great distances between games, the Patroons often got to games in a giant van with Phil Jackson driving. On game days, he and his assistant Charley Rosen ran the players through an exhausting practice at home, packed them in the van, then turned up the heat so high they would fall asleep. Then Jackson and Rosen would boom out their music, with Jackson driving very fast, very skillfully, while doing the *New York Times* crossword puzzle spread over the steering wheel. It was very crowded in the van, with nine players, all of them big, and two coaches. There were brutal trips driving in harsh weather under the worst of deadlines in order to get to games just in the nick of time, Jackson driving and playing word games with Rosen while the players slept. Once, on their way to a game against Toronto, they were stopped by a guard at the Canadian border. He gestured to the back of the van. "What is the purpose of your trip?" Jackson, exhausted, answered, "I'm smuggling runaway slaves into Canada."

If the finances on some teams in the CBA were a bit dicey, it was nothing like the Puerto Rican League. There, each coach was given a new car when he arrived, and the first thing any coach who had been there before told a rookie colleague was that no matter what else—for it was quite likely you might be fired after a few games—you were never to return the keys until you had been paid in full, because as long as you had the keys, the owners had to pay you. When Jackson first arrived he was told by friends not to worry if he was fired, because he would quickly be hired by another team. In time he was fired by the team that had brought him down and hired immediately by its archrival, from a village only six miles away.

The Puerto Rican League was even more raw than the CBA, given the greater cultural chasm between coach and players and the not-inconsiderable language barrier. Some of the handful of players who were from New York and spoke English volunteered to translate Jackson's coaching instructions to their teammates, and they took pleasure in telling them the exact opposite of what Jackson was saying. It summoned, if nothing else, the need to coach at an elemental level, to stay with fundamentals, and to reach players across a huge chasm of differing experiences. It meant that you had to try and understand who they were and what they wanted out of this, a skill that was to serve Jackson exceptionally well later in his career. It also paid reasonably well— $1,500 a week for eight weeks, if in fact the check came through.

In both the CBA and Puerto Rico, Jackson dealt with professional basketball without amenities and without room for self-pity. Jackson was good at all of it. He was smart, and he had a photographic memory so that even though they were too poor to videotape the games, he could remember each play afterward. He was very good with the players. He treated them with respect, and he treated them as individuals, not setting conditions that they would not obey, such as bed checks and curfews. He sensed the idiosyncrasies of each player and tried, within the limits allowed to a coach, to adjust to them. Something else, too, helped him as a coach, Charley Rosen thought, both here and later in the NBA, the same thing which at that time also worked against him: He *was* different. He did not think or talk like other coaches, and it was harder for the players to figure him out. He did not come at them with his rules and his need for authority. Instead, he was open, he listened, he treated them with dignity, and he did not put his authority on the line all the time as too many coaches, struggling to make a name, do. He tried to understand their purposes and see if he could create a shared purpose. He was also very smart, one step ahead of them at almost all times, and they knew they could not con him. The fact that he was not easily predictable was an asset, Rosen thought. It kept the players interested.

The other thing Jackson had going for him, Rosen thought, was that for all the sensitivity and the willingness to understand his players, he was very tough, and there was a hard integrity that backed up everything he said. He might be an unusually deft and sensitive coach, a man whose own personal experience made him extremely tolerant of the frailties and vulnerabilities of others, and gave him a willingness to see humans as they were, and not as stereotypes, but he was also a very demanding coach, uncompromising on certain things. He might be a searcher who wanted to blend Eastern philosophies of a simpler, purer life into an ever more materialistic culture, but he was also a fierce competitor.

Since they were often short a player, he frequently practiced with the team. Because he had been a defensive success, he demanded hard physical play, and he still played that way himself. Some of the players might be fifteen or twenty years younger than he was, and they might be quicker than he ever was, but he never surrendered territory. A player named Dave Magley from Kansas got some shots off against him in practice and hit more of them than the coach liked. Charley Rosen remembered Jackson deliberately putting his knee into Magley's thigh, just as a reminder of the price to be paid for playing against a professional.

Though this might be one of the lower rungs in the basketball universe, Jackson believed passionately that practices were sacred, and no outsiders were allowed in. He had learned from Red Holzman that this was where the players should be allowed to make mistakes and where a coach could criticize them without any fear that his words would go outside the family. The same was true with his huddles during games. They, too, were sacred. For one game, a rival team hired the famed San Diego Chicken, the most talented of the new mime mascots, as a promotional lure. During one timeout, the Chicken placed himself in the middle of the Patroon huddle as if he were a player. Jackson moved over to him, a big smile on his face, and said, this man of Zen, "Chicken, get the fuck out of our huddle, or I'll kick your fucking ass."

He sometimes wondered in those years if he would ever get his call to the NBA. Others of his generation, players who had not paid their dues in the wilderness of the CBA, were getting calls, and he was still waiting to be summoned. He would show up at places where the various professional basketball people assembled, like the Chicago Combine, which was one of the great tryout places for as yet marginally scouted college talent, ostensibly to see if there was some talent that might slip down to the Patroons, but mostly to see if he could be noticed by the big boys of the NBA. But nothing happened, and no one even seemed to want to make eye contact. His best chance, Jackson finally decided, was with a strange, somewhat iconoclastic man named Jerry Krause who was the new general manager of the Chicago Bulls. Krause was also very much an outsider in the world of big-time basketball, even less one of the boys than Jackson. Jackson, after all, was six foot eight, had played the game, and had a great many friends among former players and sportswriters; Krause had never played anywhere, not even in college, and was short and dumpy, perhaps five foot five, and always significantly overweight. He made periodic attempts to get his weight down: Once Jerry Reinsdorf offered a bonus if he could lose some weight; and Krause bet at least once with Michael Jordan that he could lose a specified amount of weight in a period of a few weeks, a bet he very quickly lost. It was said that while he could do many remarkable things as a basketball scout on the road, one thing he could not do was drive past a Dunkin' Donuts. The evidence for his passion for sweets was often with him in the form of small stains on his clothes. His nickname among the players was Crumbs. He was most assuredly not one of the boys, the professional basketball men who had all at one level or another played the game, knew the language of it, and were at ease with each other, the kind of men who were known as men's men, and who move in and out of locker rooms with a special confidence.

Scouting college players was not an easy job, and back in the sixties and seventies before the coming of ESPN and cable, at which point many games became available on tape, it meant endless trips in small planes and undersized rental cars to tiny gyms in schools no one but other scouts had ever heard of to judge raw talent. The men who did that fought loneliness all the time, and one way they got around it was to travel together. The top five or six scouts seemed to migrate to certain schools and certain games together: Scotty Stirling, Jerry Colangelo, Stu Inman, Jerry West, Bob Ferry. The upside was that they were less lonely, and had each other's company; the downside was that they tended to see the same things and reinforce each other's opinions. If a good player had a bad night, they tended to come down on him together, which tended to blacken the player's reputation somewhat disproportionately.

Most of the other scouts were not particularly kind to Krause. He never made it into their club. He always seemed to try a little too hard. He did not dress well, and his personal grooming, it was widely felt, left a good deal to be desired. Bob Ferry, six foot eight, who had played ten years in the league and who had clashed often with Krause when they both worked for the Baltimore Bullets, loved to needle Krause when they were at games. There was a certain edginess to the needling, much of it about Krause's poor grooming and his cars, which were believed to be filled with a vast variety of containers from the various fast-food franchises that lined the main drags of small-town America. Ferry's teasing fell just short of cruelty; it was, thought one of the other scouts, the kind of teasing that the in boys did in high school to the boys always doomed to be on the outside.

Krause never responded to the teasing. His answer was to work harder than anyone else. He was a scout, that was all. He had no other life. He knew he had a good eye; the rest of his body mattered little, and besides, there was nothing he could do about it. Over the years, he turned adversity into a strength. Fiercely determined and endlessly hardworking, excluded to some degree from the company of his peers, he created his own network of people, and he was relentless in looking into the tiniest crannies of the basketball world to find talent. First it was the small black colleges of the South, before, in the sixties and seventies, the talented black players began going to the nation's best basketball schools. As that rich vein of talent began to dry up, he moved on to Europe, where there were still occasional bargains and where he might pick up on the rumors of potential NBA stars, like the Russian center (Arvidas Sabonis) who could pass like Walton, and the Yugoslav guard (Drazen Petrovic) who reminded people of Pete Maravich.

In the early days, he on occasion talked to one of the few other scouts whom he liked and trusted about what he was going to do when he had a team of his own, as he was sure he would. The other scouts looked at this short, significantly overweight, poorly dressed and groomed man and, aware of how important looks and manner were in any front office, they would privately shake their heads and think—Jerry, you're good at what you do, and no one works harder than you, but that is never going to happen, not now, and not in the future.

When he found someone he valued, he did not call and talk for five or ten minutes, he called and talked for hours, and he kept copious notes, checking out in years to come how accurate the projections of his sources had proven. Working alone, close to no one, he became famously secretive, indeed, almost paranoiac about hiding from other scouts who might by chance venture into the same venue as he did on the same night. When by chance another scout did show up, Krause tried to make himself invisible, or at least pretend that he was not looking at the player that they had both obviously come to see. When the Bulls were champions and drafting at the very bottom of the first round and someone would ask him about one of the two or three best players coming out, he became sphinxlike and said as little as possible. Even Jerry Reinsdorf would occasionally tease him about this: "Come on Jerry, you don't have to be so closemouthed—we're not going to get him anyway, because we're drafting number twenty-seven."

On the wall of his office was an unattributed quotation: "Hear All, See All, Say Nothing." The first time Bulls assistant coach Johnny Bach saw it he was amazed. Bach was a history buff, a serious student of World War Two, and he recognized it immediately as the slogan of Admiral Wilhelm Canaris, the head of the Abwehr, or German intelligence. "Jerry," he said, "that's a very strange slogan for someone who's Jewish and from Skokie to have on his wall." Bach came away sure that his boss had no earthly idea what the origin of those words was.

The Sleuth, reporters and other scouts called him, and year by year he became more and more secretive: He registered players at hotels under assumed names, and he brought them to the Bulls' practice center for midnight workouts when no one else was around and no reporter might stumble on the scene. He once brought Will Perdue, then a senior at Vanderbilt, in for a workout, which was not a great surprise, for everyone assumed that the Bulls would be interested in a big, hardworking center. Billy McKinney, one of Krause's deputies, went to the airport at night to get Perdue and duly called in on the car phone, "This is Agent Blue calling Agent Orange. The package has been picked up and is in the process of being delivered." The workout was late at night and Perdue was registered at a hotel under a false name, which created a problem the next day when a car service came to pick him up and the driver kept walking through the lobby calling out Perdue's pseudonym, which the player had by then forgotten.

Jerry Krause had wanted the Baltimore Bullets to draft Phil Jackson back in 1967, and he still thought of Jackson as one of his finds. Krause was not a man to let go of someone he had an investment in, and he had kept in touch with Jackson over the years, respected his intelligence, and thought that one day he would make a fine coach. When Jackson went to the CBA, no one kept in closer touch with him than Jerry Krause. Krause once called and asked him for an analysis of the players in the CBA, and Jackson jumped at the opportunity to do it: a rare chance to show his intelligence. He sat down at his computer and did a detailed scouting report on every important player in the league. Krause was impressed; Jackson was just as good as he had suspected. Soon, they would have endlessly long conversations as Krause, always digging for information, loving every eccentric little bit of trivia about basketball, called Jackson regularly and pumped him for knowledge of this almost subterranean part of professional basketball. Krause's calls were soon Phil Jackson's main lifeline to the NBA; Krause for his part was extremely impressed with Jackson's reports, his knowledge of the game, and the subtlety with which he talked about the different ways to motivate different players. Phil Jackson was very smart, Krause thought. In fact, if there was a problem with him, it might be that he was too smart to be an assistant under certain head coaches, that he would create a certain anxiety among men who sensed that he was smarter than they were.

Krause had done an earlier tour for the Bulls as player personnel man back in the late sixties and early seventies. Dick Motta was the coach, and their relationship had been lethal—they were two highly emotional men who seemed to bring out the worst in each other. Motta simply hated Krause, and Krause loathed Motta. Pat Williams, the general manager, caught in the horrendous daily crossfire between them, thought his job required diplomatic skills worthy of the secretary of state. What tore it more than anything else was the 1970 draft. Krause fell in love that year with a player at New Mexico State named Jimmy

Collins. Motta, by chance, watched one of the NCAA tournament games and was wildly impressed by a small guard named Nate Archibald from the University of Texas–El Paso, whose talent had been suppressed in the past by the slowdown tempo his team favored. That night, Motta called Pat Williams saying they had to have Archibald. "He's going to be a great, great NBA player," he said. Krause was just as passionately committed to Collins. Back and forth it went, and the decision was made: They would draft Collins in the first round and Archibald with their second-round pick, number twenty-seven overall.

"What happens if Archibald's not there when we pick in the second?" Williams asked Motta.

"Then we'll play against him every year," he answered. Cincinnati took him with the second pick of the second round, and that was that. Collins was a flop, playing a total of 612 minutes in two seasons before departing, while Archibald played for thirteen years and was six times an all-star. From then on, the Motta-Krause relationship was truly toxic, and soon Motta gave management a choice: He goes or I go. So Krause left, this time to work for Phoenix.

Krause came back to Chicago as general manager after Michael Jordan's first year, brought in by Reinsdorf, who had put together a group that bought the team. When Krause named Stan Albeck as his first coach, he suggested that Albeck might want to hire Jackson as an assistant. Duly summoned from Puerto Rico for an interview, Jackson showed up in Chicago with a beard, wearing a Panama hat with a long feather sticking out of it and a loud sports shirt. In truth, he never had a shot at the job. Krause did not want Albeck's first choice, a man named John Killilea, and Albeck did not want Jackson, and so the two men were exchanged for each other, pawns taken off the board in a larger game of chess.

Three years later, Phil Jackson was still coaching in the CBA and decided that he had to get out, that he could not devote a lifetime to it. He and June had four children of their own, and he had a daughter from an earlier marriage. They were effectively subsidizing his CBA years with money he had made earlier as a player. If the NBA was still blocked, then he would have to find some other kind of work. There was the possibility of becoming some kind of academic—perhaps in philosophy or religion—or perhaps going to law school. He took a career-guidance test that showed he had aptitude in both those areas. Then again, the guidance test also showed that he might make a good trail guide or homemaker. He was pondering what to do when Jerry Krause called again. Years later, after things became more and more heated between the two men, Krause said that he had taken Jackson off the unemployment line, which was both true and untrue, for while Jackson had in fact shown up and filled out the forms for unemployment, he never actually drew a check. More important, a man of Phil Jackson's gifts was not going to stay unemployed very long in any case.

It was the fall of the 1987–1988 season, and a vacancy on Doug Collins's staff had opened up when one of the assistants, Gene Littles, went to the Charlotte Hornets to be their player personnel man. Krause told Jackson to apply for the job. He and Butch Beard, another former Knick, were the only two candidates. "This time I want you to get a haircut, wear a suit, and come in clean shaven," Krause told him. Krause had one other suggestion for Jackson: wear both his championship rings from the Knicks. Jackson seemed uneasy with the idea, because it went against his own more modest instincts, but Krause insisted and said that it would be good for the younger players on the team to see the rings. Doug Collins did not seem to have strong feelings about either Beard or Jackson, and Krause eagerly gave the job to Jackson. That Jackson was an outsider largely scorned at that moment by the basketball establishment probably worked in Jackson's favor; it meant that Krause seemed to believe, however unconsciously, that Jackson would owe a great deal of loyalty to the man who got him his first real shot in the NBA. Krause always liked to think ahead and have a coach in or near the wings.

With that, the door was opened to the NBA. Because the job came just as the season was starting, June Jackson and the children stayed at their home in Woodstock, where she had just opened a hospice, and he took a room in a hotel in Chicago. He could not have walked into a better situation. Doug Collins was a brilliant, absolutely driven coach, and he had two older assistant coaches, men already in their sixties who were extremely helpful in allowing Jackson to make the adjustment to the NBA: Tex Winter, a virtual dean of the basketball world, who had started his coaching career forty years earlier, and Johnny Bach, who was also one of the smartest and most respected men in the profession.

Jackson arrived just as the Bulls were starting to come of age. That past year, Krause pulled off the best draft of his career, the one that made his reputation. He had chosen for the Bulls the two players who were finally to give Michael Jordan the help he needed: Scottie Pippen and Horace Grant, players who formed the core of the first championship cycle. Because Pippen's game was so unrefined—looking at him, a basketball man could see the endless physical possibilities from his unique build and his great natural talent, but also how limited his training had been—it became Jackson's job that year to work with him. He worked to refine Pippen's game, trying to teach him how to get his shot and to harness his awesome athletic ability. That helped create a bond and a trust between the two men that was to serve them well in the years to come.

Phil Jackson did not start out quite as smoothly with Michael Jordan. Early on, he had been talking with the other coaches and the subject of Jordan's greatness came up. Jackson quoted Red Holzman about the fact that great basketball players were those who made the players around them better. Doug Collins immediately suggested that Jackson tell that to Jordan. Jackson, wondering whether he was being set up, finally assented. He went down to see Jordan and repeated what he said, albeit with a slight note of apology and being very careful to mention that Collins wanted him to pass this on. Jordan listened largely without comment, his face rather blank, though he was not pleased. Later, he mentioned the conversation to his teammates and added that it was a lot easier to pass off when you were doing it to Earl Monroe and Walt Frazier and Bill Bradley.

It was a refrain Michael Jordan had heard too often and would hear again and again with ever greater amplification: He might be the greatest single talent in the game, the best one-on-one player ever, but did he pass the acid test of basketball greatness, that of lifting his teammates? At about that time Jackson's old friend Bill Bradley, then a United States senator, had a visit from his old colleague Oscar Robertson, generally considered one of the two best guards of his era. "That Michael Jordan is really something," Bradley said, and Robertson dissented. "No, he isn't," he said, "not for me at least." Bradley was puzzled and he asked Robertson what he meant. "A truly great player makes the worst player on the team good," he answered, "and Michael's not there yet."

Among the elite of basketball people, Jordan was not yet perceived as the equal of Larry Bird and Magic Johnson, who seemed to carry their teammates to the Finals each year. That Bird's teammates included McHale, Parish, Johnson, and Ainge, and Johnson's, Abdul-Jabbar, Worthy, and Mychal Thompson (all three of them, like Magic himself, players who had been the number one pick in the country in the draft) plus Michael Cooper and Byron Scott, and Jordan's were Granville Waiters, Quintin Dailey, Dave Corzine, Brad Sellers, and Orlando Woolridge, was not mentioned. Michael Jordan was all too aware of this refrain; he raged to rise above it and to have the teammates who could go with him to the next level. His wrath was reserved for the basketball gods who let him flounder with so little support, but so far he had never spoken to his agent about trying to get out of Chicago in order to play with better teammates. He did see it as his job to lift his team. But it did not help his relationship with Krause that the process of improving the team seemed in his mind to be going all too slowly.

Jerry Krause thought the team he had taken over in 1985 was a disaster. Some of the players were good kids but not talented, and some were not only not that talented but were lacking in character as well. As many as five players from that early team eventually went into some form of drug rehabilitation. The prototype seemed to be Orlando Woolridge. He was gifted, powerfully built, with a body that looked chiseled from stone, but he did not, in the opinion of his teammates, play a physical game. Jordan on occasion raged at Woolridge in practice: "If I had your body, people would be flying out of there." Krause could not wait to start unloading people, and he did it quickly and cold-bloodedly, picking up draft choices here and there and creating the backlog of picks that was to give him the leverage to draft quality players in the future.

Slowly, he would create a new team. It would be something new in basketball, a team created around a shooting guard, which meant that the other players would have to learn to be unselfish. Above all, he needed some strength up front and a cop who would protect Jordan in games where opponents tried to take cheap shots at him. There had to be some kind of price to be paid for going after him.

The first real piece came in the spring of 1985, when Krause saw a kid playing for Virginia Union who had a big, powerful body and seemed willing to throw himself on the floor for every loose ball. The name of the young man was Charles Oakley, and he had, Krause thought, all the requisites to be an exceptional rebounder: good body, good attitude, and, as an additional blessing, good hands. Krause called Clarence (Big House) Gaines, the legendary coach at North Carolina Central, one of his favorite sources. Gaines's teams played against Oakley regularly, and Gaines thought Charles Oakley was the real thing: a big, strong, hungry kid with a marvelous work ethic, highly coachable, who would only get better.

The problem with Oakley, as far as Krause was concerned, was that as the college seniors went from tournament to tournament to the Chicago Combine, his stock kept rising. That year, Chicago picked eleventh. Cleveland was ninth, and Phoenix, a team with a reputation for scouting very well, was tenth. Jerry Colangelo at Phoenix swore he was taking Ed Pinckney, but Krause was nervous about Cleveland. In the end, he made a deal with the Cavaliers: He sent them Ennis Whatley and a second-round draft choice, Cleveland picked Charles Oakley for Chicago, Chicago picked Keith Lee for Cleveland, and then they switched picks. In Chicago, the fans who had gathered on draft day booed the Lee pick, and they booed the trade for Oakley as well. But the first piece was in place.

Oakley turned out to be everything Krause hoped for and more. Even better, Michael Jordan, who had begun to watch the front office with something of a skeptical, if not hostile eye, loved Oakley, and he became not only Jordan's personal cop, his protector on the floor, but his best friend on the team.

Krause was not finished dealing. He wanted to pick up some pure shooters to play alongside Jordan and to limit the double-teams he would face. He picked up Kyle Macy from Phoenix, an exceptional pure shooter with limited NBA physical ability, and though Macy played thirty minutes a game that first year, the limits of what he could do, particularly on defense, were obvious. But Krause also made a compensatory move, picking up a young player named John Paxson from San Antonio. Long before Krause signed Macy, he had been courting Paxson, the younger, shorter brother of an all-star named Jim Paxson. By this time, there were other offers on the table for Paxson, one from Atlanta and a good one from Phoenix. When Macy joined the Bulls, Paxson assumed that Chicago would pull back. To his surprise, Krause sweetened his offer: three years *guaranteed*. For a player fighting desperately to stay in the league, a player who had averaged about 4.5 points a game in his first two seasons, that was a blessing.

There was the added attraction of trying to play alongside of Michael Jordan, knowing that you were going to get more than your share of open shots because of him. Krause told Paxson that he hoped to create something new in Chicago, a team built around a shooter, and that was intriguing. Everyone on the team would have to shoot well, and the ball would move quickly. Paxson liked the idea of it and thought that his talents were well suited to that kind of game. Macy was quite possibly the better shooter, though whether he was physically strong enough to get his own shot remained a question. Though Macy played more minutes that season and averaged more points, it was obvious that Paxson was the better all-around player and athlete and, more important, that Jordan liked him better.

The most important thing with Jordan was winning his respect, if not his absolute trust, and Paxson had done that when they were still in college. They had both been on a college all-star team that had toured in Europe. In one game in a tiny gym in Yugoslavia, Paxson had hit a long jump shot at the buzzer to win. Jordan seemed to remember that shot, and he was never as hard on Paxson as he was on most of his teammates. The next year, Macy was gone, and Paxson worked his way deeper into the rotation as the perfect companion for Jordan: someone who knew exactly what he was supposed to do and what he was not supposed to do and who always stayed within his game. "He was *always* connected to Michael," Chuck Daly once said, "as if on a twelve-foot piece of rope, ready to kill you any time he got the ball."

Jordan was not so pleased with the next year's draft selection. It was not a rich draft, and the Bulls, picking ninth, chose Brad Sellers from Ohio State. He was tall and slim, seven feet and only 220 pounds, and he played a finesse game, not a power game. He could, it seemed, shoot from the outside, but he was not a man to take—or give—a pounding underneath, which was what the Bulls needed. Sellers was very much a Krause pick, and the coaches were wary of him. The player whom Doug Collins, some of the assistant coaches, and Michael Jordan wanted badly was a talented guard from Duke named Johnny Dawkins. Dawkins had played well in the ACC and been the engineer of a particularly gritty Duke victory over North Carolina when Jordan was still at Chapel Hill. For a time it appeared the Bulls would take Dawkins. The night before the draft Collins had even told Duke coach Mike Krzyzewski that Chicago was going to take Dawkins, represented by David Falk, with its pick. But Krause was not enamored of Dawkins: He was too slim, he thought, and looked to be the kind of player who simply lacked the body to take the sustained punishment of the NBA. But Dawkins turned out to be a much better NBA player than Brad Sellers, and he played for eight solid years.

It was the kind of decision that Jordan did not forget lightly. Both he and Falk thought it was a telltale sign of a significant weakness in Krause. They both believed that Krause's ego got in the way of his draft picks, that he would not go for the obvious best pick because if the obvious pick worked out he would not get adequate credit; therefore, he was driven to take chances and go for arcane picks, because if they came through, he would get the kind of special credit that they believed he needed so desperately. Much of Jordan's lingering resentment and distrust of Krause was rooted in the Dawkins-Sellers choice, and it made him warier of the situation he found himself in.

Krause made one additional mistake on the Sellers pick. He not only drafted Sellers but also hyped him to the coaches and players, talking too enthusiastically about how good a pro player he was going to be. Michael Jordan never let Jerry Krause forget a word of that hype. He decided very early on that Sellers was a soft player when the Bulls desperately needed strength. Sellers did not play like a big man, he played like a small forward in a seven-foot body, and Jordan was particularly brutal on him in practice.

It was a warning of things to come. Krause was learning all the time how hard it was to get just the right players to coexist with Michael Jordan. When Jordan got down on a teammate, he might stay there, challenging the player to do better in a way that few players, particularly on that team, were strong enough to handle. When his coaches sometimes wondered aloud if he was being too hard on his teammates, he would answer, correctly, that if they could not take the pressure in practice, how were they going to take it during the playoffs? When Johnny Bach once cautioned him that he was destroying one of his teammates during preseason practice, he answered coolly, "I have to get myself ready, Johnny."

The truth was that there was already a division in the Bulls organization that was eventually to have severe consequences. Michael Jordan had begun to bait Jerry Krause and to treat him in an essentially demeaning manner. It was by no means Jordan at his most attractive, thought even those who took Jordan's side of the battle and who did not particularly like Krause. There was a certain cruelty to it, and much of it was unnecessary. The origins of the conflict were complicated. Part of it was clearly Krause's handling of Jordan's foot injury, though Jordan could have—but did not—equally blame Jerry Reinsdorf in that matter.

Part of it as well was an innate distaste for someone who seemed to have such a terrible need to take credit for so many things, some of which he had actually done, some of which he had not. Whatever else, Krause's behavior stood in stark contrast to the conscious modesty that was the hallmark of the Carolina program, beginning with Dean Smith, who never took credit for anything.

Because his way to the top had been so long and hard and because he had been an outsider in the world of professional sports for so long, Jerry Krause had a tendency to take more than his share of credit once he made it. The stories he now told, it was believed, almost always tended to inflate his own role in things. He was wont to tell people at some length how he spotted and scouted the great Earl Monroe when he was at Winston-Salem. Though in fact Winston-Salem was the kind of small black school that scouts had traditionally overlooked in the past, Earl Monroe's greatness was not exactly a secret. When the Bullets had taken him, he was the second player taken overall in the country. Both Gene Shue, Baltimore's head coach, and Bob Ferry, his assistant, had played prominent parts in his selection. "Jerry had nothing to do with the selection of Earl Monroe," Gene Shue said years later. "Jerry was our scout—a young guy beating the bushes for us working very very hard. No one worked harder than Jerry. But Earl Monroe was not a secret—everyone knew about him and he had played in a number of games that I saw and I thought he was spectacular, one of the most exciting players I'd ever seen. The only doubts about him were from some NBA people who thought he was too much of a showboat and wondered whether he would fit into the NBA because of that. But I loved that part of his game. You have to remember that Baltimore was a tough town to draw in. So what put some people off I saw as an added bonus—I was looking for excitement for a franchise which was nearly dead. Jerry had no decision-making powers." Years later, Kevin Loughery, the coach of the Bulls when the Reinsdorf-Krause team took over, who had played in the same backcourt with Earl Monroe for four years, said that the moment he heard the news of the change in ownership, he knew he was gone. "I had been in Baltimore when Krause was there, and I knew that he had been a glorified gofer in those days, and I knew that the stories he was telling now—about how he scouted Earl Monroe—were all greatly exaggerated, and the last person he was going to want around was a witness to his past."

Hearing the Monroe stories from Krause, Michael Jordan would often yell across the bus to him, Yeah, Jerry, and if it hadn't been for your brilliant scouting would Monroe have fallen all the way to number three in the country? Jordan also told people that in a few years, when people's recollections had lapsed a bit more and there were fewer people around who were actual witnesses, Krause would take credit for drafting him as well. What bothered some of the coaches was the fact that in the beginning, Krause seemed to enjoy this byplay, or at least misread some of Jordan's baiting, as if it finally made him one of the boys. Part of the Jordan/Krause problem, however, had roots in something as old as the school yard, where some boys are popular, and some seem to be born to be targets. Jordan, talented, gifted, the best at whatever it was he chose to do, was the alpha personality, and he saw in Krause—short, unattractive, desperate to be one of the boys but lacking any of the requisite qualities—the omega personality, the person doomed to be on the very outside of any group.

It was an odd and unfortunate dynamic and it served them both poorly. Krause tended to hang around the players too much, and that only provoked more of Jordan's baiting. Tex Winter, the rare figure in the Bulls organization who got on well with both Krause and Jordan and who took no sides in the ever escalating tension between them, thought it was Jordan at his least likable and cruel. But he also thought that Krause tried to get too close to Jordan and to become his pal. Doug Collins saw what was happening and tried to warn both men off. His own position with Krause still relatively secure, Collins told him that their job was not to try to be Jordan's pal but to gain his respect, and probably the less they interacted with him the better.

16

Chicago; Seattle, 1997

IN THE EARLY weeks of the 1997–1998 season, the tensions between the team members, particularly Michael Jordan and Scottie Pippen, on one hand and Jerry Krause on the other grew worse and worse. It was no longer caustic byplay; it had escalated into out-and-out baiting, much of it quite mean and unnecessarily juvenile. It was unattractive in all ways. Some believed that Jordan was having at Krause as a way of standing up for Pippen, who was angry and embittered but not that good at verbal combat and not that good at handling his rage at this moment. Phil Jackson felt himself caught in the middle. The situation was potentially damaging to everyone involved, and if nothing else, it was very embarrassing to many of the bench players, who, with far less leverage in their contract negotiations, did not like the idea of witnessing a struggle between the team's superstar and their boss. This battle had no winning side as far as they were concerned. Part of the problem was the fact that Krause was around the players a great deal more than other general managers were around their players—in the locker room, on the bus, on the charter plane. Most general managers tried to stay away from their teams on a day to day basis. Jackson tried to warn Jordan off the heckling and the baiting, to little avail; and like Doug Collins before him, he had also suggested frequently to Krause that he try to be around the players less, as his presence was a provocative one. Jackson felt that Krause had a limited sense of proper boundaries; Krause, by contrast, felt that as the head of basketball operations he had a right to go wherever he wanted and there need be no sense of boundaries. By traveling with the team in the first five or six weeks of the season, he argued, he could get a good feel for its texture and its needs. But to the players, he was always trespassing on what they considered their domain—the bus and the plane were, like the locker room, their habitats, more by tradition than by law, and it was where they could relax and have their fun. Their rules, not the rules of management, were unofficially in effect in these areas.

This season, because of the tensions over Pippen's contract, the feelings about Krause were unusually bitter. Pippen, who was traveling with the team despite his injured foot, was seething over not just his salary but a cumulative sense of abuse from the past; on two occasions, the Bulls had almost traded him, and in his mind Krause had never been candid with him about it. At the very least, it showed to him that the Bulls did not respect his contributions to the five championships in the way they respected Michael Jordan's. When, early in the season, the team arrived in Los Angeles from Phoenix, it was believed that the Phoenix people made it clear to Pippen's agent that the player they most wanted in the future was Scottie. The contrast between their eagerness and the Bulls' seeming disdain was more fuel for his anger.

After the game against the Clippers in Los Angeles, Bill Walton, who was broadcasting Clipper games, walked out of the Bulls' locker room, shaking his head over the level of Pippen's bitterness. It was rare, he thought, to see a great player on a championship team so angry at management and talking so vociferously about wanting to be traded. That night, Pippen also grabbed Kent McDill, one of the Chicago beat reporters, and told him that he was never going to play for the Bulls again. Never. It was hard to tell how serious he was, and at first McDill did not print what he said. But a day later, when Pippen pushed McDill to write, he filed the story. With that, all the existing tensions grew more intense, and more charges and countercharges were made on both sides.

After their victory against the Clippers, the Bulls headed north to Sacramento. On the plane, there was some ugly byplay between Jordan and Pippen and Krause. There was an additional exchange in the Sacramento locker room the next day, much of it once again about Krause's alleged role in drafting Earl Monroe. Then, after a victory against the Sacramento Kings, the players boarded the plane to Seattle. On the plane, Pippen was drinking beer. When they landed, there were two buses, one for the players, one for the staff. Krause rode with the players, which some of the coaches thought was a major mistake. The bus, far more than the plane, was an explosive venue. When the players and the staff were on the plane, they tended to go their different ways and, other than a regular Jordan-Pippen–Ron Harper card game, do their separate things. Some players ate, some slept, some read, and some were cut off from others by their headphones and music. The plane offered solitude more than it did community. By contrast, the bus was a far more combustible place; the players and coaches were crowded in more closely, there were fewer distractions, there were constant communal conversations, filled with the edginess of high-powered athletes, talking about opponents and women. The level of baiting and woofing escalated dramatically on the bus. In the past Jackson had argued with Reinsdorf about Krause's traveling with the team in general, suggesting that it was obvious that he was not welcome, and that it was a constant source of tension and friction. Reinsdorf's answer was that Jackson could stop the baiting if he really wanted to. Jackson in turn, bothered by the increasingly mean-spirited nature of the baiting in the last two years, almost all of it from Jordan, had spoken to Jordan about it several times. Michael said yes, it was not something he was that proud of, but there were times when he simply could not help himself. In other words, the problem would continue.

Jackson suggested to Krause that he stay off the team bus and have a limo meet him at the airport if need be. But Krause refused. Krause's presence on the bus ride from the Seattle airport to the hotel seemed to ignite the players. The baiting began again, starting with Jordan, the subject being Krause's unlikely skill as a fisherman. Soon Pippen joined in.

Jordan was skilled at verbal blood sport; no one in the league was better at zinging other people. He seemed to know how much to bait Krause and, when there were danger signals, just when to back off. Jordan might have his own raging emotions, but he was a master at controlling them. He was mature and very tough mentally, and he had a certain high, professional coldness that allowed him to turn on his emotions as he so chose and to use his rage as an instrument. If anything, no one in the league was more skilled at creating artificial rage when needed.

Pippen was different. His emotions were always more raw and closer to the surface, and he had far less control over them. When he got into a situation like this, especially when he had been drinking, he was not nearly as good as Jordan at knowing when to let go. As Jordan began the baiting on the bus, Pippen took it over, berating Krause—*When are you going to stop taking credit for drafting me and for my career?*—then loudly and angrily demanding that the Bulls either sign him to a new contract or trade him. None of it was being done lightly, and Pippen became louder and angrier on the ride. It was the voice of anger and alcohol. Finally, Jackson held up a bottle of beer, as if to tell him that he had been drinking too much and to stop. (It was symbolic of how divided the franchise was that Joe Kleine, the backup center, thought that Jackson was toasting Pippen.) "Don't worry," Krause told Jackson, "I can take it." That, thought Jackson, was not the issue, the issue was far more serious.

It was a very ugly scene: Michael could play at this game and somehow never quite cross the line, but when Scottie did it, went after Krause, somehow a line was crossed.

The next day, the beat reporters followed up with more and more stories about Pippen's demand to be traded and his vow that he would never play again for the Bulls. It was early in the season, the Bulls were struggling on the floor, one of their great players was out, and there was a chance they would lose him permanently. It was crisis time. The other players were very upset, and before the shoot-around that day Jackson held a brief team meeting. Pippen was apologetic to his teammates for causing them any problems with his demands to be traded, but he was also very firm about his stand. He told them he would never put a Bulls uniform on again. I love all of you, he said, but I think it's all over. Pippen, Jackson feared, was moving toward a point of no return where he was going to damage not just the team but himself by saying things from which there was no turning back. Management was not going to cut him anywhere near the slack it might cut Michael Jordan.

Pippen, lacking Jordan's inner toughness, was infinitely more vulnerable to the complex social forces that often seemed to be assaulting him as he rose to an ever-higher level of athletic achievement and public notoriety. His journey from where he started to where he was today was far longer than Jordan's, and his protective mechanisms for the nonbasketball part of his life were far weaker. As such, his emotional control off the court was always something of a question. Earlier in his career, his volatility had been something of a problem on the court as well, and it had been relatively easy for shrewd opponents to throw him off his game. But during a long and increasingly distinguished career, his on-court behavior had strengthened considerably; he was now one of the league's reigning stars, with five championship rings to his credit, and it was hard to rattle him during a game. But his off-court behavior was another thing. Pippen's lack of emotional control, in a world as predatory as the contemporary NBA, where the stakes were becoming bigger all the time, could readily be used against him, Jackson thought.

In the days following, Jackson talked with Pippen several times and tried to calm him down. Pippen's various statements to reporters in the last few days contained, among other things, hints that he actually was healthy enough to play if he really wanted but he was holding back because of his contract. The coaches were sure that was untrue. They had watched him in a practice session, and he could not stop and start. But even the suggestion of malingering was very dangerous stuff, Jackson thought. Essentially, Jackson told Pippen that his day was coming, that he had to wait, that he *did* have a contract for this year, and that if there was any further escalation between him and management, he would be the one who suffered, for there would be a permanent black mark on his name around the league, particularly among the quality organizations. The only way to get his freedom was to come back this year, play at a high level, and go the free-agent route in the summer of 1998.

Jackson was quite surprised by the hostility of Pippen's reaction. Pippen, who normally listened to Jackson and accepted his judgments, seemed to be far beyond his reach this time. It was clear that in Pippen's mind neither Jackson nor Jordan had the right to tell him what to do because their big paydays had come while his had not. To the degree that they had been able to protect him from the front office, he felt, it was to keep him from being traded, not to use their leverage to improve his contract. So Pippen shrugged off their advice and seemed at least momentarily resentful of them as well as the front office.

Somewhat irritated by Pippen's behavior, both Jordan and Jackson tried another tack and spoke critically to reporters about Pippen's recent statements. They came back for this season, they both said, primarily to win one more championship, and one of the reasons they did it was Pippen. He was the only major star from the 1997 team who had been under contract, and he had asked both Jackson and Jordan to come back. Jackson remembered Pippen's words: "Don't leave me here alone." Now they had returned, and it was Pippen who seemed to be ducking out on them. Jackson was surprised by the incident, and thought that over the years far more damage had been done to Pippen than he realized.

The Bulls played well that evening against the SuperSonics—one of the two or three teams they might be expected to meet in the Finals—but lost in overtime when Toni Kukoc missed a last-second shot. When they flew out of Seattle, it was probably the low point of the season. Their record was 8–6, they were struggling, and they had yet to beat a top-ranked team. Jordan was playing very well, but he was playing far too many minutes, and his shooting percentage was down, a sure sign of fatigue; he was trying to carry the team too often too early in the season. Rodman was finally rounding into shape and beginning to play well, but Kukoc, from whom a great deal was both expected and needed, was playing not only erratically but softly. The key was Pippen. In order to make this season a success, the Bulls had to stay within striking distance while Pippen was out. Perhaps if they were lucky they would be a few games above .500. Then, when he came back, rested and healthy, they would make an all-out assault that would carry them through the play-offs. Now Pippen was not only threatening to sit out the entire season but setting up a scenario where he courted being traded in a punitive way to a cellar-dwelling team by an angry front office. As they left Seattle, Jackson was not sure whether they were going to get Pippen back, or if they did, what mental state he would be in. He now feared a repeat of the infamous 1994 playoff game.

If there was a defining event during Phil Jackson's tenure as Bulls coach, it was the one that took place in a season in which the Bulls did not win the championship, and involved not something he did but something he did not do. It was during the 1994 Eastern Conference Finals against the Knicks, in the first season in which Michael Jordan was absent, playing baseball. With 1.8 seconds left in Game Three and the scored tied at 102, Jackson called for a time-out and sketched out a play that gave the final shot to Toni Kukoc. Scottie Pippen, who had carried the team in Jordan's absence and was at the moment a legitimate candidate for MVP of the league, was enraged by the decision and refused to go back in. (One reason Pippen was so angry at that moment was that on the previous possession, the coaches had called a clear-out to isolate Pippen on the right side, but Kukoc, as had happened all too often with him that season, had not cleared out, despite Pippen trying to wave him away. In the confusion, the Bulls drew a twenty-four-second violation.)

It was a stunning moment, a great player refusing to return to a game for its climactic moment. No one could remember anything quite like it. There had been times when lesser players, pulled earlier from a game, refused to return when a coach asked them. But nothing like this: a superstar refusing to return for a deciding moment in a championship series. At first, a puzzled Jackson turned to his assistants and said, "He doesn't want to go back in. What am I going to do?"

"Fuck him," said Jimmy Cleamons, one of the assistants. "We play without him."

Most coaches at such a moment would have blown it and gone after Pippen with a certain finality. But Jackson exchanged a few heated words with Pippen at the very moment of his refusal and then essentially backed off. That Kukoc had eventually made the shot and Chicago had won seemed almost dwarfed by the fact of Pippen's act.

Essentially, what Jackson did was let the players handle it, something he had learned from Red Holzman, his coach in New York. The players were always the ones who knew; they were both judge and jury. Let them talk it out and let them decide what was the right thing, if anything, to do. As for Jackson, he knew immediately that it was something with which Scottie Pippen was going to have to live for a long time, and that would be difficult enough. The problem now was not so much punishment but containment and trying to put what happened in some kind of context, to judge the act not only of itself but alongside the other things Pippen had done for the team over the years. In that tinderbox atmosphere Jackson thought not just of himself but of the overall future of the team and, equally important, of the player involved, from whom he had gotten so much in the past. He was aware of the complete balance sheet, and he was not about to let one act, no matter how childish, wipe out all the positive contributions.

He was stunned nonetheless. He got to the locker room after the game, and there was Bill Cartwright, the veteran center, perhaps the most respected player on the team, sobbing and repeating as if to himself, "I can't believe he did that. . . . I can't believe he did that. . . . I've never seen anything like it before. . . ." Mercifully, Jackson had to take his contact lenses out, an act that took five minutes. Then he went in to meet with Pippen and the other players. He phrased his words carefully: What Pippen had just done, he said, was something terrible—it went beyond anything any of them had ever seen before. Pippen, he said, was not going to be able to wipe it out, he was going to have to deal with it, not just publicly, but first and foremost with his teammates, whom he had just so grievously let down. Then Jackson told him that he was going to go out and talk to the media, and whatever else he was not going to lie about what had happened. With that, he led them in the Lord's Prayer, because he liked to remind them that there was a higher deity. Then, while the players sorted it out without him, he went out and spoke to the press. Bill Cartwright, still very emotional, had done most of the talking.

When Jackson returned, the players had already begun to sort it out among themselves. Cartwright spoke with great emotion and effectiveness. He told Pippen, "After all we've been through, after all the sacrifices we've made to win without Michael, how could you do this?" To the degree that words were needed, they had been uttered, and not by an authority figure but by Pippen's peers. What was still to be discovered was whether he could learn from it and regain the special stature he had enjoyed with them before this all happened. But that moment, Jackson's failure to come down hard on Pippen was probably the defining act of his coaching career, and since there were a number of people in the organization anxious to trade Pippen after that, he probably helped save the core of the team for the next cycle of championships. It was typical of Jackson's view that the long run was what mattered.

That first night, Tim Hallam, the Bulls' press representative, spoke with Jackson. Hallam was very much aware that this was a crucial moment for the future of the team. He found Jackson surprisingly relaxed about the entire episode. "It just isn't going to be a problem," Jackson said; Hallam later decided that this moment, even more than winning the championships, defined Jackson as a coach.

The next day, an astonished Michael Jordan, then of the Double A Birmingham Barons, called Jackson, eager for the inside story. "I just can't believe he did it," Jordan said. "How could it have happened?" Jackson answered that there was no explanation, but there it was. "How's Scottie handling it?" Jordan asked.

"Well, he apologized but he's not really contrite," Jackson said.

It was clear that Jordan, product of an environment in which, no matter what you felt at the time, you always did what the coach said, could not believe this act of heresy. "People are never going to forget what he did," Jordan said.

"I'm not sure, Michael," Jackson answered. "People will forgive a lot of things based on a person's real intentions, and Scottie has been able to grow past a lot of things."

Now, in the fall of 1997, as Pippen was once again threatening to self-destruct, Jackson decided that it was time to move back a little, to explain the consequences of his actions to him, but even more important to cool it all down, and let Pippen's teammates be the bridge to him. Pippen's 1994 fit had been forgiven by his teammates and the basketball public, but if he now refused to honor his contract and come back and play with a championship team, potentially sabotaging it, there would be no forgiveness. Jackson wanted to keep Pippen away from Krause, so he insisted Pippen not travel with the team for a while. In addition, Ron Harper, who was closer to Pippen than anyone else on the team, slipped into a new role—that of the buddy who let his friend know they needed him, that they were counting on him and believed in him. What they needed at this point, Jackson believed, were fewer stories in the papers and more time for Pippen to confront the reality of his situation. It was time to let Pippen remember that he loved playing basketball with the Chicago Bulls.

The mood on the team began to change. Up until then, it had been relatively relaxed, almost joyous, despite the tensions with the front office. There had been a consensus that this was the last time around and they were going to enjoy it. This team was very different in one critical sense from the team that had won the first three titles. That team had been much much younger, and for many of the players coming off the bench, like B. J. Armstrong, Stacey King, and Will Perdue, it had been their first NBA team. Few of them knew what it was like to suffer on a losing team through a long, depressing season, realizing that at best you might win thirty-five or forty games. This team was very different. Bill Wennington, Joe Kleine, Jud Buechler, Randy Brown, Ron Harper, and Steve Kerr had all played on other teams and understood and accepted the limits of their places in the league and how lucky they were to be on a team that had a shot at the championship. For some of them it was their third or fourth team: They knew when they were in a good situation. By and large, their emotional balance was very good, and they accepted with good grace Jackson's changing need—or lack of need—for them. That made it an easy team to coach. It generally glowed with a benign interior mood, as the ordinary players tried to stray as far from the Krause-Pippen-Jordan wars as possible.

But now the team was struggling, barely above .500, and the confidence that it would all change with Pippen's return was gone. Perhaps he would return, perhaps he wouldn't. With their record 8–7, Jackson called another team meeting. They had already lost more games than they had in the first half of the previous season, when their final record had been 69–13, he told them. Worse, they were losing to teams they should have beaten, and they were failing at something that was critical for championship teams: They were failing to finish out close games. The trademark of champions—the trademark of the Bulls for much of this decade—had been to dominate other teams in the last few minutes when the game was on the line. Somehow, they were losing that knack. Other teams, sensing blood in the water, were coming at them and having their way.

After that meeting, things began to change, mostly because of Michael Jordan. He went into his superwarrior mode. Each game was different now: He went at these games as if they were against playoff-level teams at championship time. He escalated the level of his defensive play. He pushed his teammates to extend themselves. No one picked up on his example quite like Dennis Rodman, who also brought his game up dramatically. Jordan was aware of it and carefully stroked Rodman to the media after the games. *Dennis is our most valuable player this season*, he told reporters. *We wouldn't be doing any of this without Dennis. I've never seen a teammate play this hard*. Rodman seemed to flourish in Pippen's absence and under Jordan's praise, as if he were now the number-two instead of the number-three amigo on the team and it was Michael and Dennis together against the world. Over the next eighteen games, his rebounding average went up from thirteen a game to seventeen, one small indicator of how hard he was playing. Once again, the Bulls were tough. There was nothing artistic about these games. They were won in the pit, by smaller men outrebounding bigger men, and by superior defense, and by players coming off the bench and staying within their exact roles. If they did not look like the dominating, ever-confident Bulls of the last two years, they were nonetheless winning again. Their record was not that good yet, but they were playing hard and they were leading the league in one important category: They were holding their opponents to lower scores than any team in the league.

17

Hamburg and Conway, Arkansas; Chicago, 1982-1987

THE 1987 NBA draft laid the foundation for the first of the Bulls championships. The Bulls picked up both Scottie Pippen and Horace Grant, the former eventually to become not merely a perennial all-star but a player on the short list of the fifty best NBA players of all time, the latter to be acknowledged as one of the two or three best power forwards in the league. They were both athletic and both late bloomers. Of the two, Grant was more of a sleeper by the time of the predraft tournaments, for Pippen was attracting attention with his remarkable body and his uniquely long arms, and his stock began to rise quickly. Central Arkansas, a predominantly white school, was not exactly a basketball power, not a place to which basketball scouts made annual pilgrimages. In a day of ever more sophisticated scouting, in which scouts seem able to identify from the onset of puberty which young American males would end up as professional athletes ten years later, Scottie Pippen was the player who showed that even in the new industrialization of American sports there is room for a surprise. He had been a decent high school player in Hamburg, a small town in Arkansas, if hardly the best player on the team. He had not been that tall, about six foot one, and *very* skinny at that. He had good court vision, his high school coach Donald Wayne thought, but slow feet (a fact that would surprise his NBA opponents to hear), largely because his feet had grown early on and his body had not yet grown into his feet. In high school, he gave so few signs of the athletic ability to come that none of the surrounding colleges, all of them Division II and III, showed any interest in recruiting him, despite the efforts of his coach. A number of assistant coaches came over to look at him, but none of them was impressed.

Finally, more as a favor to a good kid than as the early touting of any great athlete-to-be, Donald Wayne called his old college coach, Don Dyer, who now coached at Central Arkansas in Conway. Wayne asked that Dyer give Pippen a chance—he thought Pippen was a good person, if not that great a basketball player, and he believed fervently that every good kid with a good work ethic should, if at all possible, get one shot at college, one real chance at beating the pervasive rural poverty of the region. Would Dyer do a favor for him? Could he offer this kid a scholarship? He couldn't guarantee anything; it was quite possible that Pippen might not be college athletic material. What Wayne wanted more than anything else was to open one more door in Scottie Pippen's life; he thought there was nothing so enriching for a young person as a chance at college—you got that chance and at least then you were free to make as much of it as you wanted to. Dyer liked Wayne and decided to take a chance; he did it thinking not so much that he was getting a great player as that he was doing the right thing for a young man he had once coached. He had no scholarships at the time, so Pippen arrived on a Pell Grant, a federal program for needy kids, and served as team manager at first. But soon two of Dyer's scholarship players dropped out, and Pippen got one of their scholarships.

Dyer remembered him as weighing about 140 pounds, but Arch Jones, Dyer's assistant and eventual successor, thought it was more like 130. But there was some talent there, Dyer thought. He had a decent freshman year, playing more and more until by the end of the year he was starting. He had a good sense of the game, in part because he had played point guard in high school and had learned to see the whole court. In addition, he was beginning to grow—to six three as a sophomore, six six as a junior, perhaps six seven as a senior. In his sophomore year, he lost half the season because his academic work slipped, taking with it his eligibility. But they had the beginning of a very good team, Dyer thought, built largely around Pippen. Suddenly, it was clear that he was the best player they had had in years. His body filled out, he got up to around 195 pounds, but he was still very quick, and he saw the court well. Dyer played him at three different positions: both backcourt spots and small forward. That served Pippen well when he reached the pros, because while his size dictated that he play small forward, he had spent so much of his time in college handling the ball that his talents were unusually varied. He was still growing as a senior, and he might, Dyer decided, play professionally. It was hard to tell just how good he was going to be when the competition was Arkansas Tech, Ouachita

State, and Henderson State, but there were moments when he seemed better than anyone in the league, when he did things that Dyer and Jones had seen only professional players do.

When Scottie Pippen first arrived at college, seventeen years old, he wrote in an essay for a physical-education class that when he grew up he wanted to be an NBA player. At that point, when he was so skinny, it seemed the most unlikely of dreams. But then by his junior year it was clear that he was the best player on the team, and possibly the conference, and as far as his coaches could see there was no real ceiling on his talent. His coaches thought his athleticism could place him at the NBA level, but they had no real way of measuring it. Both coaches talked to him about his dream, telling him that they thought it was viable, if he kept working harder. If they were doing a drill that came more easily to Pippen than to the other players and he wasn't putting out that much, Jones pushed him. "That's going to cost you," he would say, and by that he meant, That's going to cost you a place in the NBA. That was his refrain: *It's going to cost you.*

Dyer and Jones started a two-pronged campaign to give him a shot at the pros. Dyer knew Bob Bass, who worked for San Antonio in those days, and he got in touch with him about Pippen, and he also wrote the Dallas Mavericks organization. He heard back from neither. At the same time, Jones, stunned by his own brazenness as a small-time coach, picked up the phone one day and called Marty Blake, who was the head of scouting for the NBA. "Marty, you don't know me or my conference," he began, "but I've got a kid down here who's a right good player and I think can play in the NBA." The conference, the Arkansas Intercollegiate Conference (AIC), was small, but Blake, a lifer's lifer who had scouted the backwoods in the fifties, knew it well. Jones described Pippen's athleticism, and he mentioned those exceptionally long arms and the ability to play several positions. Blake took him seriously and said he would send a scout. That began the process of discovery, and in time a series of scouts found their way to the region.

Jerry Krause in turn first heard about Pippen from Marty Blake, who called Krause to tip him that there was going to be a game in Arkansas in which Pippen was going to play, that there might be some other scouts there, and that Krause should pay attention, for Pippen appeared to be an exceptional athlete. The two things he mentioned were Pippen's quickness and his uncommonly long arms. Krause thereupon sent Billy McKinney to see Pippen, but McKinney was new at scouting and had not seen a lot of Division II games, so he found it hard to calibrate what he saw. The next day, Krause asked McKinney what he thought and McKinney said he didn't really know. What do you mean you don't know? Krause asked. Well, he's a good athlete and he has got these really long arms, but the level of play is terrible, like Friday night at the Y.

(The role of McKinney in the drafting of Pippen eventually became something of a sore point between him and Krause. At one point after McKinney left the Bulls, Krause decided that he was taking too much credit for it, and the two men, who had once been relatively close, stopped talking to each other. The friendship was later repaired, only to be fractured again when McKinney, by then working for the Seattle SuperSonics, said in his curriculum vitae that he had done the original scouting of Pippen, and Krause demanded that he take it out.)

They called Pippen's coach and asked for tapes, but the tapes were inconclusive. When Krause and McKinney went to the Portsmouth tournament, the first of the showcases for players wanting to be drafted, and Krause saw a skinny young player come out on the floor, he tapped McKinney and said, "That's got to be Pippen." How do you know? McKinney asked. "Those are the longest arms I've ever seen," he answered. Krause thought of that as one of those rare electric moments in the life of a scout when he is absolutely sure that he has seen the flash of future greatness. He thought to himself, *Oh my God, that's really something different and special*. He had experienced that feeling only on rare occasions in the past: when as a baseball scout he had first seen the young Kirk Gibson, and when as a basketball scout he had first seen Earl Monroe. One of the things really talented scouts can do is take a young player and project what he will become, look at someone still growing into his body and envision what the maturation process—aided by professional trainers—will do.

It was all there, Krause thought, a slim but powerful body, and stunning natural grace and fluidity. Pippen was not yet a good shooter, but he had great hands with exceptionally long fingers, and that was to help greatly as he worked to improve his shot because it allowed him to control the ball easily. Looking at Pippen, Krause had a sense that this was a player who, not unlike Michael Jordan, could play three positions in the NBA: small forward, off guard, or, if necessary, point guard. He had enough athletic ability—quickness and strength and instinct—to become a good defender. The Bulls were already ahead of most professional basketball teams in having their own weight and strength program, run by Al Vermeil, the brother of football coach Dick Vermeil.

Pippen played very well at Portsmouth, and the secret was now out. "Coach," he told Arch Jones when he got back to Conway, "I think I really did well—they want me to go to the next tryout in Hawaii." Now, if there was a problem with Pippen as far as Krause was concerned it was that others were getting in on the secret. Pippen's stock was beginning to rise and rise quickly; in fact, in recent NBA history few players have risen so quickly in the postseason play to make their way into the top level of the first round as Pippen did. That was the ultimate nightmare for the Sleuth: His sleeper was playing himself into the first round and, worse, now seemed to be edging his way up toward becoming a lottery pick. But then, in the modern age of basketball no one of great talent or great potential talent stayed a sleeper very long. In Hawaii, Pippen's play was even more impressive, and his stock rose accordingly. And there was still the Chicago Combine ahead, which was an important showcase for players who were trying to play themselves into the late first and early second rounds.

Neither Jimmy Sexton nor Kyle Rote, Jr., Pippen's new agents, particularly wanted him to play in the Chicago Combine. They sensed Krause's hunger for him, as well as that of a number of other general managers—indeed, Krause was talking about Pippen as a potential future superstar—and if he went to the Combine, he might only hurt himself by playing poorly. An affirming cautionary voice was added to theirs, that of Krause, who was nervous about the growing interest in Pippen. Why, Krause himself was willing to pay for a vacation in Hawaii during the Chicago Combine week just to keep Pippen hidden. The only person who disagreed with the idea was Pippen himself, who was enjoying the competition and thrilled to find that after playing in such a limited field—he had never, unlike any of the players from the bigger programs, taken an airplane to a game before—he was not only as good as so many players with big reputations but in fact better and could shut them down. He was eager to go to Chicago and show that it was not a fluke. He went, and he played even better than he had in Hawaii; he was quite possibly the best player there. (Don Dyer came up for the Chicago audition, and he ran into Bob Bass of San Antonio. Bass looked at Dyer and said, "Well, you tried to tell me about him, didn't you?")

Jerry Krause was becoming more and more nervous: He had a diamond, but it was less and less in the rough. Now he wanted Sexton and Rote to limit Pippen's personal auditions for different teams. This was a year after Len Bias had been drafted second in the nation by the Celtics and then died of a drug overdose immediately afterward, and most teams were insistent about working players out and getting a sense of who they were. Krause pleaded with Sexton and Rote not to take Pippen to places, like New Jersey and Cleveland, that had very high draft positions.

Pippen was also becoming uneasy about this part of the process, flying into different cities, meeting these strange, powerful owners and general managers, trying to answer their questions and be the person they wanted him to be, whatever that was. He asked Sexton to accompany him on the trips, which was a little unusual. They had already visited Indiana and Phoenix, with New Jersey and Cleveland still ahead, when he came to Chicago to meet with Krause and Doug Collins. Collins was young and impassioned and charismatic, and he made a great pitch to Pippen: He saw him playing on the same team and in the same backcourt with *Michael Jordan for a decade!* He saw a brilliant future for a young team, not just one but several championships down the road. He did not use the word dynasty, but that was the vision. Pippen loved the idea: He liked Chicago, he liked Collins, and the idea of playing with Michael Jordan was very seductive. He told Sexton afterward that he wanted to end the traveling show and not visit any more cities: If he could, he wanted to play in Chicago.

In Chicago, Pippen underwent a workout with the coaches, and they also checked him out with Al Vermeil. Krause could tell immediately that Vermeil saw what he himself had seen. From the start Vermeil saw in him an exceptional fluidity. That meant he had an unusually efficient body, Vermeil told Krause: he's so elastic that he doesn't appear to be expending as much energy as many other players when he runs—he doesn't have to push off the floor when he's running. The more they saw in their workouts, the more impressed they became. One test the Bulls used was called a side-to-side drill. The coaches placed basketballs in different positions around the foul circle, and the player must dunk as many balls as he can in thirty seconds. It was, among other things, a test of both forward and lateral speed. Within the Bulls camp, it was known as a killer drill. Pippen broke the record: He dunked fifteen times. In another drill, Pippen was asked to jump four times in a row, and a computer helped calibrate how high Pippen jumped and how short a time he spent on the ground between jumps. Again, his performance was exceptional. At the time, he carried about two hundred pounds on a six-foot-seven frame, and Vermeil was sure that he could add twenty to twenty-five pounds without slowing down.

The question now arose whether the Bulls, picking eighth, would have a shot at him. Sacramento was interested in him, it appeared, and had the sixth pick. But Seattle was not interested in Pippen; it wanted a big man, and it had the fifth and ninth picks. At the last minute, Krause worked out a switch, getting Seattle's fifth and giving them in return a second-round draft choice and an exhibition game in the fall, which meant that they could draw a big crowd because of the presence of Michael Jordan. In a few weeks, Scottie Pippen went from a middle-round draft pick to number five in the nation.

Horace Grant was even more of a sleeper than Scottie Pippen. It was Johnny Bach, the talented assistant coach, who first picked up on him, more by chance than anything else. All the coaches were assigned film to study and were supposed to check out certain college players. Bach was studying a player named Joe Wolf, a six-foot-eleven player on a good Carolina team who might be the badly needed center they still hoped for. Johnny Bach did not like Joe Wolf's game. He saw a good but limited college player propped up by an unusually strong system. He would probably be a journeyman in the NBA. What you saw in college might be all you got, he thought, and in fact it might be less than what you got. Wolf did not seem that quick, and Bach, who had coached at different levels for four decades, did not like the way he ran the court. "I looked at him and the way he ran, a heavy run which was hard on the body, and I thought I saw a bad back coming up somewhere in his career," he said.

But in the process he watched one of Wolf's games against Clemson, and he became intrigued by the Clemson big man who was going against him, Horace Grant. Grant was not as big, not as heavy, but he was lithe and strong, and he was very quick. He ran the floor exceptionally well for someone his size. He had an instinct for rebounding, and he hit the boards very hard at both ends of the court. He had not been particularly well coached, Bach thought, nowhere nearly as well as Wolf, but he had a bigger upside, Bach believed. He was still skinny, but he had very wide shoulders, which meant that his body was likely to fill out—he would not be another Brad Sellers. Bach asked for more Clemson film, and the more he saw, the more he decided that Grant was the player they wanted. The other coaches looked at the film and agreed. Soon it was unanimous among them. Given that they had Jordan and were about to add Pippen, the coaches thought that a big man with Grant's quickness was a far better piece than Wolf for the team they were in the process of creating. When Horace Grant came in for a workout, Al Vermeil was very impressed. At that time, Grant probably weighed around 215, but Vermeil thought it would be fairly easy, given the width of his shoulders, to get him to 230 or 235 without any loss of speed.

Though Grant's performance in some of the drills was not quite so startling as that of Pippen, in athletic terms he was very nearly off the charts for a man his size. He ran the twenty-meter test in 2.98 seconds, which was very good for a big man. (A few years later, after constant workouts, he not only was bigger and stronger, he was quicker, and he did the twenty-meter run in 2.85). All in all, it was a magnificent workout: Grant was quicker than they had thought, and a better shooter as well.

As draft day arrived, the person having the most trouble making up his mind was the person whose job was on the line as much as anyone else's, Jerry Krause. He seemed at one point to have signed on for Grant, but then at the end he seemed to be wavering again. Dean Smith was pushing Joe Wolf hard, and Krause knew that Michael Jordan badly wanted him as well. Collins thought it was the shadow of Brad Sellers that now weighed on Krause, that Sellers had come in as a big man and played small and was a big disappointment. Krause had taken a good deal of abuse about that, particularly from Jordan. Now here was Grant, whose body was not yet built up. Might he not be another Sellers? They could not afford another wasted high pick on a big man. When you had a superstar like Michael Jordan, you had only a limited window in which to surround him with the right players, and Jordan's own greatness meant that they were slipping farther down in the draft every year.

If there was one person critical in the selling of Grant to Krause, it was probably Tex Winter, who was closer to Krause than anyone else on the coaching staff. Winter never got caught up in any of the endless, pyrrhic factional splits within the Bulls management, and his opinions epitomized a kind of basketball purity. On draft day, as it was time for the second of the Bulls' two picks, Krause seemed to be tilting toward Wolf. "Jerry," Winter said—he was probably the only person who could have done this without seeming to be disloyal—"the whole coaching staff wants Grant. We're unanimous. How can you still go with Wolf?" Krause came around, and they made Grant their choice.

Michael Jordan took a wary view of the entire draft. There were two Carolina players out there whom he would have preferred, Wolf as the big man, and Kenny Smith as the guard. (Smith was taken with the next pick after Pippen and went on to have a very good professional career.) Everyone else in the Bulls organization was ecstatic. Doug Collins told Jordan the next day, "Michael, I'm not someone to be overly excited about young players coming out of college, but I think these two guys could really be something."

Jordan gave Collins a very cool look, as if to say, Well, yes, he had heard all this before. "We'll see," he said. He was a good deal harder with Krause. When Krause told Jordan that he was going to love playing with Scottie Pippen, he could feel his star's doubts. "Well," said Jordan, clearly unconvinced, "you're the one who brought Brad Sellers in here, too."

If the pieces were in place, it was still going to take time. Both players were young and unfinished products. Neither was prepared for the rigors and discipline of the NBA; they were both country boys in a big city, young and suddenly wealthy, enjoying all the pleasures of their new world, the pleasures of their money and their fame and their liberation from the small-town South. In those days, they hung around a good deal with a player named Sedale Threatt, who seemed to have one of those amazing constitutions that allowed him to party all night and to show up fresh and eager the next morning. Pippen and Grant, young and impressionable, did not seem to be quite so well blessed. So Krause soon traded Threatt to Seattle, virtually giving him away in order to protect his younger players.

The coaches sensed that they had most of the pieces for a team destined for glory, but they also knew that it was going to be a difficult process. The Bulls were in the same conference not just with Boston, which was beginning to show some signs of decline, but with Detroit, which was ascending, had had several good drafts in a row, and seemed to have a particular hold over the Bulls' psyches.

Pippen and Grant's first year—1987–1988—was the first real year of the new order. For the first time, almost all the pieces seemed to be in place, and the deadwood from another time had been effectively cleared out. Doug Collins, in his second season, was an exciting coach. He was also young, thirty-six that summer, his youth balanced by his veteran assistants Tex Winter and Johnny Bach. Winter was a coach's coach, a great purist, who some people thought enjoyed practices more than games because there was a purity to practice that games often lacked, and because he simply loved the pleasure of teaching young players. Other professionals in the league like Portland's Bucky Buckwalter were impressed by what Krause had done in taking a young and enthusiastic coach like Collins, whose own connection with the game was so recent and who knew the pressure that the modern players worked under, and buffering him with Winter and Bach. It was also the season that Phil Jackson came in as an assistant coach.

It was an exciting time. Charles Oakley was blossoming as a power forward. John Paxson was emerging as a talented partner to Jordan, the man who could hit a key shot if Jordan was doubled. But there was a long way to go. Scottie Pippen might have been the hardest-working player in Conway, Arkansas, but by the far more rigorous standards that Michael Jordan brought to practice every single day, his work ethic seemed lax. Grant was a better practice player, but his work was cut out for him because from day one he was challenging Charles Oakley for the forward position.

Jordan was still, pound for pound, the toughest player on the team, and no one messed with him. Once, during the 1989 preseason camp, a would-be rookie named Matt Brust tried to challenge Jordan. Brust was a big, tough kid from Saint John's, about six foot five and 220 pounds, a physical player. He had been throwing his weight around in camp for several days, trying to make an impression, if not with his talent then with his physicality. On one play, Jordan drove to the basket, and Brust gave him a hard body shot and knocked him down. Jordan picked himself up without a word, without even glaring at Brust. But a few plays later, he drove on Brust; he had the ball in his right hand, and Brust was coming at him from the right. At the last second, Michael switched the ball to his left hand and gave Brust a ferocious shot to the head with his right elbow, knocking the man unconscious. Brust just lay there for a few minutes, his training camp over.

Though the Bulls still had a long way to go, there were occasional glimpses of the future. One was a preseason exhibition game against the Lakers. The previous year the Lakers had killed the Bulls in an exhibition game at Chapel Hill, but this game was close. Even more interesting, Pippen did a good job defending James Worthy.

Doug Collins worked feverishly with both Pippen and Grant. He pushed them hard every day to improve their games and to accept what life in the NBA was like, that winning in this league demanded a level of professionalism and commitment that they were not even near yet. Sometimes it seemed as if he were on them all the time, his voice always at an intense pitch, driving them constantly, making them work harder, pushing them to grow up, both on and off the court. They had to learn that if they were on a commercial airline flight and the hostess said for them to fasten their seat belts, they'd better fasten their seat belts, and they'd better not joke around with her. They had to learn to play every day with pain, not an easy lesson. Once, on the eve of an important game, Grant seemed to be favoring a headache, and Michael Jordan said to him—his voice just loud enough for others in the locker room to hear—that perhaps he should take an Excedrin. Once, in a game against Denver, at the time a tough team, Pippen seemed to be favoring a hurt hand, and Collins pushed him to play. Pippen was wary. Well, what if late in the game you don't have to handle the ball and all you do is play defense against Alex English? Collins asked. Pippen ultimately declined to play, but Collins made it clear to him that he thought his excuse was inadequate and that he was letting both coach and team down.

Collins himself was the product of a poor background, and he had pushed himself hard to be an NBA star. What had always driven him, as much as his pure talent, was a passion for the game. At Illinois State, he had been coached by a man named Will Robinson, who knew how vulnerable his thin, undermuscled protégé was, and had pushed him to find the physical strength that would go with his pure talent and allow him to stick in the league. Robinson made Collins take boxing lessons each day before practice. There was a reason for it, he said. "I think you're going to make it in the NBA, and when you do, there are going to be people who are going to want what you have. A lot of them will be bigger and stronger. So they're going to come after you, and they're going to fight you. And if you don't fight back, they're going to reach inside your chest and take your heart out, and when they take your heart, they're going to take your jump shot as well."

That toughness was what Collins was trying to pass on, and he seemed to succeed. The team's improvement was obvious. They won fifty games that year, but it was in practice where the sense of the team's improvement was most palpable. "The first sign of the team which was to come," Collins later said, "was in the practices in that first and second year." They were phenomenal, Oakley going against Grant, Jordan against Pippen. The former was more like a war, because there was likely to be only one winner, and the latter more like a tutorial, for Jordan had a vested interest in Pippen's success as Oakley did not in Grant's. If Pippen improved in these workouts, then Jordan would have a high-quality teammate; if Grant reached his potential, Oakley might be out of a job with the Bulls. Oakley was bigger and stronger, with an utterly admirable work ethic, and Grant was self-evidently quicker and more athletic, with a better shot. Oakley's great strength, however, was his willingness to pound anyone in his way, whether in practice or in a game. After the fourth day of preseason practice in Grant's rookie year, Horace went into the weight room for a long talk with Vermeil and asked him to create a complete weight and strength regimen for him. He knew from the beating he was taking in practice that he would not be able to fulfill his promise unless he built himself up. "I've just got to get stronger," he told Vermeil.

The Jordan-Pippen relationship was quite different, more like teacher-student. Jordan could see Pippen's raw talent, and he knew Pippen lacked all the advantages that he had enjoyed because of the richness of the Carolina program. He set out not only to work with Pippen on the most elemental drills but to teach him the sort of toughness the NBA demanded. (There *was*, though, one move Pippen could make that Jordan could not: If they both stood out of bounds under the basket holding the ball and leaped out on the court, Pippen, without ever touching the ground, could slam the ball through with his left hand, and Jordan could not. Johnny Bach thought it might be that Pippen's hands were slightly larger.)

The more Jordan sensed that Pippen was becoming serious, the more he was willing to invest in him. That took some time, because for a long time Jordan was not entirely sure of Pippen's toughness, nor of his heart, nor of the totality of his and Grant's commitment. They were teammates, bonded by their talents but not really friends, the social gap between them still very large. Jordan was innately confident in all aspects of his life, as confident off the floor as he was on it; Pippen was very tentative in so many ways, the stamp of Arkansas poverty still deep on him.

Ever so slowly, the two came around to each other: Jordan just a little wary about committing himself to a player he was still unsure of, and Pippen gradually accepting Jordan as, if not teacher, then certainly role model. More and more frequently, Collins saw the two of them together after practice, working on their jump shots, or Jordan working with Pippen on the most elemental of moves, such as how to break the double-team or how to swing either way when pressed by the defense along the baseline. Years later, after watching Pippen's game improve incrementally year after year, even after the championship years, Collins realized that in some ways Michael Jordan, working with a player who had a degree of hunger and talent that none of them fully appreciated, had virtually cloned himself. The player who came out on the floor alongside Jordan later in their careers might as well have been a product of Dean Smith's Carolina program.

If anything made his job easier in those first two years, Collins thought, it was Jordan's very presence at practice, his daily example as the hardest-working player on the team, and his unwillingness to let his teammates coast through their drills. That made him a coach's dream, because not only was he setting an example, the voice the others were hearing was often his instead of Collins's. Collins knew he was an emotional coach, and he was aware of the danger of overcoaching young players—that if he did nothing but correct them all day he would sooner rather than later lose his authority, and they would tune out. The fact that so much of the coaching was being done almost unconsciously by the team's best player allowed him to concentrate on one or two major things at each practice.

After practice every day, Collins worked for about twenty-five minutes on Jordan's jump shot, and then after that on Pippen's. Then the guards would go down to one end of the court and compete in one-on-one games. It was fierce, Jordan, Pippen, and Paxson always going at each other, always shooting against each other for money. Jordan loved it. For Pippen it was an eye-opener—he had never been in a world where the competition was so rough, and some of it was beginning to rub off on him.

Jordan liked to bet on everything, and he loved the one-on-one games with his teammates, betting on each game of Horse. The Pigeon Club, he called their shoot-outs. After practice, he put his hands over his mouth and cooed, the sign that his pigeons were to show up, go against him, and almost surely lose their money to him. It was small money usually, one hundred dollars at best when it was done each day, but it added zest to the practices.

One practice, Jordan was slightly hurt and did not work out, but he watched the practice from one of the coaches' offices, including the one-on-one betting at the end of the practice. On that particular day, Horace Grant, who was a surprisingly good pure shooter, was nailing everyone. He was in a zone: First, he zapped the shooting guards, then he inhaled Pippen. Jordan sat there in the office with an amused smile on his face, watching Grant become more and more inflated. Just at the end, when Grant beat Pippen and was puffed to the maximum degree, Jordan strolled out on the court and, as innocently as possible, asked Grant if he wanted to play a game of Horse. He had been waiting like a cobra coiled to strike at a rabbit. He suggested a winner-take-all game, and, of course, Grant, sure that he was on a roll, took the bet. Even hurt, Jordan promptly cleaned him out.

Michael Jordan still wanted and needed to win at everything. In those days, when they still traveled on commercial planes, they sometimes spent their idle time in airport game rooms playing Pac-Man. For a time, Dave Corzine, who always carried a large roll of quarters with him, was considered the Pac-Man champion. In time, however, Jordan got a Pac-Man game at home and practiced diligently, bringing his game up until he could beat Corzine.

Early on in his Chicago years, Jordan bought a Ping-Pong table and placed it in the recreation room of his apartment. He was not a good Ping-Pong player at first, and it enraged him that he always lost to Howard White, the Nike ambassador and his close friend. Charles Oakley was a good Ping-Pong player too, and it infuriated Jordan that both men could beat him on his home court. White was amused watching Oakley and Jordan, these two immense men, playing Ping-Pong in so small a room with so low a ceiling—the room seemed filled with competitive energy. If you beat Jordan at Ping-Pong, White learned, then you had to play again—and again—until finally he won.

Richard Dent, the star defensive lineman of the Chicago Bears, became a close friend, and of course Jordan had to compete with him. Dent liked to ride a bike, and Jordan heard him say casually one day that he had just ridden thirty miles. A few weeks later, when Jordan arrived in Hawaii after a trip to Japan, he got up after about two hours of sleep, called Howard White, and said he wanted to go bike riding. How far do you want to ride? asked White. Thirty miles, Jordan answered. My God, thought White, he's going to be riding against me *and* Richard Dent.

The sport that frustrated him the most was tennis. By all rights, given his speed, reflexes, and power, he should have been a good tennis player, but perhaps because he took it up later than most, the sport seemed to elude him. Howard White, even though he had bad knees, consistently beat him and ran him all over the court. Golf, not tennis, was to become Jordan's main game.

Once, when the Bulls were still flying commercial, they arrived in Portland for a game with the Trail Blazers. As sometimes happened, the baggage men came on the plane after it had pulled into the terminal because they knew Jordan was aboard and they wanted to meet him, shake his hand, and perhaps get his autograph. On this particular occasion, Mark Pfeil, the trainer, saw Michael reach in his pocket and pull out a fifty-dollar bill and give it to one of the baggage handlers. "Michael," Pfeil said, "there's no need to do that. That's my job—I'm the one who takes care of the tips."

"Mark, just watch this," Jordan said. So Pfeil made his way to the baggage conveyor, and there he found his team gathered around the mouth of it. He watched as Michael Jordan reached in his pocket and pulled out a hundred-dollar bill and put it down on the conveyor belt. Soon, the other players were putting their hundred-dollar bills alongside it. The bet was on whose baggage would come out first, and of course it was Jordan's. Jordan made about $900 on the bet, and he had a huge grin on his face when it was over. "Not a bad return on a fifty-dollar investment," he told Pfeil.

He did not just need to win, he *had* to win. When Johnny Bach had the B team in practice, Jordan would ask Bach what he was going to do against him on defense. Bach would mention one of the bench players and say that he was going to flat shut Jordan down that day. Afterward, after he had of course had his way, Jordan would smile and say, "It didn't quite work out the way you planned, did it, Johnny?"

The one major dispute Jordan had with Doug Collins in those first two years came at a practice in Collins's second year. It was, of all things, over the score of an intrateam practice. The game was supposed to go to seven, and at one point Jordan said the score was 5–4 while Collins said it was 5–3. "You've got the wrong score!" Jordan said, very angrily. The argument became incredibly heated, and the entire gym suddenly got very quiet except for these two men, a young coach engaged in a shouting match with his most talented superstar, a player who never challenged his coaches.

"Would you have said that to Dean Smith?" Collins asked at one point, and Jordan said no. That was a shot close to the heart, and if anything it might have made him angrier.

Suddenly, he started walking off the court. "I'm leaving," he said.

"Michael, we're not through for the day yet," Collins said. "I'm out of here," Jordan said. Tim Hallam, the press officer, was there and he watched Michael Jordan, the hardest-working practice player any of them had ever seen, pick up his practice bag and stomp out of the gym.

"Michael, you can't just walk out of here," Hallam said.

"You damn well better watch me," Jordan answered, and he was gone.

Nothing was said about it, and Jordan came back the next day. In effect, Collins decided to let it pass, which was probably the best thing to do. But about two days later, he was talking with the beat reporters after practice and one of them asked him if he had talked to Jordan yet. "No," he answered, "but I know Michael loves me." Even as he said it, he saw Jordan coming through the locker-room door. "Michael," he said, "would you give me a kiss just to show everyone here how much you love me?" Jordan leaned over and gave Collins a light kiss, and the incident was done with.

The Bulls were now in mid-flight, making the transition from an expansionlike team that better teams could feast on—a team with one great player whom you could let have his forty or fifty points and still beat—to a team that would win roughly half its games, to finally, in this first year of Pippen and Grant, a team that won fifty games, the benchmark for the NBA's better teams. It was young, and it was talented. It still lacked a big man, but in Jordan, Pippen, and Grant, basketball people saw three of the best young players around. Besides, in cleaning house Krause had stored up a lot of draft choices, and there was reason to think the Bulls would soon draft even more good players.

But as the team got better, Krause was showing signs of needing greater recognition. He was beginning to talk more and more about the importance of the organization. Organizations, not just players and coaches, win championships, he began to say, and this became something of a theme of his. For someone who headed a sports team that starred Michael Jordan, it was an odd theme indeed—the organization was far more important in baseball and football than it was in basketball, where the number of players was so small and where colleges served as the minor leagues. This theme grated on Jordan, and in time it began to grate on David Falk as well. Among other things, it meant that Jerry

Krause believed that he was as important to the success of the Bulls as Michael Jordan was, not the wisest of beliefs. There were signs that this attitude, which downgraded the importance of the players, would be reflected in future negotiations.

In 1988, David Falk, Jerry Reinsdorf, and Jerry Krause began to work on Michael Jordan's second contract. Jordan might be the best player in the game, and he might have made the Bulls organization immensely rich, but the negotiations were maddeningly slow, even though Falk and Reinsdorf got on quite well. Because two of the three men in these negotiations were named Jerry, Krause was called Jake. Again and again, Falk pointed out what Jordan had done for the Bulls, the vast jump in season-ticket holders, the increases in the prices of everything—tickets, concessions, parking—the handsome radio and television contracts the Bulls now enjoyed. The Bulls were making around $40 million more a year because of Jordan, Falk argued. So why was the ownership hesitating to give him the $4 million that Falk and Jordan were asking? (At the time, the optimum big salary, in terms of length and size, was believed to be Magic Johnson's ten-year, $25 million deal, which Jerry Buss had come up with to replace the earlier long-term deal of $1 million a year for twenty-five years.) "Look what he's done for you!" Falk kept saying.

Then Krause jumped in and said, "Look David, we admit that Michael is a very good basketball player. But how much credit do you give the organization? How much credit do you give us for the fact that this year we had six more women taking orders for season tickets? For the fact that more people are working in the office right now typing up orders? For the fact that Doug Collins is up until midnight every night going over film and working on new plays? For the fact that right now Billy McKinney is probably on a plane going to Alaska or Hawaii looking for new talent?"

"Jake, you want to know how much credit I give you? Zero credit. Now what else do you want to talk about?" Falk said.

Krause started to argue, but Reinsdorf stopped him. "Just shut up," he said. "Look," Reinsdorf said, "I admit he's the greatest ticket seller in the history of sports, but I'm not going to pay him $4 million a year. I'm just not going to do it."

Reinsdorf did offer $3 million, however, and they finally settled on a long-term contract, then the best in the league: eight years for $26 million, an average of $3.25 million a year. As Falk liked to point out, this meant that his client was making about 30 percent more in salary than Magic Johnson. But when it came time for the announcement, Krause seemed to want to win—they would make the announcement and say that it was for eight years (the length showed that the Bulls had done well in the negotiations, tying up Jordan for a long time) but not give out the figure. Might the size of it show that the Bulls had lost in the negotiations? Again Falk argued with Krause and Reinsdorf: It was unfair, he said, to make an announcement saying that Jordan was locked up for what might be the rest of his career without saying that he was then the best-paid player in the league. Finally, Reinsdorf had intervened again. "Jake, David's right—pick A or B."

Falk thought that the press conference would be a historic occasion, that Reinsdorf would say that he had signed up the best player in the league for what might well be the rest of his career. But instead, Krause had got up and said that they had an announcement to make, that they had signed one of their very best players, Michael Jordan, for a very long contract. My God, thought Falk, they're blowing it—they could be announcing the signing of a bench player. When Krause asked if there were any questions, one of the reporters asked, Jerry, why did you decide to sign Michael for eight years? You must not have been listening, Krause said, I didn't say anything about eight years. Yes, answered the reporter, but the release you put out did. The whole press conference set the tone for the future: The better the team did, the more difficult all future negotiations would be.

18.

Detroit, the 1980s

THE PROBLEM FOR the Bulls was that there was another team that had come together just a little earlier and was itself challenging the hegemony of the vaunted Celtics of Bird, McHale, and Parish. That was the Detroit Pistons, led by Isiah Thomas, Bill Laimbeer, and Adrian Dantley. The Pistons were a very tough and physical team (in time they were given the nickname "The Bad Boys," which made some of the NBA's executives more than a little uneasy), and they played an extremely aggressive game that seemed to challenge the very nature of how the game was refereed. "Detroit was our albatross," Bulls assistant coach Johnny Bach once said. Until they beat the Pistons, the Bulls could forget about going to the Finals.

The Pistons had come together just a few years ahead of the Bulls, put together with great skill by their joint architects, Jack McCloskey, the general manager, and his close friend Chuck Daly, the coach. As the Bulls began to elevate the level of their game, they found that the Pistons had arrived a bit ahead of them and were a bit more cohesive, a little deeper, a little more physical, and a little more determined and focused in their play. Though in 1987–1988 the Bulls added two exceptional players to a weak nucleus, it was the year after the Pistons added John Salley and Dennis Rodman to a strong nucleus. The shadow cast over Chicago Stadium as the Bulls began to get better was not that of Larry Bird and the Celtics or of Magic Johnson and the Lakers but of Isiah Thomas and the Pistons.

The Pistons' rise began in 1981, when with the number-two pick in the country they drafted Isiah Thomas out of Indiana. He was small—listed as six foot one and possibly even shorter—immensely talented, smart, and absolutely fearless. If he had been six foot six, the team's PR man Matt Dobek said, he would have been Michael Jordan. Dallas had the first pick in that draft, but Thomas deliberately tried to alienate the Dallas management during a predraft visit, saying that he did not particularly want to play there; in his immortal words, he was not into "that cowboy shit." His ploy worked well, and the Mavericks' management, thus rebuffed, took Mark Aguirre instead. If Thomas had not scared off the Dallas management, and if the Pistons had drafted Aguirre instead—a talented but not an overwhelming player—the Pistons never would have risen to the top.

Thomas tried to talk the Detroit management out of drafting him as well, but Jack McCloskey had scouted him far too carefully. He was the kind of point guard that you could build a team around, McCloskey thought. "But I don't want to play here," he had told McCloskey at their first meeting. "I want to play in Chicago."

"Well, Isiah," McCloskey had answered, "that doesn't matter because we're going to draft you, and you're going to play here."

"But who do you have for me to pass the ball to?" he had asked.

"I'll find them for you, Isiah," McCloskey promised.

They had a very good sense of how good he was going to be, the rare small player who, because of his intelligence, on-the-court leadership, and shooting ability would be able to control the tempo of almost every game. He was quick, facile, and charming, a gem culled from the very heart of the Chicago inner-city ghetto, a product of a neighborhood and family where all too many contemporaries fell into the world of drugs and where the chances of escaping to any kind of material success seemed minuscule. Perhaps because of the extremely difficult world he had left behind, he had a physical toughness to him that was unmatched for a player of his size. And there was his intelligence, which was blinding. "He's smarter than all the rest of us," Daly liked to say.

What they did not know about was his rage to succeed, his rare capacity for leadership, and finally the stunning impact of the force of his will as he applied it to those around him.

At his first press conference, he spoke about bringing the Pistons to the competitive level of the Celtics and Lakers, and a good number of people in the audience openly laughed at him. At his first day in practice as a Piston, he went up against Ronnie Lee, a very physical player known for the punishment he dished out to offensive stars. Lee put a body block on him right from the start, and then did it again and again until finally Thomas turned to him and said, "Do it one more time and we fight." That ended it. It would have been a great fight, thought Mc-Closkey, watching from the sidelines.

Thomas helped create the culture of the Pistons, though he was appalled when he was drafted by them. He came from one of the strongest basketball programs in America, Indiana University, coached by one of the most exacting coaches in the business, Bobby Knight, and he was accustomed to excellence and tradition and to meeting impossibly high standards or being tongue-lashed for his failure to do so. The Pistons by contrast had nothing: no identity, no tradition, no culture, and seemingly no purpose. He did not intend to let things continue that way, and starting in his rookie year he started going to the NBA Finals every year to study the teams that got there to see what it was that set them apart, the secret of what made them winners. Those secrets were hard to come by. Magic Johnson was perhaps his closest friend in the professional game, and he seemed to be in the playoffs every year, but when Isiah visited with him during the Finals, he said bluntly, "I'm not going to tell you what it is that allows you to win at this level, you're going to have to learn what it takes yourself."

What did it take to get to the playoffs? And what did it take to win there? He talked not only to basketball people but to football people such as Al Davis and Chuck Noll as well. He began to learn that there had to be a singularity of purpose, a common goal that everyone signed on to, an agreement that nothing mattered but winning. Players on the Celtics who had played elsewhere and who had reputations for caring only about personal statistics changed when they went to Boston and accepted the team concept. They, too, became players who sacrificed their personal stats for the team good, and played their roles, no matter how limited. Winning teams, he decided, always saw themselves as being apart, taking on the rest of the world. If they did not have enemies who were trying to take away what was rightfully theirs, then they invented enemies in order to help push themselves toward their goals.

For Thomas's first season, the Pistons picked up in one of those NBA trades that no one took very seriously a center from Cleveland named Bill Laimbeer, who seemed well on his way to becoming at the very best a backup player of modest value. No one thought it was a breakthrough trade, nor that Laimbeer was to be a critical part of the foundation for a championship team. He had played at Notre Dame as a collegian, and McCloskey had scouted him at the 1980 Olympic trials and thought him something of a joke, slow and awkward, with little feel or talent for the game. Then he went to Europe to refine his game. When he returned to the United States, he went to Cleveland where he was playing behind

James Edwards (who later became *his* backup); McCloskey, checking out the league, was surprised to see that Laimbeer had become a very different player. He could shoot, and even though, in the words of Chuck Daly, he never jumped more than two inches off the ground, he had become a surprisingly adept rebounder by dint of knowing how and where to position himself. He had his limits as a big man, but he was better than what the Pistons had. McCloskey and Daly agreed that a big man who could score and rebound, even if he was slow, was still something of a find. Quicker players could sometimes be used to protect him on defense. So Detroit made the trade.

What both McCloskey and Daly soon noticed about him was that he seemed to have little love for the game of basketball itself; indeed, Daly was never sure he even liked the game. He was a terrible practice player, and before games, when he was being taped, he often complained to Mike Abdenour, the trainer, about the degree of mental fatigue he was suffering from, as if he could not play one more game. He was the first person to leave the gym every day after every workout, almost never sticking around as most players did to work a little extra on their shooting.

But he also had a fierce competitive spirit, and if he did not like the game itself, he liked the competition of it. It sometimes seemed, Pistons assistant coach Dick Harter thought, as if he were on a quest all his own, to prove that he was not just another big, slow, disposable white center who could not cut it, but that he could play in this league at the highest level. He wanted to erase the stigma of having played in a lower tier of the world of professional basketball. Picking up Laimbeer was the second of a series of moves that in seven years was to make McCloskey look like a basketball architect of the first order, having found different pieces that by themselves seemed not only of limited value but oddly disparate, but that, when they were all added together, made an infinitely greater sum.

Laimbeer was not an easy person to deal with. He was a verbal bully off the court and something of a physical bully on it. He was deliberately rude to reporters in the Pistons' locker room, and when, before a game, the time allotted to journalists there was coming to an end, he did his own countdown, "Fifty seconds to go, media. . . . thirty seconds to go, media. . . . Get out, all media, get out." He was a dirty player, and he knew it; it was the only way, given his physical limitations, he could stay in the league. Sometimes he boasted of what he had done after a game—the cheap shots he had gotten away with and how it had caused a more gifted player, say, Parish or Abdul-Jabbar, to lose his cool. "It's a mental game, not a physical one," he would say. He was despised in most other arenas by opposing fans, and many opposing players actively disliked him, believing that he was quite willing to inflict career-ending injuries on them if it suited his purpose and that he would do it casually, out of what seemed like innate malice.

Nor did he make it easy on his own coaches and teammates. He often seemed unusually spoiled. He was willfully rude to the coaches, even to Daly, who was giving him his big chance, and in the constant byplay between coach and players he not only failed to be supportive of Daly but often seemed openly dissident. Daly could live with it: That was simply Laimbeer being Laimbeer. As for his teammates, he was often blunt and rude with them in the locker room, flaunting his conservative politics. If someone mentioned his lack of grace with them, he would say, "I don't plan on having any of these guys as my friends when I'm finished here." But if coaches and teammates were put off by his lack of grace and courtesy, they accepted him because he always played hard, and he was an unusually smart player on the court.

Laimbeer and Thomas roomed together during their first camp, and Thomas thought that Laimbeer could not have been more different from him: tall, white, upper middle class. His father was the head of a company, and therefore Laimbeer was said to be the rare NBA player who for a time did not make as much money as his father. He was a Republican and an atheist, whereas Thomas was ghetto-reared, black, a Democrat, and seriously religious. (His actual name was Isiah Lord Thomas III.) Somehow, they found common ground. What Thomas liked about Laimbeer was his passion: He was committed to his political ideas and committed to the idea of winning. He decided that they could be friends, should room together, and would form the backbone and create the new winning culture of the reinvented Pistons. One thing their synergy gave the Pistons, Dick Harter noted later, "was the power of two of the smartest players who ever played the game. What we had was not just mental toughness—that doesn't get you everything. What we had was mental toughness and a core of exceptionally high intelligence."

Bit by bit other pieces were added. The process often seemed excruciatingly slow to Thomas. Lacking talented teammates in his early years there, he had a tendency to take more shots than the coaches wanted (in his second year he took more than 1500 shots, almost 300 more than he would take in the Pistons' championship seasons). Daly pushed him to pass off more, but the problem for him, as it would be with Michael Jordan later at Chicago, was that he did not trust his teammates, and with good reason. On two occasions, Thomas became so frustrated with losing that he wanted to quit the game. Once the trainer, Mike Abdenour, called Daly to tell him he had better go and talk to Isiah, that Zeke was in his room, so depressed that he wanted to quit. "What are you going to do if you quit?" Daly asked Thomas. "Go back to college and get my degree in criminology," Thomas said. "Will you need a master's degree?" Daly asked. Thomas wasn't sure. "How much will it pay?" Daly asked. Again Thomas wasn't sure. But he was sure of one thing. "I can't stand losing anymore. I can't take any more games like this." Daly did not push it that evening, he simply told Isiah to think about it, and take a couple of days before he made up his mind, knowing that the very force that drove Thomas to this point of desperation, the passion to compete and win, would keep him in the game, that his disappointment and depression were the other side of the coin of love of the game and the need to excel.

The next important piece the Pistons added was Vinnie Johnson, a great pure shooting guard with a compact body who came in a trade with Seattle. He had been a relatively high first-round draft choice out of Baylor, but because the SuperSonics were at that time deep at guard, with Gus Williams, Dennis Johnson, and Fred Brown, he had not gotten as much playing time as he probably deserved. Besides, Seattle wanted a forward named Greg Kelser. So he came aboard, and he seemed to have the same passion as Thomas and Laimbeer for winning. That gave the Pistons a quick jump toward respectability, and they went from twenty-one wins to thirty-nine wins. Then for a time they seemed to level out. In the mid-eighties, they began to make the moves that cemented the team. The first and perhaps most critical was the drafting of Joe Dumars out of McNeese State. He was big, he could shoot, and he could play defense. If you were looking for a guard to play alongside Thomas, Dumars was everything you wanted, a good offensive and defensive player.

That year, the Pistons also grafted on an additional piece, Rick Mahorn, who made them overnight a much more physical and focused team. Mahorn was big and strong, and though not particularly talented, he was a player coaches loved to have because he was a very good teammate, smart and joyous and wise off the court, blessed with a great sense of laughter, and very good with all kinds of different players, particularly younger players to whom he tried to explain the complexity of life in the NBA. Having Rick Mahorn on your team meant that you had a healthier, happier team off the court. On the court, he was a widely feared enforcer. With Mahorn there to back him up, Laimbeer—already a talented rebounder but with a body that intimidated no one—seemed to blossom. A year later, Detroit traded Kelly Tripucka, a scorer whose defense was a problem, to Utah for Adrian Dantley, a player who was to play in six all-star games before his career was over. Dantley, relatively short to play forward, was strong and bulky and determined, one of the great low-post players in the game. If Dantley was not the perfect complement for a player as quick as Thomas, he nonetheless gave the Pistons additional firepower up front. Again and again, he took the ball and muscled his way to the basket, inevitably drawing fouls. Bob Ryan, the *Boston Globe* sportswriter, referred generically to a certain kind of box-score line as a Dantley: It was one in which the player scored, for example, thirty points on seven field goals and sixteen free throws. "The greatest Dantley of all time—it should be engraved on his tombstone," Ryan once said, "was 9-28-46, that is nine field goals, 28 free throws, for a total of 46 points." McCloskey loved Dantley's game because it got the other team in foul trouble early and allowed his teammates to set up on defense even as he was shooting free throws.

The next year, the Pistons put the last two critical pieces together for their championship run. Though they drafted in the middle of the pack, the 1986 draft was spectacularly deep. They picked up John Salley, a tall, nimble shot-blocker, and Dennis Rodman, whom they had hungered for. Even though they picked Salley eleventh in the first round and Rodman early in the second, Rodman was the player they desperately wanted. They had begun to hear about him midway through the season, a young, athletic kid who had barely played in junior college and then had gone to Southeastern Oklahoma State. McCloskey saw him at one of the postseason games and fell in love with him. He was essentially untutored but had amazing raw athletic talent. A great jumper with very quick feet, he looked like an Olympic quarter-miler who had slipped over to the basketball gym. He ran the court effortlessly. And McCloskey spotted in Rodman a passion to excel that was special. "That was what drew me, you could look at him and see it—it almost burned in his eyes. He had been neglected and scorned for so long, not merely by the basketball world, but by the rest of the world as well, that now, when he was finally getting a chance against players who had been more highly recruited, nothing was going to stop him. He was finding out he was better than they were, and you could just see the passion in his eyes."

Suddenly, the Pistons were deep. They had a strong eight-player rotation. The talent of the two rookies was obvious, as were the matchups now permitted to a shrewd coach such as Daly. No team was stronger in what Johnny Bach called "the alligator wrestling pond," the area around the basket, than Detroit was with Laimbeer, Mahorn, Salley, and Rodman. The Pistons could make adjustments to different teams, going with their players who were skilled offensively in certain situations or with their defensive stars in others. Soon they started having, Matt Dobek, their PR man said, more five-point blowouts than any team in history. A five-point blowout, Dobek added, seemed like a contradiction in terms, except that if the Pistons had a five-point lead near the end of the game, they could put Salley, Rodman, Dumars, Thomas and Laimbeer on the floor, and even if Laimbeer was slow, he played good position defense, and the others were all defensive standouts. Thus could they shut down opponents late in the game.

They became the team no other team wanted to play. They were immensely physical, and Laimbeer was regarded by other players as the league's premier cheap-shot artist, a player who liked to nail other players at their moment of greatest vulnerability, more to get in their heads and make them blow their cool than anything else. His strength was his complete immunity to public opinion—he seemed to drink in the boos for him that thundered out in arenas outside of Detroit. The team became the Bad Boys, a title taken from an Al Pacino line from the movie *Scarface*, "Say hello to the bad boy because you'll never see another bad guy like me." In the 1988–1989 season, Detroit drew $29,100 in fines— Portland was next with only $10,500. Laimbeer, Rodman, and Mahorn among them had $11,000, more than any other team.

Their practices became fierce, better, and more bitterly contested, some of the players thought, than many NBA games. At the first day of practice each year, Daly told the players that they would get their minutes based on how hard and well they played in practice. Everyone practiced hard. No one was exempt from the tough code of the team. They practiced hard, and they practiced and played in pain. "We were," Isiah Thomas said later, "the last of the gladiator teams."

Daly was the ideal man to coach this team, a man of humor and intelligence who had worked for a long time in the smaller, poorer vineyards of basketball, starting as a coach at Punxsutawney High School in Pennsylvania for eight seasons and ever so slowly working his way up, through the college ranks, mostly as an assistant. If anyone had ever paid his dues, it was Daly. He never let his newfound success or increasing affluence go to his head. Head coach or not, millionaire salary or not, he had the soul of a lifer, someone who did what he did because that was the only thing he wanted to do. He had gotten the job in Detroit, it was said, only because the team was so bad that no one else wanted it. Just a few years earlier, Bob Ryan had run into Daly at an all-star weekend, at a moment when Daly was looking for work. He had recently been let go after a brief part-season tour in Cleveland—then one of the worst organizations in the league—was unemployed, and was not optimistic about his future. He was fifty, he told Ryan, and the jobs were all going to younger guys—"Who's going to hire someone as old as me?" He liked the new affluence that came with the success of this team, the peripheral money offered by television stations and clothing stores, and he was a bit of a dude when it came to clothes. "Daddy Rich," the players called him.

But complementing his passion for winning, Daly also had learned more complicated lessons early on, and he never forgot that basketball was not war, it was a game, and only a small part of the human comedy. He had a wonderfully skeptical vision of human nature, reflecting his Irish roots, exemplified by a saying of Yeats's that in times of great joy, the Irish were comforted by the sure knowledge that tragedy was just around the corner.

It almost happened for the Pistons in the 1986–1987 season, the first year they had Salley, Rodman, and Dantley. The Celtics were beginning to slow down. Though the Celtics won fifty-nine games that year, by the end of the season Detroit, which had won fifty-two games, was coming on strong. Its players were younger, and its rotation was deeper. They lost to the Celtics in a close playoff series that year, but the Pistons were clearly on the rise. They were in the process of replacing the Celtics as the team to beat in the East, standing between the Bulls and their own special destiny. A year later, the Pistons beat the Celtics and went to the Finals, where they might have won had not Isiah Thomas badly hurt his ankle in Game Six.

The Pistons represented a particularly murderous obstacle to a team like the Bulls, which was still coming of age and where the pure talent of younger players had not yet been matched by the requisite mental and physical toughness needed to be a champion. The singular strength of the Pistons, their mental toughness and their sense of purpose, made them the most difficult opponent of all for a team on the ascent. The Pistons had an unerring ability to hone in on the weaknesses, physical or psychological, of their opponents. More, Michael Jordan's wildly competitive nature played into Detroit's hands: Chuck Daly created a defense called the Jordan Rules, deliberately designed to make Michael Jordan's games against Detroit as physically demanding as possible, to make him work for every shot and to pound him to the maximum. Jordan, warrior that he was, for a long time took the bait and rose to the challenge, bringing the Bulls ever so close to the level of the Pistons but somehow falling short.

Even as the Pistons were on the threshold of overtaking the Celtics, Chuck Daly looked out and sensed that his team would not have a particularly long reign. It was a team driven as much by willpower as pure talent. The good drafts when they had the luxury of a top pick were long gone, and not only did the Bulls have the best player in the game, but Daly saw in Scottie Pippen another superstar on the rise. The time when Jordan had to carry the entire burden, those games when he got forty or fifty points—Daly called them "astro points" because the number was so high—was almost gone. A talented cast was gradually being assembled around him. Pippen was the harbinger of the next championship team, Daly was sure. He was not there yet, but he soon would be. All he needed was mental toughness, and that, for someone who played against Michael Jordan every day in practice, would come soon enough.

19.

Chicago, 1988-1990; New York City, 1967-1971

B Y 1988, it was clear that for Chicago to do something about the Pistons, they had to add a big man. The Pistons had Laimbeer and James Edwards as his backup, plus Mahorn and Salley and Rodman. The Bulls had two very good power forwards but were playing without a center. Dave Corzine was a hardworking player, popular with both management and his teammates, but his limits were obvious, and he had become a target for the fans, who took out their frustrations over the team's failure to improve by booing him. As Jerry Krause analyzed the availability of centers in the draft, and as he saw his team reach the fifty-win plateau, he thought the Bulls had very little chance of getting the center they wanted. The next year's class included Rik Smits, very tall at seven foot four, with some skills but essentially quite unfinished, a player who would obviously become a major project; Ron Seikaly at Syracuse; and Will Perdue from Vanderbilt. They had the best shot at Perdue, but he was a long way from becoming the kind of center who could lead a team to a championship.

Krause began to look for centers already playing in the league, and the most likely place appeared to be New York, where the arrival of Patrick Ewing had created a twin-towers lineup for the Knicks of Ewing and veteran center Bill Cartwright. It had not been used with particular success there; neither Ewing nor Cartwright appeared comfortable with the other, and so Cartwright might just be available. The rise of Horace Grant had given Krause a chip to play with: Though Charles Oakley had emerged as the league's second-best rebounder for two years running, it was clear by the end of Grant's rookie year that he was the more gifted all-around player and they had to find more minutes for him. That meant that Oakley was available for a trade. Krause was willing to trade Oakley for the draft rights to Smits, but nothing happened there. So he began to concentrate on Cartwright, who had come into the league ballyhooed as a star, one of those young men who attract a lot of attention too early in their careers—he graced the cover of *Sports Illustrated* as a college player. He did not, however, have a great NBA body: He was tall and slim, with narrow shoulders, and he lacked the formidable muscle definition of players like Ewing and Olajuwon. What his body did not show was that he was a tough, smart player and that he had adapted unusually well to his limits within the NBA, evolving, oddly enough, into a defensive rather than an offensive specialist. He was unusually shrewd, he carefully studied the moves of the more talented centers he defended, and he was tenacious in holding defensive positions. No one, it turned out, defended Patrick Ewing better than Bill Cartwright. This turned out to be a major plus for the Bulls.

Cartwright had constant problems with his feet, and the Bulls checked them out very carefully. Years later, Krause called it the hardest trade he ever made. Oakley had been his first big score with the Bulls, and he had been everything a basketball executive could want as a man and as a player and more, bighearted, dedicated, and fearless. Because Cartwright had a history of injury problems, Krause played it very carefully when the Bulls picked in that year's draft. Instead of Dan Majerle, occasionally known as Thunder Dan Majerle in the media, a player he coveted badly and about whom he had become very expansive within the Bulls' organization, he picked Perdue, so as to have a backup center. Of the centers available, Krause preferred Seikaly of Syracuse, who had more of an offensive game, but Seikaly was gone before Chicago picked and Smits, to no one's surprise, went second in the draft.

Because of the timing of the trade, the Bulls were not able to tell Oakley beforehand. He and Jordan, his closest friend on the team, were on their way to Las Vegas to watch a Mike Tyson fight when they heard the news from the media. Both were furious. Jordan, it seemed, was even angrier than Oakley. Oakley had been the team cop, the man assigned to go after anyone who took cheap shots at Jordan. Now, suddenly, his protector was gone, and for Cartwright, a player whose game Jordan most decidedly did not admire. "Johnny, who's the new cop going to be?" Jordan asked Bach shortly after the trade. It was a good question.

"Horace Grant," Bach suggested.

"Hell, *I* can whip Horace," Jordan said, "How's he going to defend me?"

Jordan did not respect Cartwright as a man or as a player. He called him Medical Bill because of his past injuries. He thought Cartwright had bad hands, so sometimes in practice he threw him passes that were unnecessarily hard so that Cartwright would fumble them and prove Jordan's point. About no other player was Michael Jordan to prove quite so wrong as about Bill Cartwright, both as a man and as a player, but it took him almost two years to realize it and admit it. Cartwright gave the Bulls something they needed badly, a quality big man. There were limits to his game—he in fact did not have good hands—and his offensive skills had diminished over the years as his body, particularly his knees, wore down. But he was an intelligent and tenacious player, and he would prove a considerable asset on defense. But despite his arrival, it was not a good year for the Bulls.

Somewhere in the 1988–1989 season, his third year as head coach, Doug Collins began to lose his team. It was a hard year, because they had won fifty games the year before, and now, with Cartwright, all the signs indicated that they were on the very cusp of greatness. Collins had probably been the ideal coach for a young team. He had pushed Grant and Pippen ceaselessly, and there was no doubt that they had prospered greatly under his coaching. No one doubted Collins's intelligence. But if there was one thing he could not do—and it was a considerable vulnerability in a season as long and demanding as that of the NBA—it was undercoach. Some of his assistants cautioned him to try and let go once in a while, to live more readily with defeat, especially on those bitter nights when a coach leaves an arena sure his team should have won. If there was one critical quality to coaching in the NBA, it was the ability to let go, to accept the occasional defeat on nights when you knew your team should have won.

But Collins was not a man to let go. He was very open about it: "I am who I am, and I coach the way I am," he said. But because he was so driven and so emotional, with essentially only one gear, by the third season the players began to tune out. They started to complain about playing under him, that it was too much of an emotional roller-coaster. One day he was screaming at them, and the next he was hugging them, telling them how much he loved them. Somehow, the requisite emotional balance necessary to coach a team in the NBA was missing—normally, it was the players who were supposed to be volatile and the coach, perched on his own sturdy emotional plateau, who was supposed to steady them. Michael Jordan was always reasonably careful in his public comments, for he had been raised not to challenge authority figures if at all possible, and a coach, unlike Krause, was an authority figure to him, but those around him sensed his doubts. "A young coach—very emotional," he told friends.

At the same time, the distance between Collins and Krause went from a small seam to a chasm. When Collins first came aboard, there was an understanding that not only was Tex Winter to be his assistant but that Winter's patented offense, the triple post, was to be the team's offense. In fact, it was Winter, Krause's oldest and closest friend in the coaching world, who had given the final approval on Collins. Winter was virtually Krause's first hire. Back in 1985, the day that Krause's appointment was announced, Winter, then sixty-three, was watching ESPN, and he pointed to the television set and told his wife, "That man there, Jerry Krause—he's going to call me within twenty-four hours and offer me a job," which in fact he did.

Winter's trademark triple-post or triangle offense used multiple post positions from which players made a series of cuts as they switched to different, presumably more advantageous points from which to attack the basket. It was supposed to keep constant pressure on a defense, and the offensive players were always probing for a soft spot, an improved angle, an open shot, or a mismatch. The hope was that it would not only showcase Jordan's special offensive talents but allow Chicago to involve the other players in the offense a bit more. That hope remained stillborn.

Michael Jordan was not enamored of the triple post, and Collins's own faith in it seemed marginal. Soon, the triple post was effectively junked. Instead, the Bulls once again seemed dependent primarily upon Jordan's raw talent. Collins was always adding plays. When another team ran a play that worked against Chicago, the Bulls added it to their repertoire the next day. "A play a day" was what the players called their offense.

In the third year, there was often a bizarre scene at practice. The coaches were all together, except somewhat off by himself, Tex Winter sat taking notes, as if somehow he had been sent from some other basketball program to study the Bulls' practices. His separation from the rest of the coaching staff was not a good sign. "Doug," Winter once said, "for someone as smart as you are, I often wonder if you know what you're doing."

Worse, the relationship between Collins and Krause had become poisonous. They began by battling over draft choices and player-personnel decisions. The argument between Collins and Krause over Brad Sellers and Johnny Dawkins was particularly brutal. Other disagreements followed. By 1988, tensions had escalated to the danger point. Collins, confrontational and unable to suppress his will and emotions, was openly challenging Krause. Why was he always hanging out with the coaches? Why was he always coming on trips? Because I'm the general manager, Krause would answer, and Collins would tell him there was no need for the general manager to travel with the team. Collins would come to practice and look over and see Krause and yell at him, "Why are you here? What are you doing on the floor?" It was a quarrel over space, over personnel, and it was turning into an increasingly bitter battle of egos.

Phil Jackson knew the situation was bad. So far, Jackson managed to get on reasonably well with everyone on the staff. He and Johnny Bach liked each other, and Bach taught him a great deal about how to do scouting reports. Jackson was fond of Tex Winter and even seemed to get on well with Krause. He was aware of Krause's idiosyncrasies, his lack of a sense of proper boundaries, but he thought him smart (he had had the sense to hire Jackson, after all), and he was at ease with him. He was, without realizing it, probably the coach in waiting. Almost a decade later, in 1997, as it became clear that Krause was enamored of a coach at Iowa State named Tim Floyd and wanted him as Jackson's replacement, someone mentioned to Jackson that Krause was in love with Floyd. Jackson thought for a moment, and then said rather wistfully, "I remember when he was in love with me."

During the 1988–1989 season, things began to disintegrate. One sign came at a game in Milwaukee right before Christmas. Collins was ejected from the game early on, and he turned the reins over to Jackson, carefully scripting what he wanted done, and above all the plays he wanted run. The Bulls were quite far behind when he was tossed, so Jackson essentially scrapped what Collins wanted and, being a defensively oriented coach, put on a press, which worked. On offense, he undercoached, letting the team find its own rhythm, and eventually the Bulls came back to win handily. What made that victory particularly painful for Collins was that Krause and his wife, Thelma, had invited June Jackson to sit with them that night, and the television camera showed a picture of the three of them together that was relayed back to Chicago. ("A major political mistake," June Jackson said of her decision to accept the invitation several years later, after her husband and Krause had become antagonists, and after Krause's stepdaughter was married—a wedding to which Tim Floyd of Iowa State, his wife, and all the Chicago assistant coaches and their wives were invited, but the Jacksons were not. The Jacksons found out about the wedding because Sheri Cartwright, Bill Cartwright's wife, called up June to ask what she was wearing to the reception.)

June Jackson's presence with the Krauses inflamed Collins. To him, it looked conspiratorial. The next day, Collins, livid, accused Jackson of undermining him and his coaching philosophy. In addition, he said, Jackson was going behind his back with Krause and plotting against him, which was not true. What followed was a very long and unpleasant meeting among Collins, Krause, and Jackson in which grievances were aired. During this meeting a not inconsiderable friendship between Collins and Jackson was damaged severely.

A few weeks later, Jackson was scouting the Miami Heat in Miami, and he missed the game itself because of his travel plans. The next day, he got a call from Krause, who told him not to miss any more games for the remainder of the season. Clearly, something was in the air. The season did not end happily. The team lost eight of its last ten games. Instead of winning around fifty-five games, as some people in the front office had hoped, the Bulls slipped, winning only forty-seven. After the season, Doug Collins was fired, and Phil Jackson was made head coach.

Phil Jackson had not thought of himself as a coach in waiting. If anything, he thought Billy McKinney, a protégé of both Winter and Krause, was ahead of him, but McKinney had been offered a job by the Minnesota Timberwolves to head their player-personnel program, and he took it, although without Krause's blessing. Jackson was forty-four years old when he got the job. One of the calls that Jerry Reinsdorf made before he gave Jackson the job was to Bill Bradley, at that time a United States senator, whom the owner knew through Democratic politics. How good a coach would Jackson be? Reinsdorf asked. Bradley said that he would be very good: "He thinks group, but he always sees individuals. He's not going to be a drill sergeant trying to force everyone into the same mold. He has a real appreciation—and respect—for individuality." Jackson had been infinitely respectable in his Chicago years, and no one thought of him as a hippie anymore. In the Bulls' team picture his first year as an assistant coach he is completely clean shaven, as he offered his facial hair as a sacrifice to the existing prejudices of the basketball powers that be. By the second year, in what is clearly something of a cultural compromise, a major league mustache has sprouted. Subsequent photos, taken year by year over a decade, show his hair turning gray at an alarming rate, testimonial either to his genes or to the sheer burden of coaching one hundred games and going that deep into the playoffs annually in the NBA.

Because of his off-court demeanor, his early days as an apprentice to the counterculture, and his later fascination with the gentleness advocated by Buddhism, it was often easy to forget how driven he was, that he had two separate incarnations, high intensity on the court, and great gentleness off it. Even in his counterculture incarnation, he had, of course, been a fierce basketball player: that was very much the product of a certain kind of childhood, and those values remained a crucial part of him. The mark of that particular fundamentalist background was deeply on him. His mother had not in vain been a striver who had told him when he was two that at that age his older brother already had a vocabulary of a thousand words. He was not to waste anything; he was to push himself to the highest level of his ability.

Over the years, Jackson distanced himself greatly from the religious beliefs of his parents, although he did not go as far as his brothers. Chuck Jackson turned almost completely against Christianity, and Joe Jackson, a psychologist, become even more closely connected to Eastern religions than Phil did. Eventually, Phil Jackson ended up with a fascinating amalgam of beliefs—a blend of Christianity, Zen Buddhism, and Native American philosophy. His beliefs were the result of some thirty years of searching, sifting, trying to blend belief with ethics, and coming up with a code of human behavior the hallmark of which was tolerance for others.

Philosophically, Jackson was on a search for an ethos that would allow him to be intensely driven, a humanist, and yet not a materialist. But he also wanted to enjoy some of the better things that an increasingly materialist society distributed to its winners, and with which he as a successful coach was eventually rewarded. That took him a long way from the world of tongues, his mother's world of religious certitude— her favorite phrase was "Christ is the only answer." His mother never gave up hope, of course, that he would come back to the more narrowly focused religion that produced him. Several years ago, when writer Garry Wills was asked to introduce Jackson to a Chicago audience, he first called Elisabeth Jackson to chat about her son. She concluded their conversation by saying, "You can tell my son that I hope he still feels that he can come back here and become a minister."

That was not likely. He remained very uncomfortable with his original religious roots, and much of his life was a search to remain in some form or another a Christian and yet to escape that part of the religion of his birth he found unacceptably harsh. In the spring of 1998, Jackson went to see the movie *The Apostle*, a brilliant film in which Robert Duval portrays an evangelical minister. His wife, June, sitting next to him, could feel his body tension. As the movie went on, he became more and more rigid in his seat—the movie obviously hit too close to home. The occasions when he did return to the church of his parents—mostly done for the benefit of his mother and in keeping with a promise made to his father before he died—were not comfortable ones. A few years

ago, a local minister in Bigfork, Montana, asked those in the congrega-
tion to rededicate themselves to Christ, and he mentioned that there was
someone very famous in the audience, someone who had recently received many accolades in the secular world. "But those accolades won't
get you into God's Heaven," the minister said. Then he added, "Jesus is
calling softly, 'Sinner, come home.' "

Later, Jackson said he was less bothered by the sermon than June was.
"June," he told her, "he's just doing his job—and it's his job to make me
feel guilty."

His was a very austere childhood. Part of it was the simplicity and unsparing quality of the land itself, part of it was the unbending nature of
his parents' fundamentalist religion. Bill Bradley, his Knick teammate
and lifetime friend, himself a child of the good, solid Midwest, remembered visiting Jackson in North Dakota after his rookie year. He discovered that Jackson came from the same kind of simple background as
Bradley, except that Jackson's seemed to reflect an even more intense
kind of separation of people from each other, a far greater loneliness
than Bradley had ever known. Driving across the upper plains of North
Dakota with Jackson that day, Bradley felt a sense of being on a moon-
scape and a feeling that even more than in rural Missouri the people here
seemed to be somehow apart from each other, the words spoken fewer,
the silences between them greater. As they went through a series of
small towns, Bradley had a feeling that he could envision Jackson growing up here, as he could now see himself growing up in Crystal City,
Missouri: "He's like me, only more so," he thought.

Jackson's parents, Charles and Elisabeth, were both Pentecostal, As-
sembly of God ministers, part of the charismatic movement that swept
through the country in the years after World War One. His father was
from the Canadian East, his mother from the American West, and they
had met at Central Bible College in Winnipeg. In the churches they
served, his father was the morning minister, his mother the evening
minister. Their sermons contained a good deal of hellfire and brim-
stone, Jackson remembered. In their home, there were no movies, no
dancing, no alcohol, no smoking, no television (when finally there was
a television station in their area), no easy earthly pleasures. There was a
disdain for all other religions. When Phil met a new boy in school and
came home and mentioned it, his mother asked, "Is he a Christian?"
The answer, in that religiously judgmental family, might well be "No,
he's a Catholic." The book in the house was the Bible, the magazine was
Reader's Digest. The children were to be good citizens and they were
never to lose their tempers. Anger, his wife, June, once noted, was alien
to him, and other people's anger always made him nervous. "That

comes from his religion and from his home," she added. "In that home, anger was very much a sin."

When there was a square dance at school, Phil Jackson had to sit on the sidelines. When their contemporaries were going to the movies and the Jackson boys—Chuck, Joe, and Phil—asked their father if they could go too, Charles Jackson would say, "We don't go to the movie show." If the boys asked why not, the answer was that they were in this world but not of this world. We don't do worldly things, he would say, we don't do what other people do. Then their father would use a phrase from Scripture, "I call you to be a people separate unto Himself." Phil Jackson saw his first movie when he was a senior in high school and danced for the first time when he was in college, doing both with no small amount of guilt.

Decisions in that family were never based on pleasure but driven by obligation. When the older boys were teenagers, there was a serious family career decision to be made. They had been living in Montana, which they loved, and there was a choice of a position in a part of Idaho that was said to be beautiful and very green, much like Montana, or Williston, North Dakota, which was said to be bleak and much harsher in climate. All the kids wanted Idaho. The Reverend Jackson, of course, chose Williston: "This is where the Lord wants me to go," he said. The children, three boys and a half-sister, were PKs, Preacher's Kids, which meant they were under constant scrutiny from all the adults in their town; above all they were not to slip away from the Lord's words and their family's rules and embarrass their parents by doing the devil's work, which children of ministers so often did. Charles Jackson, intense and unbending in his beliefs, was nonetheless a gentle man of great kindness, much loved by those around him. He was the ministerial supervisor for the entire state, with some seventy churches under his watch. At one point he took away the ministry of his own nephew because of some mistakes he had made, but the nephew revered him to the day he died for the personal kindness he had shown while doing it.

Elisabeth Jackson, by contrast, was the striver who pushed her children to excel. She and her five siblings grew up very poor in Montana, and Joe Jackson remembered that until he was sixteen, his maternal grandparents' home had an outhouse, despite the almost unbearable cold. All of her siblings had been valedictorians, and it grated on her for much of her life that she had missed being one by two tenths of a point, in no small part because she always missed the first six weeks of school because of the fall harvest. There was a stoic quality to her and her life: She had taught school in eastern Montana at the age of eighteen, in a school so poor that during the winter they burned cow chips in the stove for heat. You could be anything you wanted, she told her children constantly, and she pushed them to memorize paragraphs from books and definitions of words from the dictionary. Each week some verse from the Scripture was to be memorized. In case the boys seemed ready to slack off, she would quote some long dictionary definition she had memorized herself thirty years earlier. She would have no slackers in her family, and she was not a slacker herself. Things were to be done right. There were four men in that house, and each wore a clean white shirt every day of the week, which meant she washed and ironed some twenty-eight shirts every week, knowing almost to the minute how long it would take her.

If there was one single lasting lesson that Elisabeth Jackson wanted to impart, Chuck Jackson believed, even if all the other aspects of her children's upbringing slipped away as they ventured out into the world, it was the idea that whatever else, they were not to waste anything God had given them—they were to maximize their talents.

The idea that you owed a great deal was everywhere in evidence in the home. Elisabeth Jackson created a large sign and placed it in Phil's room when he was a little boy: "John 3:16. For God so loved the world, that he gave his only begotten Son, that whosoever believeth in him should not perish, but have everlasting life."

Even as a boy, Phil Jackson was uneasy with the evangelical, highly emotional nature of their church—the people talking in tongues, the people throwing themselves on the floor and rolling around. These were people whom he knew otherwise as quiet, sober, extremely restrained neighbors, until suddenly they seemed seized by wild, uncontrollable emotions. For a young kid looking on, it was all very troubling, and he found himself pulling back from it.

All three Jackson boys, of whom Phil was the youngest, threw themselves passionately into athletics. Chuck Jackson believed they did so because it was one of the few things open to them and because it allowed them some degree of normality: It was the only time when they were allowed to do what other kids were doing. Sports were sanctioned by their parents—they were good and clean, as opposed to, say, the demon work of Hollywood. Because the other two boys had fought some of these battles before—such as for the right to play football on Friday nights— it was easier for Phil when he came along, and he was given permission to play football as they were not. At the very least, Phil noted, the long trips to play other schools often meant that they would miss church.

The boys were thus involuntarily set apart from most of their friends when they were very young—because they could not do what the other kids did, they lacked their peers' frame of reference. They could not talk about movies they had seen, television programs they had watched, or music they had danced to. "You could not go along with your peers in any easy way," Chuck Jackson said. "The separation had already been done for you early on, and you had no control over it—so you're oddly objective and distanced from a lot of things most kids automatically accept and go along with."

Phil Jackson's rejection of so much of the religion of his childhood and his own enduring search for something else made him a man of unusual tolerance as he grew older. They had all grown up in a home, his brother Joe once said, that was terribly judgmental, and Phil was uncomfortable with the finality of many of those judgments. He became fascinated by human behavior without being particularly critical of it. "Phil," his mother (a woman not given to finding grays in her world) once said, "is like lubricating oil with people." June Jackson agreed with that: Her husband, she felt, got on with a vast variety of people; he was a good listener and could see other people as they really were, accept them as they were, and, more often than not, appreciate them for it. Strikingly secure in his sense of self, acutely interested in those around him, he had become as much psychologist as coach as his career had evolved over the years.

Much of this was innate, and much Jackson learned from his New York Knick coach, Red Holzman. Only in hindsight had Jackson realized how wise a coach Holzman had been. When Jackson arrived in New York, for example, there was a potentially explosive situation on the team involving the struggle for playing time between Bill Bradley and Cazzie Russell. Bradley was white, Russell black. Both had been high-profile college stars, reputations significantly hyped because of a famous NCAA playoff game between their college teams. And neither had made an easy adjustment to the NBA: Bradley was too slow to play guard, and Russell's game turned out to be somewhat incomplete—he was a potent but streaky shooter, not a particularly good passer—and an inconsistent defender.

Each, of course, had his partisans, people who saw only the player's strengths and not his weaknesses: Bradley among the male Ivy League set disproportionately influential in the city's public life, who finally had one of their own to play in the Garden, and Russell among a small vocal claque—including some powerful and outspoken people in the local media—who hyped him and hung out with him and told him constantly he was The Man. If anything, what Russell's fans represented was something of a forerunner to what would one day be called a posse, people whose primary connection to the game was through one player and whose ego they therefore constantly inflated, and whose teammates they constantly denigrated. Members of the posse in time began to think that they were the player. It was a potentially incendiary controversy, because there was growing optimism and enthusiasm in New York about this team, because both players were highly heralded marquee players, and because one was black and one was white. Holzman never took sides, never said anything publicly, which was of itself quite remarkable. He acted as if the problem did not exist. He let the players sort it out on the floor and in the locker room. It was as if what was for some people a major struggle of personalities did not exist at all.

"I think Red knew from the start that Bill, with his exceptional intelligence, was a natural leader, and even more interestingly, he knew that Bill was already leading the team and doing it from a deficit position—that is leading when he had not yet really found his own position—but that he brought such on-court intelligence and skill to the game that the team was better with him out there," Jackson said years later. "Red was going to let everyone else see what he saw about Bill and Cazzie—first their teammates, and in time the fans."

By his second year, Bradley had moved to small forward, and his ability to create better shots for his teammates by moving without the ball had helped change the team. Clearly, the team jelled and played better when he was on the court. Russell, by contrast, had not added to his game and still seemed somewhat one-dimensional. He was still a talented player, and sometimes, when the team needed scoring, Holzman went to him. Gradually Russell's minutes went down and Bradley's went up and the issue simply evaporated, as it became increasingly clear to everyone that much of the team's unique cohesion came from Bradley's relentless movement. Within the locker room the players, primarily the black players, sorted it out as well. Russell was often talkative and given to blathering in the locker room; Bradley, by contrast, was quiet and extremely reserved, wary of being sucked into the role of the great white hope. But it was the black players, principally Walt Bellamy, who needled Russell when he used unusually long words; Bells would sit there half-naked in the locker room, and imitating the accent of an Oxford don he would ask, "Now Mister Russell, as a noted expert on the English language do you think you could explain for the unfortunate poorly educated souls on this team that very long word you just used . . . ?"

Holzman dealt deftly with Russell's ego, again by never really confronting it. He chose to see what he wanted to see and to ignore what he wanted to ignore, confident that he had mature players on both sides of the racial line who would handle most of the issue for him. The only time he came down on Russell was when he broke team rules. One of the team rules was that they went everywhere as a team. There were a lot of games with Philadelphia in those days, Cazzie Russell had a new Cadillac, and on one occasion he drove it to Philly. Right before the game, Red asked him how much the tolls were from New York to Philly, and Cazzie answered $8, and Red said, "Good—why don't you subtract the $8 from the $100 I just fined you for driving here instead of coming with the team—so the fine will only be $92, not $100." It was a gentle reminder that there were rules, and they applied to everyone equally.

Jackson faced a similar chemistry problem when he took over in Chicago. Getting the Chicago job was, of course, the chance of a lifetime for him, as difficult in some ways as the situation was. He was going to be coaching the best player in the league, as well as a group of other players whose talent was obvious and who were just coming of age in their professional incarnations but who were by the very nature of the superstar's greatness that much more tentative on the court. How to blend the pieces together, how to adjust the chemical mixture of this team, was going to be a great challenge. It was now Jordan's sixth year, and his attitude had in many ways hardened. He had grown accustomed to a lack of any offensive system, and he was somewhat suspect of almost everyone on the team, save Paxson. Jackson's problem was to figure out how much the ball was shared, what the allotment of shots for Jordan would be (or, to be blunt, how much that figure would come down). If Michael Jordan was in his own way a genius, then the ultimate challenge for his coach was to blend that genius with the gifts of mere mortals.

The team Jackson inherited was at a crossroads. If Collins had perhaps burned out emotionally, he had also brought Pippen and Grant to a much higher level of play. Years later, it was obvious that by dint of Collins's passion and drive, Jackson had picked up a team that was on the very threshold of greatness. Pippen and Grant were, if not quite all-stars, certainly close.

More than anything else, Jackson felt that the team needed an offensive system. He did not think of himself as a particularly gifted offensive coach, but he wanted an offensive system of some sort. The Chicago offense when he arrived was too dependent on Jordan's singular talents: Essentially it was throw-Michael-the-ball-and-everyone-else-get-out-of-the-way. Employing some kind of system was particularly important for the other players, who needed not only to know what their roles were but to be brought into the offense enough to make them work hard and to keep the defensive teams honest. Jackson was very much aware of how hard it was even for good players to coexist with someone as supremely talented and as psychologically demanding as Jordan. As Dave Corzine once said, Jordan was so good that if the Bulls won it was because of him, but if they lost it was always going to be your fault, not his.

How Jordan viewed his teammates remained a serious issue, particularly if he was being asked to share the ball. He saw Grant's upside, but he did not think him a smart player nor one likely to take big shots at the end of the game. Pippen was a more complicated matter. He was improving all the time, his athletic ability was in some ways beginning to rival Jordan's, particularly on defense, and he had a surprisingly good sense of the game. He was not that good a pure shooter yet, though he was improving. But how tough he was and how well he would play in critical moments of big games was still something of an issue with Jordan, and his doubts were considerable, of which fact Pippen himself was very much aware. The one player Michael was comfortable with and trusted was Paxson, which of itself was amazing, for it was particularly hard to play the other guard position alongside him. Paxson not only was a very dependable pure shooter but knew the limits of his game; he knew what he was supposed to do, and, even more important, he knew what he was not supposed to do when Jordan was on the court.

Jackson liked Tex Winter's triple-post offense. They had coached together in the summer league one season, and Jackson had become its advocate. He thought the constant movement and the clearly assigned roles that demanded that players cut from one point to another suited the nature of the talent he now had. He also thought it would make Michael Jordan a more complete offensive threat—for it would use him as a post-up player, and no guard in the league, because of Jordan's pure strength and jumping ability, posed such a threat in the post—and it would conserve his energy and extend his career. It was not an easy offense to learn, and over the years, while certain players took to it naturally, it was bewildering to others, who never managed to grasp the nature of the movement, which was at once both ordained and yet voluntary. The problem would be selling it to Jordan, and that process was to take much of the next two seasons. To Jackson, product of a Knick team that had lacked physical strength and size but that had systematically beaten more physical teams because of its movement and its team intelligence, it seemed to suit the players he had.

Jackson at that point was balanced between the powerful personalities of Tex Winter and Michael Jordan and between their two very different philosophies of basketball. Tex Winter was then sixty-eight and in his fifth decade of coaching: He had started at Kansas State as a full-time assistant in 1947 for $3,000 a year. He was a beguiling man, completely unvarnished, willing at all times to express his opinions, always on the record. He was the product of an infinitely poorer America, a man who had come into his adulthood in the worst of the great Depression and who knew an America where salaries were tiny, and the middle class was not lightly entered by that vast segment of the population that had not been born into it. He could have been the grandfather of some of these players, and his conservatism, financial as well as social, stood in marked contrast to the values of almost everyone around him. He did not waste money. Lunch for two with Tex rarely went over eight or nine dollars. If some of the other coaches regarded the free meals served by the Bulls to the press before games as virtually inedible, Tex Winter, child of the Depression, seemed to love them, and was a regular at a table before the games.

He had been chosen by Krause from the start as a kind of senior presence and guru, but he was not Krause's man—he was no one's man but his own, and he was always completely honest. That was what appealed to so many people about Tex—he was simply so straight, and he played no political games. He did not buy into the culture of modern basketball, the noise and fanfare and celebrity; he thought it all a distraction. He was in his own way an absolutist. If he was by the nature of his personality and his essential openness a great favorite of the beat reporters, he was also a very powerful presence within the organization, a man with a clear vision of what he wanted on each play. His and Michael's visions of basketball were diametrically opposite. In some ways both were right and both were wrong. Inevitably, the lines were rather sharply drawn between Jordan, with his surpassing athletic ability and his ability to change the flow of a game on his own, and then take it over, and Winter, wedded in Jordan's eyes to a concept of basketball that had emerged when players had none of his special talent—a system, he believed, that was created to compensate for the lack of talent of a different generation of players in a distant, antediluvian era. The power of Jordan's arguments was not to be underestimated—no one read a defense better than he, no one could score more quickly. And it was all done by instinct; playing in a system might cost him that instinct. Winter, of course, hated the idea of an offense that depended so much on the talent of a superstar. "I think Michael's a great, great player," Winter liked to say, "but I'm not an idolater."

The two men had their own running debate on what constituted good basketball. "There's no *I* in the word *team*," Winter would tell him.

"There is in the word *win*," Jordan would answer.

Deep in his heart, Jordan believed that the game had changed, that the sheer talent, size, and speed of the new breed of players made the old-fashioned system with set plays outdated, that it had become a player's game that favored those who could create their own shots. And no one in the league did that better than he did. So Michael Jordan resisted Jackson's attempt to reintroduce the triple post. Jordan had not been enthusiastic when Collins had made his first tentative stab at it, and he seemed to have even less love for it this time around. He was wary that it might limit his game without adding anything in return. "An equal-opportunity offense," he said, and he did not mean that as praise. Jackson tried to explain it in a different way to him. The ball was like a spotlight, and it was important to share the spotlight with his teammates. What Jackson was really counting on for leverage was Jordan's surpassing ambition, which was not for individual awards but to win the championship. What he emphasized to Jordan again and again was that they had gone as far as they could go in the playoffs doing it Jordan's way: The deeper they went in the playoffs, the more likely they were to find formidable defensive players who were finally going to limit what one great player could do. It might not be a bad idea, he even suggested, if Jordan did *not* win the scoring title, as he had for the last two years.

And so that year a struggle began between Phil Jackson and his superstar, both of them exceptionally stubborn. Jordan was still wary of his teammates, and when Jordan expressed his doubts about them, Jackson would say yes, what Jordan was saying about some of them was right, they were not yet at his level, and they probably never would be. It was possible that he would never get better teammates. But they were certainly not going to get better or contribute very much more if the show was entirely his. He had to start sharing the ball, and he had to take a chance. Otherwise, another season would end the way the ones in the past always had as they advanced to a higher and higher level in the playoffs. The better defensive teams emerging in the later round of the playoffs would figure out ways of shutting him down. Individual talent, no matter how unique, could only take them so far in this game.

Jackson's first season, 1989–1990, was a learning experience for everyone. It was a season of searching, with only partial success, for the requisite mental toughness that set champions apart from other teams. The triple post was not an easy system for many of the players to learn. "Like trying to learn ballroom dancing," said Will Perdue, the backup center, a man with imperfect footwork.

Sometimes that season Jordan played within the offense, and sometimes he slipped out of it, becoming frustrated either because it was no longer the pure, reactive game that he had mastered or because when he had trusted the offense and given the ball to his teammates in his eyes they had let him down. Sometimes, encouraged by Johnny Bach, the assistant coach, Jordan simply took over a game. Bach, an old navy man, said, "Michael, I'm not your coach, I'm only an assistant, but what Admiral Halsey would order his fleet in moments like this is, 'Attack, attack attack!' " Jordan, of course, loved it. Then playing by his own rules, he might hit three or four jumpers at the end of a game for a win. He would tease Winter afterward. "Tex—I need to apologize to you for going outside the offense at the end."

But gradually there had been some improvement, some sense that this was becoming a team, and a team that ran a triple-post offense at that. In the second half of the season, the Bulls went on a 24–3 run. What Jackson was doing was shrewdly creating a compromise between what Tex Winter wanted and what Michael Jordan wanted, a healthy compromise because no small amount of the strength of the triangle was the threat Jordan posed of exploding out on his own. Johnny Bach was somewhere between Winter and Jordan. He loved Michael's individual brilliance and he thought, like Jordan, that there were times when you simply had to go with your instincts. That season, Winter was impressed by the effort Jordan made. It was hard for someone of such incredible talent to discipline himself, to go against his instincts and try to run an alien and seemingly confining offense. Winter thought Jordan graded out at a B or a B– for that year; most important, Jordan was trying to be a good teammate. The more he reached out to his teammates, the more they seemed to respond and become a different kind of team. They were not there yet, but it was beginning to happen. In the playoffs, they beat Milwaukee 3–1 in the first round, and in the second round they won four of five from Philadelphia.

That set up another Conference Final against the Pistons, their third in a row. The first time, in 1988, they won only one game. The following year they won two. This year, they hoped they were ready. The Pistons won the first game, though, and at halftime in game two, with the Bulls down by fifteen points, Jordan gave his teammates a furious tongue-lashing for their lack of toughness. Though they lost that game as well, they closed the gap slightly in the second half and then went on to win the next two games in Chicago. Jackson believed his team was more talented, that it lacked only the confidence and the experience to win at this level. He also believed that because of Jordan's unique warrior spirit the Bulls were unusually vulnerable to the Pistons, because Chuck Daly had baited the perfect trap with his Jordan Rules defense for someone as competitive as Michael. In effect, what Daly had prepared for Jordan was the ultimate challenge: You have to beat us yourself, and you have to beat us physically. Jordan tended to respond to the challenge in the most predictable way imaginable, going right into the full force of the defense, having some monster games against the Pistons, but games scripted in the end by Chuck Daly. Jackson wanted his team and his star to play a smarter game, to use its greater quickness to full advantage, to fake at the strength of the Detroit defense—of their big men only Rodman was really as quick as the best Chicago players—and then utilize its speed to pass the ball and get good shots.

There was some accommodation to that, and the Bulls won Games Three and Four. In Game Five in Auburn Hills the Pistons hammered the Bulls again, but the Bulls, playing back in Chicago, won handily in Game Six. That meant a Game Seven in suburban Detroit again, a place where the Bulls had yet to win a playoff game. It was a disaster. Paxson had a bad ankle. Even worse was Scottie Pippen's condition. A year earlier, he had been taken out of Game Six after being elbowed in the side of the head by Bill Laimbeer so viciously he suffered a concussion in the first minute of the game. This time, just before the biggest game of their lives, Pippen suffered a migraine. With the game about to start, he could barely see. He took some aspirin but that seemed to only inflame the headache. He told Mark Pfeil, the trainer, he was having severe problems with his vision. "Can you play?" Pfeil asked him.

Pippen was about to say no, but Jordan answered for him, "Hell yes, he can play." Pfeil put an ice pack on Pippen's head, and Pippen tried to play, but he was never really in the game. He shot one of ten. Later, he said that he could barely tell the difference between the uniforms of his teammates and those of the Pistons. The game was a nineteen-point blowout. The defeat was a crushing blow to the Bulls and particularly to Michael Jordan.

After the game, Jordan was almost inconsolable. As he went through the parking lot on the way to the bus, Jack McCloskey spotted him. McCloskey was standing near the entrance and he excused himself from his wife and said that he had to go over and try to help that remarkable young man. "Mr. McCloskey," Jordan asked, "are we ever going to get past the Pistons? Are we ever going to win?"

"Michael," McCloskey answered, "your time is coming, and it's coming very soon."

Jordan got on the bus and sat in the back, alone with his father, in the depths of his own dark world. It was probably the lowest moment of his career. That day, he wept in the back of the bus. The Bulls had failed for the third time against their nemesis; once again, he questioned his teammates, particularly Pippen. Jordan was not that interested in the actual roots of Pippen's migraine, how real it had been, whether it was triggered by nervous tension or something else. To him, the thing that mattered was that Pippen had once again failed at a critical moment, and the question about him—his mental toughness, not his talent—remained unresolved.

Obscured in the immediacy of disappointment was the fact that the Bulls were on the rise, that they won fifty-five games in the regular season and that in the Conference Finals they were coming ever closer, going year by year from one victory to two and now to three. The difference between the Bulls and the Pistons was marginal, and if anything the Bulls' younger players were more talented and more complete than the young players on the Pistons. Michael Jordan, about to be twenty-eight, was coming into his absolute peak years, where his awesome physical abilities were now blended with an ever shrewder knowledge of the professional game. Pippen and Grant were on the rise, too. The Pistons, by contrast, had crested, though few sensed it, except perhaps their coaches and one or two of their players.

20

Chicago, 1990-1991

WINNING IN THE NBA more often has to do with psychological qualities than physical ones. Veteran coaches and players know that the margin of difference comes more than anything else from superior mental toughness. Quality players on great teams know how to win, how to finish a game, how to block out a hostile crowd on the road; they speak of the ability of great teams to bend the will of lesser teams to their own. If these phrases sound to the outside world like clichés, within the league they have achieved the status of gospel. In a season as long as the NBA's, where one game runs into the next, where mental fatigue is often greater than physical fatigue, what sets the great players apart is a capacity, in the dog days of February, on the road, when their bodies ache, to see a game against a lesser opponent as being important and to bring a high level of preparedness to it. Greatness in the NBA does not just require great skill, it demands the ability to go out and play hard night after night, and the ability to inspire one's teammates to play hard as well. That was what set players such as Bird, Johnson, and Thomas apart—not only their fierce will but its effect on their teammates. By 1990, the Bulls and the Pistons looked about even; in fact, if anything, in terms of pure talent, the Bulls looked superior. But so far, the Pistons owned the Bulls because they managed to get inside the heads of the Chicago players.

The one thing a championship-level team liked least to do was to give off any sense of vulnerability to a contender, particularly one that imagined its fortunes on the ascent. And so issues of mental toughness were critical: Were you mentally strong enough to expose the weaknesses of a rival team and emphasize to that team its own weaknesses before that team exposed your own vulnerabilities? Who danced for whom? If your magic worked often enough, as Detroit's had in its head-to-head meetings with Chicago, you created a sense among your own players of their own invincibility, and one among your opponents of their own fallibility. But if you showed even momentary vulnerability, particularly to a team that was getting better, it was like leaving blood in the water for sharks.

The Pistons had struggled with the same scenario against the Celtics during the height of the Bird-McHale-Parish years. The Pistons' narrow defeat by the Celtics in the 1987 Conference Finals was actually what snapped the crushing psychological hold the Celtics once held over them. So, too, did the ashes of Chicago's defeat contain the seeds of future triumph. If some of the Chicago players left the 1990 Conference Finals bitterly disappointed, convinced that the Detroit hex had worked again, the coaches were not that pessimistic. Not only had the Bulls once again narrowed the margin with Detroit, but they did dramatically better against Detroit than either Western Conference champion did in the Finals. The Lakers were swept in four in 1989 by the Pistons, and the Trail Blazers won one game and then lost three in a row at home. What that showed was that at this point the real NBA Finals were the Eastern Conference ones and that the Bulls were a tougher team than anything the West offered.

That was tantalizing. If the Bulls could beat the Pistons, the championship was theirs, and might, because of their youth, remain theirs for some time. Phil Jackson and his assistants thought that the Bulls were closing and closing fast. It was only a matter of figuring out how to go forward that final notch. What the Bulls had to learn was how to stop beating themselves. To do that, they had to believe in themselves. They would have to become tougher, physically and mentally, and they would have to stop letting the Pistons set the tone and pace of the game. And they would have to learn to win at the Palace, the handsome new arena in Auburn Hills that had opened in the fall of 1988 and where the Pistons played their home games. The Bulls had won only one game there since it had been opened.

The first step was to build themselves up physically. No one thought the Pistons were more talented than the Bulls, or for that matter smarter. But they *were* self-evidently tougher. The first sign that the players knew this as well as the coaches came the day after that last defeat in Auburn Hills. The game had been on a Sunday, and that Monday the coaches gathered at their offices at the Multi-plex, which was then their practice facility, to review the season. When they emerged from their meeting, they looked across the floor, and there were Grant and Pippen working with weights. Clearly, the 1990–1991 season had already begun. It did not take a genius to know that if each Chicago player built himself up that much more physically, he was likely to go on the court with greater confidence against a team whose players gloried in their reputation as bullies. Suddenly, that summer, all the Bulls were working out. No one demanded it; they just did it. On the July Fourth weekend, one of the coaches dropped by the practice center, and there was virtually the entire team working out, doing weight training. Clearly, the immediate disappointment of the last Detroit defeat had worn off. What replaced it was a sense of just how close they had come, and with it the smell of a possible championship. The players obviously could not wait for the next season to start.

Michael Jordan had started working out seriously the year before. After the 1990 defeat by the Pistons he spoke out to reporters about how he was tired of taking the physical punishment the Pistons handed out, and he spoke of his determination to build himself up. The article had been seen by a young physical trainer in Chicago named Tim Grover. Grover had played college basketball at the University of Illinois–Chicago, and though he was only five foot nine, he was a full-fledged basketball and physical-fitness nut. Both his parents worked at Northwestern Memorial Hospital—his mother was a nurse, his father ran one of the labs—and they had hoped he would go on to medical school after his graduation. But he had become enamored of the world of sports, and he decided instead to become a trainer, which was becoming a thriving new industry, given America's increased obsession with physical fitness. Grover took graduate courses in physiology, working toward a master's degree, with the aim of becoming a sports physiologist. When it came time to write his master's thesis, he wrote on how to create a strength program for basketball players—how to make them stronger and more immune to injury without bulking them up and slowing them down.

As part of his master's program, he chose to work with two high school programs in the area. At one school, he got the coach's permission to create a modest training program where he could test out relatively elementary concepts of fitness. At the other, he installed no program but simply monitored the progress of the team. The difference between the two programs was dramatic. In the school where he employed his ideas, the number of injuries went down dramatically, and the players performed very well in the late stages of their games; at the other school, the number of injuries was higher, and the team played poorly late in its games. It was, he was sure, a valuable if primitive confirmation of many of his ideas.

He received his master's degree in 1986, and three years later he was working as a trainer in a local health club when he read about Michael's dilemma. It struck him that he could be of considerable value to him. What Jordan wanted was help in an area about which Tim Grover had been thinking for six or seven years. It was a tantalizing prospect—the possibility of employing his skills and his passion for physiological improvement on the greatest player in the game, a player who was able to do all the things Grover would have loved to do if only he had Jordan's size and talent. Grover called Dr. John Hefferon, the Bulls' team doctor, who was associated with the hospital where his parents worked and something of a family friend. Hefferon immediately started to laugh. "Why are you laughing?" Grover asked. "Because Michael and I have been talking about this for a few months," he said, "and your name has come up several times. I was just telling him that I thought you two should meet."

Grover met first with Mark Pfeil, the trainer. He explained his philosophy, how he would work to build up the upper body while not sacrificing speed and elasticity in the lower body, thereby making Jordan stronger but not slower. In addition, he said, he would concentrate on strengthening the areas where basketball players were traditionally vulnerable to injury. Pfeil, who knew the special vulnerabilities to injuries induced by a demanding professional basketball season, was impressed. At the end of their meeting, he said, "I like you, and I know John Hefferon likes you, and I think you ought to meet Michael."

After practice that day, Grover met with Jordan, and the only thing that Jordan said was, "You're younger than I am—I've never worked with anyone younger than me before."

Grover told Jordan that he could not make him a better player, but he could make him stronger, and equally important, he could almost surely extend his career. That was no small incentive, since Jordan was aware that players such as Julius Erving had turned to weight training only very late in their careers. Grover was suggesting that he start sooner rather than later. That obviously made sense. Grover also told him he thought there was a right and a wrong way to do this, and that instead of trying to do too much too soon, they should try and do it over several years, adding a little weight and strength each year and thus incorporating the new strength into the existing body incrementally rather than overloading it in one assault. Jordan had come into the league at about 185 pounds, and by the time he met with Grover he was near 195. The two of them talked about what the ideal weight for him would be, and

Jordan thought it would be 215, which turned out to be a very accurate estimate. Grover estimated that it would probably take three or four years to reach the optimum weight. Five pounds a year was probably the ideal target increase, because that way the body could adjust, add the muscle, and yet maintain its skill level. "If we try and bulk you up too quickly, your game will suffer and you'll lose something," he said.

Grover also warned Jordan that if he signed on, the first few months would be, if not painful, certainly disorienting, because the new program was bound to throw his shot off. Basketball, he said, was a muscle-memory sport, and he was going to be messing with that memory. "Your timing will be off, and you'll be missing your jump shot, and you'll be furious—you're just going to have to trust me when I tell you that eventually it will all come back." Michael Jordan laughed at that, sure that his shot, which had always been so true, would not desert him just because he was working out. He said he would try Grover's regimen for thirty days, and he gave Grover ten days to get the equipment they needed to get started. Grover asked what his budget was for equipment, and Jordan told him whatever he needed. Later, Grover thought there were several reasons why Jordan had wanted to work with him instead of Al Vermeil. Jordan wanted complete privacy, and he wanted someone absolutely committed to him and loyal only to him, not to the Bulls' management, which made him a little wary of Vermeil, who, whatever his strengths, worked for Krause.

They began the program. Grover's warning was prophetic: For a time, Jordan's game seemed to disintegrate—his jumper disappeared and he was even missing layups. If anything, however, this added to Grover's overall credibility: What he had predicted had taken place.

Jordan and Grover worked not just to build up his upper body but also to strengthen the parts of the body most vulnerable for a basketball player: the ankles, the wrists, the shoulders, the knees, and the hips. That was the real grunt work, Grover thought, and most big-time basketball players scorned it because there was no obvious reward. It did not make your body sleeker or more powerful looking. It gave you at best a partial immunity to certain draining injuries. What impressed Grover was that Jordan was so committed a pupil that he went along willingly with all the donkeywork. There was, for example, the problem of groin pulls. Because of the way basketball players have to move their feet on defense—a constant lateral movement—they are particularly susceptible to groin pulls, and that had been a nagging problem for Jordan in the past. Grover did some testing, and he discovered that the muscles on the insides of Jordan's legs were much stronger than the muscles on the outsides. That imbalance probably caused some of the groin pulls. They worked in a series of exercises designed to balance out the muscles and thus reduce the number of Jordan's pulls.

Not everyone thought the weight and strength program was a good idea. Jordan's close friend Howard White thought it a mistake. "You're a thoroughbred," he had warned, "so why screw it up? You might lose some of your speed."

But Jordan was adamant. "Howard, you're not the one who's getting pounded. Those guys are beating me to death. I have to get stronger."

He was a good student working with a good trainer. The most obvious thing about Jordan, Grover thought, was that he was willing to pay the price of his ambitions. He was not only a great practice player but unusually faithful to his workouts. He didn't cheat. At first, they scheduled the workouts after practice, but Jordan drove himself so hard in practice that he was too tired to do them properly afterward, so they switched their sessions to the mornings. Eventually, it became known as the Breakfast Club. By the late nineties Ron Harper and Scottie Pippen worked out with Jordan at the gym in his home every morning when the team was in Chicago, and then they had a breakfast prepared by a chef according to Grover's specifications. Grover alternated sessions, upper body one day, lower one the next. Under their agreement, he was not to talk to the media because Michael Jordan did not want anyone to know what he was doing. He was a trendsetter, and he knew other players keyed off him, whether it was his hairstyle or the length of his shorts, and he saw no benefit in taking something he now regarded as a distinct advantage and advertising it for the benefit of the players he wanted to destroy.

The long-range benefits of Grover's training were not known until much later, after Jordan left basketball, played baseball, returned to basketball, and extended his career at a rare level of excellence well into his thirties, an age when most basketball players, except for big men who can coast a little, are in considerable decline. In the seven full seasons Jordan played with Grover as his trainer, he missed only six games. In the three full seasons he played after his return from baseball, he did not miss a single game.

The immediate signs of the success of Grover's program were obvious. Jordan was bigger and more powerful, and his shoulders and arms reflected it. "You're costing me a lot of money," he told Grover annually. Grover played the straight man and asked why. "Because I have to keep throwing out my entire wardrobe—my clothes don't fit me anymore." By the end of the first year, it was clear that his body was stronger. One of the early signs was that Jordan became a much stronger finisher on his drives to the basket. In the past when he had driven to the basket, if he took a hit he often failed to finish the play because the player pounding him was so big. Now he could drive, take a hit, absorb the punishment, and summon the strength to finish the play and make the shot.

Now when he played against teams that had deliberately beaten up on him in the past, he was more often than not the pounder, and the defensive guards were becoming the poundees. It was a memorable change in roles. Nor was it just Jordan who was bigger and stronger. Grant and Pippen had worked out hard as well, and they too returned stronger and more committed. During the 1990 Eastern Conference Finals, when the Bulls were down two games, Jordan had seen the two cavorting around in practice in what seemed to him a lighthearted manner, and he became furious, because he did not think they were taking the game seriously enough. That was no longer true. Pippen came of age in the 1990–1991 season. He had made the all-star team for the first time the previous season, and now strength begat winning, winning begat confidence, and confidence begat more winning. In the NBA, these things built on themselves. Pippen had a breakout year, averaging eighteen points, seven rebounds, and six assists a game while becoming a brilliant defender.

Watching Chicago that year, Chuck Daly knew that time was working against his own team, that the Bulls had probably caught up, more because of Pippen's improvement than anything else. Pippen's coming of age was a double blessing, because as he emerged as a great player in his own right, he changed Jordan, making him more of a team player. They were becoming more comfortable with the Tex Winter offense, which allowed them both to move the ball and make slashing drives to the basket. It was going to be harder for the Pistons to catch Jordan in a net the way they had in the past. Nor was Daly's own team on the ascent anymore. They lost a critical piece when Rick Mahorn was taken by Minnesota in the expansion pool a year earlier. Without him, they were simply not as tough or as intimidating. Laimbeer was heard several times that season complaining that the hunger was no longer there, that what drove him in the past was gone.

What was surprising that season was how quickly it all changed. The Bulls were playing well before the all-star break, winning more than two out of three games going into a road swing. They won in Sacramento, then flew to Detroit to play the Pistons at Auburn Hills in the final game before the all-star break. They had lost twelve of their previous thirteen games there; if there was ever an ideal time to win, Jackson thought, this was it. His team was 31–14, the pieces were all there, and wondrously, Isiah Thomas was out with a wrist injury. The Pistons were very much aware of the game's importance—before the game, Chuck Daly had spoken of how important it was because it might decide home-court advantage in the playoffs. The Pistons' John Salley, one of the more quotable players in the league, told the Chicago writers bluntly, "They've got the same syndrome we used to have against Boston—the inner feeling that every time we went there we'd lose. But one day we realized they're just normal people like the rest of us. That's the way Chicago has to feel when they come in and play us."

Still, it was a very hard game. Bill Cartwright was ejected in the third quarter: There had been a brief collision with Laimbeer, and Laimbeer had instantly flopped. The referee called a foul on Cartwright, he protested and was immediately thrown out. In the fourth quarter, the physical nature of the play escalated. During a time-out, the Chicago coaches feared that Horace Grant might be wilting under the Detroit assault: He had begun to turn and look to the referees when the Pistons pounded him, as if beseeching them for help. Jimmy Cleamons thought that it was a sure sign of defeat. He, like the other coaches, knew all too well how the refs would view it—as whining. At that level, playing the defending champions at home, Cleamons knew, you had to prove to the refs that you were tough enough to be a champion yourself. If you wanted their crown, you had to work harder and you could not look to the refs, because they were not going to give it to you. The more you asked them for calls, the less likely you were to get them. The way of the world was unfair: Champions did not ask for calls, champions *got* calls. During the next time-out, Cleamons told Grant, "Just play! Don't complain!"

With about four minutes left, the Pistons were ahead by five points, which, given the nature of their defense, was a considerable lead, especially at home. In the past, the Pistons almost always closed out games better than the Bulls had, and they were at the point where all too often the Bulls folded. But Pippen made a jumper, and then Jordan scored off a Grant offensive rebound. Somehow, in the final two minutes the Bulls got the calls from the refs. On the sidelines, Chuck Daly was screaming at the refs—pleading if not his case then the fact that his was the home team and was entitled to the calls. The Bulls won 95–93. Johnny Bach, who had always spoken of Detroit as Chicago's albatross, was exuberant after the game. The albatross was finally gone, he said. The monkey is off our backs, Jackson said in a postgame interview. Bird or beast, both were gone.

With that victory, the Bulls went on a run. After the all-star game, they won nine games in a row, lost one to Indiana, and then won nine more. When both streaks were over, they were 50–15, an incredible mark. The previous season, the Pistons won fifty-nine games, but that fell this year to fifty; by comparison, the Bulls had won fifty-five games the previous year, but this season they won sixty-one, the franchise's best record ever. That was a swing of fifteen games. The orbital curves had finally crossed.

In the playoffs, the Bulls continued their run: They swept the Knicks 3–0 in the first round and took four out of five from the 76ers in the second round. They had earned what they wanted most, a return match against the Pistons but with the home-court advantage.

The Pistons team that arrived in Chicago for the 1991 Eastern Conference Finals still had the bark, but much of the bite was gone. So was some of their leverage with the refs. Phil Jackson had sent the league office a carefully edited tape of the cheapest shots the Pistons had taken against the Bulls in the past, and there was no doubt that it struck a responsive note—the league was not pleased with the Bad Boys image, nor the larger implication that brute force was becoming more important than pure skill in a game whose most critical selling point was the artistry of its players. So the Pistons still talked trash, but they did not intimidate, particularly with Mahorn gone. If anything, the Bulls got in the first shots physically, like a sharp elbow to the chest Jordan gave Joe Dumars as a welcome-to-the-game introduction in Game One. In this game, it was Jordan who screamed trash at Rodman, hoping, his coaches believed, to give greater confidence to his teammates. At one point, Jordan, guarded by John Salley, was holding the ball, threatening to drive on the basket. Salley, whose nickname was Spider, shouted, "You don't go near the Spider's web!" At that, Jordan drove forward, reversed his direction at the last second, and slammed the ball home for a basket. "Block that, bitch!" he yelled at Salley, and with that, Salley knew the old Pistons magic was gone. The Pistons tired in the fourth quarter, and the Bulls won.

By the second game, the Bulls seemed even more in command. Jackson had Pippen bring the ball up the court: He was a smooth ball handler, as quick as any smaller guard, and if the Pistons contested him, they risked matchup problems in the front court. The Pistons seemed unable to apply pressure to the Bulls, who were now getting the calls and going to the line far more than Detroit. Chicago won Game Two handily. But the Bulls had yet to win in Auburn Hills in the playoffs. In Game Three, the Bulls had a number of big leads—sixteen points at one moment in the third quarter—but the Pistons narrowed the gap to eight in the fourth quarter. Detroit made its last run, closing to five points with 2:30 left. During the next Bulls possession, the Pistons stole the ball. Vinnie Johnson drove to the basket. Jordan chased him, closing quickly. Johnson looked over his shoulder, sensing Michael's approach, and at the last second he slowed to let Jordan fly by him. Jordan somehow anticipated the move, and made a beautiful adjustment, forcing Johnson to throw up a weak, off-balance shot, which Jordan rebounded. The Pistons' rally fizzled; the Bulls won. They were up three games to none.

The Pistons had little left for Game Four. Laimbeer took a cheap shot at Paxson as Paxson was driving to the basket, and Paxson immediately jawed back at him, made the free throws, and then hit three jumpers in a row. In the second quarter, Rodman took a vicious shot at Pippen on a drive, pushing him so hard out of bounds that he could have suffered a career-ending injury. He suffered a gash to the chin that took six stitches to close. As Sam Smith later wrote, Rodman (who in his subsequent incarnation as a campy media provocateur was to emerge as a cross-dresser and a frequenter of gay bars) kept screaming at the refs, "You think that's something, I'll do it again. We don't want no fags out here and he's a fag. . . . We don't put up with none of that fag-ass shit out here." Pippen played through it. If anything, as a sign of their new toughness the Bulls in their own way talked every bit as much trash.

The Bulls won handily. They had swept the Pistons; the demons were exorcised. Led by Isiah Thomas, the Pistons players walked off the court in the final seconds without shaking hands with the Bulls. There apparently had been a debate over that. It was Isiah's idea, and most of the other players had agreed. Originally, Isiah was going to grab a microphone and thank the Detroit fans for their loyalty, but Daly, appalled, had pleaded with him not to do it and had managed to talk him out of using the microphone, saying if they did it, their behavior would never be forgotten. So what happened was something of a compromise: They walked off, without using the public-address system but without the traditional respect for the winners as well. That scene, more than anything else, was what many fans outside of Detroit remembered about the Bad Boys.

21

Chicago; Los Angeles, 1991

A FTER THEY defeated Detroit in the Eastern Finals, the Bulls then took on the Los Angeles Lakers for their first shot at the championship. It was the Lakers' ninth visit to the Finals in the age of Magic Johnson, which began in 1980, eleven years earlier. Both Kareem Abdul-Jabbar and Michael Cooper were gone, and by all odds this should have been the twilight of Johnson's career, but he was still a superb player on a powerful team. If there was a decline in his on-court play, it had yet to be exploited by opposing teams. Johnson still had a stellar cast, including James Worthy, Sam Perkins, A. C. Green, Mychal Thompson, Byron Scott, and Vlade Divac. The Lakers, coached by Mike Dunleavy, won fifty-eight games that year. Some of the old razzle-dazzle from the earlier Johnson years was gone, and the Lakers used a more deliberate offense now, designed as much as anything else to conserve energy, but they were still a formidable team, and their players were accustomed to all the media hype and the accompanying disruption of the NBA Finals, unlike the Bulls, save of course for Michael Jordan, who dealt with that kind of media pressure every day of his life. This matchup was exactly what NBA and NBC executives had long wanted: the raw young gunslingers from Chicago up against the savvy old pros from Los Angeles, the older, incumbent superstar against the ascending one, the player much of the country longed to see in the Finals.

In a way, it was a battle of two great smiles. Magic Johnson had a brilliant smile, which if anything seemed more a permanent part of his countenance than Michael Jordan's. Jordan's smile was more controlled, as befit his character—it might have a higher wattage, but he flashed it more sparingly, only on select occasions such as championship-award ceremonies, and photo shoots for his varying commercial sponsors. That selective rationing made it more effective with the public—the fierce face of the warrior suddenly gone, replaced at the end of the game by a smile that reflected the incandescent pleasure of the victor. Johnson's smile was much more his signature on the court; he seemed to take constant joy from the sheer pleasure of playing, and it was easy to forget how intense and demanding he was, how hard he pushed his teammates, coming down on them immediately if he sensed some slippage or carelessness in their game. "Forget Magic's smile," his longtime teammate Mychal Thompson said. "That's not who he was. He was like Ali, and Ali smiled a lot too. But what they both wanted was nothing less than to kill you."

The Lakers-Bulls Finals gave basketball people a chance to compare two very different superstars. Johnson was a natural leader on the court, and he played the right position for it, point guard. In the shrewd assessment of Mark Heisler of the *Los Angeles Times*, who had covered both men for a long time, Jordan was by contrast not a natural leader, he was a natural *doer*. His game did not evolve naturally from sharing the ball and making other players better. One of the few men who knew them both very well, James Worthy, once said that if anything, Johnson was more intense than Jordan: "Michael is more intense within himself, Magic is intense for everybody."

The stories of Jordan pushing his teammates were well known, in no small part because he had labored so long in such difficult circumstances with lesser players. There was less a sense of Johnson as someone who pushed and punished his teammates, for he had from the start been fortunate enough to be surrounded by greatness. The Lakers team he joined was like a very good, very well crafted automobile that lacked only one thing, an ignition system. He was that system. Winning was very serious business to him: He won in high school, he led his Michigan State team to the NCAA championship when he was all of nineteen years old, and he took the Lakers, who had not been in the Finals since 1973, to the Finals in his first year, winning as a rookie at a time in his life when there were a great many states in the union in which he could not legally drink.

He was not a great one-on-one player, not a great pure shooter, and his ability to jump was quite limited. But he was passionate about winning, joyous about playing the game itself, and his instinct on the court—when and where to get the ball to a teammate—was almost unmatched. He had great peripheral vision, he was a superb ball handler with huge hands, and his height—six foot nine, unprecedented in a point guard—meant that not only could the defensive man not block his vision but he was constantly causing matchup problems. His sense of the court, his capacity to make the right pass at the right time as the play unfolded, was special. Coaches and scouts who did nothing during a game but focus on Johnson, trying to figure out where his weaknesses were, often came away shaking their heads, believing that there were no weaknesses.

Magic Johnson was the prototype of the alpha personality as basketball player, a born leader, his manner on the court a natural extension of his personality off it. Knowing him, it was hard to imagine a field of endeavor in which he would not have taken command. He made the Lakers *his* team almost from the start. "We thought he was very good when we drafted him," Jerry West said years later, "and we thought he would distribute the ball very well to his teammates. But we had no idea that he would take over the team and exert his leadership that quickly—that he would do it midway through his first season."

His nicknames reflected different aspects of his personality. To the fans at large and most sportswriters he was Magic, reflecting the wizardry of his game. It was the nickname for those who did not know him well, the outsiders who wanted to feel like insiders. To those who knew him better, the elite, he was Earvin (his given name), a name he liked to be called. His teammates and those very close to him—the select few— called him Buck, for young buck, a nickname bestowed on him by teammate Norm Nixon when he first arrived in Los Angeles because of his energy and drive and passion to win.

In time, as the team crystallized and after Pat Riley became the coach, the Lakers became a very tough team. Riley was endlessly driven, a young man with blue-collar roots who had always been aware of his physical limits as a player. Riley knew that this was his one great chance at the brass ring. One day, his career over, he had been virtually out of a job, absolutely unsure of his future, when he lucked into a marginal position as assistant broadcaster to Chick Hearn, the Laker announcer, a man who neither wanted nor needed an assistant; the assistant's principal responsibility was to say "That's right, Chick" several times a game, as Mark Heisler noted. Then Riley stumbled into a job as a Lakers assistant coach, and when Paul Westhead was fired, it became his team, because Jerry West wanted no part of coaching. Riley was stunned by this series of events, but once they won their first title under him, he was not about to let this opportunity slip away—he was going to push it for all it was worth.

Riley himself was always aware of to whom he owed the most. One day, he was with a group of nonbasketball friends, and he asked them if they could name two words that set him apart from everyone else. So they tried—Honesty? Loyalty? Toughness? Simplicity? Preparation? All wrong. Finally he told them. "Magic Johnson."

Riley and Johnson pushed that team hard: If Riley was the general, as James Worthy once pointed out, then Magic Johnson was the drill sergeant. The drill sergeant, Worthy added, knew that his job was to take as much pressure as he could off the general. Lakers practices were serious business. Everything was scripted, and no time was to be lost. The enforcer was Johnson. He was the first player there every day for practice, wanting to get his own head right, sitting there by his locker, thinking of what he needed to do himself, and then checking out the other players. He did not want a lot of noise in the locker room, particularly before a game. He wanted nothing to break his concentration. No boom boxes—if someone wanted music, let him use earphones. The lesson was clear: This was a business office, not a social or athletic club. If you were late to practice, it was Johnson who got down on you: "Let's look at you. Is everything OK? Nothing wrong? No one in your family died? You didn't have a car wreck on the way over here? Thank God!" A message was being sent. He was very hard on A. C. Green because Green did not have good hands and could not handle some passes, and he was very tough on Vlade Divac, who arrived from Yugoslavia a bit soft for the American game. On occasion he addressed Divac, said one teammate, the way you talk to a dog—a dog you did not particularly like. If the Lakers lost two in a row, Johnson was in a terrible mood, worse even than Riley.

The Laker team that emerged in that decade was a great team. At its best, only the Celtics at their best were its match. Because of its speed, because of its capacity to play a finesse game, and because it played in Los Angeles, which was not considered a tough city in the way that Chicago or Detroit were considered tough cities, it was said to be a soft team. Nothing could have been further from the truth. Pat Riley did not coach soft teams, and Magic Johnson did not play on them. The Lakers were very tough. Though Dunleavy had since replaced Riley, the Lakers were still very tough, and they were the team Chicago was to face for its first championship. How well they would match up against the Bulls was a fascinating question.

Because of Jordan's brilliant offense, few noticed that the team's real trademark was its defense. "You don't know how lucky you are," Don Nelson, then the coach of Golden State, told Phil Jackson a year later.

"I think I do, but what do you mean?" Jackson asked him. "Your two best offensive players are your two best defensive players," Nelson answered. That was true, and it was very rare. Phil Jackson had no illusions about his ability to coach an offense, but he knew he was a very good defensive coach. When Jackson got the team in the fall of 1989, he pushed all his players at camp to play pressure defense. That first camp was brutal. They were all to be in great shape and push hard on the defensive end; their energy there would create opportunities at the offensive end. They most assuredly had the talent for it.

Michael Jordan was a very good defensive player. Some, like Mike Dunleavy, considered him the best ever at his position on defense. It was part of the singular completeness of his game. Here credit went to Dean Smith, who, sensing Jordan's offensive brilliance and surpassing natural ability, had pushed him to excel on defense as well. Out of that early pressure evolved the rarest of players, a brilliant offensive star who also had a hunger for the exhausting and often neglected gritty work at the other end of the court. Early in his professional career Jordan mentioned casually to reporters that he hoped one day to be named defensive player of the year as well as the MVP. Jan Hubbard, then with *The Dallas Morning News,* wrote that it could not be done, that it took too much energy to play his kind of offense and an equal amount of energy to be that kind of defensive star—no one could have enough energy to do both. But then, in 1987–1988, Jordan was named both the MVP and defensive player of the year. Hubbard wrote that he had been wrong, but Michael, who always wanted the last word, never let Hubbard forget what he had written, forget that he had, however momentarily, underestimated Michael Jordan, certainly more than a journalistic misdemeanor and perilously close to a felony.

Scottie Pippen emerged that season as perhaps an even better defensive player than Jordan, or at least a more versatile one. With those unusually long arms, a wingspan that exceeded Jordan's, he was able to play in the backcourt with the footwork of a guard and the reach of a center. Nothing in those early years helped him more than playing against Jordan every day in practice. The equation was simple: If Pippen could guard Jordan, then he could guard anyone in the league. The two of them, plus Horace Grant, arguably the quickest power forward in the game, made the Bulls a formidable presence on defense. "The Dobermans," Johnny Bach called the three of them, because they were so young, quick, and fierce on defense. In addition, though Cartwright had lost much of his offensive game, he was a skilled positional defensive player; it was hard for any other team's center to have a dominating night against Cartwright. No matter what the tempo, they were a hard team to beat: They played very good defense and so could win low-scoring games, but they were also explosive and good in the open court, so they could also win if the score went well over one hundred.

As the two teams prepared to meet, very few people knew how good the Bulls were. They knew how good *Jordan* was, but that was a different story. Yes, they had swept the Pistons this year, but only the people who played against the Pistons knew how tough they were, how much was required to beat them. By contrast, people knew how good the Lak- · ers were, or thought they did, because they had been around for so long.

The first two games were played in Chicago. In the first game, the Bulls seemed a little tentative and surprisingly slow on their defensive rotations. Sam Perkins hit a three pointer at the end to give the Lakers a two-point win. Phil Jackson had a sense that his team had played beneath its level, that it had struggled with first-game jitters; he was confident that there were some defensive adjustments he could make that would impede the Lakers' flow on offense. He was not that unhappy. A game had slipped away, but he liked most of what he saw, and he was sure they could get the game back. In Game Two, an early second foul on Jordan pushed Jackson's hand. He would have Pippen guard Magic on defense, something he had pondered doing earlier on. It was a marvelous move: Pippen was nearly as tall as Johnson but much quicker at this stage of their careers, and Johnson was unaccustomed to that combination. Pippen's defense of Johnson seemed to throw the Lakers offense out of sync. The Lakers were also hurt by the absence of James Worthy, who was suffering from a badly sprained ankle—he was a better ball handler and thus a better press breaker than Byron Scott, the off guard. Without Worthy on the court, the pressure applied to Johnson was harder to handle. Sensing that, the Bulls stepped up the defensive pressure.

At the same time, the Bulls were finding their own rhythm: In the third quarter, they hit seventeen of twenty field goals to take over the game. When the game was over, Jordan had hit fifteen of eighteen, Paxson eight of eight. One of Jordan's fifteen baskets was a highlight-film special: driving to the basket with the ball in his right hand, he saw Sam Perkins, his old Carolina teammate, coming at him. In *mid-flight* he seemed to pause for a moment, and then he switched the ball to his left hand and slammed it home. No one else in basketball could have made that shot. It was part of a 107–86 blowout, and it ended the idea that the Bulls were too young and inexperienced to play the Lakers. They had split in Chicago. Now, as they were going to Los Angeles, Phil Jackson said he wanted to win two out of three there. "What about making it three of three?" Jordan asked.

In Game Three in Los Angeles, Jordan hit a fourteen-foot jump shot over Byron Scott with 3.4 seconds left to tie the game and send it into overtime. The Bulls, younger and fresher, went on to win, but Jordan had injured his big toe when he landed after making the tying shot. The pain was immediate—he thought at first that it was broken—and it affected his ability to start and stop. Chip Schaefer, the Bulls' trainer since 1990, tried to construct a special shoe, designed to give his toe extra protection, but when he tried it out he found that he could not make his normal cuts. Just before the tip-off for Game Four he turned to Schaefer and said, "Give me the pain." He would wear his regular shoe, would deal with the pain. He did, scoring thirty-six points in Game Four, the third straight Chicago victory. In the second half, Magic Johnson screamed at his teammates to play harder. Sam Perkins made just one of fifteen shots. It was not just a shattering blowout, 97–82, but a blowout driven by great defense. The Bulls simply shut down the Laker offense, holding Los Angeles at home to its lowest point output since the introduction of the shot clock. That the old order was changing was dawning on the Lakers. After Game Three, Johnson had said it would be a long series: "Nothing's been decided." But after Game Four, he was clearly shaken. "An old-fashioned ass kicking," he said. "Never dreamed it would happen." What had been the inconceivable, a sweep of all three games in Los Angeles, now seemed possible.

The Bulls got the sweep in the Los Angeles Forum in Game Five. This time, however, Los Angeles made it a game. With about six minutes left, the Lakers had a one-point lead. The Chicago coaches were wary that Jordan was slipping out of the team offense and trying to do it all himself. That was the last thing they wanted, particularly because Magic Johnson had a tendency to play a kind of zone defense, dropping off Paxson and leaving him open in order to be able to lay back and stop potential drives to the basket by Jordan or Pippen. Jackson had pushed Jordan during the entire series to look for Paxson. "Michael, who's open?" Jackson asked near the end of Game Five. There was no answer. "Michael, who's open?" he asked again. Still no answer. Then he asked a third time.

"Pax," Jordan finally answered.

"Then get him the fucking ball," Jackson said. To the players it was a critical moment in the evolution of the team, if not in this game and this series, then for the future. (Years later, when the division between Jackson and Krause was absolute, Jerry Reinsdorf recalled that as one of

Krause's happiest moments—"Jerry kept saying that it was one of Phil's great moments, that no other coach could have gotten Michael to do that.") The Bulls went on to win, 108–101.

They had won four in a row, sweeping Los Angeles in Los Angeles as they had swept Detroit in Detroit: They had gone 8–1 in the two series, and they had won all five games they played on the road. Much of it, people discovered, was about defense: They held the Lakers, who year after year averaged around 110 points a game in the Finals, to 90 points per game in regulation. The torch had truly been passed.

After the game, after winning his first championship seven years into the league, Michael Jordan broke down and wept. Reporters asked Magic Johnson if he had been that emotional when he won his first title. No, he answered, "I was so young, so unschooled in what it took to win the NBA title back then. So I know exactly what Michael is feeling now, because I felt that way later in my career, when it took much more effort and sweat to win it."

22.

Chicago, 1997-1998

SLOWLY, STARTING IN DECEMBER 1997, Scottie Pippen began to mend, both physically and psychologically. Ron Harper had stroked him as a friend and teammate. Phil Jackson had stayed in touch, as carefully as possible, without seeming to be threatening him or taking management's side, outlining the dangers of Pippen's proposed strategy, pointing out that the real victim would not be Jerry Krause or Jerry Reinsdorf, but Pippen himself and, of course, his teammates. By late December, he had swung around mentally and decided to return. But his foot had healed slowly. The operation was successful, but when Scottie started to work out on his own, the Bulls' coaches and trainers were stunned to find that his legs had atrophied so much during his four-month absence that he had lost two thirds of his vertical jump. The way back was going to be harder than anyone had expected, and it was weeks after his foot had technically healed before he was ready to play.

Pippen missed thirty-five games, or just under half of the eighty-two-game season. His teammates had held turf surprisingly well in his absence: Their record was 24–11, and since its low point soon after Pippen's explosion in Seattle they had gone 16–4. But those games had been exhausting, particularly for Michael Jordan, who was being double- and triple-teamed night after night and who found himself having to carry much of Pippen's share of the offense and defense. Any hopes that Jordan could pace himself in this season were now gone. It was going to be a season that demanded maximum minutes from all the starters, and as

Michael Jordan neared his thirty-fifth birthday, he was playing thirty-nine minutes a game—thirty-nine *hard* minutes a game.

Pippen returned for a game at home against Golden State on January 10. The Bulls were a different team with him on the floor. In the past, Chicago had been a team without a pure point guard; that was by design, to keep Jordan from having to handle the ball too much while bringing it up but also to make sure that he touched the ball often enough once the ball was in the frontcourt. In the past, much of the ball-handling fell to Pippen, with other players also sharing the duty. But without Pippen, the Bulls often looked awkward and stiff. With him back, that changed. If there were few athletes in the NBA more artistic than Jordan, there were also few more beautiful to watch night after night than Scottie Pippen. There was an elegance and a fluidity to his slightest movements; his grace, his ease of direction, his almost perfect timing possession after possession obviously affected his teammates. Now, with Pippen handling the ball again, the Bulls' offense looked completely different, fluid and comfortable. With Pippen on the floor, the players seemed to know where they were supposed to be at all times, as if their movements were preordained by a skilled watchmaker.

The Bulls immediately went on a 10–2 run for the rest of January and into early February. The old confidence, indeed arrogance, was back. In early February, the Bulls arrived in Los Angeles for a game with the talented young Lakers. The Lakers, with Shaquille O'Neal, Kobe Bryant, Nick Van Exel, Robert Horry, and Eddie Jones, were probably the most physically talented team in the league—they exuded a sense of raw power. Whether that power and athleticism could be distilled at the right moment into a mentally tough, winning team was very much a question. They reminded basketball writers of teams in the past whose physical strength was an immense asset during the monotony of the regular season but who, when confronted with the much tougher defenses of the playoffs, often unraveled in the face of teams that were less talented but more disciplined. The Bulls came into Los Angeles in these dog days of the season in a winning rhythm that any coach would envy. Despite Pippen's long absence, they were 33–13 and contesting their division with a team that was looming larger and larger in their minds, the Indiana Pacers, coached by Larry Bird.

The Lakers game was billed as a matchup against the team the Bulls might meet in the Finals. The first half was close, and the Lakers held a four-point lead, 57–53, at the break. Then in the third quarter, Los Angeles came out and scored the first fifteen points, blowing the game open and eventually outscoring Chicago 34–10 in the quarter. "It was like a layup line out there," Jackson later said. Afterward, the Lakers were talking about the power of young fresh legs, and the Bulls were licking their wounds. Toni Kukoc played nine minutes, scored two points, and complained about an injury that Jackson described as a mystery illness—it turned out to be a minor back injury. Jackson was furious about the poor showing on defense, but later he decided that the team had relaxed from the moment it had arrived in Los Angeles, and there had been too much partying the night before. He decided not to read too much significance into the defeat.

If there was a sense of frustration at this point for Phil Jackson, it revolved around Toni Kukoc, the talented, enigmatic Croatian. Now in his fifth year, Kukoc had yet to play at the level the coaches and scouts expected from him and knew he was capable of. Kukoc, who had been the best player in Europe before coming to Chicago, was the most tantalizing of players. He was immensely talented, a backcourt man who stood six foot eleven and had exceptional distance on his jump shot and great court vision. He could shoot and pass beautifully. In Europe, his nickname had been the Waiter, because he served his teammates with the ball so skillfully. There were times when he was on the court with Jordan, Pippen, Rodman, and Harper when the Bulls were simply awesome; they came down the court and the passing was so good that the ball did not seem to touch the floor. There were other times when Kukoc stood on the perimeter, faked a jump shot, and then drove to the basket, his long arms extended, and made a left-handed scoop shot that was impossible to defend. On those occasions, it seemed as if he could score twenty points a night simply driving. But such moments tended to be the exception. What was missing from his game were two things: first, a certain toughness required in the NBA, and second, a consistency of effort. He went in and out of focus; on good nights he looked like an all-star, then the next night he virtually disappeared.

Kukoc himself was a pleasant, almost sweet, if slightly vulnerable young man, with a tendency to sulk when things did not go well. America often seemed hard for him, and the coaches noticed that he played better at home in Chicago than he did on the road. It often seemed to his American coaches that he had been raised in Yugoslavia less to be a basketball player than to be a young prince. Once, when Chip Schaefer was talking to him about why the coaches were down on him, he likened it to a spanking parents give to their children when they are young. Kukoc looked quite puzzled. An interpreter was summoned, but the problem proved not to be the language but the concept—Kukoc had never been spanked as a boy. Nor had he ever been tongue-lashed by a coach. From the time he was a young boy he had always been so gifted and so tall that his different coaches congratulated themselves on their good fortune in having him on their teams and had not worked to make him a more complete or tougher player. What he did on offense was more than enough, and on defense, in a league where the players were a good deal less athletic than in the NBA, he was not a step slower, as he often was in America, and his height was sufficient to allow him to defend and rebound adequately.

He arrived in America immensely gifted, but in the eyes of his coaches virtually untrained. His fundamentals, for a player of such compelling skills, were surprisingly poor, particularly on defense. He was a specialist in what the coaches called the toreador defense—reaching in with his hands instead of moving his feet and his body. It was a sure way to draw fouls in the NBA. Nor did he box out properly. He knew nothing about how to train and get his wind up, even what and how to eat before a game. Once Chip Schaefer had a pregame meal with him and was stunned to watch Kukoc put away a seven-course meal including salad, pasta, and steak. "A sure four-thousand-calorie meal," Schaefer noted later, almost admiringly. Like many European players, he was accustomed to drinking wine with his pregame meal, even if he did water it slightly. His body fat when he arrived was about 20 percent, very high for the NBA. Eventually, the Bulls got it down to the midteens, which was pretty good for Kukoc. At first, aware that he was not physically strong enough, the Bulls tried to bulk him up, and he lifted weights. But while that did not make him noticeably stronger, it certainly made him noticeably slower. So finally they accepted him for what he was, although they did work to get him in better shape, and to have him eat more wisely.

Because of his height, he had the capacity to create havoc in the backcourt against men much shorter than he. But there was a downside as well. He often caused the Bulls serious matchup problems. He was a defensive liability in many situations, and Jackson did not like to start him. He was a soft player in a very physical league. He hated to take the charge of an offensive player. When the Bulls reviewed game films in sessions at the Berto Center, the other players often laughed and teased Kukoc when the film showed him stepping aside when it was time to take a charge, or when it showed players about to rebound, and there under the basket was Kukoc clearly wincing and protecting himself. Pippen and Jordan were very hard on him in the film room, as was Jackson. Finding the right way to use him, finding the situations in which he was a plus and not a liability, was tricky. The previous year his ability to come off the bench had won him the league's coveted sixth-man award, something that most players in the league would have cherished, understanding that being a starter meant less in this league than being a finisher. But Kukoc was stubborn, and he hated coming off the bench. As far as he was concerned, it meant that he was not good enough to start on a great American team. So he fought Jackson's use of him, complaining openly and bitterly when he did not start.

Of all the talented players Jackson dealt with in Chicago, Kukoc more than anyone else eluded his reach. There were moments when Kukoc flashed talent of a dazzling kind, and moments when he seemed completely out of sync with his teammates, shooting when he should pass, passing when he should shoot, holding the ball in a way that caused the rebounders gathering underneath to get three-second violations. In one memorable sequence in a playoff game against Miami, he was being guarded by Chris Gatling, who had just sprained his ankle. The Heat had not been able to call time-out, which meant that Kukoc was being guarded by a very vulnerable defender who was hopping around on one leg. Kukoc held the ball on the perimeter. The other Bulls cleared out so that there would be no one to double him when he drove to the basket. Then, instead of driving, Kukoc took a long three-point shot and missed it. "Toni," Jackson told him later, "that's why Croatia has never won a war."

Over the years, Kukoc had become one of Jackson's two principal whipping boys, the player he repeatedly stopped the film sessions to criticize. The other was Luc Longley, the big center who seemed to have constant problems with his footwork. But Kukoc had emerged as a far more irritating project than Longley, for when Longley was captured on videotape in some misdeed, he acknowledged his mistake and vowed to play better. Kukoc, by contrast, almost always had some excuse, or would claim that it hadn't happened, that they hadn't seen what they had all just witnessed. He was viewed on the team as a whiner. Jackson stayed on his case throughout the season: "If I don't do it, Toni," Jackson told him, "then your teammates will. So it may as well be me." When Jackson substituted for him during a game, he often came out mumbling in Croatian, a sure sign that he was complaining and quite possibly cursing the coaches, though of course no one could be sure.

Jackson's relationship with Kukoc was complicated by the fact that Kukoc was Krause's last great coup from the draft. Therefore, there was an unusual emotional attachment on Krause's part and, the coaches thought, an unwillingness to see Kukoc's weaknesses. Nothing pleased a talented scout more than to find a great player in the second or third round, a selection that in the future has the scout's name all over it and tells as much about the talent of the scout as it does about the talent of the player.

Twenty years earlier, in the ice age of the NBA, before the coming of

ESPN and the mechanization of the whole scouting process, that kind of big strike was relatively frequent, and many talented scouts made their reputations by finding talented players in small backcountry colleges and drafting them in the second and third rounds. In the new age, however, such a delight was rarer and rarer. Therefore, getting a high-quality player with nothing more than a second-round pick was a great triumph for Krause.

It was Leon Douglas, a former NBA player, who had first tipped Jerry Krause off about Kukoc. "He's an amazing kid," Douglas said. "He plays like he's been in the ghetto all of his life—he's got all the moves." Why would I want a white ghetto kid from Yugoslavia? Krause asked. "Because there's something special about him," Douglas said. What position does he play? Krause asked. Guard, Douglas answered. "So why would I need a guard who's a white Yugoslavian ghetto gym rat?" Krause asked. "Jerry," Douglas said, "*he's six eleven.*" That got Krause's interest, and he began to scout him, and in time to try to sign him.

Never had Krause been more amorous in going after a player than in his pursuit of Kukoc. It was the Sleuth at his stealthiest. Bucky Buckwalter of Portland, who also liked to work the basketball back alleys, was also checking out reports about Kukoc. Kukoc played in a tournament in Rome, and Buckwalter spotted Krause in the stands, which did not surprise him, since their taste in finding a certain kind of player was so similar. Then he looked again and Krause was gone. Krause literally fled the stands in order to hide, Buckwalter realized. That charmed Buckwalter, a considerable basketball eccentric himself, and after the game he eventually found Krause and decided to tease him. "Jerry," Buckwalter said, "you can't be looking at Kukoc, can you? Because if there's one thing I know, it's that he's not your kind of player—he's not nearly athletic enough."

Krause quickly agreed; Kukoc was much too soft a player. "He'd be a defensive liability for us," Krause said. "Besides, we don't have a position for him." And Buckwalter agreed, thinking, Jerry, have it your way, but we both know that you and I are both looking at the same man for the same reason: He's a great talent, likely to be a steal, and besides, when can't you find a place for a six-eleven guard who can handle the ball, shoot, and pass?

The Bulls drafted Kukoc in 1990, the second pick of the second round. He was only twenty-one. If they could sign him, he was a virtual freebie. But he was a big star in Europe, and he was very well paid there. His family was in Yugoslavia as it was being torn apart by civil war, and his fiancée (later his wife) had no desire to come to the United States. Krause courted him relentlessly. There were many visits and presents and impassioned talks of what it would be like to play against and with the best. But for a long time it was a very difficult sell. The offers included figures larger than those paid to members of the Bulls such as Pippen, which added to the tensions back in Chicago. To some players, Krause's ardent courtship of Kukoc seemed in direct contrast to the way they were treated by management. Their boss was showering affection on some foreign player who had never showed that he could play in the NBA, while treating them, NBA champions, with great coldness. The more Krause pursued Kukoc and the more contract problems with his other players simmered, the greater the resentment of Kukoc became. When Krause asked Michael Jordan as part of the recruiting process to call Kukoc and try and get him to America, Jordan answered coldly that he did not speak Yugoslavian. The feeling that Kukoc was not the Bulls' equal came out in the 1992 Olympics, when the Dream Team played Croatia. Pippen and Jordan seemed to play against Kukoc as if they had a vendetta, and the game was perilously close to a humiliation. In the end, it was as if they had been playing not against Kukoc but against Krause.

Eventually, at no small cost to himself, Kukoc bought himself out of a very good European contract and came to America—just in time to hear the news of Michael Jordan's retirement. He wept at the news. But there was no doubt that Krause felt a special commitment to Kukoc, and therefore he had unusual status on the team. Of all the players on the Bulls, the player, other than Michael Jordan, whom Jerry Krause was most loath to trade was Toni Kukoc.

After Horace Grant's departure, Michael's return, and Orlando's defeat of Chicago in the Eastern Conference Finals, it was obvious that the team desperately needed a big man who could both rebound and score. That year, New Jersey was willing to take Kukoc for Derrick Coleman. Coleman was an immensely talented player with a very big contract who had become something of a symbol of the Generation X basketball world: big no-cut contract, big body, big talent, and yet slim and often erratic commitment to team goals. He was then in the process of making his reputation more for defying his coaches rather than for his skill on the court. Told that he had to adjust to a dress code for team travel, he immediately sat down and wrote out a huge check to cover his fines for the entire season. He was six foot ten, 240 pounds, and he could, when the moment seized him, play defense, rebound, and score. On those occasions when he came to play, rare though they might be, he was an awesome player, a far greater offensive threat than Grant. Jackson was sure he could handle Coleman, sure that part of the problem was that Coleman was the best player on a very weak team, and that playing on a championship team under Michael Jordan's demanding glare would change him. No one, he was sure, really wanted to be like Coleman when the alternative was to be a winner. No one, no matter what he said to the media, wanted to make all that money but leave the game tagged as a perennial loser. Jackson desperately wanted the trade. Because of Coleman's big salary, $7 million a year, there were some problems for Chicago under the salary cap, but Jackson thought they could be worked out if Krause really wanted to make the trade. When Krause declined, Jackson was convinced that Kukoc would never be traded.

Kukoc's melancholia grew worse during the 1997–1998 season. When he had first arrived in Chicago, he often went out for dinner with some of the other players, in time Longley, Wennington, Kerr, and Buechler, but by this season, he was going out with them less and less, and when he did, only because they were making an effort to bring him out of a funk, he often seemed as if he was there but not there, off in another place. He became the least pleasant of dinner companions, and after a while the others stopped asking him out. But that didn't work either—he seemed to go deeper into his funk. So, like it or not, they started working harder to reach him, afraid he might be nearing some kind of crisis.

Kukoc made it clear to his teammates that he thought he deserved more respect from his coach. If anything, Jackson came down on him harder and harder. Some people who knew both men wondered if part of the problem went beyond Kukoc—that the player had become an extension of Krause in Jackson's eyes and that his dislike for Krause affected his handling of a talented player. As a coach, Jackson was known more than most as someone sensitive to players and exceptionally well tuned to the fragility of their psyches. But if there was one area where he was a hard man, it was with players who did not live up to their potential, and in his eyes Kukoc was playing well below his potential. Certainly, Krause saw Kukoc not as a player who had disappointed so far but as one who was having a hard time finding his niche because instead of being the first offensive option, he was now the third one. Clearly, Krause saw Kukoc as the centerpiece of the post-Jordan team, and Jackson was not very interested in some distant era in which he would have no part.

For whatever reason, Jackson needed Kukoc to come through in this season, and so far he had failed to do it. In early February, Jackson's tongue got sharper. Finally, the night before they played the Lakers, Frank Hamblen, one of the assistant coaches, told him he had to back off, that he had been so hard on Kukoc in recent weeks that the player could not take any more and they were in danger of losing him completely. Jackson heard him and in fact did back off. But the next day he said to a friend with some irritation, "Losing Toni?—I've been in danger of losing him the entire five years he's been here."

23.

Chicago; Portland, 1992

GRADUALLY, AFTER THE FIRST CHAMPIONSHIP, people began to realize how good the Bulls were, particularly the Bulls themselves. The championship, so hard to attain, was not something they would relinquish lightly. In the 1991–1992 season, they won sixty-seven games. Grant had his best season yet, averaging fourteen points and nearly ten rebounds a game, and Pippen became an all-star starter for the first time. His statistics revealed the completeness of his game: twenty-one points, seven assists, and almost eight rebounds a game. It was, Phil Jackson thought, one of the best basketball teams of modern times: deep, complete, versatile, and confident. Young players such as B. J. Armstrong were just coming of age, and Grant, Pippen, and Jordan were at the peak of their abilities.

In addition, the NBA leadership elite was in transition. The Celtics, Lakers, and Pistons were all slipping. Of the next generation of potential champions, the Bulls seemed to have arrived first. That did not mean that the way to the championship was easy. In 1992 and 1993, it was arguable that the toughest playoff matchups the Bulls faced were against the New York Knicks. The Knicks had replaced Detroit as the new Bad Boys of the league. They were big, and if they were not that talented—they lacked anything like a backcourt of Isiah Thomas and Joe Dumars—they were nonetheless very tough and very physical. Their only possible advantage against a team as talented as the Bulls was their sheer muscle. Like the Pistons, no one wanted to play them, and like the Pistons, if you showed them any weakness, they found it and beat you. They not only had Ewing and Oakley, formidably physical players, but in 1992 they had rotating at small forward Xavier McDaniel and Anthony Mason, who both played like power forwards. They were coached by Pat Riley, and there was an underlying tension between him and Jackson, particularly because Jackson had been outspoken in his criticism of New York's physical play.

These Knicks banged their opponents relentlessly, and often their opponents wilted under the duress. In Game Seven of the Conference Semifinals in 1992, McDaniel, built far more powerfully than Pippen, had made it his business to beat up on Pippen and taunt him throughout the course of the game. Finally, in a crucial moment, Jordan stepped in and took on McDaniel face-to-face and ended the abuse. ("It's like when you're in school and the school bully picks on your little brother and you have to step in," he said later.) A photographer caught the moment—the much smaller Jordan, absolutely fearless, in McDaniel's face and then, as the much bigger Ewing joined the scuffle, right in Ewing's face as well, not backing down for an instant. It was a moment, the other Bulls felt, that helped turn the tide psychologically. An enlarged print of that moment hung thereafter in Jackson's office. Game Seven turned into a Chicago blowout.

In the 1992 Finals, the Bulls faced the Portland Trail Blazers, a team of remarkably gifted athletes who tended to unravel at certain times and who did not play as well in a half-court game as they did on an open court. A Portland-Chicago series had an added degree of attraction because it matched Jordan against Clyde Drexler. Some people even believed that Drexler, coming off his best season ever, runner-up to Jordan for the MVP award, was in the same class as Jordan. According to this line of thought, Drexler might well be just as good as Jordan, perhaps even better, but because he played in Portland he simply had not gotten the same amount of publicity. Those who argued for Drexler pointed out that he was certainly a better rebounder, he might be a better passer, and he was a better three-point shooter. That year, for example, he had taken more than three times as many three-point shots as Jordan, and his percentage of accuracy was significantly higher.

The fact that the ever-more-powerful media spotlight did not reach all the way to Portland had not bothered Drexler at all, and even as the hype about the Glide playing against the Airman, their hyped nicknames, began to grow, he seemed curiously oblivious to it. In contrast to Jordan, who seemed to feed off the spotlight and use it as a motivational tool, Drexler never sought the spotlight. If anything, he seemed uneasy with it, as if aware that it was a two-edged weapon, something that brought you a veneer of fame and more money but that once turned on could not so readily be turned off. Drexler on occasion said quite re-markable, almost un-American things such as, "Personally, I'd rather be out of the spotlight."

Jordan, the most passionate of competitors, said all the right things before the Portland-Chicago series: that it was not about him against Drexler, it was about the teams. No one handled this part of the media game with more skill. He was being very careful not to say anything that might motivate Drexler. But of course, it *was* intensely personal for him, the perfect challenge for a man who always wanted and always needed challenges, and he used all the comparisons with Drexler, all those nonbelievers who thought Drexler as good as he was, to motivate himself. He set out to do nothing less than destroy, not just Portland, but Drexler as well: *After all, here was someone that people were saying was Jordan's equal, maybe his better. Worse, here was someone whose presence on the Portland team in 1984 had caused the Portland management to pass on drafting Michael Jordan. That meant Jordan had gone third in the country instead of second. Someone should pay for that.* For a young man like Michael Jordan, it was the perfect situation, particularly because he did not for a minute think that Drexler was as complete a player as he was.

Basketball aficionados thought Jordan had two advantages over Drexler that would be critical in the series: First, he was a far better de-fensive player; second, he was one of the best jump shooters in the league. He had been a reasonably good jump shooter in college, but no one ever worked harder once in the league to improve his shooting than Michael Jordan, even after he was already a superstar. By 1992, his eighth year in the league, he was one of the two or three best jump shooters in the league; more, unlike a lot of talented jump shooters, he worked hard to improve his shot for difficult situations, such as playoff games when both teams play tough half-court defense. He shot excep-tionally well when closely guarded.

Drexler, by contrast, was not that good a jump shooter, although he liked to think he was, and when friends and team officials pushed him to work on his shot, he cited his overall shooting percentage (around 50 percent) as evidence that he shot well. That was a deceptive figure, however, bolstered by the fact that many of his field goals came on high-percentage drives to the basket. He never developed into the feared jump shooter that Jordan was, and the general belief in the league was that he was a streaky rather than a consistent outside shooter. More, it was one thing to shoot well during the regular season and another to shoot well in a tough half-court playoff game when he was guarded by one of the league's best defensive players—namely, Michael Jordan.

Further, Jordan was not bothered by all the media people who said that Drexler was a better three-point shooter than he was. It gave him what he wanted more than anything else, an additional challenge. On the morning of the first game, he came out and very quietly worked on his threes. If anyone asked him about it, he said later, all he had to do was say he was just fooling around, playing Horse with his pals.

Later, Danny Ainge, who was Drexler's Portland teammate that year, said that there was a certain inhumanity to what took place on the court in that series. Drexler chose to give Jordan the outside shot in the beginning and Jordan hit six threes in a row. He scored thirty-five points in the first half as part of a Chicago blowout. "My threes felt like free throws," he said afterward. The Bulls won the game by thirty-three points. At one point, in a clip made famous because it was replayed so often, Jordan hit one of his threes and, as he ran back downcourt, he looked over at the sideline where Magic Johnson was broadcasting the game. He caught Johnson's eye and then looked up and raised his hands with an expression that seemed to say, "I don't understand it either, but isn't it sweet?"

Nor was all the damage done on offense. When the Trail Blazers had the ball, Ainge thought, it was as if Jordan had a terrible personal vendetta against Drexler. If it was not personal, it most certainly looked that way. Jordan barely let Drexler touch the ball on offense. Ainge sensed that it was as if Jordan had taken all those newspaper articles and television stories about Drexler as nothing less than a personal insult. It was like watching a killer on the court, he decided, "an assassin who comes to kill you and then cut your heart out."

Phil Jackson was privately aware of Jordan's need to dominate Drexler, and he later thought that if anything it might have hurt the Bulls, that it was a rare moment when some of the team's concentration seemed focused too much on one player rather than the larger purpose of winning. Thus, in a later game when Drexler fouled out with four minutes left and the Bulls ahead by nine, Chicago seemed to relax. But Ainge, a potentially better half-court player, came in, picked up the slack, made nine points in overtime, and Portland won. Nevertheless, the Bulls won the series relatively easily in six games. The question of whether Clyde Drexler was Michael Jordan's equal rarely came up again among serious basketball fans.

24.

La Jolla; Monte Carlo; Barcelona, 1992

I N A WAY, it was the 1992 Olympics that lifted Michael Jordan's fame to another level, because of the worldwide focus on the American team, known as the Dream Team—because for the first time professionals were allowed to play. Jordan had not particularly wanted to go to Barcelona. He was exhausted from two long championship seasons that seemed to run into each other. Even the summers, brief as they were, were not entirely his—they were given over increasingly to his existing corporate responsibilities. Playing in the Olympics would cost him most of the precious time when he could rest his body, retreat from some of the pressures around him, and recuperate. Certainly Jerry Krause did not want him or Scottie Pippen to go—it did nothing for the Bulls to have their best players worn out by the extended season, and it increased the chance for injury. Phil Jackson was ambivalent. He saw no upside for Jordan, who had already played on one Olympic team eight years earlier, but he thought it might be a big plus for Pippen, a chance to get recognition long deferred because of playing in Jordan's shadow. Both would go, of course, because it was never really about basketball, it was about showcasing the NBA and above all else about pleasing its corporate sponsors, who wanted to use this special platform to maximize exposure for what were now the most famous athletes in the world. It was never about beating Angola or Croatia or even Spain, it was about putting on an exhibit of basketball as an art form, and that could not be done without the league's premier artist.

He was on the team, but he did not want to be a leader. When he arrived in Portland for the Tournament of the Americas, the pre-Olympic selection process for the Western Hemisphere, Brian McIntyre, the NBA's head of media relations, mentioned to him that he had picked him for his team in a rotisserie league. "That's a mistake," Jordan said. "I'm here to take it easy—it's been a long season. I'm going to coast a bit while I'm here." He seemed to prove as much with a relatively casual performance in the first game. The next day, McIntyre saw him and said that based on Jordan's own warning, he had traded him. "Who for?" Jordan asked. Karl Malone, McIntyre said. "You screwed up," Jordan said. "It was classic Michael," McIntyre said, "somehow what I did was a challenge—I had slighted him—and so he went out and got about forty points against some poor Latin American team the next night."

There was something special, the players thought, about being named to the Dream Team, a team of the best players in the world. The competitive juices ran dangerously high from the start. At one of the early practices, in La Jolla, California, Michael Jordan brought the ball up against his most recent nemesis, Clyde Drexler. Only a few weeks before, the two had dueled in the 1992 NBA Finals. Like most NBA players in a situation like this, Jordan did not pass up the opportunity to talk some trash as he brought the ball upcourt. "Didn't I just kick your ass? . . . Anything here look just a little familiar? . . . Think you can stop me this time, Clyde? . . . Better watch out for the threes, Clyde." Eventually some of his Dream Team colleagues, notably Charles Barkley, suggested that Jordan cut back on the trash talk with Drexler because they were all teammates now and there was no need to reopen wounds still so fresh. Back off he did, but the coaches noted that every time Jordan guarded Drexler in scrimmages, he took the defensive level up more than anyone else. If the talented Portland team again faced the Bulls in future Finals, Jordan did not want Drexler for a moment to think that what had happened in June was a fluke. To Mike Krzyzewski, one of the Dream Team coaches, Jordan was already thinking of next year's Finals.

Krzyzewski's instincts were confirmed later by Jordan himself upon his return from Barcelona. Michael reported gleefully to the Bulls' coaches that one day Clyde Drexler showed up at practice with two left sneakers. Unwilling to admit his mistake and borrow a shoe from someone else or go back and get another one, he went out and played with a sneaker on the wrong foot. To Michael Jordan, who always looked for psychological weaknesses in his opponents, that was a sure sign of Drexler's insecurity. He carefully filed it away, to be used some other day if necessary.

During the weeks they handled the Dream Team, the American coaches marveled day after day at the collegiality of the players; for all the woofing and barking and gamesmanship, they felt a palpable pride about being a part of the greatest group of basketball players ever assembled. The pride was about more than individual accomplishment, the coaches thought. It was about what these players had done as a group, not just for themselves or even for their teams but for the league and for basketball as a whole. For this was the generation, the Larry-Magic-Michael generation, that had helped take the NBA from something of an athletic backwater, almost unsalable to network television and to corporate sponsors, to the zenith of its popularity and affluence.

Still, there was edginess in the air. These were the greatest players in the world, and they were eager to prove something, if not to the juggernauts from Angola and Germany, then most certainly to each other and their NBA compatriots who had been left behind. The best ever had to prove as much, even if there was really no one worthy of proving it against. Early in the pre-Olympic schedule, before they left for Europe, the coaches arranged for them to scrimmage against a team of college all-stars, most of whom were expected to enter the NBA in a year. It was a team loaded with talent, albeit immature young talent, including Chris Webber of Michigan, Jamal Mashburn of Kentucky, Penny Hardaway of Memphis State, Rodney Rogers of Wake Forest, and Allan Houston, a gifted pure shooter from Tennessee. It was coached by Roy Williams, now the Kansas coach, and George Raveling. On that particular day, the professionals were flat, and the college kids were eager and played well. They won the controlled scrimmage 58–52, with Houston hitting seven three-point shots. That was bad enough, but the college kids, more audacious than they were wise and sadly innocent of the pride that marked the upper levels of the world they were just about to enter, began to celebrate. They jumped around a great deal and did a great deal of trash talking, a cardinal sin given their place in the basketball hierarchy. Watching them bounce around and talk too much to their superiors as if they were equals, Roy Williams knew they were making a great mistake.

Later that day, Williams played golf with Jordan, Chuck Daly, Charles Barkley, and John Stockton, and he apologized for the impetuous behavior of his young players. "I can't believe our kids were bragging and trash talking like that," he said to Jordan, whom he had coached in college and with whom he had always been quite close. "Don't worry about it, Coach," Michael said. "We'll take care of it tomorrow." At the next day's scrimmage, just as the referee was about to throw the ball up for the tipoff, Michael Jordan pointed a finger at

Houston and said, "He ain't getting any seven threes today." He covered Houston as if he were out to suffocate him, and late in the first half, when it was time for him to take a break and Drexler came in for him, Jordan pointed at Houston and told Drexler, "Make sure you keep it going." What transpired was nothing less than a massacre; at the end of the twenty-minute scrimmage, the Dream Team won by thirty-eight points. Daly wanted to play a little more, so they decided to add ten minutes to the clock. The professionals then added an additional eighteen points to the lead, winning by fifty-six points.

That set the tone. No team, not even one composed of the best young American players, was going to beat this team when it paid attention. Everyone knew that. Mighty Angola fell 116–48 in the early rounds. In the medal round, the Americans beat Lithuania by fifty-one points, and in the gold-medal game Croatia lost by a mere thirty-two points. To the degree that there was any real competition during the games, it was not between the Americans and any other team, it was between Nike and Reebok. Nike had the players—Jordan, Barkley, Pippen, et al.—but Reebok was the official sportswear company of the Olympics. The Olympians, even the men of Nike—were supposed to wear the Reebok logo. In this era of sneaker wars, that was like asking the American players of just a few years earlier to wear the uniforms of the Soviet Union. The Nike players were adamant; they would not play for a hostile, foreign power such as Reebok. Barkley, ever quotable, said he had "two million reasons not to wear Reebok." If he had two million, Jordan by then had somewhere around twenty million, and he, the great star of the show, took the hardest line of all against Reebok, harder even than Phil Knight, who was uncomfortable with escalating questions by the media about putting greed ahead of patriotism. "I guess Phil doesn't realize how loyal I am," Jordan said at one point, and then he asked Howard White, "Is Phil going to back me up on this?" There was a compromise, of course: They would wear Reebok but could cover the logo, which they did, Jordan draping an American flag over his shoulders.

There was a certain pecking order within the team. Larry Bird and Magic Johnson were the captains, the reigning great players from the previous era. Though their teams and their skills were beginning to slip, they were still the respected champions, credited by their peers not just for their greatness but for their pioneer roles in bringing the league to a new position of wealth and popularity. In that same pecking order, Jordan was now the dominant player, two championships already under his belt, obviously by now the best individual player in the game. Chuck Daly asked Jordan if he wanted to be a captain, too, because in any real way this was his team. But he deliberately deferred to Bird and Johnson. "No," he answered, "let the two old guys be the captains."

To some degree, the hierarchy, and the right to speak trash, were determined by championship rings: who had them and how many. Those who had them could do the talking; those who did not were supposed to do the listening. Rings at that level of the game were what set you apart. Bird, Johnson, and Jordan never missed an opportunity to give teammates such as Patrick Ewing and Charles Barkley hard times because, though they might be ferocious competitors, they did not yet have rings. But the ring holders also talked trash to one another. One night, Jordan, Bird, and Johnson went at it in the players' lounge in Barcelona. "You know," Jordan said to Bird, "when I go to the Garden, I like to look up and see all those great championship banners hanging from the ceiling." He paused—was this to be an homage to Bird and Celtic greatness? "And then I think how sad it is, knowing that there will never be another one up there."

Bird, who had three rings to Jordan's two, struck back. "Michael, let's talk about banners when you have your third ring."

"I don't know, Larry," Jordan answered, "you used to be such a great player. And now you're right down there at the end of the bench waving your towel—just like another M. L. Carr."

Then Jordan turned his attention on Magic Johnson, who had retired during the summer of 1991 after testing HIV positive but had come back to play in the Olympics. "You know," Jordan said, "it isn't very much of a challenge going out to L.A. anymore—the games out there just aren't much fun. In fact, from now on I'm going to take both of my kids with me, because it's such a real sleeper out there. It's not like the old days when you were playing. There's no real test anymore." Then he smiled at Johnson. "But in deference to you, if you come back and play again, just as a sign of respect, I'll only take one of my kids with me."

Johnson came right back that evening and began to talk about having a one-on-one game with Jordan, which was not the best idea in the world because while Magic Johnson could do many remarkable things with a basketball, no one ever thought of him as a great pure shooter or a great one-on-one player.

Larry Bird jumped in. "Are you crazy?" he asked Johnson. "He's probably the best one-on-one player in the country, and you think you can beat him? Get real." It became Bird's sad job—Bird who had been bothered by a bad back all week and who did not score a point in what would prove to be his last game—to try and explain to Johnson that their era had passed, that thirteen years after they had both entered and changed the league, it was time for them to go.

That kind of macho, edgy competitiveness came to a head during one now legendary practice game in Monte Carlo. The tiny handful of people who happened to watch it thought that what took place that day constituted the greatest basketball game ever played, between the greatest players of all time, playing at a fever pitch. That it took place behind closed doors was regrettable; that it took place in of all places Monte Carlo, hardly a citadel of basketball, was a fluke. No official box score was kept, and there was even some dispute about the final score, but there was no doubt about whose team won, and even less about who the best player on the court had been.

These were the best players in the world going all-out against each other, not, as they were wont to do in the all-star game, playing only marginal defense so that the offensive skills of all the players could be showcased and no one would be injured. Instead, this game was played with an intensity more likely to be found in the seventh game of an NBA Finals. It was to be known afterward as Michael's team against Magic's team.

The last thing Chuck Daly wanted was an injury to some other coach's best player on his watch. But some of the other coaches, notably Lenny Wilkens, Daly's longtime rival and now one of his assistants, thought the players needed a tougher workout. The players themselves also wanted a hard practice, particularly Magic Johnson. Here, as with the Lakers, Johnson was not merely a player but a de facto coach, a player to whom the coaches listened and with whom they consulted. Somewhat apprehensive about unleashing that much power, ego, and talent in an intrasquad scrimmage, Daly reluctantly agreed to an all-out practice. Mike Krzyzewski, wary of the emotions that might be let loose, volunteered to lead the morning drills, hoping thereby to escape being a referee. It was the smartest move he made all week, he thought, getting himself out of the line of a good deal of verbal fire.

The players seemed pleased to be letting loose after so many controlled, soft practices. Johnson's team jumped out ahead and took an early lead, said to be 14–2, although some claimed the score was actually 14–0. It was like a playground game at the highest level. Johnson's team included Chris Mullin, Charles Barkley, David Robinson, and Clyde Drexler. Jordan's team included Patrick Ewing, Karl Malone, and Scottie Pippen.

Later, because exact records were not kept and the number of witnesses present was limited, some people thought that it was Magic Johnson who first mouthed off and talked trash to upgrade the level of play.

But others who were there, such as Josh Rosenfeld, the Lakers' PR man, believed that Johnson was too smart for that, too aware of what Jordan's reaction would be. Rosenfeld insisted that it was Charles Barkley, a woofer's woofer, who talked the first trash, as Johnson's team was running downcourt after scoring a basket. Johnson gave Barkley a little shot with a forearm to make him stop, saying, "Stop it—you're not the one who has to guard him." It was a terrible mistake, Johnson later told some of the reporters allowed in to watch the tail end of the practice, because it woke Jordan up.

The game became raw and physical, all territorial and all ego. Michael Jordan more than anyone else set the tone. He simply took over the game, driving to the basket every time he got the ball, rebounding, stepping in the passing lanes for steals, hounding Johnson on defense, screaming at everyone, opponents and teammates alike, pushing himself. There was one stretch where he made twelve points in a row, though some witnesses claimed that it was actually sixteen. When a call went against his team, Johnson yelled out, "What is this, Chicago Stadium? Are you going to get all the calls here, too?"

"I'll tell you what it is," Jordan shouted back. "It's the nineties, not the eighties."

The play on both sides was frenzied. After watching them all week, Krzyzewski sensed that they would play with a level of ferocity almost unmatched in basketball history, but even he was amazed by the intensity. It was, he thought, like being in a house and hearing a terrible hurricane outside, then opening the door and seeing that the storm was even more powerful than you'd envisioned. Watching from the sidelines, Daly was at once in awe of the quality and intensity of the play and decidedly unhappy: It was out of control, he thought, and he was sure that something terrible was going to happen—some great star was going to get hurt.

Jordan's team rushed past Johnson's team and eventually took a ten-point lead. With a few minutes left in the game, Jordan was standing at the line, about to shoot two foul shots, when Krzyzewski innocently yelled out from the sidelines, in the manner of a thousand coaches wanting to encourage their players, "Plenty of time, plenty of time left." Jordan slammed the ball down and said, "Fuck that, there's no time left at all! It's over!" He then made both foul shots. The game ended with his team winning 36–30. Daly was more than eager to call it off. The players wanted to continue, but he had seen enough. His team was ready, if anything too ready.

After the game Jan Hubbard was one of a handful of journalists who went out on the floor to talk to the players. Jordan seemed to be on some kind of competitive high, he thought. He had recently switched his soft-drink endorsement from Coke to Gatorade, and he had already done a commercial in which different people dreamed of being like him. There he was on the sideline saying like the others in the spot, "Sometimes I dream," holding up a Gatorade bottle, enjoying the moment, knowing that he had dominated the play among the best players in the world. As Jordan danced, Magic Johnson sat thirty yards away telling a few reporters, "We just screwed up. We got him mad. We all did too much talking. You'd think by now we'd know better."

Jan Hubbard walked over to talk to Jordan. "You just have to win every time, don't you?" he said.

Michael smiled that wonderful, radiant smile. "I try to make a habit out of it."

25.

Chicago; Phoenix, 1992–1993

IN THE FALL OF 1992, the Dream Team experience was over and it wasn't. There were people who covered the NBA who now divided its history into two phases: pre–Dream Team and post–Dream Team. David Stern had sought commercial legitimacy for his great athletes and his sport, and he had achieved parity with other American professional sports; if anything, he might have overachieved it, for not all of this was a blessing. His athletes were now the most famous ones in the world, far more famous in a setting such as Barcelona than a dozen great baseball or football players might have been. They were the great stars of a sport that was becoming steadily more internationalized, and they were stars of countless brilliant commercials as well. And because of their height and in most cases their skin color, they were often immediately identifiable. The American basketball players were such an attraction at Barcelona that they had not been able to stay in the Olympic Village; it was not just tourists and fans who mobbed them whenever they appeared, it was the other athletes. Whether this represented the Olympic ideal was questionable, but it reflected reality in the new epicenter of the global village. As a result, they could barely move around Barcelona. (Even someone who conformed to the visual stereotype of an NBA star as little as John Stockton, who was neither tall nor black, had his movements limited.)

Success affected everything. Sometimes the NBA seemed a league that had grown far too much in too short a time. Its economics had changed so dramatically that it was top-heavy and lacked a solid foundation: It was a wonderful sport for producing five or six good and sometimes great teams at playoff time, but it was built on stilts, its underpinnings shakier than those of the two other big-time sports. Because of steady expansion over the last thirty years, there were not that many good teams and not that many teams with at least three very good players. There were still perennially weak franchises and other teams that seemed to be mired in mediocrity. That set a considerable ceiling on many of the regular-season games. If anything, it seemed to be a three-tier league, with a handful of very good teams at the top, a larger group of mediocre ones in the middle, and a smaller group of truly hapless ones at the bottom. In all-too-many arenas, the teams were selling more sizzle than steak.

As the hype began to exceed the reality, there was a sense, city by city, of the rising power of the marketing people in each organization: in every arena, the noise—not real noise made by enthusiastic and knowledgeable fans, but artificial noise amplified electronically to seem real and to make fans feel a part of something larger—was boomed out at ever-more-deafening levels, as if to assure fans that even if the game was not that good, they could at least feel as though they had attended the equivalent of a rock concert. Above all else, they were at a hot event.

A visitor to the United Center hoping to see a great basketball game between Chicago and Houston got a good deal more—or perhaps a good deal less. It was as if the architects of the modern game did not entirely believe that its new fans, unlike those who had attended the old Chicago Stadium, found the game adequately entertaining. Even as the music boomed out ever more loudly, more and more idiotic games were being played either on the Jumbotron or on the floor, as the players waited in the locker room. On the floor, there might be minibike races between toddlers two or three years old, acrobats firing T-shirts into the crowd, or fans who were brought out, blindfolded, spun around to make them exceptionally dizzy, and then told to shoot baskets for prizes. At time-outs, young, scantily dressed dancing girls rushed out on the floor to do numbers that were supposed to be sexual. The Jumbotron flashed singing contests between fans who could not sing and other contests equally thrilling, such as an electronic chase each night between a doughnut, a bagel, and a piece of cheesecake. The Jumbotron was the symbol of the rising level of narcissism in the society: Bob Ryan of the *Globe*, appalled by the fact that so many fans had left an overtime game between Boston and Atlanta before the overtime period began, wrote that too many modern fans were more concerned with seeing themselves on the Jumbotron than in seeing the game. What was amazing, he noted, was that these endless banal promotions did not take place merely during the regular season between two teams down on their luck but even during the Finals.

Acute observers of the Bulls felt that they had lost a significant edge in their move from the old Chicago Stadium to the United Center. Not only did Michael Jordan and a number of other players hate the lighting in the United Center, but there was believed to be a considerable loss in home-court advantage. Chicago Stadium was a fearsome place in which to play a big game, wildly intimidating to referees and visiting players alike, a place where, in the words of Dick Motta, the noise was so thick you could actually reach out and touch it. The United Center crowd was far wealthier—it had to be because of ticket prices—and far more genteel, with less pure instinct for the tempo of the game. The Bulls still won, but much of the noise was artificial. They had never, in the old Chicago Stadium, had to fake crowd noise.

The combination of the new rock-star fame and the giant salaries also contributed greatly to separating the players from the people who covered them and removing them that much more from traditional forms of accountability. Just a decade earlier, most teams traveled commercial, and the handful of beat reporters covering them traveled with them, although in the economy section. The players and writers stayed at the same hotels and often ate together at coffee shops. The bus going from the airport to the hotel and from the hotel to the arena transported the players and the reporters alike. In the best of circumstances, there was a mutual respect and an awareness on the part of the players of which writers were serious. Now that had all changed. The players went by charter flight, which made sense in many ways, for it was restful, conserved time, and improved the meals they got after a game. Nor were the reporters any longer welcome on any bus going to the arena. An important connection had been cut. Press sessions now tended to be dominated by quickie radio reporters in battalion strength. In every real way, access was becoming more and more limited.

Sustaining success in the modern NBA had always been harder than attaining it in the first place. Winning brought its own special set of pitfalls and ever greater expectations. The more you won, the more the pressures against sustaining success grew—not just from other teams that wanted what you had and came at you with ever greater determination, but from the forces on your own team produced by that very same success. Success in contemporary sports does not, as some might imagine, create greater harmony. It almost always creates a greater need for individual recognition. Everyone wants a greater share of the glory.

Egos that had been suppressed at least partially during the original championship assault surface. Pat Riley called it, fittingly enough, "the disease of more."

The ingredients for the disease had always been there, but through the seventies it had been relatively easy to control: There was no free agency, so players were at the mercy of the owners and contract leverage belonged entirely to management. Dramatic changes in the sport's labor laws made teams less stable: Players could now choose where they wanted to play and had far greater leverage in attaining their salary demands. Agents entered the equation and were now more powerful than coaches and as powerful as owners. How a player felt about his front office was now important; how players felt about each other became equally important. The division of glory became more and more sensitive. Perpetuating a dynasty became increasingly difficult—the phenomenon of five or six very good players arriving at roughly the same time and staying together for most of their respective careers was rarer and rarer. What was striking in retrospect about the Celtics and Lakers championship teams was how many of the core players stayed with the teams for their entire careers. The difficulties of repeating as a champion were all the more challenging for the Bulls because of the unique quality of Michael Jordan's greatness. Anyone else was doomed to live in his shadow, and few very good players liked even the slightest glimmer of a shadow on them.

Michael Jordan, propelled by his talent, his beauty, his championships, and his growing number of commercials, had long since transcended mere athletic fame and was on his way to becoming the most famous American in the world, an icon of almost unparalleled national and international fame. His only rival globally was England's Princess Diana. Jordan's fame, like Diana's, had become a monster, a living, organic thing that seemed to feed on itself and grow ever larger. The more successful he became, the greater the expectations he created; the greater the challenges he faced, the more he pushed himself to excel; the more he excelled, the bigger the monster became. He was no longer competing with his brother Larry or Leroy Smith in the backyard, or Patrick Ewing in college, or Magic Johnson and Isiah Thomas in the pros. He was competing now against the most deadly opponent imaginable: himself. The more he accomplished one year, the more he was expected to accomplish the next.

The monster—endless demands to endorse products, to pose for magazine covers, to be something larger than life, to be a hero—grew exponentially in the late eighties and into the nineties. Only someone as focused as Jordan, with his special ability to concentrate on what was authentic, could have handled these mounting pressures so well. Everyone he met, it now seemed, wanted a slice of him, some for benign reasons and some for exploitive ones. Every phone call was a request for him to do something, more often than not something he did not particularly want to do, even if it brought in a million dollars. The monster might easily have crushed and devoured a young man less intelligent and of less inner toughness.

In some quite stunning way, he never gave in to this monster. It changed him, certainly, making him at first warier, and then in time more cynical, and on occasion more brusque in his dealings with the outside world. He carefully studied those around him and judged them on many scales, not the least of them the measure of what they wanted from him. One of Phil Jackson's great strengths and a tribute to his shrewdness in dealing with Jordan was that he never asked him for anything—no autographs, no signed sneakers, no appearances at his children's high school fund-raisers. The only thing he asked for was performance on the court and to share the ball a little. It was one of Jordan's special gifts to understand that basketball was the one true thing at the center of all this madness, that it was real while almost everything else was artificial. That in itself reflected uncommon wisdom and inner strength—many other athletes who had attained far less and had received far less in the way of adulation came all too readily to believe the myth of who they were and to believe that the inauthentic was the authentic, that they were every bit as important as that most transitory of images—the mirror that is contemporary media—said they were. Jordan was far too smart and too emotionally balanced for that; instead, as the burden of the exterior responsibilities grew, he took genuine solace primarily in the game itself. Freedom became basketball: the practices and the games were the real fun in life. Here he could, for a time at least, shut out everything else and follow his heart.

If all of this was hard on him, it was also hard on his teammates. They were in the odd position of being both caught in his spotlight and doomed always to be in the shadow of it, never quite in focus. Yes, the media laser beam touched them, but it was never about them, and their brushes with it were filled with no small degree of insincerity. They had to accept the harsh knowledge that no matter how good they were, how well they played, much of the world that now paid attention to what they did was not very interested in them, except perhaps as a conduit to reach *him*.

Some players handled this reasonably well, understanding instinctively the disingenuous if occasionally seductive quality of modern fame. John Paxson, the most likable and mature of athletes, had his minor brush with it and decided very quickly that he did not like it at all. Not only did it make him uncomfortable and intrude on the simple life he preferred, but he discovered to his horror that he was unconsciously changing for its benefit, and not for the better. He found himself trying to become the person the spotlight wanted him to be, always pleasant and charming in public, always exceptionally nice and gracious to strangers who came up to him in restaurants. The trouble with that, he realized, was that he was on occasion nicer to strangers than he was to his own family, to whom, because of the pressure now being applied to his life and the illusion that he was more important than he really was, he had become grumpier.

The Bulls player who most skillfully handled the contradiction caused by the special nature of this success was Scottie Pippen. "The vice president," Gary Payton of the SuperSonics once called him, "not the president." It was, thought one teammate, as if Pippen was more comfortable in the role of talented partner than full-fledged star. Pippen did on occasion chafe under the difficulty of playing with Michael Jordan, the demanding nature of Jordan's personality, and the troubling burden of losing just enough of his privacy to make his own life more difficult. He was all too aware in those early years, even after they won the championship, that there was a part of Jordan that had not yet embraced him and his game and that waited in judgment on him, still wondering if he was real. But Pippen had a sixth sense of his own limits, of what he did well and what he did not. What Jordan did every bit as well as he played basketball—dealing with the media hordes, handling the immense amount of nonbasketball responsibilities—Pippen had the most marginal talent for. The gap in their abilities—not that large on the basketball court—was immense off it. Jordan was an innate media sophisticate, seemingly born to have the camera trained constantly on him; he liked it and though eventually there was too much of it, he also missed it when it was gone.

Pippen, by contrast, had little natural instinct for dealing with the growing number of image makers who followed the fortunes of the Bulls. When the media hordes entered the Bulls' locker room, they were searching for that part of Scottie Pippen that he was most reluctant to reveal; what took place was an ordeal for everyone involved. Pippen adapted well to the triple post—no one shared the ball better with his teammates. If you missed a few shots, Jordan tended to cut you off, but Pippen worked even harder to get you the ball. Jackson was convinced that was the outgrowth of being the youngest child in so large and poor a family—sharing everything came naturally to him.

Pippen had been burned by the media early on: He had struggled coming of age in Chicago, and he had done much of his growing up in the public eye. Unlike Jordan, who had arrived in Chicago from an extremely polished program where a great deal of time and energy went into helping its graduates deal with the world that awaited them, Pippen had come to the city a poor rural kid from a small athletic program. In his early years on the Bulls, he wore glasses with clear lenses, apparently in order to make himself look more serious.

He had arrived at once raw and unfinished and yet rich and famous, the most dangerous equation imaginable, and Chicago had been full of temptations. He, like many an NBA player before him, had succumbed to many of those temptations. He and his close friend Horace Grant, who had arrived in the same season with a very similar background, had been, one team official noted, like kids in the world's biggest candy store. Pippen's judgment in his relationships with women was not always impeccable; at one point he was dealing with simultaneous paternity suits from two different women. On another occasion he was picked up by the local cops for possession of an unregistered gun, which he had been carrying in his car. But as he matured and became more comfortable with himself, his pleasure in the game grew year by year. Few NBA players seemed to relish the game itself quite so much. When the television camera zoomed down the bench after Pippen had just come off a game, more often than not it seemed to find him laughing and joking with teammates, taking a singular pleasure out of this part of his life. Someone once asked Phil Jackson to define Pippen in one brief phrase, and he immediately answered, "the joy of basketball." But when it was time for the nonbasketball duties, for dealing with the media, a mask seemed to come down over his face. He might answer a question, but what his answer really said was, Please don't ask me any more questions. He gave answers that deliberately closed doors rather than opened them. In time, the mask worked, and the media people came to pay only the most limited attention to him before going on to other players.

Pippen did not seem to begrudge Jordan his special position. Early in their careers, he was aware that Jordan was withholding his approval and somehow sitting in judgment on him, but that didn't seem to bother him either. Unlike his close friend Horace Grant, who resented both Jordan's special status and his lack of enthusiasm for Grant's game, Pippen accepted that Jordan was a level above him but that it was important to keep working together, learning and improving. If in their early years together Michael was occasionally hard on Scottie during practice, thought Chip Schaefer, who watched them day after day, Pippen was smart enough to know that he was a beneficiary of what Jordan was doing and could learn from him, not just on the court but off it as well.

On the Dream Team, Pippen finally reached superstar status. Alongside the most ballyhooed players in the league, he had played at the highest level, a level above most of the rest of the team, most members of which arrived with far greater reputations than his. In the view of Chuck Daly, he was just under Jordan and equal to Charles Barkley, who had also enjoyed a brilliant Olympics. Pippen's play surprised almost everyone, including Jordan and Daly. "You never really know how good a player is until you coach him," Daly said later, "but Pippen was the great surprise in Barcelona—the confidence with which he played and the absolutely complete nature of his game, on offense and defense. No one else really expected it."

Pippen even surprised Jordan by his play. For when Jordan first arrived he talked with the coaches about the different players on the team, and it was obvious he still was not sure how high a level his Chicago teammate would reach. But after Jordan returned to Chicago, he talked with Jackson about the games. The best thing, he told his coach, was the degree to which they had showcased Pippen's greatness. "Scottie came in as just one of the players, and none of the others really knew how good he was, but then he kept playing, and by the end of the week it was clear he was the top guard there—over Clyde and Magic and Stockton. It was great for people to see him in that setting and to see how good he really was."

If Pippen handled playing in Jordan's shadow the best, the player who seemed to have the most trouble with it all was Horace Grant. He sometimes seemed to seethe with resentment over what he perceived as Jordan's special status within the organization. Why it was so much harder on him than on others, no one was quite sure. Certainly part of it was the nature of his role on the team. It was his assignment as the one agile and quick big man on the team to do a large share of the heavy lifting, playing tough defense against bigger men and working the boards. In return for his blue-collar work, he felt, very few plays were being run for him.

Some of the coaches thought that Grant's problem was that he was not as quick a student of the basketball-entertainment world as Pippen had become, and so he coveted what would never be his and what no sane person would want in the first place: Jordan-like fame. Nor did he understand that Jordan's special status on the team was not created by Phil Jackson or the organization but by the gods and could be controlled by no one, least of all Jordan himself. Some people in the organization began to sense that a sort of virus had taken hold in Grant, a belief that

in some ill-defined way he was being held back by Jordan, and his own
personal goals were being obscured by Jordan's fame.

There was also some history between Grant and Jordan, going back
to when Jordan was dubious about him as a draft choice. Later, Jordan
made clear that he did not think that Grant was that bright. For whatever reason, Grant obviously had a smoldering resentment of Jordan.
After the 1991 championship, when the team was invited to the White
House to meet President Bush, Michael Jordan went to dinner with
Grant and mentioned to him that he planned to skip the event and play
golf instead. At the time, Grant did not say anything, but then when
Jordan's absence became a public issue, Grant seized the occasion to
criticize him. Jordan was quietly furious. If Grant had had anything to
say, he believed, he should have said it that night at dinner or remained
silent.

A clear tip-off that Horace Grant was so unhappy that he would leave
the team came on the first day of training in the fall of 1992. One of the
staples of Jackson's training camps was a conditioning drill he called the
Indian run. The players ran single file, and every time Jackson blew his
whistle, the person who was last in the line had to sprint to the front of
the pack. It was a killer drill—jog and sprint, jog and sprint. Because
Jordan and Pippen were still resting from the extra practices and games
of the Olympics, Jackson excused them from the run. Somewhere in the
middle of the drill, Grant blew up and stormed off: He simply could not
handle the fact that the other two musketeers had been on the Dream
Team while he had to run in this drill. Jackson went to the locker room
to calm him down. It was not a good sign.

Grant's unhappiness was only part of a larger malaise that now
threatened the Bulls because of their growing success. Some of the tensions had existed since the late eighties, part of the inevitable undertow
of any championship run. But as the Bulls became more famous, as success mounted so quickly, the spotlight following Jordan began to focus
on tensions and divisions of the sort that might exist on any team but
which on any other team no one beyond players themselves would care
very much about.

Later, when some of the divisions within the Bulls organization became chasms, and ever more public ones, a reporter asked Phil Jackson
how and when it all started. The answer was an unlikely one. He said it
began with a book. After the 1991 championship, Sam Smith, the beat
reporter for the *Chicago Tribune*, wrote a book on the championship season called *The Jordan Rules*, which was published during the fall of the
1991–1992 season. Smith was a smart, hardworking reporter who had
covered the team for three years, and his knowledge of the team's fac-

tions and interior disputes was, not surprisingly, encyclopedic. His book was a basketball junkie's delight, full of inside stuff, and while admiring of Jordan's greatness, it also effectively represented the first attempt to demythologize him. Jordan, it turned out, was not always perfect. He had flaws. He was hard on his teammates and was all too aware of his corporate image. It was a warts-and-all portrait of someone on whom very few people had in the past wanted to see any warts. It showed his lesser, occasionally petulant side and how difficult he could be toward certain teammates.

In some ways, what Smith reported was not that unique to the Bulls. Beat reporters are often witness to all the petty jealousies and inevitable ego conflicts that take place during a long and difficult season. Not many great players are great pals with the other great players on their teams. Jealousies abound. Some players resent the closeness of their teammates to the owner—as Kareem Abdul-Jabbar resented Magic Johnson's palling around with Jerry Buss. On many teams, the rivalries begin with something one wife has said to the wife of a teammate. Probably every team could produce a comparable book, but rarely are those petty jealousies and incidents worth writing about. What made this special was that it was about a team that included Michael Jordan. In no small part because of Jordan's fame and the hunger for information about him, the book became a best-seller. That in itself was not without its ironies: Smith was in effect amplifying the feelings of people critical of Jordan's special status, but his book was a best-seller in no small part because of that same special status. Clearly, Horace Grant was one of Smith's prime sources, as were, it was believed, Phil Jackson and Jerry Reinsdorf. The book made all too tangible and all too visible different rivalries and divisions that had always been there but that people had been able to avoid discussing before. Now these tensions and factions were very public.

Michael Jordan was not pleased with the book, but he was also aware of his near invulnerability to criticism—the nature of his fame left him largely immune to any assault by a print reporter, in no small part because his team kept on winning. He had long since graduated to a world where the real media world for him was nothing less than network television, and where many television reporters, hungry for access, became as much ambassadors from their networks to him as journalists. What mattered for him was image, and his image glistened; facts were less important, because the only real fact that people cared about was that he and his team kept winning and he remained quite handsome.

The book was absolutely devastating to Jerry Krause, however, for it described in considerable detail the tensions between Krause and the players, particularly Jordan and Pippen, and the way the players baited and mocked him. Even before the book came out, Krause was undergoing some degree of fame deprivation: Though his contributions to creating the Bulls were considerable, to the television camera sweeping the sidelines during the games he was invisible. Television cameras tended to take little notice of a general manager and fastened instead on the players and coaches. This meant that Phil Jackson, *who worked for Krause and had been brought there by Krause, who owed his job to Krause,* was becoming far more famous than Krause and was being given far more credit for the team's success than Krause.

That was hard enough. Now here was this book that seemed to denigrate Krause in the public mind and portrayed him as a man despised and belittled by his players. To the public, any dispute between Michael Jordan and Jerry Krause was an easy one in which to take sides: Krause always got to wear the black hat. Krause hated the book and became obsessed by it. Others, finding something so unpalatable written about them, might have walked away from it or pretended it had never happened or even suggested that they actually enjoyed it. Not Krause. The book seemed to eat at him. He went around to everyone in the organization complaining about what Smith had written. He underlined nearly two hundred passages that he said were lies. (They were more often than not opinions of others that he did not share.) He quoted unflattering passages about himself to his staff and asked them to confirm that these were not true. Krause, whose dress code earlier in his career was not a model of neatness or decorum, grabbed one member of Jackson's staff and barked, "Sam Smith calls me slovenly. Have you ever seen me slovenly?" He once trapped Jackson in his hotel room and started systematically going through what he said were the lies one by one, an agonizing and demeaning process, until Jackson told him that what he was doing was unseemly, that these were all petty things. "Jerry, you have to let go," Jackson finally said. But it was as if Krause was unconsciously determined to make the book more important than it was.

Sam Smith's book not only deepened the breach between Krause and the media, but it began to separate him from Jackson and some of the coaches as well. Krause was convinced that a principal source was assistant coach Johnny Bach, and he began to push Jackson to get rid of him. He had long disliked Bach, who was immensely popular with almost everyone in the way that Krause could never hope to be. Bach was a talented coach and an important figure in the Bulls' success, but even more important Bach, in contrast, was a charming, worldly man, extremely attractive, a combat veteran of World War Two. He was a military history buff, and very well read. He was also very close to the players. He got on exceptionally well with Horace Grant, and Horace Grant was best man at Bach's second wedding.

Bach also got on very well with the working media. The beat reporters liked and respected him, in no small part because he was smart, honest, and very good at coming up with just the right colorful one-line quote. Krause, ever secretive, hated Bach's closeness to the writers and was sure that he was popular because he was giving away state secrets. "Johnny," he would say, "assistant coaches should be seen and not heard." Even before the publication of Smith's book, Krause had been on Bach's case because the reporters were so close to him. After the book came out, Krause needed a villain, and he became convinced that the negative material was Bach's work. It was not. What the players and others in the organization felt about Krause was hardly a secret, and a smart, hardworking beat reporter like Smith was inevitably the recipient of endless stories to that effect. The book was not so much Bach's work as it was in some sad way mostly Krause's, and Reinsdorf's for having as the head of the organization someone bound to create constant conflict. But it did begin the process that would see Bach squeezed out as a coach.

Krause was in general more wounded than ever, needier of publicity, and above all, some people in the organization thought, even more jealous of Jackson. Krause seemed to believe that the turmoil within the organization was Jackson's fault and that he had failed some kind of loyalty test by allowing the players to feel so negatively about Krause. Jackson was not yet at war with Krause, but he felt that Krause made things difficult by crossing boundaries into places where he was neither needed nor wanted. Krause, for his part, seemed to feel that when there were tensions between him and the players, it was Jackson's job to stand up for him. The lines within the organization were hardening; loyalty tests were beginning—even if unconsciously—to be applied.

Loyalty was an extremely important quality to Krause, particularly because of the hard road he had traveled to the top. If he had said little when he was a young man about the scorn he had felt from most people in the world of sports, from all those other scouts, he had most certainly heard all the taunts and he had been acutely aware of the endless dinners on the road to which he had never been invited. His true feelings—from the wounds he had so quietly suffered—showed in the unbending loyalty he felt to the handful of people who had been kind to him in those early days, those people who accepted him for his passion for the game and his work ethic, and did not reject him because of what he looked like. Those men, people like Tex Winter, Big House Gaines, John McLeod, and (when Krause was a baseball scout) the old Detroit shortstop Johnny Lipon, would be able to count on his commitment to them whenever they wanted it—Winter had a lifetime job, and Gaines's son worked for Krause as a scout. He himself was blindly loyal to Reinsdorf, and spoke again and again of Reinsdorf as the best owner in sports, an assessment not many other people in sports, while granting Reinsdorf's intelligence and toughness, shared.

Krause had little sense of the complexity of the loyalty of talented men. If he hired people, yes, they were obligated to remain loyal to him, but they did not owe him their lives or their personal honor or their inner belief in personal truth. Nor did he understand that in the increasingly convoluted and factionalized politics of the Chicago Bulls, loyalty to him could regularly put a man in a collision with loyalty to others in the organization—most specifically the players themselves. Nor did he accept the idea that his omnipresence caused a great many unnecessary incidents. Thus he tended, almost consciously, to administer loyalty tests that no talented, self-respecting person would ever pass. Others had failed him in the past; now it was Phil Jackson's turn.

The tensions within the organization rarely showed on the court. Still, the 1992–1993 season was a hard one. The coaches and trainers thought they sensed both mental and physical fatigue. Both Cartwright and Paxson were still recovering from operations when the season started, and both Pippen and Jordan suffered from nagging injuries, as well as exhaustion from the Olympics. The number of team victories dropped that year from sixty-seven to fifty-seven. Sometimes the exhaustion of the schedule and of always defending the championship seemed to wear them down. On occasion, the level of prepractice bitching reached new heights. Once, during a tough, long road trip as some of the other players were getting ready and there seemed to be more grumbling among them than usual, Jordan simply turned to them and said, "Let's go, millionaires," a quick reminder that theirs was not yet the worst-case scenario and that they owed something for those big paychecks. It remained a tough, confident team, however, one that played well in big games, played very well on the road, and had a sense of what it took to finish games off. In truth, Michael Jordan had become the best finisher in league history. He wanted the ball in the closing minutes of a game, and no matter what defense an opposing team threw at him, he was better at creating his shot than anyone else in the game.

In the 1993 Finals, they played Phoenix, without the home-court advantage because of the drop-off in regular-season victories. The series provided a chance to watch Jordan play against his friend Charles Barkley, who had been named the league's MVP that year. Phoenix had won sixty-two games during the regular season, five more than the Bulls. Before the series started, knowing how tough Phoenix was in its brand-new arena, Jackson talked about how important it was to steal one of the two games there. We won't win one there, Jordan told his coach, we'll go down there and win two.

Then they journeyed to Phoenix and did precisely that. If Jordan needed extra motivation, his teammates and Jackson thought, he had it in Barkley's MVP award. Starting with Game Two, he scored, successively, 42, 44, and 55 points. Even so, Phoenix, down 0–2, shocked the Bulls by winning two out of three games in Chicago. The Bulls would have to go back to Phoenix and win there to retain the championship.

Boarding the team plane, almost everyone seemed a little down. "It was a lot like a morgue," Bulls broadcaster Johnny Kerr remembered. "They had their chance to put it away at home and they had let it slip. They didn't think of themselves as a team that lost two of three at home. It just wasn't like them." Then Jordan boarded the plane wearing dark glasses, a loud hat, and an even louder sports shirt, smoking a huge cigar. "Hello, World Champs," he said. "Let's go to Phoenix and kick some ass." With that, the mood on the plane changed, and in Game Six John Paxson hit a game-winning shot at the buzzer to give the Bulls the title in Phoenix. They had their three-peat.

One of the special pleasures of playing Phoenix for Jordan was the chance to go against Dan (Thunder Dan) Majerle. It was not anything Majerle himself had done—again, it was about Krause. Jerry Krause was a huge Majerle fan and had wanted to draft him when he first came into the league, though he eventually held off and drafted Will Perdue instead only because he was worried about Bill Cartwright's feet. But as far as Jordan was concerned, Krause had spoken too often and too enthusiastically of Majerle, of how great and how complete a player he was, defensively and offensively. Krause even compared Majerle to Jerry Sloan, one of his all-time favorites. Michael Jordan, his teammates believed, always took his game up an extra notch if Thunder Dan Majerle was on the court. It was, thought Lionel Hollins, a Phoenix assistant coach at the time, a man who knew very little about the tensions between Krause and Jordan, as if Michael Jordan had some kind of personal feud with Dan Majerle during that series. Every time he got the ball he seemed determined to drive by Majerle, as if to show he couldn't guard him. It was like a vendetta that transcended the game, Hollins thought.

After Game Six of the Finals, as Paxson's shot went through the net, Michael Jordan raced to the basket to get the ball. He held it up high above his head, and his teammates thought he was going to say something about a prospective trip to Disneyland. Instead, he yelled out, "Thunder Dan Majerle—my fucking ass!"

26

Chicago, 1993

CHAMPIONSHIP NUMBER THREE, coming just a year after Michael Jordan's Dream Team exposure, increased his fame and enhanced his legend all the more. Some estimated that Jordan's annual earnings went from roughly $20 million a year before the Dream Team season to about $30 million afterward. No one associated with sports had ever witnessed a phenomenon quite like Michael Jordan as a salesman. And then, gradually, things began to go wrong. It would turn out that in a way he had become too successful—he was becoming more and more a prisoner of his fame. The pressure was too much, the scrutiny too great, the sources of relaxation, of freedom from his fame, too few.

It began with the gambling stories. Jordan had always liked to bet on all kinds of contests. Back in college he bet on practice drills and games of Horse. The bets were small—twenty-five cents a free throw—and not officially sanctioned. At practice one day, Jordan rather casually said something to Dean Smith to the effect that Roy Williams now owed him one more free Coke, and Smith asked Williams what Jordan was talking about. Oh, we bet Cokes for the drills, Williams answered. He bet on the outcome of a handheld video game with David Falk, and when it was Falk's turn to play, he began talking to him about serious business matters, deliberately shattering Falk's concentration.

He always needed to win. He bet with his Chicago teammates on games of Horse, and on the endless card games that they played on the planes. Jordan possessed unusual mathematical skills that readily translated into his being a very good card player. Soon, the Bulls' coaches tried to warn the younger players not to play cards with him, that he was too good at it, but to little avail.

If there was a trademark to his nonbasketball activities, it was the fury with which he pursued them, his need to play one more game of cards or round of golf until he won. Part of it was his sheer competitive instinct, and part of it was the need for relief as his life became more pressurized, as he was more and more under the microscope before first the sports nation, then the entire nation, and then in time much of the world. That made him more and more the prisoner of his hotel room. Because he could not go out without causing some kind of mob scene, his friends now came to him. His hotel room became the center of the action. His father was usually there, some of his old pals from North Carolina were usually there, and his bodyguards were always there, and they all played endless games of cards. "The one thing that's weird about Michael," said his close friend, the ever joyful and exuberant Charles Barkley, "is that whenever we're together, we're in a hotel room, because he doesn't ever go out."

Golf became increasingly important to him, his great escape from all his other numbing off-court responsibilities, the one place other than practices and the games themselves where he could find some measure of freedom and could let go. In a world where more and more people wanted something from him, his very freedom and sanity were now at stake. What was interesting about Michael Jordan, as the world of fame and commercial requests around him began to close in and steal his privacy, was that it was happening to a young man unusually needy of his physical freedom. His friends, going back to high school and college, had always been aware of his remarkable energy level, the almost unique metabolic machinery that allowed him to work twice as hard, play twice as hard, and get half as much sleep as anyone else. The first sign of that metabolism, a kind of energy overdrive, had come when he was still in college. Carolina had scheduled some preseason games in Europe and because of a scheduling fluke the Tar Heels were forced to play back-to-back games one night against two tough veteran European teams. The first game went into overtime, and during a time out Michael told Roy Williams, "Coach, this has gone on too long—I'm going to end it now," and he took the game over and got them the victory. Then, after a brief thirty-minute break during which he gobbled down a couple of candy bars, he dominated the second game as well. For some of his teammates it was the first demonstration of a special energy level. Then, it had shown in his first year in the NBA, when he had defied the expected behavior for a rookie and instead of wearing down midway through the season, he had thrived on the tougher schedule and gotten stronger. Now

closed in, constantly pressured by more and more nonbasketball responsibilities, most of which were harder for him than the actual games, he
needed the solace of the golf course more than ever, and when he had a
chance he seemed to explode there with amazing bursts of physical energy. "Why does he play golf?" Magic Johnson once asked rhetorically.
"To get away from the world. . . . Why does he play thirty-six holes,
forty-two holes? . . . Michael will go from seven until the sun goes down
in the summer. He doesn't come off the golf course, he stays
all . . . day . . . and . . . night . . . why? Because when he's out there, no-
body can bother him. He's having fun. The world is shut out."

As he became wealthier, his golf bets became bigger and eventually
more reckless. At first, he bet $100 a hole, sometimes $100 a putt. Later,
the bets reached $1,000 a hole. These games became more and more
fierce. "Man, it's like World War Three playing with Michael," said
Gene Ellison, a man who played golf regularly with Jordan. "He'll
wear you out. He'll drive you crazy. But there's no harm in what
Michael's doing. He's only having a good time."

Over the years, Jordan became something of a mark for shrewd golf
hustlers prowling for raw meat. The public found out about the mania-
cal intensity of his games only because after the 1991 season he played
with some dubious companions at Hilton Head, South Carolina, where
he had a home, and one of the people in the group was subsequently arrested on drug and income-tax charges and another murdered. Because
some of what took place was eventually made public in the courts, there
is a rather accurate record of the obsessive quality to Jordan's golfing.

One of the men he played with, James (Slim) Bouler, was already a
shady figure when they all connected. Bouler carried an earlier conviction for selling cocaine, along with two probation violations for carrying semiautomatic weapons. He was, it turned out, in addition to
everything else something of a high-stakes golf hustler—someone who
would play golf with a targeted mark at the behest of big-time gamblers
and in return for playing him just right get a handsome cut of their win-
nings. Bouler owned a pro shop and driving range in Monroe, North
Carolina. One day in 1986, someone came to Bouler's driving range to
tell him that Michael Jordan was playing down on the nearby golf
course. That meant little to Bouler, accustomed as he was to being
around celebrities at different golf tournaments. But the person then
said that Jordan was betting hundred-dollar bills on different holes, and
Bouler smelled the kind of action he thrived on. He went and got his
clubs.

When *Washington Post* reporter Bill Brubaker interviewed Bouler in
1993 in a federal prison in Texas, he asked Bouler if he would describe

himself as a golf hustler. Bouler seemed rather proud of the description: "If you want to call me that, I won't get mad. All I'll tell you is: When you come to play, bring a lunch because you're not going to no picnic." During the five years he and Jordan played together and bet together, Bouler said, he often carried $30,000 in cash with him. For five days after the championship season of 1991, Jordan and a group of his friends played a kind of ongoing marathon of cards and golf—golf all day long, cards at night and into the early morning—at Jordan's Hilton Head home. A bunch of them would meet at 7 A.M. for breakfast and be out on the course by eight. They played as many as twenty-seven holes a day. The bets were generally $100 a hole, but they could reach as high as $500 and $1,000 a hole. The high rollers, the players who were wealthy, played in one group called the Big Group; the others with more limited resources played in another group where the bets were much smaller. When the five-day spree was over, Jordan owed $57,000 to Bouler and $108,000 to Eddie Dow, a local bail bondsman whose job it was to hold Bouler's money. When Jordan eventually sent Bouler his check, the feds seized it, claiming that Bouler intended to avoid paying income tax on it. A few months later, in February 1992, Dow was murdered in his home during a robbery, apparently unrelated to any of the gambling. One hundred and eight thousand dollars of Michael Jordan's money in two checks was found in his briefcase.

The NBA was quite uncomfortable with the idea of its signature figure enmeshed in a gambling scandal with unsavory characters, and it moved slowly and perfunctorily to check out what happened. Jordan's wrists were slapped, but the investigation seemed marginal. Jordan somehow managed not to talk about other gambling problems, but a year later a man named Richard Esquinas, a self-proclaimed gambling addict, self-published a book in which he said that he had won $1.25 million from Jordan during a ten-day golfing spree and that they had negotiated a $300,000 settlement. Jordan admitted that he owed Esquinas $300,000.

None of the gambling was connected to basketball games. Unlike Pete Rose, who bet in the abstract, Jordan bet primarily on his own golf ability. To those familiar with Jordan's intensity, it all seemed familiar— the ferocious need to win; the need, when he lost, to keep playing and up the stakes—just a part of the same predatory impulse that carried him to so many basketball triumphs. "Michael doesn't have a gambling problem," his father, James Jordan, told reporters at the time, "he has a competitiveness problem." Jordan was, David Falk noted, because of his competitiveness, almost the ideal person to catch in a golf sting. He had a ferocious drive, he always thought he could win, and he almost surely thought he was a better golfer than he actually was. Later, Jordan told Bob Greene of the *Chicago Tribune*, "Was I gambling with goons who had bad reputations? Yeah, I was. Should I not gamble with goons anymore? Yeah, I shouldn't gamble with goons."

Things came to a head during the 1993 playoffs when the Bulls were playing the Knicks in New York. Jordan had ventured down to Atlantic City one night to gamble, and the resulting response had bordered on media overkill. It had also underlined the split personality of a television network that wanted to both entertain and report. During a half-time break of one of the playoff games, Bob Costas, the esteemed NBC broadcaster, had started questioning David Stern about the story. This was serious stuff, a point where a powerful, very rich network was caught between its conflicting roles as journalistic instrument and entertainment purveyor. It was doubly important because the league and the network had so much tied up in Jordan's public image, especially at a time when so many younger players were behaving like punks. Dick Ebersol had asked Costas beforehand to make sure to mention all the positive things that had happened to the league during the year as well—the success of the Dream Team and the high ratings of the previous Finals. Costas thought he had mentioned the good news as the interview unfolded, but apparently not at sufficient length or enthusiasm for Ebersol, who thought Costas was going right at Stern. In the NBC production truck, Ebersol's voice was immediately heard on the private producer's wire redirecting Costas on the interview. Costas paid no attention. Other warnings were issued, Costas plunged ahead. By the end of the interview, Ebersol was in the truck shouting at Costas, who, undaunted, continued to pose the questions that any good journalist would ask. Stern seemed to take little offense and in time the furor died down.

It was a bad time for Jordan, and it was soon about to get worse. The media coverage of the gambling scandal offended him. In the past, the media had been largely adoring, if a bit too intrusive. Now he saw them as the enemy. He was hardly the first or the last person to go through this particular metamorphosis of the supercelebrity in the contemporary culture: to think of himself no longer as a young man who was the fortunate beneficiary of a number of forces that had come together and made him wealthy and famous far beyond anyone's previous expectations, but instead as a victim of that same machinery. That both of these results, the immense wealth and the parallel loss of privacy, were produced by the same forces, the two faces of the same coin, seemed lost in the mounting pressure on him. (He told Bob Greene, a writer in whom he periodically confided, after the fact, that he had hated the Barcelona Olympics because of how commercialized it was. "It was one long sales call and we were the salesmen," he said, a comment made without irony by the world's most highly rewarded salesman.)

His talent and attractiveness, which had worked so well for him, were becoming a burden. He was dealing more and more with the terrible scrutiny that came with superfame and the concurrent loss of privacy, the inability to make mistakes. His slightest flaws were now magnified for the rest of the world. In contemporary America, as part of the same explosion in communications—the coming of cable television—that had served the NBA so well, there was now an enormous increase not just in the coverage of sports but in the tabloidization of news. A number of new celebrity-driven tabloid television shows were now part of America's daily diet of news, aimed at reporting the triumphs and—even more eagerly—the failures of America's celebrities. This tabloid machine was new, it was powerful, it was predatory, and it had to be fed every day. If sports coverage in America took a quantum leap forward with the coming of cable, so too did trash celebrity coverage. But it had an old and familiar dynamic: Whom the tabloids first inflate, they eventually attempt to destroy, or at least try to diminish. That would affect Michael Jordan now as well.

The new media lusted after each bit of news about him, whether it had anything to do with basketball or not. Stories that in another age might have been considered off-limits by the beat writers assigned to the team, men who accepted old-fashioned covenants of what was and what was not germane, were now considered legitimate news. He was beginning to deal with the price of being the ultimate media star in America: There was no place to hide.

In the beginning, as his star ascended, Jordan had been appreciative of the media—it seemed to be part of the key to unlocking all the good things that were entering his life. But then he climbed the mountain and become very famous and flush with commercial endorsements. That of itself changed the relationship. He was there atop the commercial and professional world, and he wanted to preserve his position. He needed the media less, and he now saw it as an instrument that could no longer help him but that was trying to knock him out of his hard-earned place. At the same time, the media itself changed and became bigger. What had been a handful of familiar reporters whom he knew personally and more often than not trusted and who were covering his basketball activities had morphed into a giant mob of strangers who cared nothing about basketball but wanted to put his private life under greater and greater scrutiny. Jordan became more and more wary. The dynamic had changed: He wanted to hold on to what he had, and the media, he now believed, was there to separate him from what he had rightfully obtained. Many a president and movie star had undergone much the same process before him—but his withdrawal, his occasionally hostile tone, and his lack of time for them surprised some of his old friends in the press corps. He was, they sensed, for all his immense success, beginning to think of himself in some way as a victim of the very system that had helped create him.

All of this came to a head in August 1993 when his father, James Jordan, was murdered. The senior Jordan had driven to the funeral of a friend in Wilmington and was driving back to his home when, somewhat tired, he pulled over at the side of the highway near Lumberton to rest. It was something he often did, a throwback probably to a time when blacks had trouble getting into quality motels. Two area hoodlums came upon him, murdered him, and stole the car.

It was a devastating blow to Michael Jordan. He had always been unusually close to his father. After Michael had become a huge success in Chicago, James Jordan had retired from his job at the GE plant and effectively set up shop in Chicago, becoming an important part of Michael's retinue. In the years that followed, James Jordan became his son's close friend and pal, a parent who had in some odd process turned into a beloved sibling, able to share many of the pleasures of his son's new life.

He was a warm, easygoing man, unpretentious, quick to make friends. He was the son of a sharecropper himself, and he had been raised in very hard times. As a young man, with the odds stacked greatly against him as a black rural son of the South, he had worked hard for everything he had ever obtained. Because of that, because of the harshness of his roots, he had a highly developed sense of irony that protected him from many things that might have bothered other, more privileged men. Like many Southern blacks of his generation, he had learned long ago to laugh through the hard times and to enjoy the rare moments of good times; now late in his life, to his surprise, the times were mostly good.

In the highly pressurized atmosphere of the high-level NBA, James Jordan was an affectionate, genial presence, and he was much liked by everyone: custodial people at Chicago Stadium, reporters, other players, coaches. Pops, he was called by everyone. He was immensely affable, enjoying this unlikely ride to fame and affluence late in his life. His presence eased the pressure on his son. Michael was devastated by his death, by the fact that his own fame made his father's death and funeral—normally the most private of events—a semipublic one, and by the fact that some people in the media dementedly connected it to his own gambling problems.

For the moment it seemed to be the final straw. The pressure on him had been mounting for three years. But he had begun to live in an airless world, a place so pressurized that he was allowed no mistakes. The scrutiny of his life had become brutal and unforgiving. He dealt every day with other people's expectations. Others watching the team that year noticed some of the differences in him. The season had been harder, in no small part because of all the injuries, and because when you were champions everyone came at you, and because of the subtle and not-so-subtle tensions between Jordan and Grant, which created a certain uncomfortable silence in the locker room early on. Jordan was not so joyous this season, the coaches thought.

On the court, Jordan was as ever all business—the game itself was still a place where he could find solace and freedom—but in practices he was less attentive, less joyous. The exuberance he had always brought to practice, which was an important part of the Bulls' success, was gone. It was as if it all was becoming a job. Some of the taste for it was clearly gone. Part of it was the ever-escalating nature of the fame, the need to excel all the time, which all the Bulls felt now whenever they entered an arena; and some of it was the hangover from the gambling stories. He talked more and more to close friends about leaving basketball. Late in the 1993 season, in an important sign that he might be leaving the game, Dean Smith came up from Chapel Hill to see a Bulls home game. Smith had always told Jordan that he would come to see one of his professional games, but up to that point he hadn't. It was as if they both knew this might be Smith's last chance.

Magic Johnson had a sense of what was happening to his colleague. He was watching from a different perspective now, as a broadcaster, but he sensed that something was missing. Johnson had, after retiring, begun to join the inner circle of Jordan's pals, mostly men with Carolina roots who hung out at his house and played golf and cards with him. Johnson had been warning his colleagues at NBC for some time that Jordan was going to pull out. Jordan loved playing basketball, Johnson said, but he was becoming exhausted by all the ancillary parts of his fame—the parts that were also critical to the vast amount of money he was making in corporate endorsements. Johnson thought it was not merely the gambling stories, but the vacuum of celebrity around him—both Johnson and Bird were departing the scene, and the young potential replacements such as Grant Hill and Shaquille O'Neal had not yet arrived as superstars. The burden of being the signature figure of the sport fell entirely on Jordan.

Jordan now had three rings, and it was harder to find the challenges that were so important to him. They had beaten Detroit. They had

PLAYING FOR KEEPS · 325

pulled off the fabled three-peat. No one spoke anymore of him as a great individual player who could not lift his teammates and could not win a ring. He always talked about challenges—in one memorable postgame press conference, reporter Mitchell Kruegel noted him using the word *challenge* a dozen times in about forty-five minutes—but for the moment the challenge seemed elsewhere. In that third championship season, he began to talk more and more about his desire to try baseball. When he was a boy, it had been his favorite sport for a time, and his father believed it was his best sport, which was not a small factor in the late summer of 1993, after James Jordan's murder. For a time he had wanted to play both sports at Chapel Hill, but Dean Smith would have none of it. It remained a lingering dream.

There were hints that something was up. With writers he barely knew, he talked more and more about trying baseball. When this writer wrote a cover piece on him for *Sports Illustrated* in January 1992, Jordan took the opportunity to go on at length about wanting to try major-league baseball, and he talked about his recent dreams of batting against some of baseball's most feared power pitchers. (He had also mentioned trying professional football—one more challenge—and had talked about it with his friend Richard Dent. He would be a wide receiver but would not go after passes coming across the middle, he noted.)

Even as he was celebrating the 1993 victory over Phoenix in the locker room, Michael turned to his trainer, Tim Grover, and told him to start preparing a baseball program. Phil Jackson was not that surprised—he had sensed that basketball was becoming, if not an ordeal, at least a job for Jordan, and the childlike enthusiasm needed to carry him through so demanding a season was missing.

Jerry Reinsdorf, informed first by Jordan of his intention to leave, had asked him to meet with Phil Jackson before he made his final decision. At first, Michael was reluctant to talk to him, fearing that Jackson, always so subtle, might talk him out of leaving. Finally, Jordan, quite wary, went by to see his coach. But Phil Jackson wanted none of the responsibility of talking a player out of going where his heart took him. He simply mentioned the amount of pleasure millions of ordinary people took from Jordan's great gifts, and let it go at that. Inside, Jackson thought there was a great likelihood that Michael Jordan would miss what he did so brilliantly and would one day come back. His handling of Jordan that day took their relationship to a new level; it was as if Jackson had passed an acid test—of being willing to do what was good for Jordan, not Jackson.

So Jordan retired. At the press conference announcing his retirement, he was surprisingly churlish; he referred to the media as "you guys" twenty-one times. The media, he said, were not driving him from the game, but he noted that this was the first time there had been so many people around him when there had been no scandal. There were other things he wanted to do with his time, he said, friends and family members whom he had neglected in his search for excellence and with whom he now wanted to spend more time. "So you guys can go somewhere else to get your stories and hopefully I won't see too many of you guys in the future," he said. To the reporters who had covered him regularly over almost a decade in the league, the hostile tone of his farewell conference was jarring. In fact, the reporters who covered Jordan had always cut him a good deal of slack, in no small part because they liked him, in part because he was so attractive, but most of all because he was a winner.

Birmingham; Chicago, 1994–1995

ASEBALL TURNED OUT to be very hard. No one knows, given his exceptional gifts and his singular determination, how good a baseball player he might have been had he played at North Carolina and then opted for a pro career, either forgoing basketball or trying to balance both, as Deion Sanders and Bo Jackson did. But by the time he switched over in 1994, he had been away from it for a critical thirteen years, since his senior year at Laney High. Besides, his height was a disadvantage in baseball, for he offered pitchers a vast strike zone without any compensating power. His reflexes, wonderfully attuned to the slightest movement of an opponent in basketball, reflexes that were built so completely into his game that he could make decisions without even thinking about them, now had to be retooled, and rather late in his career. The task was to prove to be very difficult. There was something quite admirable about what he now set out to do, a player at the very top of his game, a uniquely proud man—arguably the best ever—walking away from one sport and willing to begin at the lower rungs of another very demanding sport, willing to endure the possibility of failure. That would be hard enough, but given his fame, he was going to have to do it in the most public of ways—to risk failure under the scrutiny of the media. Not many people whose success is so hard-won will risk ridicule in so public an attempt, even if it is in pursuit of something they love. Private failure is one thing, public failure is another. A cover of *Sports Illustrated* with the headline BAG IT, MICHAEL, which said that he was a disgrace to baseball, angered him greatly. He did not forgive *SI* and its people, and was unwilling for a long time to cooperate with its writers. To *The Washington Post*'s Tom Boswell, one of the nation's very best sportswriters, what he was doing was a form of grieving for a beloved father. This sport had bonded them together when Michael was young and a mere Little League player. This was the sport his father had thought Michael was best at, and so he was trying baseball as if to go back to another time and find solace. Interestingly, Phil Jackson agreed with Boswell.

He played for the Birmingham Barons, a class AA team owned by Jerry Reinsdorf. He was a good teammate. Most of the other players were ten years or more younger than he and a good deal poorer. (In addition to his $850 monthly baseball salary and $16 daily meal money, he was making by 1993 an estimated $30 million in endorsements as well as his $4 million salary from the Bulls, which Reinsdorf kept paying him. Among other things, he chartered a luxury bus and leased it to the Barons for the team to travel in—a far better bus than most minor-league teams had when they ventured out on the road for the twelve-hour trips on long, hot summer days and nights. He enjoyed Rogelio Nunez, a catcher, and worked with Nunez on his English—he called out certain words and if Nunez could spell them, Jordan paid him one hundred dollars. No one worked harder at trying to lift his own game. He was the first to practice each day, working with his hitting instructors, and the last to leave. No pupil had ever listened more avidly to the words of a hitting coach than he did to those of Walter Hriniak.

But it didn't happen. That was the surprising thing. He was such a surpassing athlete in basketball, so quick, so powerful, so committed, that he always managed to overcome whatever obstacles stood in his path. Jordan did not seem likely to fail at *anything* to which he committed himself. Somehow, the nonbaseball sporting world expected him to succeed here as well. He had started reasonably well, hitting around .300 in the early weeks, but then the pitchers started throwing him curves and sliders, and his batting average dropped. He had trouble adjusting to breaking balls, and his bat speed, for someone so powerful and lithe, was oddly disappointing. For all that size and muscularity, he could not translate his strength into baseball power. Could hitting a baseball be that much more difficult than anything else in sports, as Ted Williams had suggested years earlier? The answer seemed to be yes. In 436 at bats, he hit only three home runs and fifty runs batted in. For a time, he hovered near the Mendoza line, the legendary line of failure in baseball, batting below .200. That was bad enough, but to fall below it for a man of his pride would be extremely painful. With his average at .201 near the end of the season, his manager, Terry Francona, offered to hold him out of a game, but he played, got a hit and stayed above the line.

One problem, baseball scouts thought, was that his body was all wrong. The best body in basketball was a poor baseball body. Jordan's training program had deliberately left his legs as slim as possible, and baseball players get much of their power from their thighs and legs. Baseball players were by and large chunkier, thicker in the lower body and thicker in the chest than basketball players. That was where the extra power came from. Jordan, they felt, was built more like a race-horse. One of the things Jordan took away from his failure was a respect for the athletic ability of those shorter, stubbier baseball players who did not look like athletes, at least on the scale of body prototypes found in the NBA. These were guys five foot eight and nine with body-fat percentages of 20 percent, not 4 or 5 percent. But they could see things he could not see, do things he could not do, and they had a power to drive the ball that he lacked.

Jim Riswold of Wieden and Kennedy joined him to shoot his first baseball commercial in the fall of 1994. Riswold was impressed by the fact that although the baseball experiment was not going very well, Jordan seemed infinitely more relaxed, a man very much at peace with himself. It was as if by playing baseball Jordan had released himself from all the pressure and all the expectations of being the main man in basketball, the person who every night was supposed to do something spectacular and lead his team to yet another victory. Here he was an apprentice, and little was expected of him, so he could learn and enjoy himself, frustrated as he was by the fact that he was not doing as well as he had expected.

The first baseball commercial featured Spike Lee as Mars Blackmon, Jordan's multisport amanuensis and narrator. In the ad, a chorus of baseball greats and near greats evaluate Jordan's efforts. There is a shot of Jordan at bat, swinging and missing. "He's no Stan Musial," says Mars. Cut to Musial himself with Mars: "But he's trying," Musial says. Then a shot of Jordan catching a fly ball. "Say hey, he's no Willie Mays," says Mars. Cut to Willie Mays: "But he's trying, man," says Mays. "He's no Ken Griffey," says Mars. Cut to Ken Griffey, Jr., who says, "But he's trying." Then a shot of a ball rolling through Jordan's legs. "He's no Bill Buckner," says Mars. Cut to Buckner: "But he's trying."

Phil Jackson had always thought that Michael Jordan's love of basketball was special—that there was a purity to it that was rare at any level. Jackson never believed that Jordan was leaving basketball completely. He thought he was just exhausted. When Jordan called Jackson after Scottie Pippen's failure to go back in the game against the Knicks, it served only to convince the coach that Jordan was still a Bull. More than anything else, it was a teammate's call.

The one person from the Bulls' organization who was in close contact with Jordan during his nearly two-year baseball sabbatical was B. J. Armstrong. They had been friends but not intimate ones during their playing days. As his professional career had advanced, Jordan had increasingly limited his contact with his teammates. The old days, when he could pal around with someone like Charles Oakley, were long gone. Because of his increasingly blinding celebrity, the gap between the orbit of his life and theirs widened every year, and any kind of easygoing camaraderie was ever more difficult. There were a number of other factors contributing to the gap: Basketball was something he loved, but it was also a job, and as he matured there was a growing desire to separate his office life from his personal life. And there was one other reason: As the media assault upon him and his privacy had grown, what his teammates did not know about him was an asset, because they were in the path of an endless stream of journalists every day, journalists who might pretend to be writing about them but were *always* ready to write about Jordan. He preferred to hang out with his old North Carolina buddies, people who never found themselves in the path of reporters, who got back to him immediately if a reporter called and got his permission to talk, and who were not jealous of him.

But in the nearly two seasons he was away, he was in constant contact with Armstrong, the boyish young player from Iowa who had once found playing with Jordan so difficult that he had gone to the library to check out books on geniuses. That he chose Armstrong was in retrospect not surprising: Armstrong was smart, analytical, and very much independent of the other players and the coaches. Armstrong thought that Jordan left basketball because he had lost his innocence, the special childlike quality that great athletes have that allows them to play their sport deep into their careers, long after the money stops mattering that much, and long after they have been garlanded by sufficient titles and awards. Though he did not operate at as high a level as Jordan, Armstrong knew how important that innocence was to success in an arena as difficult as the NBA, and there were different times in his own career when he came close to losing that quality in himself. But when his pessimism was at its greatest, he would drive past a playground and watch a bunch of kids playing even as darkness fell, and he could envision the young B. J. Armstrong playing into the night and dreaming of playing in the NBA. Then he would remember that he had been lucky enough to live out his dream. That always helped him balance his priorities. He was sure that as the burdens and the expectations had mounted during the 1993 season for Michael, somehow the real pleasure of basketball had been lost.

Back in the fall of 1993, when Michael Jordan first told his teammates that he was leaving in a private meeting at the Berto Center, Armstrong told him, "Man, you now have the two scariest things imaginable: all the money in the world, and all the time in the world." But Armstrong always suspected that baseball was a temporary source of direction for someone who had momentarily lost true north on his inner compass. So when the phone calls started coming from Jordan, he was not surprised. They came at odd hours—often early in the morning when Jordan was up before anyone else to take extra batting practice or late at night after a game and a bus ride. Even when Armstrong put a do-not-disturb request in to the hotel operator, Jordan managed to get through. When Armstrong quizzed him on how he got through, Jordan laughed and said, "Come on, man," which was to say, I'm Michael Jordan. You think a telephone operator is going to stop me from getting through?

Armstrong never asked Jordan how he was doing in baseball, but what he heard in Jordan's voice at first was the sense of exhilaration at being set free of the burden of being Michael Jordan. It was all talk about how much fun it was being with young, eager kids hungry to make it to the big leagues, still caught up in their pursuit of their dreams. There were no big egos, Jordan said, only dreams and hopes. In the card games you won a few dollars at best. He was finding some form of regeneration at being with kids young enough to dream of having careers like his in their sport. The baseball experience, Armstrong was sure, was allowing Jordan to regain his innocence once again and to reassert his real priorities, just as driving past a playground at night occasionally allowed Armstrong to regain his, and to rediscover the person he had been when he was young.

That was the first note that Armstrong heard. The second note, lower at first but then mounting in pitch, was that Michael wanted to talk about basketball, wanted to be updated, particularly about young players coming into the league. Latrell Sprewell was beginning to emerge as a player to be reckoned with, and Jordan wanted to know about him. Armstrong told him that he was a terrific athlete, *very, very strong*. Some people had written that Sprewell was the next Michael Jordan. Armstrong was not surprised that a few weeks later Michael just happened to be in the San Francisco area, where Sprewell happened to play, because Michael just happened to be visiting Rod Higgins, a friend who happened to be an assistant coach there, and he just happened by the Golden State practice, and just happened to work out with the Warriors. Checking out the scene, Armstrong thought, very much the Michael Jordan he knew and admired and everyone else feared. Soon the calls became more frequent and more precise. He wanted to know about Penny Hardaway, just beginning to make his reputation. What about Jason Kidd? He wanted to know about all the young players on the Bulls and how Jackson was handling them.

Armstrong was careful never to ask Michael about his own plans—somehow, without either of them talking about it, that was deemed to be off-limits—but he was sure that Michael was coming back, that his heart had come back to basketball, that the time away had in some way cured him.

That Jordan was getting ready to return did not come as a complete surprise to Phil Jackson either. In the winter of 1994–1995, as baseball seemed headed for a strike and the owners talked of using nonroster players for their major-league teams—a form of strikebreaking—Jackson sensed that he might hear from Jordan. In early February, Jordan dropped by to see Jackson, and they talked about the likelihood of a baseball strike. "You know," Jackson told him, "if there's a strike, you have to think about what you're going to want to do. You don't have a lot of time left in your basketball career. You could come back at the tail end of this season for twenty-five games."

"That's too many," Jordan answered, "how about twenty?" Jackson heard that and knew that Jordan was thinking along the same lines that he was—and that if the baseball owners misplayed their hand, as they seemed likely to, he might soon have his man back. Eventually, the White Sox management tried to force Jordan and other minor leaguers into being replacement players, and Jordan stomped out of baseball, extremely angry over what he thought was a betrayal of a private agreement.

One morning in March 1995, Armstrong got a phone call at about 6 A.M. It was Jordan, asking B.J. to meet him at the Berto Center. Armstrong did not want his friend to come back and fail, and he asked him first if he was sure if he wanted it and second if he was sure he could still do it. Jordan said he had been working out in recent weeks. When Armstrong got to the Berto Center early that morning, there was Michael working out alone, practicing rebounding and shooting. Suddenly, at Jordan's suggestion, they started playing one-on-one, B.J., somewhat smaller than Jordan, in his sweats and sneakers, Jordan in street clothes and shoes. At first, Armstrong was taken by the pleasure of it all. It was low-key and relaxed; he scored and Michael scored, and suddenly it was just like old times with Michael Jordan, kill or be killed, both of them calling fouls on the other. "Are you sure you want to do this?" Armstrong asked, looking at Jordan in his shoes.

"This is great—just keep going," he answered. In the end, his street clothes soaked with sweat, Jordan won, 10–7. "You still can't guard me," he told Armstrong, "and I had shoes on." The next day, Jordan called Nike and ordered a bunch of sneakers, and the day after that he issued his terse statement: "I'm back." Armstrong was not surprised. He later told Bob Greene that he always thought Jordan would return to basketball. Why? asked Greene. "You are who you are," he said.

Before Jordan came back there was one preliminary call that he and David Falk made: to Dick Ebersol, the head of NBC sports. Both Jordan and Falk came on the phone for the call, but Falk did the talking. Jordan, he said, was strongly considering coming back to basketball. What did Ebersol think about it? Ebersol, who had been picking up rumors along these lines and who was all too aware of what Jordan's presence did for ratings and what his *absence* did to them, thought it was a simply grand idea, and he said as much. Then came the next question. "What do you think it's worth to NBC to have Michael come back?" Falk asked.

It was worth a great deal, of course. Ebersol remembered giggling at the question. They were suddenly in unexplored territory. "You guys want to know how much we're willing to pay for Michael to come back?" he asked. At that point, Ebersol thought he heard laughter at the other end of the call. Then Ebersol explained that the previous NBC contract, which was supposed to run out in 1994, had been extended in 1993, when Jordan had still been playing, and it had been extended at a very high level. "We did the last one thinking you'd still be in the league and you'd still be playing. So we're thrilled by the idea of your coming back, but we feel we've already paid for it," he said. To their credit, Ebersol thought, Falk and Jordan immediately dropped the idea. He would be glad, Ebersol added, to work out a deal for Jordan to work for NBC as on-air talent, say for the 1996 Olympics. They would be able to pay as much as $750,000 a year.

Michael Jordan wanted none of that. "Me, sitting at half-court at a volleyball game, and all those people coming up behind me and trying to press near me—that's what I hate more than anything else in the world, that loss of privacy," he said. "So the answer is no, thank you." But it was not an uninteresting exploratory call, Ebersol reflected later—in fact, it was a very original one, based on the knowledge that Jordan's value was not just to the Bulls and not even just to the entire league but to the network.

He came back in mid-March, bringing a new dimension of media madness with him. His return was an event of national significance: the first game was on March 19, a double-overtime loss at Indiana in which he shot only seven of twenty-eight. It was a Sunday, and NBC had previously scheduled the Bulls-Pacers game for half the nation, but when it was clear that Jordan was returning, it expanded the coverage to all but a few local markets. It was NBC's highest-rated regular-season game in five years. After the game, when a few reporters finally reached Pacers coach Larry Brown in the Indiana locker room, he told them, "You guys made my day. The Beatles and Elvis are back, and you came to talk to me."

Jordan was even willing to make fun of the aborted baseball run. Jim Riswold sketched out an ad in which Jordan, back in basketball, is practicing his foul shots. Slightly dazed, as if awakening from a nightmare, he shakes his head. He's had this dream, he says, in which he retired, played AA baseball, and became a weak-hitting outfielder with a below-average arm, traveling from small city to small city by bus and making sixteen dollars a day meal money. "Why do you want to refer to me as a weak-hitting double A outfielder?" Jordan asked Riswold.

"Michael," Riswold answered, "what else do you call someone who's batting .200 in double A ball?" There was a pause.

"Oh, the hell with it, I'll do it," he said.

Riswold filmed an even better commercial at the same time that portrayed Jordan living the rather grim blue-collar life of a minor-league baseball player. There he is, eating at the counter of a small-town greasy spoon while on the road. The commercial projects a sense of his loneliness and frustration. A friendly, middle-aged black waitress has been both serving and observing him. As he gets up to leave, he reaches in his pocket and puts a limited tip on the counter, perhaps a dollar in change. "You know, honey," she then says, somewhat kindly, "there ain't no curve balls back in the NBA." He stops, gives her a long, sharp look, and then takes away half the change. Riswold loved it, and Jordan approved it, but the Nike people decided not to go with it.

He was gone from basketball for twenty-one months. He was not in basketball condition, which was very different from baseball conditioning, by a long shot. And he returned to a very different team. Bill Cartwright, plagued by bad knees, was gone. Horace Grant, involved in a bitter salary dispute with management, was gone, to become the star power forward of Orlando. Toni Kukoc had arrived but was making a slow, uneasy adjustment to the NBA. A number of the new players had never played with Jordan before, were in awe of him, and did not adjust readily to his presence. Still, the Bulls, who had been 34–31 before he came back, went 13–4 upon his return. In one memorable game against the Knicks, he was his old self, scoring fifty-five points. In the playoffs, they took three of four from Charlotte but then lost to Orlando in a series in which Jordan's lack of conditioning was a crucial factor. In the first game, he turned the ball over eight times, and his mistakes led to an Orlando victory. He had been embarrassed. Most important for the future, the Bulls had not been able to match up against Horace Grant.

After the last game against the Magic, Jordan lingered for more than an hour talking to reporters. He was open and candid and accepted personal responsibility for the defeat. He had not been in game condition, he said, and it had been hard for some of his new teammates to adjust to him. He accepted the blame, and those who knew him sensed that he could not wait for the next season to begin, to regain his high-level conditioning.

That first summer back, he went out to Hollywood to shoot a goofy movie in which he costarred with Bugs Bunny and other cartoon characters. But coming off the humiliation of the playoffs, he also pushed himself to be in the best condition of his career. As part of the deal, Warner Bros. built him a basketball court so there would be no downtime for him; all sorts of pro and college players came by to play in pickup games. The others might be out there to play, have some fun, and keep their wind from slipping, but Jordan, aided by Tim Grover, did a singularly demanding welcome-back-to-basketball workout first, to make up for his added years and his time away from the sport. Only then and when his movie duties were done did he play full-court games with the others.

Old friends noticed that he was also working particularly hard on a shot that was already a minor part of his repertoire but that he was now making a signature shot. It was a jumper: He held the ball, faked a move to the basket, then at the last second jumped up while falling back slightly, giving himself separation from the defensive player. Given his jumping ability and his threat to drive, it was a virtually unguardable shot. It was also a very smart player's concession to the changes in his body wrought by time and the fact that he was entering a new stage of his career. He was older and wiser now, and what his body could no longer accomplish in terms of pure physical ability he could compensate for with his knowledge of the game and of opposing players. Nothing was to be wasted. He let younger stars like Gary Payton of the SuperSonics talk about what they were going to do to him, and he kept his mouth shut, using their words to motivate himself. Then he inevitably went out and dominated them on the court. There was a new quality, almost an iciness, to his game now. It was as if his game had undergone an even more refined distillation process, in which less went in at one end than it had earlier on, but even less was wasted.

Immediately after the playoff loss to the Magic, someone asked him—because the Magic seemed so overpowering, with O'Neal, Grant, and Hardaway—if a new generation had ascended in the NBA. He did not think so. "We're a rebounder away—a power forward away," he said.

28.

Chicago; Seattle; Salt Lake City, 1995-1997

As THEY PREPARED for a new season, power forward was obviously their most glaring weakness. It was particularly important on this team, which lacked a dominating center—Will Perdue, Luc Longley, and Bill Wennington shared the job. When Horace Grant left for free agency at the end of the 1994 season, Chicago became a much smaller and more vulnerable team.

Grant's departure was bitter, if not surprising. He never bought a house in Chicago, and he seemed to loathe Krause. His general alienation had grown over the years—he was angry at Jackson for not running enough plays for him, and he seemed to envy Jordan and eventually Pippen, who for a long time had been his closest friend, not just on the team but in his life. More than anyone else on the team, Grant had a hard time accepting the fact that any other player on a team with Michael Jordan was doomed to the shadows. Grant seemed to have a hard time accepting the most basic rule of existence: Life is unfair. Late in the 1994 season, as his existing four-year contract was coming to an end, he seemed wary of sustaining any injury that might affect his ability to sign with another team, and he missed a number of games with what the coaches and management thought was the basketball equivalent of the blue flu. His teammates were irritated with him. Trainer Chip Schaefer asked Pippen one day, "What's with your boy?"

"He's not my boy," Pippen answered curtly. "He's my teammate."

The circumstances of Grant's departure eventually became bitterly disputed. Not in dispute are the basic facts. Unlike Pippen, Grant had settled four years earlier for a relatively short-term contract, ending in 1994. He had asked for a longer contract, but the Bulls had been wary. As time passed and his exceptional abilities became ever more clear and he became a vital cog on a championship team at a position where great and complete players are hard to find, his comparatively low salary was clearly a plus for the Bulls, while the brevity of the contract was a plus for Grant. A very good payday was soon to come. He was not yet thirty-one, in the very prime of his career, one of the handful of top power forwards in the league, a good defender, a good rebounder, and an all-around player. With Jordan gone, his scoring had increased slightly, up to fifteen points a game in the 1994 season. That year for the first time he made the all-star team. Because the contract he was completing was his second, he was an unrestricted free agent, which meant if he went elsewhere, Chicago would get nothing in return for him.

That was not a scenario the ever-shrewd Bulls' management favored. Reinsdorf and Krause's ability to dominate all negotiations had always been something of a plus—all of their top players had been signed for comparatively small salaries. But those who thought there was something shortsighted about the Bulls in their negotiations could point to their handling of Grant as an example. The special trademark of the Bulls in their business dealings was a certain toughness, a need to *win*, which was one thing in normal business but another thing in a world of talent, where if you won, you won at the expense of your own prime resources. There was a downside to that, some thought, a certain almost inevitable long-term unhappiness on the part of their best players. The Bulls' front office, these dissenters thought—and many of them worked for the organization—was too smart and tough by half.

As the end of Grant's contract neared, it became more clear that with unrestricted free agency coming up, Horace Grant held the whip hand. He had waited his four years, played at a high level, and the moment was his. The Bulls' management realized that Grant was slipping away. After the all-star game, Jimmy Sexton, Grant's (and Pippen's) agent, met briefly with Krause and asked him to leave Grant alone and not to try to negotiate with him because they were going to test the free-agent market.

Then, one day in late April 1994, just as the playoffs were about to start, a surprising thing happened. Jerry Reinsdorf, a man who seemed to have as little contact with most of his players as possible, much of whose strength seemed to come from his lack of emotional involvement with the players, made a surprise visit to the Berto Center. Nothing could have been more unusual. The Berto Center was located far from Reinsdorf's downtown office, a drive of some fifty minutes. Because

Reinsdorf was so distant a figure, there was little of the personal animosity toward him that existed toward Krause among so many of the players.

There are two very different accounts of what happened next. According to Jimmy Sexton, Reinsdorf almost immediately sought out Grant, who was working in the weight room. There, he suggested moving ahead on Grant's contract, just the two of them. "Why don't we leave Jerry and Jimmy out of it," he allegedly said, "and why don't we see if we can get this done between the two of us." A tentative meeting between the two of them was set. Upset by the approach, Sexton immediately called Reinsdorf, who said it was not about making Grant an offer, but only about talking to him and finding out whether he wanted to remain a Bull. Negotiations between the two men might be an owner's delight and an agent's nightmare: Reinsdorf's very profession and single greatest strength was his ability to negotiate, and Grant was a player known even to teammates for his innate simplicity, honesty, and lack of sophistication. Grant, it was believed, liked to please everyone around him, and hated to say no: He was the perfect mark to be snookered in a situation like this. Sexton was not pleased by the idea of a two-person meeting, but he believed that you could not order a player not to talk to an owner.

In Reinsdorf's version, it was Grant who wanted the two-person meeting and said that they could pull it off only if Sexton and Krause were kept out of it. Two days later, the two men met. According to Sexton, Reinsdorf suggested they both write down a future salary scale that would be fair for Horace. Grant wrote down $22.5 million for five years, and Reinsdorf wrote down $20 million for the same period. Then Reinsdorf juggled the figures and added some incentives, and Grant allegedly agreed. In Reinsdorf's version, "Horace's eyes lit up like I've never seen before. He walked over and shook my hand and said, 'This is great. I don't want to go through a whole summer of not knowing what's going on. I probably can't get this anyplace else. We have a deal.' " Reinsdorf then suggested that they sign or initial the agreement. At this point, Grant said he wanted to clear it with Sexton. That was where it all unraveled. Reinsdorf did not want him to call Sexton, and the meeting broke up. Whatever else, Grant signed nothing, and initialed nothing.

The meeting had lasted about twenty minutes. When it was over, Grant, highly emotional, called Sexton and told him what had happened. According to Sexton, the first question he asked his player was, "Horace, did you sign anything?" Grant said no; in addition, he said, he had not made any verbal agreement. Grant then faxed Sexton the rough sheet Reinsdorf had used, with the owner's signature at the bottom, and sure enough there was still an empty space where Grant was supposed to sign. Sexton thereupon called Reinsdorf, and heated words were exchanged.

In Reinsdorf's version, it was Grant who had sought him out and who wanted the deal. In Reinsdorf's mind he was the wounded party, exploited by Grant and Sexton after he had made a generous offer and had a handshake deal with Grant. He eventually held a press conference accusing Grant of breaking his word. To some people knowledgeable about how the Bulls operated, the idea of Grant snookering and manipulating Reinsdorf seemed quite unlikely; but there was also no doubt that Reinsdorf, who was rarely emotional about contracts, was very bitter about what had happened. Reinsdorf liked to think of himself as a man who made deals based on a handshake and in his mind a handshake deal had been violated.

From then on, Grant insisted that in his future dealings with other teams he wanted to meet with every owner. Though Orlando had limited room under the cap that year, Grant liked and trusted Rich DeVos, the Orlando owner, and he signed with him. The Orlando contract eventually became a five-year, $50 million deal.

So in the summer of 1995, as the Bulls prepared for a full season with Michael Jordan back, the truly glaring hole in their lineup was still at power forward. There were other changes—B. J. Armstrong had left in the expansion draft—but their vulnerability was up front. Power forward was a particularly difficult position to fill, for it demanded strength, size, and agility. The Bulls' recent drafts aimed at finding an additional big man had not panned out. Both Stacey King and Scott Williams had shown occasional flashes of talent, but both had finally disappointed. King, a high first-round draft choice, was traded for Luc Longley, and Williams departed via free agency to Philadelphia. Corie Blount, drafted as a power forward, was clearly not the answer, nor would Dickey Simpkins, the newest draft choice, prove to be.

There was, however, one power forward available. Very available. He was immensely talented and equally difficult. His name was Dennis Rodman, a former Detroit Bad Boy of all things. He had once been the Bulls' nemesis but at that point he was regarded as nothing other than a coach killer, and quite possibly a team killer as well. He was also a very talented basketball player, a brilliant rebounder, perhaps the best in the game, and a skilled defender. Nor would the price for him be very high: After the debacle of the 1995 playoffs, when Rodman seemed interested more in his relationship with the singer Madonna than in his teammates, whatever else San Antonio was going to do that year, it was most assuredly going to do it without Rodman. At a preseason Bulls practice, Rick Telander, a columnist for the *Chicago Sun-Times* and a writer for *Sports Illustrated,* ran into Krause and asked him if he was going to pursue a trade for a power forward. Krause asked him if he had anyone in mind. Just being goofy, as Telander later wrote, he suggested Rodman. "He looked at me as though I had nominated Jeffrey Dahmer for head chef."

"No, no. Never," Krause answered. "Not our kind of person."

He was not the kind of person for many teams at that moment. Mike Dunleavy, then the general manager and coach of the Milwaukee Bucks, was after him. Dunleavy was in a good position to get him—he had a fair amount of room under the cap, and he badly needed rebounding. Dunleavy's reasoning was simple: As crazy as Rodman was, he was a talented player, and he played hard. "He brought back the concept of garbage player, but he's made it an art form," said Scott Hastings, who had often been matched against Rodman. Besides, the word was that the main reason Rodman caused so much trouble in San Antonio was that one set of owners had promised him a big contract, and then the team changed hands and the new owners had not honored the verbal commitment. With a player as volatile as Rodman, with his own special sense of being exploited by all forms of authority, that was a fatal mistake. San Antonio seemed interested in making a trade with the Bucks. Dunleavy flew out to meet with Rodman. Aware of Rodman's capacity to self-destruct, Dunleavy offered him an intriguing incentive-laden contract: He would pay Rodman $1,000 for every point, $1,000 for every rebound, and $1,000 for every minute he played. That, given his better years, was about $5 million a year. It was a good deal for someone whose salary was then around $2 million. Rodman seemed pleased by it. "I could do that," he said. But while Dunleavy was there the phone rang. It was Jerry Krause. The Chicago Bulls were interested too.

If he came to Chicago, he would come with a lot of baggage. In San Antonio, he tended to miss practice or arrive very late or come wearing a great deal of jewelry. It was thought that his first coach there, John Lucas, had cut Rodman too much slack and was too permissive; it had cost Lucas his job. His second coach, Bob Hill, was deemed to have tried to keep the reins too tight. In Rodman's second year, it was as if he set out to create a record for team fines. During the 1995 playoffs, when the Spurs seemed to have a genuine chance to go all the way to the Finals, he not only separated himself from his teammates, journeying around town with Madonna in a limo, but he drew costly technicals at critical moments and even got himself suspended for the vital fifth game. He fought throughout the year, not only with management but with his teammates, most notably David Robinson, whose squeaky clean Christian life seemed to cause Rodman an unusual amount of grief.

Yet if there was one team well positioned to deal with Dennis Rodman, it was the Bulls. There were three key ingredients that were to help in dealing with him. One was that the Bulls were certain to contend for the championship, and whatever else, Rodman had a passion to excel. The second was that Michael Jordan cast the most powerful peer shadow of anyone in the league, and no player, not even Dennis Rodman, no matter how cavalier he might seem in public or with the media, wanted to let Michael Jordan down or be the object of his scorn. The third factor was that Phil Jackson, subtle and flexible, was always intrigued by people who were different from the norm, and he was very skilled at not drawing lines that would provoke a dissident player. He was therefore probably as well suited as anyone in basketball to deal with Rodman. Krause asked Jackson what he thought of getting Rodman, and Jackson said shrewdly that it was not just a coach's decision, it was a team decision, because no matter how well you did, there were inevitably going to be problems, and the team leaders would have to be brought in.

The players had to be in on the decision. Jackson talked with both Jordan and Pippen, and they were positive about the idea, Jordan perhaps more than Pippen. (Jordan in fact later said that the second wave of championships would not have happened had they played with Grant again because Grant was a problem in big games.) The past was the past, as far as Jordan was concerned, and both he and Pippen knew that Rodman played hard, practiced hard, and provided exactly the talents they badly needed: rebounding and defense against talented power forwards such as Karl Malone.

Jackson called Chuck Daly, Rodman's Detroit coach, to whom Rodman had been devoted. Daly told him, well, he's selfish but selfish in an unusual way. He's selfish about rebounding. He'll cheat a little bit about his positioning on defense in order to get his rebounds. But he's hardworking, and he's coachable. To Daly's surprise, Rodman, starved for affection and grateful for any kindnesses, grateful for any sign of fairness from an authority figure, had come to think of Daly as a kind of father figure and had been shattered when he left Detroit. (Much later, Dennis Rodman presented his old coach—by then coaching New Jersey—with a life-size portrait of Dennis Rodman.) Daly understood Rodman's skills and his passion from the first and told him that if he worked hard on his defense and his rebounding—all the things, Daly said, that no one else wants to do—he would be able to stay in the league a very long time and make a very good living.

But when Rodman was in the midst of his San Antonio struggles, he and Daly ran into each other at Gibsons, a Chicago steakhouse, and Rodman seemed disconsolate. He was clearly unhappy with the Spurs. He resented being singled out locally as the bad boy, and he was bitter over his contract struggles. "Coach," Rodman said, "I don't know what to do. I've got a new agent. I've been defensive player of the year. I've been an all-star defensive player. I'm always among the top rebounders in the league. I've done everything they've asked me to do, and no one knows who I am—and they're still paying me only two million a year. They tell you they want you to play like this, give yourself up for the good of the team, do all the dirty work, but they pay you like it doesn't matter." He paused for a moment. "I've got to reinvent myself," he added.

From that frustration, Daly was sure, emerged the new Rodman, aware of the shock value of what he did, of the tattoos, and the hair dyes, and the seductive hints that he might try a gay lifestyle. He clearly learned from Madonna—one of the great automythologists of contemporary culture, a person who refined a certain skill in provocation into something of an art form. "He studied under her teaching," Mike Dunleavy once said. "It's a course—Madonna 101." Thus was born the Rodman who showed up at a book launch wearing a bridal dress. He had always had a good deal of authentic eccentricity, Daly believed, so why not escalate it with a dose of artificial eccentricity for the benefit of a culture, increasingly artificial itself and celebrity driven, that seemed to thrive on a celebration of false eccentricity? After all, it worked in music—the more provocative a rock band was, often the more successful it became. Sports and entertainment were merging. Why not bring that same provocative behavior to basketball?

Behind the audacious, provocative veneer was someone who was almost childlike, painfully shy, not just with strangers and people from predominantly white worlds such as management, business, and the media, but with his own teammates as well. John Salley, who was as close to him as anyone in basketball, had first met him when they had each been invited to Hawaii to play in the annual exhibition tournament for college seniors and were assigned to room together. On a beautiful sunny day, Salley walked into his room for the first time only to discover his new roommate bundled up under the covers with the air-conditioning going full blast and cartoons blaring on the television. He was apparently suffering from a cold. Salley, one of the most joyous and verbal men in the game, tried to talk to him. He got a monosyllabic answer back. He tried another subject. Again the answer was monosyllabic. He tried a third time, got another brief answer, and finally decided to let it go. Salley later decided that he had seen the real Dennis Rodman; shy, uncomfortable with people, very tense, the least verbal of men.

Sometimes when he saw some of his old friends from the Detroit days, people who knew the real Rodman, if there was a real Rodman, they teased him, now that he was covered with tattoos and had colored hair. "Come *on* Dennis," one of his former teammates might say, "what's this hair stuff?"

"I know, I know," he would answer, "I'm just trying to get paid."

When he ran into Maureen Malone, the wife of Brendan Malone, one of his Detroit coaches, she would say, "Hey, Dennis, I see you're fooling a lot of people these days."

He, the little boy caught in the act, would grin and tell friends, "See, I'm not fooling her."

Sometimes it seemed as if he were living his childhood and his adulthood at the same time, making up for unhappy, lonely years. He communicated well with children, poorly with adults; he seemed to get on better with the children of his coaches than he did with many of his teammates. When he was with Detroit, he became attached to the young daughter of Brendan Malone; she often gave him a bandanna before a game, and he wore it afterward. It was as if they had a bond and did not need to talk to each other. When he came to stardom in Detroit, he bought a huge suburban house that he had barely bothered to furnish but that had a considerable number of electronic games. A large number of white suburban teenage kids always seemed to be hanging out there—the perfect companions to play pinball and Pac-Man with him.

Rodman flew to Chicago to meet with Krause and Jackson at Krause's house. When Jackson arrived, he found Rodman slumped back on a couch, dark glasses and a hat on. Jackson walked over to Rodman, hand extended, and said very gently, "Stand up, Dennis—you need to stand up to shake my hand." Rodman stood up and shook Jackson's hand. "Now Dennis, could you please take your sunglasses off, so I can see you?" Off came the sunglasses. Whatever else, Jackson was not going to let him hide. Their meeting went well, as had Rodman's private meeting with Krause. So yes, the Bulls, who prided themselves that their players were good people, would swallow a bit of their pride and trade for him. Will Perdue, hardworking, limited in his gifts, less provocative in his behavior, went to San Antonio for Dennis Rodman, wildly talented, very eccentric, either a very gifted player or a time bomb, or perhaps both. Was there any signing the Bulls could have made, given the team's history, that would have been a bigger surprise? Scottie Pippen was asked. Yes, he answered, Bill Laimbeer.

Perhaps no other player underlined the vast gulf between the high-glitz world of the NBA, with its celebration of black athletes and its multimillion dollar contracts, and the harsh, unsparing world where so many of its best players came from than Dennis Rodman. He was born in Dallas. His father, who was in the Air Force, abandoned his wife, Dennis, and Dennis's two sisters early on and went his casual way, later boasting to reporters that he was the father of seventeen children, none of whom, it seemed, he had bothered to raise. Rodman was painfully shy as a child, small, vulnerable, often picked on by other kids. His two sisters grew tall and were considered excellent basketball players and won college scholarships. His own growth was very late in coming. He did not make his high school basketball team. His prospects for any kind of life other than one on the margin seemed quite bleak.

He was a young, black American who seemed without any skill and any future, one of those people who are somehow always invisible in contemporary America. His job prospects appeared slim—at best he might work in some fast-food franchise or park cars in a lot. At eighteen, he worked as a night custodian at the Dallas–Fort Worth airport but was arrested for breaking into one of the gift shops and stealing sixteen watches, valued at $470. His future did not seem very bright.

And then in one year he grew eleven inches, and the world changed. People became interested in him. Off he went to a local junior college to play. In time, a recruiter from Southeastern Oklahoma State saw him and knew he was a gem—a Division I player who had somehow slipped through the cracks of America's recruiting network. At Southeastern Oklahoma, playing for the Savages, at a level not unlike the one at which Scottie Pippen had played, he was a great player, a small-college all-star for three years. He was a brilliant rebounder there, but professional scouts remained wary—he was posting up big numbers but against limited opposition. A number of teams, including the Pistons, were interested in him and might have taken him in the first round of the 1986 draft, but he played poorly in both the Hawaii and Chicago try-outs, because of asthma attacks. The Pistons were the only ones who knew he had been sick, and they took him early in the second round.

He turned into a truly talented player. He never seemed to tire, he could run and rebound all day, and when the game was over he often went back to the exercise room and rode a stationary bike for an additional hour. When Isiah Thomas was the guardian of the Pistons tradition and got on other players if they were not working hard enough, Rodman periodically got on Thomas if he thought Thomas was slacking off just a little. He studied Bill Laimbeer, a big man who rebounded well even though he could not jump; since Rodman was a far better athlete, he soon became a skilled rebounder. He was a smart player, and he had incredibly quick reflexes: When rebounding, he often seemed to be several critical split seconds ahead of the other men gathered around him. He studied film endlessly, watching the trajectory of the ball off the shots of different players so he could position himself better, and he learned to compensate for his lack of height—he was listed as six foot eight, but he looked shorter than Pippen, who was listed as six foot seven—by playing volleyball with himself, tapping the ball up again and again until he could get clear possession of it. For the past four years he had averaged seventeen rebounds a game.

He was a truly exceptional athlete, and a great basketball player. One could look at that slim, powerful body that never seemed to wear down and imagine him as an Olympic-level quarter-miler or half-miler. "World class," the Pistons coaches had called him for a time, because they thought that if he had run the 440 he'd have been a world-class athlete. There were certain limitations to his game. He was not a bad shot early in his career, but over the years he largely stopped shooting, in no small part because he did not think he shot fouls well and did not want to be fouled in the act of shooting and thereby embarrass himself in front of the crowd at crucial moments.

He was a perfect piece for the Bulls, if he could stay focused. The Bulls already had two of the best defensive players in the league, and Rodman gave them a third. The one place where they were still vulnerable was at center, but Rodman's quickness could cover for Longley's lack of agility. Because of Rodman's speed, the Bulls were now prepared to attack teams in two different ways: When the mood suited them, they could run the floor with great bursts of speed, or in deference to the growing age of their best players, they could play a fierce half-court defense and grind other teams down. To basketball people, the addition of Rodman meant that the Bulls were on the threshold of becoming a great team. Bill Walton, by then an NBA analyst, said early in the season that the 1996 Bulls might become one of the greatest teams in NBA history. Hubie Brown, a former coach and an analyst for TNT, said that the Bulls had become the best defensive team in the history of the NBA.

That season was something of a dream. "You won't have any problem with me," Rodman told Phil Jackson at their first meeting. Then he added, "And you'll be getting an NBA championship." Everything came together. Michael Jordan, humiliated by his performance in the 1995 series against Orlando, returned not just in great shape but with a sense of vengeance. He had become, some of the coaches and people around the Bulls thought, a somewhat easier person to play with since his return from baseball. Until his failure in baseball he had been on a fifteen-year run of continuous ascent. In baseball, for the first time since he had not made the high school varsity basketball team, he had run into limits and found something important to him that he could not master, no matter how hard he tried. That changed him, it was believed, and made him more tolerant. In the past, he had been hard on his team-mates because he believed that they were not trying that hard, not putting out that much effort. To some of them, that had always been an unusually cruel judgment. He was so naturally gifted that he did not un-derstand that the game came easily to him. Very few players had his raw physical gifts, and very very few of those who did had in addition the amazing eyesight and kinetic reactions that catapulted him to the top and made the game seem, as someone who knew him well once said, as if it were played in slow motion for him. Now on his return, playing with a new set of teammates, he seemed less judgmental. The one thing he demanded was that they practice hard and play hard. Coasting in practice or in a game was still something he could not abide.

The rest of the team seemed to fit nicely around him. Pippen was thrilled to have him back and to be relieved of the role, always ill fitting and surely unwanted, of team leader and team spokesman. If Jordan's sojourn in baseball had made him more tolerant of the frustrations faced by lesser players, the same period had taught Pippen how hard it was to be Jordan and to deal with all the endless off-court responsibili-ties that went with being the star of the Bulls. Ron Harper, once a great scorer himself with Cleveland and the Clippers, had come over the pre-vious year and was a singular disappointment; he was not in good shape and struggled with the offense on a somewhat dispirited team, mourn-ing the loss first of Jordan and then of Grant. For this season, Harper came back in great shape and, knowing that Jordan's return changed his role—that he was not, as he had been for most of his career, the primary shooting guard—reinvented himself at this late moment as a defense specialist, and in fact a very good one. That meant that in addition to Rodman the Bulls could throw three big, talented defensive guards at their opponents. They would kill other teams with their superior de-fense.

The eagerness to get on with the new season showed on the first day of camp. On that day, most of the Bulls were already in better shape than most players were at the end of training. The other players greeted Rodman cautiously. His reputation at San Antonio had preceded him. At the first day of practice, Jackson called a team meeting. "Dennis," he told him, "I don't give a shit about what you do off the court, but we do have a few rules, and they matter." Then he outlined a very short list of rules, essentially about being on time for practices and games and playing hard all the time. A preseason cover of *Sports Illustrated* featuring Rodman was being shot, but there was a question of which player would pose with him. In the end, Rodman posed for it with Jordan. The caption read "Air and Space." On occasion in those early weeks, his teammates tried to talk to him, but they found he rarely responded or kept the conversation to a minimum. He was the quietest, most reserved of teammates; more often than not he seemed apart from everyone else, in the film room by himself, wearing a Walkman, watching film, a man thrilled to be hidden away in his own world. But he was also easy to play with on the floor. He was a very smart basketball player, he was able to learn a complicated offense quickly, and he almost always played hard. Quick, and athletic, with no need to score, he seemed not just the missing piece but the *perfect* missing piece for this team.

Suddenly, the Bulls, so vulnerable the previous season, seemed to have little in the way of demonstrable weaknesses. The other players who had arrived after Jordan left to play baseball steadily made adjustments to play with him. There were several critical new pieces: the center was Luc Longley, talented but awkward, his court vision better than his footwork, still learning how to maximize his massive body; Steve Kerr, who had replaced Paxson as the pure shooter, ready at all times to nail the three if Jordan was doubled; Bill Wennington, the quintessential backup center, but one with a good shooting touch; and, of course, Toni Kukoc, thrilled that Jordan was back but endlessly struggling to find his niche in the American game.

They won twenty-three of their first twenty-five games. They lost their first meeting with Orlando, on the road, and Jordan was outscored by Penny Hardaway, hailed by many as one of his legatees. But when Orlando came to Chicago for the return match, Jordan blocked Hardaway's first shot as a fitting welcome and went on to outscore him 36–26. The rites of succession were clearly going to take a little more time. Rodman had gotten nineteen rebounds. The Bulls' confidence soared game by game. In one long stretch during December and January, they went 31–2. They had the belief, Bill Wennington said later, that all they had to do was go out on the court each night and play their own game, and they would win. It did not matter that much what the other team did, as long as the Bulls brought their game and played to their own expectations.

At the all-star break, they were 42–5, on track for a seventy-win season. People began to speculate on whether or not they were the best ever and how they matched up against great teams from the past. Bill Bradley watched them play and spoke of the terrifying matchup problems they caused for their opponents. If they were to play against the old Knick championship teams, Bradley noted, he would be matched up against Scottie Pippen, who was taller, stronger, faster, an immensely versatile player, and a vastly superior athlete. "All I could think of," he said, "was 'Help!' "

When the Bulls beat the Lakers by fifteen points in Los Angeles, Magic Johnson, back for a brief run after leaving the game because of his illness, said he had never seen a better team. "They're as good as our championship teams. They're better than their three title teams. They're scary, man." That now seemed to be the majority view. Rodman was rebounding better than ever, and in mid-season *Sports Illustrated* put him on the cover again, and posed the question, "The Best Rebounder Ever?"

The media madness around them grew in amazing increments. Added to the Michael-Is-Back mania, which was wacky enough, was the Rodman mania, and, gradually, the Seventy Wins mania. Michael madness was, of course, the given, the backbone of the huge throngs of media people who seemed fascinated by even the tiniest developments. Watching the fascination with Jordan's every move and word, Tim Hallam, the Bulls' press representative, started referring to the team as "Jesus and the Apostles." Mimicking the style of local news shows, Hallam told reporters, "Jesus takes a light pregame meal by himself in his hotel room. Details at eleven."

Rodman madness seemed to grow during this season, as if the media needed some fresh blood after too long an obsession with Jordan and as if Michael's innate goodness was becoming boring. Sports fans often liked to see certain contests in terms of good versus evil, white hats versus black hats. So it had been with the young Cassius Clay against Sonny Liston, and a series of different basketball teams against the Detroit Pistons. But Jordan and Rodman on the same team was something new—you could root for the Bulls and root for both good and evil, a Prince of Darkness playing alongside the Prince of Light. Suddenly, it appeared, the entire nation was fascinated by this shy, troubled, remarkably nonverbal young man, largely because he dyed his hair, covered his body with tattoos, and set an NBA record for pierced orifices. The Rodman fascination revealed modern media at its worst, with its new fascination—and hunger—for the aberrant; it was enthusiastically playing the game with a provocateur, even if the provocateur himself did not entirely understand it. If one great wing of the media cared nothing about the authenticity of its new cultural heroes, that was quite all right with Rodman. He wrote a book, albeit a bad one, which sold some 500,000 hardcover copies, and he posed naked on a motorcycle for the book's cover; during the book's promotion tour he did publicity for it wearing a bridal dress. Aware of the ambiguity of the persona he was now creating, he started hanging out at gay bars. One local paper kept a daily record of what color he dyed his hair, game by game, and what the total was, color by color, for the season. Ejected periodically from games by referees, he started taking off his shirt and throwing it into the stands; these were soon coveted as collectors' items of great value, and fans began to appear with signs begging for Rodman to throw them his shirt.

Rodman went on the nation's leading late-night talk shows, where, of course, he had nothing to say and where he was more often than not interviewed by people who had nothing to ask him. With millions of American insomniacs watching avidly in their bedrooms, Rodman sat there, slumped back in his seat, dark glasses on, and mumbled monosyllabically. "Do you think," an amused General Colin Powell once asked David Stern, after one of these performances, "that the average NBA fan knows that when Dennis Rodman goes home at night he actually sits in his darkened room by himself and listens to Vivaldi?" As the cult grew ever larger, Rodman went out at night after games to certain restaurants, surrounded by pals and well-wishers; there he would sit quietly, saying very, very little, while others vied for his attention; he was in effect letting those around him perform for him. His commercial endorsements increased; almost bankrupt before he joined the Bulls, he was now becoming a wealthy young man.

Rodman's teammates were amused by it all. It was a great game, they thought; he was not playing for the world, he had tricked the world into playing for him. In general, his teammates liked him: He was a good if remote teammate, he was incredibly quick around the boards, and very determined as well. The truth was that no one knew who was really there, because no one knew him very well. Luc Longley, who got on well with everyone, had dinner with him a few times and seemed to like him. He told the others that Rodman was rather quiet and pleasant. That was good enough for everyone else.

No one, of course, wanted to let Jordan down. That was no small part of the cumulative leverage available to Phil Jackson in keeping Rodman focused. Even more than any words of any of the coaches, it was Jordan's stern, demanding countenance that drove the team and compelled everyone to be at his best. The stunning thing about Jordan, his new teammates were learning, was that he played every single game as if it were a playoff game. He did not take nights off. Only once that season did Jordan seem to play without his normal intensity. It was early in the season, on the sixth game of a long western trip. The Bulls were 11–2 when they arrived in Vancouver to play the expansion Grizzlies. On that evening, Jordan seemed to be coasting; entering the fourth quarter, he had scored only ten points, and the Bulls were trailing by two. Then Darrick Martin, a young player who was guarding him, made a fatal mistake, one made all too often by young players new to the league and eager to make a good impression. Martin started talking trash to Jordan. "You ain't so hot," he woofed, "I can stop you any time I want."

Almost immediately, the Grizzlies' coach pulled Martin from the game, but it was too late. Martin woke up the lion. With Vancouver leading 79–73 with 5:37 left, Jordan went on a roll. He drove and scored on a dunk. Then he hit a jumper. Then a driving layup with a foul shot. Then a jump shot and a foul shot. His run was broken when Kukoc hit a three pointer. Then, on the next three possessions, Jordan hit a running jump shot, a driving layup, and, off his own steal, a dunk. That made the score 91–83 Bulls. He made nine of twelve from the field and scored nineteen points in the fourth quarter. Darrick Martin did not reenter the game. The Bulls won 94–88.

Still, for all the success they were enjoying, it was not always easy to keep Rodman focused. Not all of Rodman's dissidence was artificial; there was real paranoia there. What he had was a shtick: Some of it was a skilled act, and some of it was genuine anger rooted deep in his soul, and no one—not his coaches, not the referees—always knew which was which. It was not always clear that even Rodman knew when he crossed the line from artificial provocation to genuine anger. He might, night after night, push his right to wrestle and hold an opponent to the absolute limit, and he might get away with endless fouls, but if the refs called him for pushing or holding, he was enraged and sure he was being victimized. "I'm being screwed so much I need a chastity belt," he once said. What saved Rodman and kept his behavior largely in bounds, assistant coach Jim Cleamons thought, was the contrast between Chicago and San Antonio. In Chicago, the coaches and teammates tended to yawn at most of his act; in San Antonio, almost everyone had come down hard on him, prompting him to escalate the aberrant behavior.

The main burden of keeping Rodman tuned was Jackson's. Their relationship was wonderfully complicated: It was filled with admiration and affection, but it was in addition a deft psychological tug-of-war. Rodman threw out a series of small challenges to see how much he could get away with, and Jackson, as the semistern but very supple parent, let his player know there were limits, though he was still loved. Often, the provocations were small. Sometimes, it was about coming on the court with his shoelaces untied. Everyone was supposed to appear on the court with them tied, but Rodman pushed it, tying them even as he came on the floor. No one was supposed to wear jewelry at practice, and on occasion Rodman tried to smuggle some bracelet on, and Jackson, a big smile on his face—this was always a game, remember, and Jackson had to catch him in a way that minimized the entire thing—would go over and say, "Dennis does this look like jewelry to you?" If Rodman threw a relatively minor tantrum on the court, Jackson was relaxed and on occasion smiled and told his assistant coaches—but not the team—"He reminds me of me."

Their two-person game allowed Rodman to be just a little dissident, still something of a bad boy, worthy of the commercial rewards he was now reaping, for his image demanded that, without threatening the agreed-upon team ethic. They both played the game very well. What saved her husband in dealing with Rodman, June Jackson liked to say, was that they had already raised a number of teenagers, and therefore whenever there was a crisis, they had some kind of idea of how not to push too hard. You had to pick your battles and make sure they were over important things, she said. (Her husband did not completely agree. "Is Dennis like my kids?" Phil Jackson asked two years later. "Not *my* kids, my kids are well behaved.")

Rodman's good behavior did not last the entire season. In mid-March, frustrated during a game in New Jersey, he head-butted a referee. Then he indulged in a tirade against the league officials, including the commissioner. He was fined $20,000 by the league and suspended for six games, which meant a loss of an additional $183,000. Someone asked David Stern about Rodman's comments, in light of Stern's oft-repeated remarks that the NBA was a family. Was Dennis Rodman really in the NBA family? And if so, what kind of a family was it? Stern handled it deftly. Yes, he answered, Rodman was family. "Some families have an Uncle Moe, some have a Cousin Dennis. We have Cousin Dennis. You know, a lot of players and coaches like that us-against-them mentality. It's a tried-and-true sports motivation technique. Rodman may have taken it to a new art form."

The danger of all that celebration was believing in it and believing in your own myth of greatness, based on winning seventy-two regular-season games, breaking the record of sixty-nine by the 1971–1972 Lakers. At the end of the season, Ron Harper came up with their slogan: "Seventy-two and ten don't mean a thing / without the ring."

For Jordan, the playoffs were nothing less than a countdown: It took fifteen victories to win the title, three in the first round, and then four each in the next three rounds. That became his real calendar. After each playoff victory, he came into the locker room and he said *twelve*, meaning twelve victories still to go, or *nine,* or finally, *four, three, two,* and *one.* Those were the only numbers that really mattered.

In the playoffs, they swept three games from Miami, then took four of five from New York. That set up the series they wanted most of all, the return matchup against Orlando in the Conference Finals and the chance to avenge the previous year's defeat. It was over almost before it started. The previous year, the dominant player had been Horace Grant, playing against a team essentially without a power forward, matched up as much with Pippen as with anyone else. This time, going against Rodman, Grant virtually disappeared. Late in Game One, he was injured in a collision with his own teammate Shaquille O'Neal, but even before that he had no points, no steals, no blocks, no assists, and only one rebound. Rodman ended the game with thirteen points and twenty-one rebounds. The Bulls swept the Magic in four. "They have the talent to be champions," Rodman said of Orlando before the series started, "but they don't know what it takes to be champions." It was one NBA generation speaking of its putative heirs.

In the Finals, they met the SuperSonics, a team that had won sixty-four regular-season games, a team of considerable physical ability, but not known for the cohesiveness of its half-court game. The Bulls won the first two games at home, and then, when they went to Seattle, they raised their intensity, as they often did for important away games. It was 62–38 Chicago at the half of Game Three. The final score was 108–86. The Bulls had, George Karl said later, "killer eyes." Then, with a 3–0 lead, they began to relax. Seattle blew them out in Game Four, and then, in Game Five, Seattle won again. That meant the Bulls were going back to Chicago with a 3–2 lead. That brought back their focus. Game Six was more like the first part of the series, and Chicago played much tougher defense and showed far more concentration on offense. The Bulls won relatively easily, 87–75.

George Karl said admiringly after the game that the Bulls were a throwback to another era because of their unmatched mental toughness. They gave you nothing, he said: They knew exactly when to turn the defensive pressure up, and they sought out your weaknesses with a certain unforgiving cruelty. What drove them, he said, as much as their talent was that mental toughness and their heart. Karl was right, and he had caught something important in the evolution of Michael Jordan and the Bulls. In the beginning, what caught the eye and admiration of fans was Jordan's sheer talent, the balletic quality of his feats. In his early years, when he had struggled with lesser teammates, the Bulls were still one of the best shows in sports because of Jordan's individual brilliance.

That had been a time of great individual honors, matched by equal frustration over the failure to win. And then, surrounded by better teammates, he had gone to stage two; he had learned how to win. He had become a champion, or as Bryan Burwell, a reporter who covered him in those years, said, he had gone from being a gracious loser to becoming a very tough, determined, merciless winner. In those years, it was still his sheer talent, the fact that he could do things that no one else could do on a basketball court, and the talents of his teammates Pippen and Grant, that had shone through. When he returned from his baseball sabbatical, though, it was for stage three of his career. In his next three full seasons, from the 1995–1996 season through the 1997–1998 one, he was different, older, even more focused, even tougher.

What professional basketball men saw in Jordan now was something that had been partially masked earlier in his career, and that was his consuming passion not just to excel but to dominate. He was the invincible man: His focus was unsparing. For fans who had watched him grow since that championship game against Georgetown in 1982, what emerged now was not the talent—though the talent was still majestic and he could still dominate an all-star game—but the willpower. "The athlete you remind me the most of is Jake LaMotta," Jerry Reinsdorf told him one day, referring to the great, rugged, fearless middleweight fighter of another era, "because the only way they can stop you is to kill you." "Who's Jake LaMotta?" Jordan answered.

No one monitored his performance more harshly than he did. He was acutely aware of the possibility of slippage, and he was aware as well of the fact that the media was *always* watching, eager to write that he was not the Jordan of old. There was a constant theme now to many of his postgame interviews: I-know-you-guys-think-I'm-slipping-but-I-know-I'm-still-getting-the-job-done. But he was an infinitely proud man, and he was all too aware of those athletes who, loving the game a little more than they should have, had stayed on too long after their skills had begun to erode. He was aware as well that the athlete was never the best judge of when that process had begun. He had hated watching Larry Bird at the end of his career, his back killing him, a great player being outplayed by lesser ones. Jordan and Johnny Bach spoke of this often. Bach told him of the great athletes he had seen who stayed too long: Joe DiMaggio in his last season, when his foot was hurting and he could no longer pull the ball as readily; Joe Louis, when lesser men were beginning to beat him; and Willie Mays, falling down in the outfield. When Bach spoke in this vein, he knew Jordan was listening very carefully. "Johnny," Jordan said, "you've got to let me know if you ever see me slipping—if you catch some sign of decline that the others don't see, you've got to tell me." He wanted to be the first to know when it was time to go.

His attitude, as always, was contagious for his teammates. The only exception was Rodman, who generally played with an intensity virtually equal to Jordan's, but who occasionally slipped out of focus completely. Playing mind games with others, Rodman occasionally became caught up in these games himself and became his own victim, slipping over the fine line between control and wildness. But other than that the Bulls reflected Jordan. They were consummate professionals who understood not merely the game but the league, which meant they understood the exhausting subterranean pressures of the season: They were smart, they were talented, and above all they were focused. They knew exactly what they were supposed to do each night when they went out on the court, and more often than not, they managed to do it.

The 1996–1997 season was not unlike the previous one. The number of victories fell by three, to sixty-nine. But essentially there was no drop-off in talent or focus. There was little evidence of what other coaches and players were hoping for: a sign that this team was finally showing its age. The one major break in concentration came from Rodman, and it was typically Rodmanesque: In midseason he dove for a loose ball, and then, lying down among the semiscattered cameramen in plain view of what later seemed like the entire world, he chose to kick one of the photographers in the groin, an utterly stupid and gratuitous act inflicted on someone who had done nothing but help to amplify Rodman's deeds over the years, and which cost Rodman a suspension of eleven games. While he was out, his teammates rallied to fill the potential vacuum and won ten of the eleven games. But Rodman also missed thirteen games at the end of the season with a collateral sprain of the knee, four of which Chicago lost. With him in the lineup the Bulls were clearly a great team with no identifiable weaknesses: 48–7, on track to break their own record from the previous year, if they so desired. Without him they had a record of 21–6, and were merely a good team that had to work extra hard on defense, and had a certain vulnerability to teams with quick, powerful big men. The statistics told part of the story: With Rodman in the lineup the Bulls averaged almost seventeen offensive rebounds and forty-seven total rebounds a game; without him it was about thirteen offensive rebounds and forty-two total ones.

In 1997 the Finals were a little harder, because Pippen had seriously injured his foot in the last game of the playoff series against the Miami Heat and was well below his normal effectiveness, and because Rodman still seemed to be recovering from his knee injury and was somewhat off his game. But a late-season pickup of Brian Williams by Krause made a critical difference, giving them badly needed size and quickness around the basket, and they defeated Utah in the 1997 Finals. In the end, the drop-off from the previous season was marginal: In 1996 the Bulls had gone through the playoffs with a record of 15–3; in 1997, despite the injuries, they went 15–4.

If there was any game that marked Michael Jordan's transformation late in his career, and allowed sports fans to understand how remarkable his status was—that it was talent, but also far more than talent—it was Game Five in the 1997 Finals, that day when the deathly ill Jordan not only played, but dominated the game. He seemed barely able to stand, much less get up and down the court, and yet he had scored thirty-eight points, fifteen in the last quarter.

He was very aware that he was nearing the end of his professional journey. He was no longer a boy playing a boy's game; he was a full-fledged, thoughtful grown-up, a millionaire many times over, experienced in sports, experienced with the media, experienced in business, a shrewd tough negotiator in all three fields. When Jim Riswold of Wieden and Kennedy came to him and suggested a joint commercial, which would show him and Tiger Woods as kids—driving go-carts and playing miniature golf—he vetoed it. He understood the idea, knew immediately it was a great idea and potentially a wonderful commercial, and he was fond of Tiger; aware of the media crunch that Woods was being subjected to, he had become something of an adviser to him. But it was not who he was anymore; he was not a kid, he was very businesslike in all aspects of his life, and it was not by surprise that the commercials that Nike ran in the last season were about Jordan as a CEO.

He was a very good teammate: A certain cruelty, a determination to destroy certain teammates in practice that had marked him when he was younger, was now gone. Typically, the coaches thought, Jud Buechler was the kind of player Michael might have gone after when he was younger, but he was different now, able to see not just Buechler's limitations but his strengths, and the fact that he was a very good and valuable teammate. There had been a vicious little preseason fistfight in the fall of 1995, with Michael going after the significantly smaller Steve Kerr. No one was sure what exactly caused it, but it was obviously a combination of things: Jordan's frustration from his poor showing the previous spring, some differences over Kerr's role as the team union representative, a sense that Kerr had not tried to hide his displeasure over Jordan's failure to pass when he was open. But Kerr, a *very* tough, gritty player, had stood his ground, which was important with Jordan. He had matched Jordan cheap elbow shot for cheap elbow shot, and then punch for punch, and that night Jordan had called Kerr to apologize, something he might not so readily have done in his earlier incarnation. From then on the two men had no problems.

Yet if he got on better with his teammates, he remained more distanced from them than ever. They were all businessmen who shared the same address: They all went to work together, and when the job was done each night, they went their separate ways. His teammates understood that, understood that the pressures on him and the demands on him were so different that it was impossible for him to share very much with them. They knew that in some ways he could not reveal himself to them for fear that no matter how small the confidence, it would soon end up in some newspaper or magazine.

He understood that in all of this, the great circus that surrounded his life, the one true thing was his love of basketball. Normally, as the playoffs neared, the last thing he ever wanted to bother with was a commercial, but one year Nike approached him with what was in effect a love-of-the-game commercial.

It was something Jim Riswold had written and rewritten until he finally got it right. The first draft had gone something like this: "You can find my face everywhere, but there's only one place you can find my soul—on a basketball court." Riswold liked it, but he kept working on it until one night he scribbled these words on a cocktail napkin: "What if my name wasn't in lights? What if my face wasn't on television every other second? What if there wasn't a crowd around every corner? Can you imagine?" Pause: "I can." It was to be shot in a darkened gym with Jordan, alone, shooting foul shots. Jordan loved it. He told Riswold that it was exactly how he felt, about the game but even more about the celebrity that was engulfing his life. Playoffs or not, he told Riswold to go ahead with it.

He lived relatively quietly in suburban Chicago. His private life remained very private, which was remarkable in itself, given the intensity of the scrutiny he was subjected to, and the American media's seeming belief that nothing was private anymore. He had married Juanita Vanoy, an attractive former model and secretary, in Las Vegas in 1989, ten months after the birth of their first son, Jeffrey; two more children, Marcus and Jasmine, would follow. He kept as low a profile locally as he could. Ahmad Rashad, the NBC commentator who became his close friend, was once asked by his network to do a special on what Michael Jordan did on his days off. "You'll be surprised," he told them, "how normal it is. He does what a lot of men do with their families on their days off. He takes the kids to school, and he runs a lot of boring errands." The difference, Rashad thought, was that his neighbors tended to understand the burden of his celebrity. They were used to the sightings, his comings and goings by then, and they granted him the privacy he wanted. It was only when he ventured out to other areas of Chicago or to other cities, where his visits were unexpected, that the madness began to take place, and where crowds that knew no restraints began to gather.

For his many social—and some business—occasions, the world tended to come to him, because it remained so much more difficult for him to go out. Among those who often made the journey was his old friend and suitemate from the Dean Smith camp that first year, Buzz Peterson. They had remained very close over the years, and their families had become close as well, and on occasion they would vacation together in Hawaii. Buzz Peterson's career had been marred by a series of injuries, and he had never fully blossomed as a player. He was a seventh-round draft choice of the Cleveland Cavaliers and played briefly in Europe before realizing that his future was as a coach, not as a player. For a time he followed where the Carolina connection led him, working for Eddie Fogler, one of Dean Smith's old assistants, at Vanderbilt. By the mid-nineties Peterson was coaching at Appalachian State in Boone, North Carolina, and doing very well.

One spring, Michael Jordan invited Peterson up to Chicago to be with him during the playoffs. They were immensely comfortable with each other, and the vast difference in their career curves had in no way affected the quality of mutual affection. This was quintessential Michael Jordan, a reflection of his intense sense of loyalty and friendship. He and Peterson had been friends for almost fifteen years, and nothing had come between them, not Michael's stunning wealth and fame and success, and they could pick up as friends exactly where they had left off, even if a year had passed. If there was any point of tension between the two men it was over dress codes: Michael cared desperately about clothes, and even on the golf course he wanted to look stylish, whereas Buzz was quite content to wear knock-around clothes, so they would often argue before they set out, Michael trying to force some of his more stylish clothes on Peterson.

One day, out on the golf links, while they were waiting to tee off, Jordan told Peterson, "I want to thank you for something." "What's that?" Peterson said. "You made me a very, very good basketball player." "How?" asked the puzzled Peterson. "Well, you were the golden boy of North Carolina basketball and I wasn't. And you were going to be the big starter, and everyone back home was saying that you would start and I wouldn't. All those people had told me that I was never going to play because I was behind you, I was never going to leave the bench. So

every day we went to practice at North Carolina I woul[
'You've got to be better than Buzz. You've got to improve. [
do all the drills better than he does. You've got to shoot [
got to work on your defense.' Every time there was a dri[
myself that I had to do it better than you." The confession stunned Buzz
Peterson, and he was not sure he knew how to answer it, but finally he
said, "Why didn't you tell me then so I could have competed back
against you?" But later he thought to himself that if he had been by
Michael's standard complacent, he had also been happy to be himself,
happy to be at Chapel Hill, and he had not thought you needed to be any
better. He was, he decided, missing a certain rage to excel.

Jordan was not in any way political, and he was uncomfortable with
the new part of American celebrity life that demanded that its celebrities
take stands on all kinds of political and social issues, qualified or not. He
tended to turn down almost all requests for noncommercial endorsements, except for an occasional special cause such as urging young people to stay in school. No small part of his wariness toward any political
endorsements was a fear that he might taint his value as a commercial
spokesman. When Harvey Gantt, an early black civil rights leader, ran
against Jesse Helms, the nemesis of Carolina blacks (among many
others), for a Senate seat in North Carolina, it seemed like an easy call
for someone who was black and who was still so amazingly popular in
the state. But Jordan would not take a stand, pointing out that Republicans buy sneakers too.

Because of that, there was a certain resentment of him among many
black activists who felt that unlike other prominent black athletes in the
past, like Muhammad Ali or Arthur Ashe, Jordan had not done enough
for the black community. That seemed something of an unfair test; after
all, accomplished white athletes were not put to any comparable test of
their speaking out on broader social issues. No one had ever presumed
that the much-revered Joe DiMaggio should speak out on civil rights.
But it was always a little different for black people: Arthur Ashe once
said that being black in America was like having a second full-time job.

But perhaps Michael Jordan was different. He was representative of a
different generation of young blacks in America, for whom many doors
once closed, not only educationally but commercially and socially, were
now opened, and he as much as anyone had in his way helped open some
of them. To the degree that he was capable of making a statement about
the black condition, it was not so much with his words but with his
deeds, the way he played in big games under unrelenting pressure, the
way he comported himself on and off court in front of the most intru-

.ve media scrutiny in modern history, and finally how shrewd a businessman he had become. It was, in his case, as if some things did not need to be spoken because they had been *done*.

The other reason he did not speak out much on politics was because he was clearly not very good at it. Some people had a natural feel for it, grievance was in their souls, while others did not. Often those who had a feel for it had been raised in families where at least one parent was in some way or another quite political; Jordan had been raised in a family where there were powerful internal codes, but they were middle-class codes, about how to comport yourself, how to do well and become a success in school and business, not about manifesting any political or social grievance. If anything, the teachings in the Jordan family had been quite the reverse. He and his siblings were taught about the greater possibilities that awaited them if they worked hard, rather than about the historic prejudices that had damaged people in the past; he was taught that it was important and natural to have friends on both sides of the racial line and that was what he had always done. When this reporter once mentioned to Deloris Jordan, his mother, about how remarkable Michael's climb was for a young black athlete in becoming the best-known and best-paid commercial spokesman in the world, her immediate reaction was to say that there was too much being made of the black-white thing and that was one of the things wrong with the country. Everyone ought to remember, she said, that people were just people.

The natural ease and confidence Jordan showed with reporters in the easy byplay before and after games—talking about subjects he had mastered, always getting in the best last shot with men who made their living using words—and the poise he had shown in dealing with the directors and cameramen shooting a hundred different commercials, deserted him when the subject came to politics. It was not something he knew much about, cared much about, or had any real feel for. He became uneasy and awkward. Besides, as one of his friends pointed out, his political ideas might not be the same as those of the people urging him to speak out on a good many issues. He might be a good deal more conservative than they expected. Jordan's good friend Charles Barkley once announced to his grandmother that he was going to run as a Republican for governor. She had been shocked. "Son, the only people who vote for Republicans are millionaires," she said.

"Mama," he explained, "*I'm* a millionaire."

Nothing quite revealed Michael Jordan's maturation over the last three years than the change in his attitude toward Scottie Pippen. For much of the early period, Jordan remained quite reserved about Pippen, and upon occasion in private sometimes quite negative. His doubts after the migraine game in 1990 were obvious, and even after the Bulls won three championships it sometimes seemed to others that he was oddly distanced from Pippen. What bothered him about Pippen in those years, their teammates thought, was the latter's inconsistency. There were great games—Pippen would have a triple double, say, posting double figures in points, assists, and rebounds—and the next night he virtually disappeared. True greatness in the NBA depended more than anything else on consistency. The Bird-Parish-McHale front line seemed to get its sixty or sixty-five points every single night.

But after Jordan returned from baseball, he was far more generous about Pippen, who himself had clearly matured that much more. "Scottie is the best player on this team," he said in those first few weeks after coming back. He seemed more appreciative of Pippen now, talking about him as though they were brothers on the court. The difference, thought B. J. Armstrong, was that when Jordan was younger there was nothing he could not do on the court by himself. He could score fifty any time he wanted, and he could bring the ball from one end of the court to another, take whatever shot he wanted, and do it all game long. He needed good teammates to win, but he did not need good teammates to be Michael Jordan. But now, older and needing to conserve energy and to set just the right pace for a game, he realized that in order to be Michael Jordan, he needed Scottie Pippen. For the first time, there was a codependency. He needed Pippen to bring the ball upcourt and get it to him where he wanted it, to control the tempo of the game to an acceptable Jordan-like pace, to create an alternative threat to the basket and an additional threat on defense. By the time of the second round of championships, Armstrong said, they knew each other so well and what the other wanted and needed to do at all times that they were in each other's brains, like twins.

One of the reasons Jordan continued to be hard on Jerry Krause was because of the way Krause dealt with other members of the Bulls who were important parts of the team but somewhat vulnerable in their contract leverage. It was Jordan's way of being a good teammate. In these instances, he believed, Krause was not only unnecessarily tough and ungenerous but also demeaning. It was a feeling that went back to Krause's negotiations with John Paxson, even after Paxson had proved to be a valuable member of a championship team. Paxson was by NBA standards badly underpaid for a starting guard on a champion team, making perhaps $500,000 a year, and it was Jordan's belief that Krause was much too tough in their dealings, as if Paxson had no value elsewhere in the league. One year, appalled by the way they were treating Paxson, Jordan had asked David Falk to represent Paxson, and Falk in time secured a very nice offer from San Antonio, almost three times what Paxson was making in Chicago, as a way of keeping the Bulls competitive. Those dealings in time hardened feelings on both sides of the line.

29

Chicago, 1998

As THE 1997–1998 season reached its halfway mark with Scottie Pippen's return, the Bulls were once again the team to beat. Pippen's long absence had meant that the early part of the season took a good deal more out of Jordan than anyone wanted. The upside of Pippen's absence was that he was well rested.

The team was a little more erratic than in the past; intensity of focus and mental toughness were now more important than pure talent, and the bigger the game, generally, the better they played. The corollary of that was a tendency to slip out of focus in games that were not so important. Tex Winter, the organization's resident pessimist, was always brooding, always sure that things were not going well. He remained quite pessimistic for much of the season and was fond of issuing doomsday predictions. Coach No, the players liked to call him. Typical was a preseason game against Philadelphia, a young team trying to define itself with some talented young players who might or might not mesh. Philadelphia played well that night, and Winter had come away concerned about how good the 76ers were going to be. "Tex," Jackson had said, "they're going to be lucky if they win thirty games."

"Phil," Winter said, "they're more talented than we are."

"Tex," Jackson said, "it's not about talent—it's about toughness of mind, and about a collective attitude. They're going to be lucky if they win thirty games." (In fact, they won thirty-one and were last in their division.)

"How many games do you think we can win without Scottie?" Winter asked him.

"Sixty, if Scottie's back for half the season," Jackson answered.

Jackson thought that if things went well the Bulls could easily win fifty-five games and had an outside chance at sixty. The lift Pippen gave them, the new cohesion on offense, gave them a fluidity they had lacked earlier, and meant that opposing teams could no longer concentrate on Jordan as they had before. Gradually, as the number of wins mounted, all the players became more confident. There was, however, a sense that Dennis Rodman was slipping out of focus a bit more as the team depended on him that much less. There had been a game in late January, when Rodman missed a pregame practice in New Jersey, and Jackson sent him home.

The better he got to know Rodman, the more sure Jackson was that his player was struggling with what was known as ADD, or Attention Deficit Disorder, almost surely a genetic condition that placed sharp limits on an individual's ability to concentrate and caused all sorts of frustrations and parallel social disorders. All of Rodman's symptoms— he was quickly bored; he immediately reacted negatively against even the slightest surfacing of authority; his instinct was to place his career in jeopardy again and again in needless, gratuitous ways; he had bursts of hyperactivity—were classic manifestations of ADD. So was the fact that when he had realized that he was a good basketball player—the one thing he was good at—he had worked so hard at perfecting his game. That was typical of ADD people: Frustrated in other endeavors, they were relentless when they found their one calling. Even Rodman's love of Las Vegas—he tended to go there every time he got a chance—was a sign of having ADD, Jackson thought, because for someone so readily bored, Las Vegas, with its constant noise and artificial action, was a kind of heaven. During the playoffs each year, as the Bulls came more and more into national focus, Jackson received letters from special-education teachers around the country who dealt primarily with ADD kids. They noted that their students shared many of Rodman's symptoms and that he was something of a poster boy for them; they could show their students that someone struggling with their problems could have a useful career.

Nonetheless Rodman was becoming more and more of a dissonant force without really wanting to be, and Jackson talked on occasion to the rest of the team about him, about trying to understand him. The remainder of the season was going to be difficult, he said. Rodman was obviously slipping away, and yet they needed him badly. They not only needed him, Jackson reminded them, they liked him as well. Almost every Indian tribe has someone like Rodman, he said, often referred to as the backward-walking member of the tribe—*Heyokah*, in the Sioux language—the tribe contrarian, someone who always had to go against the grain. It was a tribute to the maturity and professionalism of the other players and the skill and candor with which Jackson had midwifed a difficult player into a strong, thoughtful team that the other players rarely resented Rodman's behavior or the fact that Jackson cut him considerable slack. There was a consensus on the part of the other players and coaches: They had all sacrificed a great deal for this last shot at the championship, they needed Rodman to win and they liked Dennis in spite of himself. In their view, no other coach in the league could have gotten so much out of him for so long. But the act was wearing thin. "I don't know how you stand it," Tex Winter told Jackson late in the season. "I could never deal with a player like that. I would never have the patience." The irony of that, Jackson thought, was that although no fellow American was culturally more different from Rodman than Winter, the last great square produced by the Great Depression, no one worked better or more lovingly with Rodman day after day, often staying late after practice to work on parts of his game. Rodman seemed to love Winter, and Winter seemed to like Rodman.

Despite Rodman's waning concentration, the Bulls held together for the rest of the year. Late in the season, in a move that surprised every player on the team and a great many other professional basketball people, the Bulls traded Jason Caffey to Golden State, getting very little in return. Caffey was six foot eight and 250 pounds, the backup power forward, physically impressive, a good rebounder, but limited in other ways, and someone who had trouble with the triangle offense. In return for Caffey the Bulls got a player named David Vaughan, who was quickly let go, and in time a player named Dickey Simpkins, whom they had gotten rid of in an earlier incarnation. On paper, the trade seemed inexplicable, particularly for a team driving for the championship. Whatever his limitations, Caffey was a strong, physical presence on a team that badly needed his strength and athletic ability in certain key matchups. Krause did not like Caffey for a variety of reasons, not least that he was about to be a free agent and was represented by Jimmy Sexton. What upset some of the players was that Jackson had been willing to get rid of Caffey. He later said he saw it as a means of putting more responsibility on Rodman's shoulders. For as long as Caffey was there, Rodman had a competent rebounding backup, which allowed him a touch more irresponsibility in his behavior. Jackson also later said that he had agreed to trading Caffey in the belief that they would get some-one of value. That, he felt, had not happened. If anything, the trade sharpened the existing tensions between Krause and Jackson.

Sometime that season the Bulls seemed like a team patched together with Elmer's glue and Scotch tape. Whether they *had* to become that old was an interesting question. Because of free agency, the way you put together a basketball team was different these days. The draft was less important, and whether or not you signed talented free agents was more and more about your skill in recruiting them—it was more like attracting high school stars to a great college program. Obviously, the Bulls had a great potential advantage in recruiting because they could use Jordan, Pippen, and Jackson to help seduce the right free agents and get them to Chicago—almost everyone wanted to play with Jordan. But that was a hard path for Krause to follow. He had spoken openly of his plans to build the post-Jordan team, and to have Jordan play a principal role in putting it together would therefore taint it. The only player Krause had asked Jordan to help recruit was Kukoc, and Jordan had wanted no part of that.

The Bulls were rarely brilliant on offense, but there were frequent moments when they turned the ratchet up and were truly murderous on defense. Their number of victories mounted steadily. In early February, Michael Jordan came to New York to play in the all-star game. Though he was fighting the flu, and though there was much talk about the rising young star from the West, Kobe Bryant, Jordan put his signature on the game and was named its most valuable player.

Though the undertow from the front-office squabbles was always there, it never affected the performance on the court. If anything, Jackson, ever shrewd, used the tension as a means of building team cohesion by encouraging an attitude of us against them: Not only were the Bulls going to fight off the Lakers, the Pacers, the Knicks, the Jazz, and the SuperSonics, but they were also going to fight off their own front-office. Much of that had been implicit in Jackson's calling the season the Last Dance, with the idea being that they were essentially orphans in this quest, defending champions or not. Jackson and the players from Jordan on down believed that the ownership had brought the team together for one last try with the greatest reluctance, as if not wanting the onus of breaking the team up to be placed on them.

Certainly the fans believed that this season was the end of something they would never see again. Driven by a spreading belief that this might be Jordan's last season and that therefore his appearance at many arenas might be his last, Michael Madness reached new heights. At least two documentary film teams were constantly tracking him, one from the

NBA. Almost everywhere the Bulls went, the game was sold out. When they played in Atlanta, 62,046 people bought tickets, many with obstructed views. In Philadelphia, a local newspaper printed a fifty-two-page special section about Jordan. When he came to New York City to play what might be his last game at Madison Square Garden, Jordan wore an antique pair of Air Jordans, which many reporters saw as Michael's exquisite (and quite commercial) way of saying that this was his final appearance. After the game, hundreds of media people crowded into a converted press room, and a number of hardened and accomplished New York sportswriters were seen not only accompanied by their young children, but holding them up so that they would be able to say, some day far in the future, that they had seen Michael Jordan.

In each city where the Bulls stayed on the road, a large number of people rented rooms in the team's hotel just so that they could say that they had stayed at the same hotel as the Chicago Bulls. Thousands of others of the cognoscenti simply gathered around the hotel at the hour when the Bulls were to leave for the arena, in order to watch them make the brief walk from the hotel door to their waiting bus.

Everywhere, of course, there were the photographers. Not just the thirty or forty hired by varying news organizations to shoot pictures of Michael as he soared to the basket for a slam dunk, but the thousands of others, pure amateurs, armed only with their Instamatics and other baby cameras, who snapped him walking to the bus, or exiting the bus, or best of all when he came out on the court. They sat in their seats and fired away as Michael came on the court before the center jump, making each vast arena look like a giant Christmas tree for a moment. They intended to preserve that special moment as a souvenir for the future: Jordan was only a tiny dot shot by a tiny camera from a great distance, but it was proof nonetheless, like a million photos of the Eiffel Tower or the Statue of Liberty, that yes, one day they had been there, had seen Michael Jordan play.

The mob of journalists, American and foreign, crowded around Jordan's locker grew larger, the questions more esoteric. Jonathan Eiger, a young magazine writer working on a piece on the press, found himself behind a French reporter. He glanced surreptitiously at the reporter's questions. They were: "1. What is the most important thing? 2. Do you have any heroes? 3. What is it like being MJ? 4. What historical figure do you most admire? 5. Do you believe in God?"

After starting the season 8–7, the Bulls went 54–13 the rest of the season, playing over .800 ball. Their final record, 62–20, tied them with Utah for the best record in the league. The day after the season ended, Jackson walked into a coaches' meeting with a huge grin on his face. "I don't know about you," he said to his assistants, "but I have a clause in my contract calling for a $50,000 bonus if we have the best record." During Jackson's heated contract negotiations the previous year, management had argued that the $6 million they were paying Jackson to coach the team ought to be incentive enough and there was no need for any bonus clauses. Jackson and Todd Musburger had agreed, but when the contract was drawn up, the incentive clauses had been left in by mistake. Jackson was much amused by his good fortune, a mistake that was worth more than his entire salary for some of his CBA years. Reinsdorf was not so amused; he argued that the Bulls did not have the NBA's best record, since they had lost the home-court advantage to the Jazz, so the clause was not applicable. They eventually settled for a $25,000 bonus.

As the team was getting ready for the playoffs, Jackson called the players, coaches, and trainers into a special team meeting. Jackson believed deeply that as much as the championship was a reward, the true reward was the journey itself, the friendship and human connection they shared together in good days and bad days over the past few years. Since it was likely that this was the last time they would all be together, he asked everyone to help bring some measure of closure to a difficult but successful season by writing something, a few words, perhaps a poem, about their time together and what the season had meant to them. Fifty words or fewer. He had learned this from his wife, June, who worked in a hospice and sometimes did a similar exercise with older people who were dying. At the end, the team would burn all the messages together in a coffee can.

That, thought trainer Chip Schaefer, was the quintessential Phil Jackson. First, very few coaches would think of doing it, and of the few who might, even fewer would have the courage to do it because it might seem unmanly. Even if they had the courage to do it, he wondered, would any other coach be able to get a group of hardened and somewhat cynical young millionaires to go along? In fact, it turned into an incredibly moving moment. Everyone participated. Some of the players had written out statements, and some simply got up and spoke without notes. Some spoke of how the years in Chicago had changed their lives, of children born here, of the pleasure of playing alongside great teammates like Jordan and Pippen, and of the thrill of being part of two championship teams. Perhaps the most moving speaker was Ron Harper, who talked about what it was like to be playing the limited, unglamorous role of defensive specialist on this team after years of being the main man on weak teams. It was so much sweeter, he said, being just a cog on a winning team than being the superstar on a weak one.

What was surprising was how intimate it all was. Men like this, professional athletes, were not accustomed to opening themselves up emotionally. Part of the unspoken macho code of the locker room was that you did not show certain emotions. Anger was all right—anger at refs, opposing players, coaches, even teammates occasionally—but any more complex emotion that might be viewed as a sign of weakness was not. Even Michael Jordan got up and spoke. He had written a small poem, which surprised some of his teammates, because Jordan was usually so buttoned up, so much inside his own cocoon, someone who liked to know about other players' emotions and feelings and weaknesses but wanted no one to know of his own. But his poem was gentle and sweet: Is this the end? it asked, and if so, what does the future hold? That he had participated mattered greatly to all the others.

The Bulls faced the New Jersey Nets in the first round of the playoffs. Long one of the league's disaster areas, New Jersey now fielded a good team of talented young players: Jayson Williams, emerging as one of the league's best rebounders; Keith Van Horn, an exciting rookie with an explosive move to the basket and exceptional outside shooting range; Kerry Kittles, a much-admired young player; and Kendall Gill, long one of the better guards in the league. The point guard, Sam Cassell, was both talented and occasionally something of a problem, a player who had a tendency to distribute the ball first and foremost to himself. The Nets were young, hungry, and on the rise; they were much more fun to watch than their neighbors across the river, the Knicks, who played a very physical game, designed as much as anything else to wear—or beat—down opponents. With luck, if no one chased free agency, the Nets would be one of the league's better teams in a few years.

Whether the Bulls were ready for the early rounds of the playoffs was an open question. They had won sixty-two games, but they had not been as impressive as in seasons past; other teams were becoming aware of their age and of the fact that they sometimes seemed to play well only in spurts, rather than for entire games. "They got a year older but not a year better," Seattle coach George Karl said. A preplayoff headline to a *Chicago Tribune* column by Bernie Lincicome read, BULLS MARATHON LIKELY TO SUCCUMB TO TIRED FEET. The Bulls, Lincicome wrote, "must face the passing of their own time. . . . Dead men dribbling." In Game One, Chicago seemed almost careless, not really taking the Nets seriously until it was almost too late. Even though Willams played with a broken thumb and his hand in a cast, and Van Horn missed much of the game with the flu and was hooked up to an IV in the locker room when he came off the court, the Nets outrebounded the Bulls 53–39 and played with more enthusiasm. The Bulls should have opened up a big lead in the third quarter but let the visitors stay in the game. The Nets stayed close and might have won in regulation if Kittles had hit a fifteen-foot shot. He missed, and they went to overtime tied 89–89. Even in overtime, the Bulls still played badly. With more than four minutes gone in overtime, the score was tied 91–91 when Kittles brought the ball up-court. He came over the mid-court line with forty-five seconds left. Jordan was guarding him and began to push him left, toward his weaker hand. As Kittles began to move left, Jordan beat him to the spot, stole the ball, and went down the court for the dunk, Kendall Gill flying behind him. As he went into the air, Gill came over his back and fouled him, but Jordan made the shot. The free throw gave the Bulls a three-point lead. On the next sequence, Gill drove the lane and went up for a dunk, but Pippen made a great defensive play and blocked the shot. The Bulls had a win, but it was hardly an inspiring one. Jordan had not shot very well, eleven of twenty-seven, but he had gone to the foul line twenty-three times, almost as many times as the entire New Jersey team, and made seventeen free throws.

If the first game was a wake-up call, the Bulls did not seem to hear it. In Game Two, the Bulls played better early, and with about four minutes left in the third quarter they had a twenty-point lead. Then they went to sleep, playing erratically on offense and missing free throws. By the end of the third quarter, the lead was down to eleven, and early in the fourth quarter it was cut to seven. Then Toni Kukoc and Chris Gatling exchanged baskets, and Steve Kerr put an end to the Nets' run by hitting a three. They went on to win but hardly in a commanding fashion. They were up two games, but looked sluggish and seemed to lack a killer instinct. In New Jersey for the third game, they finally played like champions. They ran a clinic, both on offense and defense. Everything they did seemed right. Jordan hit fifteen of twenty-two, for thirty-eight points. The Nets, young, boisterous, and joyous, were gone. Now the magic number was twelve.

The Charlotte Hornets were next. It was a troubled team and a troubled franchise. Only a few years earlier, Charlotte had started out as the very model of the new, modern expansion franchise in a new, modern arena in a new, modern Sunbelt city. Here the owners and managers and players and fans were going to do everything right. The Hornets did well in their early drafts, brought in talented young players and skill-fully built up fan support. Then in the fall of 1993, Larry Johnson, one of those perplexing modern all-stars who might or might not really be a very good player, was given an inexplicably large and long contract— one of the early ones that changed the nature of NBA payrolls: twelve years for $84 million. This happened at almost the same time his back began to bother him, and his ability to rebound began to decline precipitously. His behavior off the court began to decline as well: He had been one of the principal offenders, one of the ugly Americans on Dream Team Two, whose behavior at the World Championship Games in Toronto in 1994 had managed to offend almost everyone—their coaches, the media, and foreign players. Johnson did not seem to get along with his Charlotte teammate Alonzo Mourning, the team's talented young center, and after Johnson's new contract was finalized, Mourning, represented by David Falk, soon left Charlotte for Miami. Johnson's tenure in Charlotte grew less and less happy, and he was traded to New York for the equally troubled Anthony Mason, one of the most physical players in the league, a young man who in his own way always seemed to be unhappy about something.

Mason had a football body—at six foot eight and 250 pounds he looked like a tight end—and he played a very physical game. He could play solid defense, particularly against somewhat bigger men, whom he could force away from their favorite spots, and he had a decent ten-foot jump shot. Like many NBA players, however, he had no real sense of his limitations. Because he handled the ball reasonably well for a big man, he liked to dribble; one of the great mistakes Don Nelson made as a coach was, during his brief New York tenure, to tell Mason he was a point forward, a big man who could and should handle the ball. Mason had little sense of court direction and team flow, and he tended to handle the ball too much, dribbling it endlessly while grateful defensive players welcomed the opportunity to set up against him and his teammates. Mason had thus spent much of that year feuding with Dave Cowens, the Charlotte coach, a man who was a throwback to a plainer, less ego-driven era.

The Bulls had faced Mason in the playoffs before, when he was with the Knicks, but in this series he was tailor-made for Rodman, who was much quicker of foot and more nimble of both body and mind, to play against. Mason was a very difficult player for certain teams to match up with, but in this series the matchup was bound to go to the Bulls, without, it sometimes seemed, Mason ever understanding why.

In the first game, the Bulls started slowly, and Charlotte led after the first quarter, 23–15. But then Jordan began to take over, and Chicago went on a 16–0 run. After hitting twelve of their first twenty-three shots, the Hornets hit a prolonged dry spell in the second and third quarters, when they made only four of twenty-three. Chicago, if not exactly in sync, played reasonably well on offense, and Pippen, guarding Glen Rice, the Hornets' talented shooting guard, limited him to nine of twenty-five shots. The Bulls won easily, 83–70. Defense had done it again.

Charlotte made a brief comeback in Game Two. Apparently sure they had the Hornets measured and now somewhat overconfident, the Bulls played very badly. Chicago was if anything too confident of its defensive abilities, as if they could *always* shut another team down whenever they wanted. This time, struggling and playing listlessly once again on offense, they nonetheless entered the fourth quarter with an eight-point lead, after holding Charlotte to only forty-nine points in the first three quarters. Then the Charlotte guards took over: B. J. Armstrong, the former Bull who had been let go in an expansion draft, scored eight points in the fourth quarter, and Dell Curry scored thirteen. Charlotte won in a grim, inartistic game. It was to be the high-water mark for the Hornets. It meant that Chicago had lost the series home-court advantage. But the Bulls' defense rose to the task, and the remaining games were not close. Charlotte, which had averaged ninety-six points a game during the regular season, was held to an average of eighty-two during the series. Mason, imposing and threatening against most teams, seemed slow and awkward around Rodman, who outrebounded him by an average of seventeen to seven; Rice, one of the top scorers in the league, was held to an average of twenty points a game, after averaging twenty-two in the regular season; in the NBA at playoff time, it was important for the great players to play above their regular season level.

30.

Chicago; Indianapolis, 1998

HE INDIANA TEAM that met Chicago in the Conference Finals was full of surprises. First there was the Pacers coach, Larry Bird. It surprised many that he had wanted to coach at all, and more, that he turned out to be a very good coach indeed—the NBA's coach of the year in his rookie year. That went against one of the prevailing beliefs in all sports, that superstars were rarely good coaches or managers because the game had come too easily to them, because they had little sense of the frustrations that burdened ordinary players, and because, having climbed to the highest part of the mountain themselves, they had less drive to excel as coaches than men whose careers had been far more limited and who needed to prove things they had not been able to prove as players.

In addition, there was the perception among many people that Bird was somehow not very smart, an image that no one worked harder to perpetuate than Bird himself. Smart as a whip and savagely funny, with an unusually stinging wit, Bird had hidden his intelligence as best he could from the media and the rest of the world for a long time, pretending to be nothing more than the backward hick from French Lick. He quite deliberately let very few sportswriters get to know him well, and those whom he did let in had to prove their own love of basketball over a long period of time as a kind of rite of initiation. One of the few who knew him well was Bob Ryan of *The Boston Globe*, and part of his job description, it sometimes seemed, was to interpret Bird and what he did and said for the rest of the basketball world. Ryan once called Bird willfully uneducated, a phrase that had caused a great stir among the politically correct when first used. Actually, it was a wonderfully accurate description, for Larry Bird wanted to know only what he needed to know and nothing more. He was much more comfortable letting the world think that he was stupid than dealing with the greater obligations he would inevitably incur if people thought that he was smart. Those who had played with him and against him, however, knew how smart and in fact calculating he was. Over the last few years, he had made it clear that he was interested in coaching—under the right circumstances.

Indiana was his home, and in 1997, when the Pacers went looking for a coach, Donnie Walsh, the head of the organization, met with Bird. They talked for about an hour and a half and Walsh was very surprised by how well prepared Bird was and how much he wanted the job. He told Walsh exactly what he would do: He would run a very tough training camp. His players would be in great shape to play when the season started. He would get two assistant coaches, and he would lean heavily on them—otherwise, why pay their salaries? He would prepare his team very well, but he was not going to be a ranter or raver on the bench. Once the game started, they were going to play, and he was not going to run the game from the bench. He was not going to have a lot of rules, but he was going to be very tough on certain infractions, such as lateness. It was the key to discipline. Walsh was immediately impressed, and gave him the job; Bird was clearly eager to coach, he knew the strengths and weaknesses of everyone on the team, he knew the sources of authority, and he knew the game better than almost anyone around. Though the current NBA players had little sense of the league's history, Bird's own magical deeds were still recent enough to exist in what passed for a basketball memory bank among the young, and there would therefore be some carryover of legitimacy and authority from his playing days. And there was an absolute straightness and simplicity to Larry Bird. Walsh already knew that, and now he sensed it more clearly than ever. No games were going to be played with people. He did not fancy dealing with the media, but smart reporters who showed that they loved the game would get smart answers. There would be very little conning or spinning. His players would never doubt where he stood or what he expected. From the start he was very tough on lateness. The first infraction brought a $1000 fine. The second time it would be $2500, and the third time the player would be suspended. Perhaps the players' union might challenge the last part, but it never came to that. Once, in the preseason, almost all the players were aboard the charter plane and the stairs were coming up when Travis Best and Dale Davis arrived at the airport and started racing across the tarmac. "Do you want to lower the stairs and let them on?" someone asked Bird. "No," he said, "Let's go." It was a lesson picked up on by everyone. A few days later Reggie Miller, the star shooting guard, asked Bob Ryan, "Does the coach have a military background?" No, Ryan answered, remembering that in the old days when the Celtics played in San Antonio there would always be a lot of fans at the games in uniforms from the surrounding military bases, and Bird would look up in the stands, see those uniforms and would always put on a show. "But he loves the military and he loves authority."

Bird had been absolutely true to his word, and he coached completely in character. Team discipline improved significantly. When the Pacers began the season, they were in very good shape. Other teams had a large number of assistant coaches—the Bulls had four, for example—but Bird had only two. Walsh offered him a slot for a third coach. "What do I want a third coach for?" he said. "I don't have enough work to do myself as it is." He remained a fierce competitor. Before one game with Cleveland, coached by Mike Fratello, he refused to do the traditional pregame interview with Hubie Brown. Walsh was quickly summoned to see if he could straighten the problem out. "Don't you like Hubie?" he asked.

"I like him a lot," Bird answered, "but he's a close friend of Mike Fratello, and he's going to tell Mike everything I say." It was pure Bird, thought Walsh: He was not going to do an interview that wasn't straight, and he wasn't going to help an opposing coach.

The team he coached became more and more an extension of him; for one thing, it was dramatically tougher that year than in the past. It was hardly a perfect team, though, and there were certain obvious weaknesses. Rik Smits was tall and a very good shooter, but he was not athletic; and both the power forwards, Antonio Davis and Dale Davis, were athletic, but they were not considered skilled players or scorers. Point guard Mark Jackson ran the offense exactly as Bird wanted, but he was a step or two too slow for an NBA point guard. Reggie Miller might rank with Michael Jordan as the best pure jump shooter in the game, and he had even greater range than Jordan, but he was not quite as good at creating his own shot as Jordan, and he was nowhere near the defender that Jordan was.

What Bird and his assistants did was skillfully cover up the various weaknesses of the team game by game, depending upon who the opponent was, maximizing strengths, minimizing weaknesses. It was a surprisingly deep team, and Bird was clearly getting a great deal out of players who up to then had not shown much in the NBA. That was most notably true of Jalen Rose, whose NBA career had so far been a major disappointment and who seemed on the verge of being a prime candidate for the NBA all-punk team. He had been a member of the Michigan Fab Five, a team that became better known in time for what its players did not accomplish than what they did, for talent wasted, rather than talent maximized. It was a team disliked by many fans and coaches for its on-court arrogance, and it had been believed that for better or worse—often worse—Rose was the true team leader. Rose was a big guard, six foot eight, physically very strong, but his early tour in Denver, where he had been a first-round draft choice, had been something of a disappointment, and he was being written off by much of the league: too much ego and too little mental toughness. The previous season, then-Pacers coach Larry Brown had barely concealed his scorn for Rose. But Bird had always seen his upside, and he now began to blossom. When he played in a way that Bird did not like, the coach simply pulled him off the floor. His presence added greatly to the Pacers' backcourt rotation. They won fifty-eight games, and they were younger and deeper than the Bulls.

The Bulls won Game One both because of and in spite of themselves. Their offense was simply terrible, but they were brilliant on defense. In the first half, they could barely shoot: They made four of twenty-two shots in the first quarter, which translated into 22 percent shooting. The drought continued in the second quarter, but the Bulls gradually tightened up their defense. Even though they were not shooting very well, they managed to keep the game close. With 1:40 left in the first half, Mark Jackson hit a basket to put the Pacers up 40–31. Then the Bulls went on a brief run before the half, most of it ignited at the defensive end, and closed the score to 40–37 at the half. Instead of being down by twelve or fifteen points, as they might well have been, they were down by only three, yet Jordan was one for nine, and Pippen and Kukoc each one for eight. That meant their three top scorers shot 12 percent in the first half, and they were still close.

In the second half, Chicago continued the run until they had scored a total of sixteen unanswered points, again largely triggered by their defense. The Bulls had a 47–40 lead, and they held on for an 85–79 win. The Bulls shot only 35 percent for the game. It was a typical evening when they won when most teams would have lost. The key was Pippen, but no one looking at a box score would know it. From the field he was only one for nine, but he had absolutely dominated Mark Jackson and disrupted the Indiana offense. The Pacers had to start their offense farther out from where they wanted and with less time left on the clock. That meant that the Bulls had plenty of time to set up on defense and the Pacers' Chris Mullin, an all-star pure shooter who was slow and not very athletic, was not getting the ball where and when he wanted it. He scored only two points in twenty-six minutes. The Pacers came in with a reputation for executing their offense extremely well, with the fourth lowest average of turnovers per game in the league. In this game, they turned it over twenty-seven times. Jackson's assist-to-turnover ratio during the season was an admirable 4:1, but against Pippen, a player who was bigger, stronger, and much quicker, he had six assists and seven turnovers. "Scottie's amazing," Steve Kerr said after the game. "He scores four points and totally dominates the game. That's what makes him one of the best ever to play—he doesn't have to score a point to win a game for us." Mullin just shook his head. "[The Chicago defense] screwed us up a lot," he said. "At times it seemed like there were seven or eight of them out there."

Game Two in Chicago was more of the same, except this time the Bulls played better on offense. Again, Pippen hounded Jackson and disrupted the Pacers' offense. The matchup seemed almost unfair; once again, Jackson had seven turnovers. The Bulls had fifteen steals to two for the Pacers in the course of an easy victory. In his postgame press conference, Bird made a move to stop the hemorrhaging: He took a deliberate shot at Pippen's defense for the benefit of the league and the referees. He would like, he said, to see Scottie Pippen guard Michael Jordan from one end of the court to the other and see how many fouls the refs called. A few minutes later, Jordan, holding his own press conference, was told what Bird had said. He flashed his biggest, warmest smile, the one he reserved more and more for his commercials. "Larry said that? Well, he's really sounding like a coach now," he said.

The series switched to Indianapolis, and from the opening tip-off Bird's finger-pointing at Pippen seemed to have paid off. The refs called two quick fouls on him, at least one quite dubious, and Pippen had to back off slightly on defense. That allowed the Pacers to run their offense better. Bird began to change his rotation and go deeper into his bench, giving young players like Jalen Rose and the very quick guard Travis Best, and Derrick McKey more minutes. Bird was a loyalist of the first order, and his instinct was to go with the players who had brought him this far, but he realized the limitations of Jackson and Mullin against the quicker Bulls. All year, the Bulls had problems with small, quick guards; it was their one significant vulnerability on defense, because while Steve Kerr was a smart defensive player, he was not a quick or physical one and Best was much quicker. Rose was big and strong, and he came in well rested at different points of the game when Jordan tended to be tired. More, because Jordan had not played that much against him, he was not exactly sure how to deal with him.

In the third quarter, the Bulls had ground their way to an eight-point lead. It wasn't pretty, and it was hard-won. Then, with 1:53 left in the third quarter, they got careless. Perhaps it was fatigue. Perhaps it was arrogance, perhaps because their defense had worked so well for them so far in the series, they were sure they could always turn it on. They began to be careless with the ball and took jump shots instead of driving to the basket. They committed fouls on defense, which not only gave Indiana easy points but allowed the slower Pacers to set up on defense. Suddenly, as the fourth quarter began, the score was tied. The Pacers' turnover total came down to thirteen to the Bulls' fourteen, and the Pacers' bench outscored the Bulls' bench 40–25. The Pacers won, 107–105.

With that, the chess game was on. Bird's strength was his bench and the comparative youth of his players. His game plan was to wear Jordan out by rotating different defenders at him and playing him as physically as possible, and above all to run fresh bodies at the Bulls at those important moments when normally they sensed fatigue in their opponents and their killer instinct traditionally allowed them to put games away. After Game Three, Phil Jackson spoke to his team in private about how they had let the game slip away at the tail end of the second and third quarters, when they normally put the dagger into their opponents. Jackson's plan was to hide his lack of a bench as best he could, trying to buy breathers for Pippen and Jordan when he could, to run the offense in a way that allowed his starters to conserve energy, and to try to exploit Chicago's mental toughness in big games. From the middle of Game Three on, the Pacers arguably outplayed the Bulls, winning three of the remaining five games and almost winning the seventh in Chicago. ("But, they never won in Chicago," Jackson noted, "and that was the test.") Bird used his rotation and his deeper bench shrewdly, and the deeper they went into each game, the more the matchups that had so heavily favored the Bulls early on seemed to favor Indiana.

The Bulls seemed to be tiring as the series progressed, and it showed in their steals. In Game One, they had nineteen steals, including four by Pippen and five by Jordan; in Game Two, they had fifteen; in Game Three, it was eight; and in Game Four, it was only three.

Game Four went back and forth, until a Jordan shot near the end gave Chicago a 94–91 lead. But then Best scored to make it 94–93. But with a chance to put the game away with 4.7 seconds left, Pippen missed two free throws. There was a battle for a loose ball after the second miss, and the ball went out of bounds. One ref called for a jump ball, but another overruled him and gave it to Indiana with 2.9 seconds left. The Pacers inbounded the ball at mid-court, and Reggie Miller came off a screen, shaking free of Ron Harper and giving Jordan, who had picked him up on the switch, a hard shove. He hit a long three pointer with seven tenths of a second left for the lead. Jordan took a final split-second shot that rimmed in and out, and Indiana had the win. Phil Jackson, trying to match Bird in the mind games played for the refs, said the Bulls were being jobbed by the refs and compared the game to the infamous title game at the 1972 Olympics when friendly refs helped give the Russians several extra chances to win. Still, it was hard to blame the refs for Pippen's missed free throws (he went two for seven at the line) or for the fact that the Bulls looked like they had old legs.

Game Five, back in Chicago, was a complete blowout. It was as if Indiana decided not to show up. Midway in the first quarter, the Bulls went on a 19–6 run, and they ended the quarter leading 29–16. They stretched it out even more in the second quarter until it was 49–24 with four minutes left. The halftime lead was 57–32 and the Bulls ended up winning 106–87.

Indiana quickly regrouped in Game Six. It was ever more clear that Chicago was in a war for survival. Using a defense drawn up by Dick Harter, their assistant coach, the Pacers were physically pounding Jordan as much as they could, defending him the way the Pistons once had, making him pay for every point and deliberately trying to wear him down physically. Near the end of the game Michael Jordan could increasingly be seen bent over slightly at the waist, hands on his shorts, a sure sign of his exhaustion. Antonio Davis and Dale Davis were playing very well, at the least neutralizing Rodman, and Phil Jackson was beginning to wonder if he had made a fatal error in signing off on the Jason Caffey trade. In Game Six, the Pacers again used their bench as the key to victory. They got twenty-five points from their bench players, including eight from Rose and six from Best, compared to eight for the entire Bulls bench. The Bulls kept it close, but in the end they were not able to contain Best, and they lost 92–89.

They were headed for Game Seven, and it was clear, as Phil Jackson said later, that this was the toughest series the Bulls had ever faced in their championship years. ONE FOR THE AGED, read the banner headline in the *Trib* before the game, and under it a subhead asked: "Bulls' vets too weary to survive?" The Bulls were lucky they had the home-court advantage. They were clearly exhausted, and the Pacers were showing little nervousness about playing in Chicago against the defending champions. One bright note for the Bulls in the series was the play of Toni Kukoc. Phil Jackson had started him in four of the five games, using Rodman to come off the bench, and by and large Kukoc was responding. It was not just that he was shooting well, for he was always capable of that. It was that he seemed far more in sync with his teammates, playing with more audacity and greater toughness. In this series, he seemed not merely a talented young man who wore the same uniform, but a real teammate, a man whose will as well as his uniform was cut from the same cloth. His defense was better—he was not a very good man-to-man defender, but his anticipatory feel for the game on defense was good, and that allowed him to play good team defense.

The Pacers took an early 20–8 lead, but Rodman gave Chicago a lift coming off the bench. The Bulls were up by two at halftime, and in the locker room Jordan unleashed a tirade at his teammates for not playing hard enough. In the third quarter, Kukoc played big, hitting three threes. But Indiana would not go away, and late in the fourth quarter the game seemed to be slipping away from the Bulls. Jordan in particular looked exhausted, and his shooting reflected it—he made only nine of twenty-five shots and only ten of fifteen free throws. But he refused to be defeated, here on his home court in a game whose loss would deny him his rightful chance to go to the Finals one more time. Exhaustion might affect his jump shot but not his drives, and again and again he drove to the basket. In the huddle, he barked to his teammates, "*We are not going to lose this game!*" Watching his great player, Phil Jackson saw all the telltale signs of fatigue, and he also saw a great player who simply refused to be defeated. Chuck Daly, who had coached against him for years and then coached him on the Dream Team, had once called him the bionic man because of a career of games like this, in which he became stronger when others around him, many of them younger, were unraveling. "Cut him open," Daly had warned, "and you won't find blood and muscle and sinew, you'll find nothing but wires and electrons and circuits."

Jackson knew all too well what Dick Harter was doing—putting up a defense that punished Michael every time he went to the basket, not just to stop him but to wear him down and take his legs from him in the fourth quarter, and he understood that Jordan was willing to take the pounding in order to win. It was a small price. It was no longer about talent, it was solely about heart. Later, Jackson edited the videotape of the last six minutes of the game for a film clip to use for the Utah series, because he knew they would face some of the same problems of fatigue, and he wanted to show his team Jordan's willpower in action.

Four times in the final 7:28 of Game Seven an exhausted Jordan simply took the ball and drove right through the heaviest traffic in the lane, trying to draw the fouls. Each time he drove he got the call, and he ended up making five of seven free throws. It was one of his great games, spiritually if not artistically. After the Bulls managed to hold on and win by five points, 88–83, Jordan was like a little kid. He rushed off the court, not just ebullient but almost giddy, like a schoolboy liberated from the last day of class. He was equally gleeful on the flight out to Salt Lake City to play Utah. They were not only back in the Finals, but they had dodged a bullet: They had beaten the Pacers in a series that by all rights the Pacers appeared to be on their way to winning. It had not been luck—the Bulls had earned every bit of it—but Jordan more than anyone else knew how close it had come, how exhausted he was at the end. Jordan was thrilled to be back in the Finals and to be getting one more shot at Utah. After going against the Pacers, he hungered to go against a team whose guards were shorter but not quicker, and in the case of John Stockton and Jeff Hornacek, not younger.

31

Chicago; Salt Lake City, June 1998

MICHAEL JORDAN HAD wanted Utah for the Finals all season, in no small part because after last year's Finals too many people had said that if the Jazz had had the home-court advantage, they would have won. He was eager to prove them wrong and to show that though Karl Malone was a great player whose abilities he greatly admired, there was a significant difference in their abilities. The Chicago coaches, glad to see the last of Travis Best, Jalen Rose, and the Davises, were pleased about Utah as well. They thought the home-court advantage meant little to their own players; with their superior ability to focus, the Bulls rose exceptionally well to the challenge of playing very good teams on the road. They also liked the matchups.

Still, Utah was a very good, very smart team, a cohesive group of veteran players who executed their offense as well as any team in the league. Unlike other, more talented teams, Utah almost never beat itself. It made remarkably few mental mistakes during a game. The man most responsible for putting the Utah Jazz together, keeping the franchise alive in bad days, and eventually turning it into a high-quality team was Frank Layden, the team's president. Perhaps the two best decisions he made in two decades running the team occurred in back-to-back years, 1984 and 1985, with the drafting of John Stockton and Karl Malone. Layden had scouted Stockton at Gonzaga and was not terribly impressed, but because Utah had a low first that year, number sixteen, they felt they did not have a better choice and so they took him. "After all," Layden recalled, "he's Irish, he's Catholic and his father runs a bar. Perfect: I'm Irish and Catholic and my father ran a bar. So in time I look like a genius." A year later, drafting thirteenth, they picked up Karl Malone. "Right before the draft we go to a retreat in Ogden to decide on our choice," Layden recalled, "and my son Scott says 'I'm going to show you some film of a *man*,' and it's Karl Malone, playing for Louisiana Tech against Oklahoma, and Oklahoma bodies are flying in all directions. A one-man wrecking crew. So I love him, but I know we don't have a chance at him because we pick too low, and then on draft day he starts to drop, I ask Scott what's wrong—does he have an incurable disease we don't know about? Did you check his medical records? But it's the herd thing. One scout tells another he's sulky, and pretty soon everyone knows he's sulky. A lot of guys lost their jobs passing on Karl Malone. He's not sulky—he's the hardest working player I've ever seen."

In the Conference Finals, Utah had gone up against the awesome Lakers, a team with vastly more physical power that had just wiped out Seattle, and the Jazz made them look like a group of befuddled playground all-stars. "Playing against them is like the project guys against a team," Lakers point guard Nick Van Exel said after the series. "The project guys always want to do fancy behind-the-back dribbles, the spectacular plays and the dunks, and they're a bunch of guys doing the pick-and-rolls and little things. They don't get caught up in the officiating, they don't get down on each other, they don't complain. They stand as a team and stay focused. I don't think they're fazed by talent. They stick with what they've been doing. They come with a game plan, nothing fancy, and they do it and do it well."

But when they played the Bulls, they were not playing a bunch of project guys. If anything, the Bulls were so mentally tough that they might be able to expose certain vulnerabilities inherent in the very strengths of the Jazz. Age, which had been such a factor against Indiana, was not expected to be a factor in this series. Utah's three best players were essentially the same age as the Bulls' veterans: Stockton was thirty-six, Malone was almost thirty-five and already doing commercials for a baldness treatment, and Hornacek was thirty-five.

It was not by chance that the two teams reaching the Finals placed two of the league's oldest starting lineups on the floor. The five most important players—Jordan, Pippen, Rodman, Malone, and Stockton—were all in different ways late bloomers, if only in their own minds. Despite their various histories, all five players had maximized their abilities and improved dramatically *after* they entered the league. That itself was becoming more and more rare. What allowed these two teams to reach the Finals was the shared work ethic among their best players.

In truth, many of the league's young stars had not blossomed as expected and were proving less and less attractive to the general public with their petulant attitudes. It was a source of immense concern within the league. Within the NBA, even though its older players were only in their early or mid-thirties, there was a distinct generational divide. The older generation, men such as Jordan, Malone, and Barkley (himself hardly a poster boy for good behavior earlier in his career but always bighearted as a player), had spoken out publicly about the careless attitude of the younger players, who enjoyed from the beginning of their careers the benefits that had been won by their predecessors. Malone had been furious at the start of training camp this season when two young Jazz players, after signing large contracts, had showed up out of shape, and he had publicly referred to Greg Ostertag, the big center, as a lard-ass.

If anything, this was supposed to have been the year when Juwan Howard and Chris Webber, both immensely talented, would take the Washington Wizards forward, but they had both regressed. They played defense when it suited them, and their off-court behavior was a cause for concern. By the end of the season, Webber, as gifted a young player as the league had, was traded by a frustrated management to Sacramento, his third team in his unsatisfactory (though lucrative—his first contract had been for $75 million for fifteen years and it had soon been upgraded) five-year professional career. (He, of course, immediately threatened not to report and wanted to force a trade to the Lakers.) The league was so concerned about the failure of its young players to meet expectations that at the all-star game it put considerable pressure on NBC to highlight three of the most attractive young players—Keith Van Horn, Kobe Bryant, and Tim Duncan—as if to say, they're not all punks.

The older players thought the younger ones just didn't get it. Michael Jordan, Magic Johnson, and Larry Bird were basketball players whose fame and skills so transcended the normal boundaries of their sport that in time they were treated like rock stars, but they always remembered that good things had arrived because of how well and hard they played the game. That was not necessarily true of the next generation: Some of them seemed not to understand the difference between being a rock star and a basketball player and believed they were both. Shaquille O'Neal, formidably talented, touted as a potential heir to Michael Jordan, but as yet incomplete as a player, had arrived in the league as a full-service entertainment conglomerate. He could sing and did; he could act in movies and did; he could sell products and did; and perhaps he might also play basketball. He and his agent struck a major sneaker deal with

Reebok (he showed up for his Nike meeting wearing a Reebok jacket, which left Phil Knight underwhelmed), a soft-drink deal with Pepsi, a movie deal, and of course, a deal as a rap singer. He was a very wealthy young man before he played his first game.

Not everyone thought O'Neal's game was complete. Several years into his career, when people pointed out that he had yet to win a championship, he said that was not a fair comment, since he had won everywhere but in college and in the pros. He did not seem steeped in the league's history, and when a major event was held on the fiftieth anniversary of the league, he was the only living player who did not show up. When he once worked out with Lenny Wilkens, the fabled Atlanta coach, soon to be the only man in the Hall of Fame as both player and coach, he told a friend, That old guy's pretty good—did he ever play? When Rick Majerus, the University of Utah coach legendary for his ability to coach big men, had once tried to teach O'Neal something about footwork, O'Neal walked away saying it was nothing but baby stuff. By 1997–1998, his game had finally begun to improve, and there were occasional signs of greatness, but his team was swept by Utah nonetheless, and there were people, serious students of the game, who thought that given O'Neal's size, strength, and quickness, he was a shadow of the rebounder he ought to be. More significant, perhaps, he also turned out to be a shadow of the salesman he was supposed to be, and at the end of the season it was announced that Reebok was pulling back from its shoe contract with him. There were many basketball lifers who thought that was the best news of the season.

It was unfair to single out O'Neal as the generation's poster boy, but the new, younger players *were* different. There was plenty of evidence that too much had been won too soon and that the value system most of the senior players in the league had learned from their elders—coaches or teammates or both—was not being passed on. Unlike most of the players on the original Dream Team, some of whose careers dated back to a more difficult era in the history of the league, none of the young could remember the time when the league was struggling and not supremely affluent. Coaching a team of modern players was more like dealing with twelve corporations than twelve players, Chuck Daly once said. The wealth of the league, as well as the right of players to take a sizable share of it, was a given. The question often seemed to be not how much effort the players were going to give but how much money they were owed. Their elders spoke openly of their arrogance.

Levels of perceived entitlement were higher than ever. During the 1994 World Games in Canada, Dick Ebersol, the head of NBC sports, sent as a gift to each player on the American team (a team that had largely disgraced itself publicly with its crude on-court behavior) a Sony television set as a courtesy, a not inconsiderable gift. He did not receive a single word of thanks from anyone, a response that contrasted sharply with the tone of his personal dealings with Michael Jordan and players like him. The editors of *Playboy* magazine, who annually brought a group of college All-Americans to Chicago for a preseason all-expenses-paid trip, were thinking of giving up the idea. When they first started it, back in another era, it had been great fun, and they enjoyed being hosts to bright, optimistic, enthusiastic young men. But now the players arrived having been courted all their lives, wanting no part of the carefully prepared schedule—going to a musical, to the House of Blues, and on a boat trip—but instead demanding a requisite limo to take them on their own nighttime odyssey of Chicago. Their attitude from the moment they arrived seemed to be: What are you going to do for us?

Most of the new players had been coddled since the time they were in high school, going to special camps, being stroked by sneaker companies, college recruiters, and, in time, agents. As Bob Ryan pointed out, most of them, unlike many of the players before them, had never held any job other than basketball and therefore did not know how lucky they were. Babied as they had been from the start, given guaranteed contracts, stroked constantly by their agents no matter what they did, they were harder than ever to coach and to reach. They had always held the leverage with their high school coaches, their college coaches, and, in time, their professional teams. They arrived having spent less and less time in college, not only being less socialized in the broad sense by that experience than their predecessors had been, but possessing games that were significantly less complete.

Because of the current NBA rules that placed limits on rookie salaries, young players now came out earlier and earlier, drafted by the league's weakest teams. They used their first contract as a kind of de facto substitute for college, and were ready to move on to the highest bidder when it was over. In fact, many of them were already pushing for trades by the end of their second year, letting management know they would not stick around in order to force the issue. The Bulls and the Jazz, however, had been less affected by these changes than most, choosing to rely on the last holdouts from the older generation. It was not surprising, therefore, that they had both reached the Finals.

Some of the matchups between the Bulls and the Jazz were rather favorable to Chicago. Rodman, with his amazingly quick feet and remarkable physical endurance, generally played Malone well, and Jordan, Pippen, and Harper could give the Utah guards serious problems. But the key to beating the Jazz lay in coming to terms with their greatest single skill: the way they ran their offense.

No team in the league executed its offense with the discipline of Utah, particularly the two-man games between Stockton and Malone. That was how they cut up lesser teams, such as the immature Lakers. But if there was a downside, it was that they were very predictable. Against a team of superb defensive players, players who were very patient and who anticipated exceptionally well and took away the capacity to execute, the Jazz might flounder because they might not have the alternative offensive options. What worked night after night for them against ordinary teams during the regular season might not work in a prolonged series against great defensive players. The price of their discipline might be a certain gap in pure creativity, the ability to freelance when the disciplined offense was momentarily checked.

This was reflected in the difference between Jordan and Malone. They were both great players, both incredibly hardworking, and both had improved greatly after they entered the league. Before the beginning of this season, the Denver rookies had come to Salt Lake City to play against the Utah rookies. One day, Bill Hanzlik, the Denver coach, rounded up all his young players at 7 A.M. and herded them into a van without telling them what the purpose of this early-morning mission was. He drove to a posh physical-training center in town, and there, sweat pouring off him, deeply engaged in a brutal workout, was the NBA's most valuable player, Karl Malone. "Gentlemen," Hanzlik said, "that's what the NBA is all about."

Both Jordan and Malone were admirable, old-fashioned players, and both had the ability to carry their teams night after night. But there was one major difference between them. Jordan's ability to create shots for himself and thereby take over at the end of big games when the defensive pressure on both sides escalated significantly was dramatically greater than Malone's. Malone had become a great NBA player, improving year by year not only as a shooter but as someone who could pass out of the double-team, but he was very much dependent on teammates such as Stockton to create opportunities for him. He was big, he was strong, but he was not explosive. Thus, when the Bulls slowed down Stockton, they also limited or isolated Malone. What Jordan and the Chicago coaches believed was that they could limit Karl Malone in the fourth quarter of tight games in a way that Utah could never limit Michael Jordan.

The Chicago perspective on Malone differed from that of most other people in the league. Malone, the Chicago staff believed, had not come into the league as a scorer or shooter. But he had worked so hard that in time he had become one of the premier scorers among the league's big men, averaging just under thirty points a game in recent years. But deep in his heart, they thought, he did not have the soul or the psyche of a shooter. At the end of big games, they suspected, with the game on the line, that would be a factor. He was a little reluctant to keep shooting in the way that players who thought of themselves as shooters—Bird, Jordan, Reggie Miller—would keep shooting.

The Bulls coaches also believed that Utah was vulnerable because Stockton was slowing down just a little, losing, if not an entire step, then much of one. If that limited him, it would limit Malone as well, and late in the series, as the Bulls began to assert their superiority and Malone came in for a great deal of criticism from the media, there were serious NBA basketball people who thought the finger was being pointed at the wrong player, that the dropoff was more in Stockton's level of play than Malone's. The one thing the Chicago coaches did not want to do if at all possible was double Malone. They intended to let him have his points—thirty-five or forty if need be. Even if he was shooting well, if he was responsible for most of Utah's shots, it would tend to take his teammates out of their games. Utah, the coaches believed, was most dangerous when Malone heated up, other teams started doubling him, and he got the other players involved.

Because the Bulls had such a hard time with Indiana and the Jazz players were well rested, the Jazz were the favorites as the series started. Jordan thought it was the perfect role: "We're the underdogs, but we're still the champs," he said. Jackson considered Utah a daunting opponent and thought what they had done to the Lakers was incredible, but he also thought Los Angeles had been the perfect target for them, singularly vulnerable to Utah's disciplined, controlled game.

Going into Salt Lake City, Jackson hoped to steal Game One; the Jazz had ten days off and were rusty. But exhausted from the Indiana series and perhaps struggling with the altitude, the Bulls seemed more than a little slow and a little tired, a step behind on their defensive rotations. Perhaps it was the air. Tim Grover, Jordan, and the others in the Breakfast Club had worked for some time trying to prepare themselves for Salt Lake City and the change in altitude, trying to build up their oxygen reserves, and it had been, Grover said, like trying to prepare a halfmiler to run a full mile in tough competition. Too often, Stockton beat them down the middle. Even so, the Bulls made up eight points in the fourth quarter to force Utah into overtime before losing.

In Game Two, the Bulls' scheme started to work. The battle plan was to stay close, play tough defense, conserve energy throughout the game, let Malone have his shots, and let Jordan take over the game at the end. Malone ended up shooting five of sixteen, for sixteen points. He did not score a basket in the second half. Jordan, by contrast, shot fourteen of thirty-three, and, even more important, he made nine of ten free throws. How and when he made them told the story of the game. He had twenty points and only four free throws going into the fourth quarter, when he began to take the ball to the basket. He hit four baskets in the fourth quarter and equally important, shot five of six free throws. The Bulls stole Game Two; with that, the Jazz lost the home-court advantage they had worked so hard for all season. Worse, the series now seemed to be playing out the way the Chicago coaches wanted it, the Chicago guards limiting Stockton's freedom of movement, thereby isolating Malone, separating him from being a part of a fluid offense, and turning him into an above-average jump shooter, limiting his ability to go to the foul line, and preventing him from dominating the game's tempo.

Game Three, back in Chicago, was a nightmare for Utah. For the first time since the middle of the Indiana series, the Bulls seemed truly rested. On defense, they played an almost perfect game: They stole the ball, they cut off passing lanes, and their defensive rotations were so quick that Utah's shots almost always seemed desperate, forced up at the last second. It was as if they knew on each Jazz possession exactly what Utah was going to try to do. Stockton, one of the toughest and most skilled players in the league, seemed to be showing his age that night. Sometimes the Bulls used the bigger, quicker Pippen to help slow Stockton down and drive him into a corner, and then they would slip Pippen back in the defense and let him work against a lesser player so he could be a rover, playing what was perilously close to an illegal defense. The Jazz simply could not handle him, and it reminded some in Chicago of what Stockton had said after the previous year's Finals, that Utah simply had not been able to come up with an answer for Pippen and particularly for his versatility on defense. The Jazz were determined to get Malone involved in the game—he was only fourteen of forty-one in the first two games—and they did. He hit his first six shots. But the rest of the Utah players went one for sixteen from the field in the first quarter. It was 17–14 Chicago after the first quarter, 49–31 by the half, and 72–45 after three quarters. The final score was 96–54, the largest margin in the history of the Finals. Utah's fifty-four points constituted the lowest total in *any* NBA game since the introduction of the shot clock. "This is actually the score?" Jerry Sloan, the Utah coach, said in his postgame press conference, holding up the stat sheet. "I thought it was one ninety-six. It sure seemed like one ninety-six." Bob Costas, the

NBA announcer, said afterward, "All that was left for the Jazz was to put on a blindfold and ask for a cigarette."

Game Four was more respectable, but in the end it was more of the same. The Bulls controlled the tempo, and the Jazz were forced to respond. Again, the Bulls managed to keep Malone from taking over the game (he had twenty-one points), and the final score, 86–82, reflected the fact that they had again done it primarily with defense. The player who was most responsible for disrupting the Utah offense was Pippen, and afterward, Sam Smith of the *Trib* suggested what was virtually sacrilege in Chicago: Perhaps this time Pippen should be the series MVP. He had scored twenty-eight points, with nine rebounds and five assists, and played another marvelous defensive game. He helped turn a smart, tough, confident team into a vulnerable one, unsure of what it really wanted to do and gradually unsure of what it could do. Smith's words symbolized what other Chicago writers thought, that with the margin 3–1, one more game to be played in Chicago, and Utah playing as if in a daze, the series was effectively over. "Now that the Jazz has been rendered irrelevant," wrote Skip Bayless in the *Trib*, "the Friday night stage is set for a much more intriguing game than Utah versus Chicago. The one to watch is Michael versus Scottie for Finals MVP." The headline over the account of Game Four in the *Trib* said: CHILL THE CHAMPAGNE.

The Jazz came back in Game Five. Malone, bottled up so long and the target of considerable criticism, had a big game, hitting seventeen of twenty-seven shots for thirty-nine points, and Chicago seemed off its game, its concentration slipping. Jordan made only nine of twenty-six, and Pippen was a dreadful two of sixteen. There was a sense that the tide might be turning. Jackson later said he thought there had been far too much pregame hype, too much talk of winning at home, too much talk of champagne, of how to stop a riot in case they won, and of whether this was Jordan's last game ever in a Bulls uniform. Jackson was sure now he knew why no playoff team ever won three in a row at home. Part of it was that teams at that level were smart and constantly made adjustments game by game, but part of it was the pressure from all the hype. Instead of the typical thirty-minute drive from their suburban homes to the United Center, it had taken most of the Bulls players about two hours just to get to work. If there was ever a next time—though there was not going to be a next time, Jackson said—they would take hotel rooms downtown or come in by helicopter. There was too much stuff going on that had nothing to do with playing basketball. After Game Five, Jackson told Jordan, "Michael—we'll need one more game. We'll have to win it on the road. I think it's better that way." Jordan agreed.

Though Chicago needed only one win, Salt Lake City loomed as a particularly hard place to play. The Utah crowd, Phil Jackson liked to say, reminded him of those back in Puerto Rico in their intensity; no NBA crowd, he thought, had the ability to bend the will of the refs quite like the Utah one (though some thought the combination of the Chicago crowd and Michael Jordan was equally formidable). Suddenly, the series was turning a little grim for the Bulls. Game Six was very important, for if Chicago lost, it would force Game Seven in Utah against a Jazz team that by then would smell blood. That was not a pleasant prospect, not in the Delta Center.

Writers who only a day or two earlier had virtually written Utah off now sensed a potential switch of momentum. It was a reminder of how fragile victory was at this level and that more often than not the difference between victory and defeat was only a few points. A game later judged by fans to be a major victory might turn on one tiny play, as in Game Two when Steve Kerr had stolen a crucial rebound from Karl Malone. A blowout like Game Three was a rarity. It showed again how important the texture of the officiating was—how much freedom, for example, a player such as Pippen was allowed in defending his man. And it underlined again the Michael Factor, how important a player such as Michael Jordan was. A very good team that lacked someone with Jordan's willpower and toughness might easily unravel on its return to Salt Lake City. But Jordan was different: He seemed to have been put together at some special genetic test center for just such a task. He exuded confidence, and it was contagious.

Just before the game, two Chicago players missed the pregame shootaround, Ron Harper because he had been up all night with a violent stomach illness from something he had eaten, and Pippen because he was barely able to walk. Pippen had severely injured his back in Game Three while taking a series of charges—seven, the coaches believed, including two very hard ones from the 255-pound Malone. He was in great pain, and his mobility was severely limited. He had received some cortisone shots on Saturday in preparation for Game Six, but the shots gave him little relief. In no other game except one this important would Pippen have played at all. Before the game, with Pippen stretched out on the trainer's table and Chip Schaefer working on him, Jackson, very much wanting Pippen to hear their conversation, wanting him to know how much it all meant, turned to Jordan. "Do you think you can go the full forty-eight?" he asked.

"If you need it I can," Jordan answered. Pippen gave it a good shot—he started the game, drove for an early dunk and made it—but he felt the pain immediately and with it the limitations: He could play, but he seemed like a geriatric patient allowed into a young man's game. After seven minutes on the court, he went to the locker room and stayed there for the rest of the half. Now the Bulls were faced with an overwhelming challenge: beating Utah at home with Pippen barely able to play.

At this late point in Michael Jordan's career, certain people thought of themselves as Jordanologists, students not only of the game but of the man himself, and believed that they could think like him—that is, they could pick up his immensely sensitive feel for the rhythm and texture of each game, his sense of what his team needed to do at a given moment, and what his role should be. Now, on this night, it was as if he had reverted to the young Michael Jordan who had carried that bottom-feeding Chicago team in the early days of his career, who had gone into Boston Garden twelve years earlier and dazzled the basketball world with his heroic sixty-three-point performance. That was the Michael Jordan who essentially told his teammates to get on board because he was going to do it all himself. Pippen was virtually a basketball cripple. Rodman was not a scorer. Kukoc had played well lately but he was always problematic. Harper was a designated defender, unused to carrying an offensive load, and he had already turned a shade of gray from his stomach illness. Longley was in the midst of a wretched playoff performance, tonight playing only fourteen minutes, scoring no points, and picking up four fouls. Kerr was dependable, but Utah would be able to cover him more closely with Pippen out.

So it was very clear from the beginning of the game that Jordan would carry the team. For much of the first half, Jordan had to ration his energy on defense. At one point Tex Winter had even turned to Phil Jackson and said, "Michael's giving defense a lick and a promise," and Jackson had replied, "Well, Tex, he does need a bit of a rest." By all rights Utah should have been able to grind the Bulls down and take a sizable lead, but it never did. The Bulls team that started the second quarter included Kukoc, Bill Wennington, Scott Burrell, Kerr, and Jud Buechler, an unlikely championship five. Yet somehow the Bulls stayed close. Even with their bench players on the floor, they played very tough defense, and they never let Utah break the game open, never let them go on a twelve- or fourteen-point run that, given the limited nature of the Chicago offense, might have put this game out of reach. On offense, Michael Jordan carried the load. He was rationing out his energy as best he could, playing less defense and doing less rebounding than normal, but at the half he had twenty-three points, on nine of nineteen from the field (three of six on his threes), and two of three from the line. Utah led at the half, 42–37. Malone had eleven points.

Later, Jordan said that he remained confident throughout the game because Utah had not broken the game open when it had the chance. A game like that, he said afterward, a two- or three- or four-point spread, you're always in it. The great strength of Michael Jordan, thought B. J. Armstrong as he watched that game, was that he had the most acute sense of the tempo and mood of every game of any player he had ever seen. A lot of players and coaches can look at film afterward and point to the exact moment when a game slipped away, but Jordan could tell it even as it was happening. It was, thought Armstrong, as if he were both in the game playing and yet sitting there studying it, completely distanced from it. It was a gift that allowed him to monitor and lift his own team with great skill and to put away other teams as well, when he sensed their moment of vulnerability.

Now, watching him against Utah in the second half, Armstrong had a sense that Jordan knew Utah had already failed: They could have put the game away by exploiting the obvious Chicago vulnerabilities, but they had not. If they had, Armstrong thought, Jordan might have conserved his energy and regrouped for Game Seven. Instead, the Jazz were leaving it out there for him to take. Offered such a gift, he was surely going to try and take it. They were, Armstrong thought, playing into his hands.

In the second half, Pippen, still extremely limited, came back and played nineteen minutes, more as a decoy in the offense than anything else. Yet as the fourth quarter opened, the Utah lead was marginal, 66–61, and the low score itself favored the Bulls; it meant that they had set the tempo and remained in striking distance. In the fourth quarter the Bulls began to come back very slowly, until, with under five minutes to play, the score was tied at seventy-seven. Jordan was obviously tired, but so was everyone else. Tex Winter grew alarmed after Jordan missed four jump shots in a row. "Look, he can't get any elevation on his shot," he told Jackson, "his legs are gone."

Two minutes later, during a time-out, Jackson told Jordan what he already knew: Just take it to the basket. "I know," Jordan agreed. "I'm going to start going to the basket—they haven't got a center in now, so the way is clear."

So once again it was Michael Jordan time. A twenty-foot jumper by Malone on a feed from Stockton gave Utah an 83–79 lead, but Jordan cut it to 83–81 when he drove to the basket, was fouled by Bryon Russell with 2:07 on the clock, and hit a pair of foul shots. Back and forth they went, and when Jordan drove again he was fouled, this time by Stockton. He hit both free throws to tie the score 83–83 with 59.2 seconds. At the last time-out, Jackson and Jordan talked about what kind of shot he might take, and Jackson reminded him that his legs were tired and it affected his jump shot. "I've got my second wind now," he answered.

"If you have to go for the jumper," Jackson said, "you've got to follow through better. You haven't been following through."

Utah brought the ball upcourt and went into its offense very slowly. Stockton worked the ball into Malone, and Chicago came quickly with the double-team. Malone fed Stockton on the opposite side of the court with a beautiful cross-court pass. With Ron Harper rushing out a split second too late, Stockton buried a twenty-four-foot jumper that gave Utah a three-point lead, 86–83. The clock showed 41.9 seconds left. The Utah crowd began to breathe a little easier. In the previous time-out, because Jordan no longer had his jumper, Tex Winter drew up a variation on a basic play of theirs, called Whatthefuck, an old New York Knicks play from Jackson's era. It called for Chicago to clear out on one side in order to isolate Jordan against Bryon Russell. Jordan took the ball out near the backcourt line, moved almost leisurely into his attack mode on the right side, and then, with Utah having no chance to double-team him, drove down the right side, laying the ball up high and soft for a basket. It was a tough basket off a big-time drive. The score was 86–85 Utah, with thirty-seven seconds left.

That gave Utah one wonderful additional possession, a chance either to hit a basket or to use Malone to draw fouls. Stockton came across the halfcourt line almost casually, bided his time to let the clock run down, and then finally worked the ball to Malone with about eleven seconds left on the twenty-four-second clock. Even before Malone got the ball, Jordan was absolutely sure of what Utah was going to do, where the ball was going, and how Malone was going to hold it. He snuck in behind him for the steal. What was fascinating about the steal was Jordan's poise at so feverish a moment: As he slipped in and made his move behind Malone, he had the discipline to extend his body to his right and thus get the perfect angle so that when he swiped at the ball he would not foul. "Karl never saw me coming," Jordan later said. There were 18.9 seconds left on the clock when he made the steal. He held the NBA playoff record for steals, but this might have been the most important one of his entire career.

Jordan did not call time-out, for the Bulls rarely did in comparable situations; their coaches were as much on the floor as on the bench, and Michael Jordan was not about to give Utah any assistance in setting up on defense. The crowd, Jordan remembered, got very quiet with his steal. That was the moment for him, he later said, the moment he had wanted and was ready for. The moment, he explained, was what all the Zen Buddhism stuff (as he called it) that Jackson constantly pushed was about: how to focus and concentrate and be ready for that critical point in a game so that when it arrived, you knew exactly what you wanted to do and how to do it, as if you had already lived through it. When critical moments like that happened, the Bulls were supposed to be in control, to use the moment, not panic and let the moment use them. The example Jackson liked to use was of a cat waiting for a mouse, patiently, biding its time, until the mouse, utterly unaware, finally came forth, and the cat was perfectly prepared.

The play at that instant all seemed to unfold very slowly, Jordan said, almost as if it were scripted. He saw it all happening with great clarity—the way the Utah defense was setting up, what his teammates were doing—and he knew exactly what he was going to do. "I never doubted myself," he said later, "I never doubted the whole game."

Utah decided it could not afford to double-team him. Steve Kerr, in for Harper, was on the wing to his right, ready to kill Utah if Stockton went to double Jordan. Kukoc had to be watched on the left. Rodman, out high on the key, made a good cut to the basket, and suddenly Bryon Russell was the loneliest man in the world, out there isolated one-on-one with Michael Jeffrey Jordan. Jordan let the clock run down, from about fifteen seconds to about eight. Then, when Russell made a quick reach at the ball, Jordan started his drive, moving to his right as if to go to the basket. Russell bit, going for the drive, and Jordan suddenly pulled up, giving Russell a light little tap on the ass with his left hand just to make sure the fake worked, nothing at all like the hard shot Reggie Miller had given him in the Indiana series. Russell was already sprawling to his left as Jordan stopped, squared up, and shot. He got a great look and an easy shot, he later said, and his elevation was perfect, as was his form. Normally, he would say later, he tended to fade just a bit as he took his jumper, just for the extra degree of separation, but this time, because his previous jump shots had fallen short, he did not fade—nor did he need to, for Russell, faked to the floor, was still desperately trying to recover.

There was a remarkable photo of that moment in *ESPN* magazine taken by the photographer Fernando Medina. It is in color, covers two full pages, and shows Russell struggling to regain position, Jordan at the peak of his jump, the ball high up on its arc and about to descend, and the clock showing 6.6 seconds left in the game. What is remarkable about the photograph is the view it offers of so many Utah fans. Though the ball has not yet reached the basket, the game appears over to them. They *know* it is going in. The anguish——the certitude of defeat——is on their faces, as if the arrow has already pierced their skin and is entering their hearts. In a number of cases, their hands are extended as if to stop Jordan and keep his shot from going in. Some of the fans have already put their hands to their faces, as if in a moment of grief. There is one exception to this, a young boy on the right in a Chicago Bulls shirt whose arms are already in the air in a victory call.

The ball dropped cleanly through. Utah had one more chance, but Stockton missed the last shot, and the Bulls won, 87–86. Jordan had carried his team once again. He had scored forty-five points, sixteen in the last quarter to Malone's six, and he scored his team's last eight points. In the second half, exhausted or not, he scored twenty-two points, and the key was that ten of them came from the line——a reflection of his willingness to drive to the basket as his jumper tailed off. A great player had written a great last chapter to his career.

Statistics rarely say that much about big-time basketball games, but in this case, the fourth-quarter statistics for Jordan and Malone are exceptionally revealing and show that the Chicago coaches were prophetic in their sense of how the fourth quarters in this series would unfold and which player would be able to create for himself with the game on the line. In only one game, the first, when Jordan was obviously still exhausted from the Indiana series, did Malone outscore Jordan, 8–5. Game Three was a blowout, and neither man played in the fourth quarter. In Game Five, which Utah won and in which Malone had his best game, they both had eight points. But in three close games, two of them played in Salt Lake City, Jordan played much bigger. In Game Two (13–1), Game Four (11–2), and Game Six (16–6), Jordan put the team on his shoulders. In those three decisive games, he had, fatigue and all, averaged thirteen points in the fourth quarter to Malone's three points.

Afterward someone asked Jerry Sloan about Jordan. He should be remembered, Sloan said, "as the greatest player who ever played the game."

Dick Ebersol watched the final minutes of Game Six in the NBC truck. He had started the game sitting next to his pal David Stern in the stands but had become so nervous that he had eventually gone down to the control truck to be more in contact with his own people. Ebersol liked Michael Jordan very much and was well aware that he and his network were the beneficiaries not just of Jordan's athletic greatness but his charismatic appeal as well. Michael Jordan in the Finals was worth about eight or nine million viewers to NBC. Ebersol was delighted by the ratings for this series so far, for they would end up at an 18.7, the highest ever by almost two full ratings points, translating into 29.4 million Americans watching, some four million more than had watched the previous World Series. But at this point, Ebersol, good broadcast man that he was, was not rooting for Michael Jordan but for a seventh game, which meant that he was rooting, however involuntarily, for Utah. A seventh game would bring NBC and its parent company, General Electric, an additional $10 to $12 million in advertising revenues. Michael Jordan's exploits had brought many benefits to NBC over the years, but he was such a killer that none of his Finals had ever gone to a seventh game.

When John Stockton hit the shot that gave Utah a three-point lead with 41.9 seconds on the clock, Ebersol was thrilled. He was going to get his Game Seven after all. He was already counting his money, he later admitted. "Well, guys," he said to the production people in the truck, turning his face away from the screens, "we'll be back here on Wednesday, and the home folks (the GE management people) are going to be very happy with the $10 or $12 million more we get for it." But by the time he turned his attention back to the game, Jordan was already driving on Bryon Russell, with no one over to double, and the lane to the basket seemed far more open to Ebersol than it should have been. Jordan was going to score, and somehow Ebersol knew, even though that basket only closed the Utah lead to one point with only thirty-seven seconds left, that it was over. Jordan was going to steal Game Seven from him again. He was not sure exactly how, but when Jordan stole from Malone and made the final jump shot, he was not surprised.

Harvest Leroy Smith, who made the Laney High team when Michael Jordan was cut and who shared so much of Jordan's early career with him, was watching at his home in Torrance, California. Earlier that day, Smith, an uncommonly joyous young man, talked with this reporter, and at one point he laughed and said, "Now you tell Michael when you see him that when he goes up against Utah not to worry because there's no one on that team who can stop him." In fact, Smith added, there's only one man who's ever been able to stop Jordan. Who was that? "You're talking to him right now," Smith said, with a rich laugh, "but that was about twenty years ago."

Smith was sure that Chicago was going to win, whether Pippen was at full strength or not. Some ten days earlier, he argued with a friend who was from Las Vegas and seemed to be under the impression that this was Utah's year. It was never going to be Utah's year, Smith said, not as long as Michael Jordan was playing. Chicago would be able to handle Malone, but no one on Utah could handle Jordan, not in the fourth quarter.

As he watched the game unfold, Smith was reminded of his junior year in Wilmington when they played New Hanover High, an archrival, in a Christmas tournament. "They had this big lead, but then in the second half Michael went ballistic. Just made it his game. Wasn't going to be defeated, not on something that important." And so, surprised by nothing that was taking place in front of him, he watched as Jordan brought the ball up for the final shot against Bryon Russell. "This time he goes right and then pulls up to the left for the shot. A year ago it's the reverse—he goes left and comes back right for the shot. No way that man Russell can win."

Tim Grover was there in Utah, watching his prize pupil defy the odds once again, aware that the Indiana series had been unusually draining on him and that in Game Six against the Pacers fatigue had cost Jordan badly. There had been very little lift in his legs when he took his jump shot at the end of the game, and that almost always spelled a miss. Now, with Pippen not able to carry his share, this Game Six had been unusually fatiguing for Jordan, but Grover thought he had paced himself brilliantly. Yes, there had been one stretch in the second quarter when the fatigue had shown, and he had briefly gone out of sync, but then Jordan had made adjustments, and he played well in the third and fourth quarters, although his jumper flattened out a bit for a time. The pure exhaustion that showed in some of the Pacers games was absent.

Grover more than most people knew the signs of Jordan's fatigue, but now as the Utah game wound down, Grover thought he looked in good shape. The driving layup he made off Russell for the next-to-last basket, Grover thought, was impressive, Jordan at his best, picking his spot perfectly, driving when he was well guarded. Utah was still ahead, but Grover was oddly confident. Michael had done this so often, Grover realized, that the players on the court—particularly the opposition players—must assume that he was going to do it again.

Grover had watched Jordan bring the ball up the court after his crucial steal, knowing that he was going to run the clock properly, giving Chicago enough time not just for one shot but for a rebound shot as well. Before Jordan released his last shot, Grover was sure it was going to go in because his elevation was perfect and the follow-through was flawless. Grover loved the moment: All that exhausting training all year long had allowed Michael to be the dominant player in a deciding game when by all rights his legs should have been disappearing on him. What Grover the teacher had learned from Jordan the pupil was the most critical lesson of all, the price for greatness: Only from endlessly practiced technique, enabled by carefully stored-up energy and singularly determined training habits, did great last-second shots go in. If there was one thing in the world a shot like that was not about, it was luck.

Buzz Peterson, Jordan's close friend and college roommate, watched Game Six with his wife at their home in Boone, North Carolina. With the game winding down, with Pippen severely limited and Utah ahead, his wife, Jan, turned to him and said, "They're going to lose." But Buzz, who had played with Michael in countless real games and even more practice games, knew all too well Jordan's supreme confidence. Moments like this were what he lived for: His team would be behind, he would predict victory to his teammates, and then he would take over the last part of the game.

"Don't be too sure," he told his wife. "Michael's got one more good shot at it." Just then, Jordan made his driving layup to bring the Bulls within a point. The key play, Peterson was sure, was going to come on the next defensive sequence, when Utah came downcourt with the ball. Peterson was sure he could track Jordan's thinking: He would know that they would go to Malone hoping for a basket or at least two foul shots. Peterson had seen his friend so often in the past in this same role, encouraged by Dean Smith, playing the defensive rover. He was sure that Jordan was going to try to make a move on Malone. He watched Jordan make the steal and he was sure, as Jordan came upcourt with the ball, that the game was over, that the next shot was as close to a sure thing as there was in sports.

Roy Williams, the Kansas coach who had picked up on Michael when he was still back in Laney High School, was at his own camp for high school players in Kansas watching the game in the coaches' locker room. He understood better than almost anyone Michael's indomitable will to excel and to triumph: After Michael's rookie season with the Bulls, when he had been named rookie of the year, he returned to Chapel Hill and sought out Williams, the coach he was closest to in personal terms. He wanted, he said, a private word together, and so the two of them left Williams's crowded office, and went to sit on the outdoor bleachers. "What do I need to do to work on my game?" he asked. "Well, Michael," Williams answered, "you were just made rookie of the year—what more do you need?" "No—I know you'll be honest with me—what can I do to improve myself?" So Williams told him to work on his jump shot—if he could improve his jumper he would be unbeatable because no one could drop off him. And so he did, in that summer and in the years to come. Everything with Michael, Williams knew, was the product of design and hard work. He was a great player with the best work ethic he had ever seen, which was why he *always* rose above everyone else in games like this. It was never by chance. So it was that in the final minute, as Williams watched Jordan drive to the basket for the first of his final two killer baskets, he was in no way surprised. Then, as the Jazz came down the court for their last big shot, knowing Michael, Williams had an anticipatory sense of what Jordan was going to do on defense. He could actually see it happening before it happened. He was yelling to his colleagues seated with him, *Look, Look,* as Michael moved on Malone for the steal. Then, after the steal, as Jordan brought the ball upcourt, Williams remembered saying that some Utah defender better run over and double him quickly or it was all going to be over. You forced someone else to take the last shot, he thought, you did not allow someone as great as Michael to go one-on-one for it. But no one doubled him. What Roy Williams remembered about the final shot was the exquisite quality of Jordan's form and how long he held his follow-through even after releasing the ball. It was something that coaches always taught their players because it encouraged the concentration that coaches wanted. Watching him now as he finished his follow-through, as he seemed to stay up in the air, defying gravity for an extra moment, Williams thought it was Michael Jordan's way of willing the ball through the basket. And then it was over. Three of Williams's Kansas players were at the camp, and he, this man who had told friends eighteen years earlier that he had just seen the best six-foot-four high school player in the country, turned to them and told them that he had just seen the greatest basketball performance he had ever witnessed. "And I'm afraid it's the last performance, too," he added.

On the day of the final game, Chuck Daly played golf at Isleworth, a well-known club in Orlando. There he ran into a man named John Mitchell, who had golfed frequently with Michael Jordan in the past. They talked for a few minutes about the upcoming game. Mitchell told Daly he had a bad feeling about it. "I think Chicago's in trouble out there," he said. "I don't think the signs are good. That's a tough place to win."

"Forget it," Daly said, "it'll be close at the end, and then with about twenty seconds left, Michael will have the ball and he'll bring it upcourt, and he'll keep his eye on the clock, and then with a few seconds left he'll go up for a jumper and hit it. The Bulls will win, and the legend will live. It's who he is, and it's what he does."

The next day, after Jordan had played out Daly's scenario almost flawlessly, Mitchell called Daly. "You're in the wrong business," he said. "You should be a seer."

Frank Layden, the principal architect of the Utah Jazz, had thought that this was his team's year, particularly after their annihilation of the Los Angeles Lakers. He thought the Jazz was a better team this year and that Michael Jordan, while self-evidently the best player in the league, had slipped just a bit. Not a lot, but just enough to open the door for the Jazz. But midway in the third quarter, he became uneasy because Utah had not put Chicago away: He did not want to enter the fourth quarter against Michael Jordan with the score close. He watched the final sequence in the fourth quarter with a sickening feeling. First there was Jordan's driving layup. Then Jordan went behind Malone for the steal. Even as Jordan had popped out, leaving his own man, Jeff Hornacek, behind, Layden was impressed, because it was the first time Jordan had done that all game as far as he could remember. A quick pass from Malone to Hornacek and the Jazz would win, but there was no time for that—the arrival of the ball and the steal seemed part of the same moment. As Jordan went up for his final shot, Layden knew even before Jordan released the ball that it was going in, because Jordan did not miss shots like this and because his form was absolutely perfect. As the ball went in, there was little to give solace to Layden, but he did remember thinking, "We were just beaten by the greatest athlete I've ever seen in my lifetime—in any sport."

Dean Smith, retired from coaching at Chapel Hill at the end of the 1997 season, did not have any great affection for the pro game, but he watched if he could whenever one of his boys was either playing or coaching, and he had watched the Indiana series with great admiration. He thought Game Seven of that series was one of Michael's very best ever. He was impressed that a young man who was so exhausted could still provide so much leadership in a crucial game, particularly at the defensive end. In Game Six against Utah, after Jordan made the driving layup, Smith was absolutely sure that Jordan was going to try to make a major defensive play at the other end. "I just knew he was going to try and sneak right over behind him," he later said. So the steal against Malone did not surprise him. What did surprise him was that as Jordan came up the floor with the ball Utah did not double- or triple-team him and make Chicago beat them with a lesser player. Michael, he knew better than almost anyone, lived for moments like this.

That summer, Smith and Jordan got together, and the first thing that Smith had told his star pupil was, "Michael, you're still getting better." By that he meant that he was playing with even greater knowledge of the game every year, with little apparent physical drop-off.

In the summer of 1998, a brochure was prepared for Michael Jordan's fantasy basketball camp in Las Vegas. On the left side of a two-page spread was a photo of the slim, young Jordan hitting the deciding basket against Georgetown in 1982; underneath the photo it said, "Some Things." On the right was a photo of the mature, well-muscled Michael Jordan sixteen years later hitting the deciding basket against Utah. Underneath it was written, "Never Change."

Perhaps thirty minutes after Michael Jordan hit the game-winning basket, Phil Rosenthal, a columnist for the *Chicago Sun-Times*, found Jerry Krause on the floor. Rosenthal got on better with Krause than most Chicago writers and was always intrigued by him, by the complexity of a man who wanted to do good things but who somehow usually ended up offending people. In the great din of celebration that followed the victory among the Chicago people rushing onto the Delta Center court, what Krause said at that moment did not receive a great deal of attention at first, but as it was circulated and recirculated it gradually drew more notice and became a source, albeit small, of lingering resentment among some people close to the team. "Jerry [Reinsdorf] and I have done it [won the championship] six times," Krause said. It was pure Krause, thought Rosenthal: He had always struck Rosenthal as someone who deserved more credit than he got but wanted more credit than he deserved.

32.

Chicago, June 1998

AFTER THE BULLS returned to Chicago there was a huge rally in Grant Park to celebrate championship number six, and that night there was a dinner at Michael Jordan's restaurant, just players and coaches and wives. Everyone was there, or at least almost everyone. Somehow Dennis Rodman had managed to miss it, but that did not surprise anyone very much—every tribe had to have its backward-walking Indian. It was a joyous and noisy evening, because the accomplishment had been so great, and because this was probably the end of the run and many of them were going to be somewhere else next year. At a certain point, the men and women separated, and the men's party became more emotional and more raucous.

The toasts were quite emotional. Jackson toasted Ron Harper and spoke of how much he had given the team, how he had made the transition from great offensive star to defensive specialist, and how when Jordan had returned from baseball Harper went further down in the rotation but fought back. Harper, one of the few people under contract for the coming year, said it was never a problem because he had a $5 million contract to fall back on. "Yeah," said Scott Burrell, "you can fall back on your peg leg." At that point Steve Kerr toasted Harper's agent, a wondrous man who could get so much money out of the Chicago ownership for a one-legged player.

The last toast was given by Scottie Pippen. It was almost certain that he was not coming back, and so everyone sensed this represented the last toast at the Last Dance. He got up and toasted Jordan. "None of this could have happened without you," he said. It was a very nice moment, a great player toasting an even greater player at what was supposed to be the end of a phenomenal run, and the others stood and cheered. The moment seemed to symbolize both the extraordinary nature of what had been accomplished in the last eight years and the fact that the members of this particular team had finally reached the end.

In the fourteen years that Michael Jordan played in the NBA, no one other than a handful of players benefited more from the league's rising affluence and the shift in power from owners to players than David Falk. A relatively junior sports agent in the beginning of the era, Falk was by 1998 not merely the most affluent agent ever to represent basketball players but one of the two or three most influential men in the sport of basketball, a man whose power was said to rival that of David Stern himself. If the legal, economic, and technological changes that took place in the eighties and nineties had been good for players, they were arguably even better for agents. Since he first surfaced as an agent, he had split twice with partners: Early on, even before he was part of Jordan's team, he and Donald Dell split from Frank Craighill and Lee Fentress, and eventually he split off from Dell in what was considered a rather bitter professional divorce. In 1998 he sold his company to a larger firm, one that specialized in producing live entertainment in arenas around the country. The price was an estimated $100 million, and as part of the deal, Falk stayed on to run his part of the company. A press release announcing the sale noted that Falk's old company, FAME (Falk Associates Management Enterprises), "represented an unprecedented 6 first-round draft picks in the NBA, negotiated over $400 million in contracts for its free-agent clients, and negotiated four of the five largest contracts in team sports history."

No one doubted David Falk's ability and intelligence, but if there was one thing that bothered people who cared about the league and the game in the broadest sense, it was whether he had any sense of a larger good, a belief that the greater good and health of the game was still something of an issue. Some felt that there was a danger that the size of some players' contracts exploited the vulnerability of varying franchises and threatened the long-range stability of the league. Falk seemed to enjoy his power as much as his wealth, the ability *not* to return calls and to make other people, particularly owners, feel vulnerable to him. "Be wary of David, and be particularly careful when he starts telling you how much he respects you," an owner once noted. "That's when you're going to either lose your wallet or your franchise player—it's his way of telling you he's more powerful than you are."

In the summer of 1998, as the league and the players' union prepared for a major battle over contract rules and the owners prepared for a lockout of the players, a number of Falk clients, including Patrick Ewing, Dikembe Mutombo, and Alonzo Mourning, had risen (hardly by chance) to positions of leadership in the union. That did not mean that it was simply Falk against the owners, for there were a number of other agents equally active on the players' side, but the issues, particularly the question of a soft or hard salary cap, seemed more about the contract freedoms enjoyed by the elite of the league than the earning power of most players. Certainly a number of people knowledgeable about the NBA saw the lockout as something of a struggle between Stern and Falk, and certainly when David Falk spoke to reporters that fall, he implied that Michael Jordan might be willing to come back for one more season—if David Stern did not block the way. As the lockout continued, it became increasingly clear that Falk was a critically important figure on the union side and that the issues seemed to affect his handful of elite clients more than they did most of the players. In an unusually scathing column the influential *New York Daily News* columnist Mike Lupica wrote, "There may be worse phonies in sports than David Falk, but it is hard to come up with one today." Falk was, Lupica wrote, "a Rasputin coming off the bench" in these negotiations, the rare person who could make a writer root for a sports owner.

As for David Stern, in the late summer of 1998, as labor tensions escalated and a lockout became ever more likely, he seemed to some of his friends to be significantly sadder, if not actually melancholy. It was as if he was lamenting the loss of a once-vital human connection to the league's players, what he thought of as a special partnership with them. He grew a beard, which he vowed he would not shave until a new labor agreement was worked out. At the same time, ever a world-class marketer, he opened a giant new NBA store on Fifth Avenue in New York City, filled with almost any kind of clothing and trinket that could carry an NBA logo. Soon to come are NBA restaurants in a large number of cities.

Stern was very much aware that his longtime critics, people who hated the way the game had evolved in recent years—with its Dream Team conquest of lesser mortals at the Olympic competition, its affluent corporate-sponsorship deals, its big television contracts, its fancy new arenas with their luxury boxes and mandatory deafening noise, its growing separation of players from the media—thought he was being hoisted with his own petard. They believed that the league, with Stern as its master image maker had become too marketing-oriented in its struggle for parity with other major sports. Worst of all, in the process of gaining such stunning success, it had inevitably helped create the attitude among altogether too many players that they were beyond traditional norms of accountability, economically and socially outside the reach and control of society, and that the NBA's phenomenal (and unlikely) growth of the eighties and nineties was not some benign technological and societal fluke but nothing less than their just due. As their salaries had grown at such a remarkable rate in the past decade, so had their separation from reality.

Stern sometimes joked privately with friends that he could be arrested for operating under false pretenses in having for so long minimized the warts and maximized the artistry of the players and the game and above all for having tried to diminish the idea that modern athletes were, well . . . greedy. He liked to talk nostalgically about his early days as a league executive, when he worked with an earlier generation of labor leaders and players, men who felt a sense of partnership and shared objectives. Everyone was learning the hard way that a shared partnership was a good deal more difficult in flush times than in hard times. What bothered him now, Stern told some associates, was that players' and agents' memories were so short—almost no one seemed to remember how recently the league could not get itself on prime time for playoff games.

What made Stern's sadness particularly poignant was the fact that he had never been simply the owners' man, as was so often the case in big-time sports. He loved the players and the game itself and was committed to both, and he always had a broad sense of the larger health of the sport, a health that he believed began and ended with the public's respect and emotional investment in the players. In the words of Bob Ryan, "In that critical period when the NBA was just beginning to become successful, and a critical ingredient of it was the labor agreements which the league worked out with the union, I could as easily have envisioned

David Stern heading the union and Larry Fleisher [the head of the union] being the commissioner—because there was no real difference in their love of the game, and the vision they both had of what they wanted to happen."

That was certainly no longer true. It all changed under the weight of so much prosperity. Revenue and salaries had gone up in staggering increments in recent years, tearing asunder all kinds of partnerships. When Stern came into the league as a relatively junior executive in 1978, the total of all players' salaries was around $40 million; only twenty years later, Michael Jordan made close to that much himself in one year, his team's payroll was roughly twice as much, and the total for the league was around $1 billion annually. That meant that salaries had gone up roughly 2500% in the twenty-year period. But a new generation of players represented by a new generation of agents had little interest in the hoary stories from what seemed like another century about how far they had all come in so short a time. There was no small amount of irony in the fact that the agent who had pulled off the Kevin Garnett deal, which more than anything else united the owners in bringing on the lockout, was Eric Fleisher, son of the late Larry Fleisher, the first head of the union and an agent in his own right, a man once despised by the owners of his day but now regarded as the very model of decorum and fairness by a new generation of league owners and executives.

The negotiations between league officials and owners on one hand and players on the other moved slowly in the fall of 1998. It was a most unusual labor dispute: on one side a large number of billionaires, on the other, countless millionaires. Tony Kornheiser of *The Washington Post* said it was a strike between tall millionaires and short millionaires. And Sam Smith of the *Chicago Tribune* wrote that watching the strike was like watching a collision between two limousines. "One guy gets out of the backseat of one limo complaining that he spilled his glass of Château Lafite Rothschild wine in the collision. And the guy from the other limo gets out mortified that his gold Rolex was scratched." By 1998, the average player's salary was $2.5 million. David Stern himself made $7 million a year, a sticking point for many of the players and agents. And Patrick Ewing, the head of the union, was making $18.5 million this year as part of a handsome four-year contract, a sticking point with owners. The issues seemed less about how much money was being made at the moment than whether salaries would be kept open-ended in the future. Would there be any ceiling on a team's ability to sign its best players? Could some formula be engineered that justly rewarded very valuable players after a certain period of service and yet did not threaten the very stability and balance of the league? Did the issues at stake affect 80 percent of the players or just a small handful of elite players who might be worthy of giant salaries?

The truth was that with the salaries so large and getting larger, the players were inevitably the losers in a showdown like this. They had lost something crucial from their earlier public struggles with the owners: public support. Few young American sports enthusiasts, after all, had ever rooted for the owners or idolized them, and few American youths had grown up in their teens hoping one day to own a sports franchise. The owners had no popularity to lose. The players did. Out of touch with the world around them, strangers even to the better sportswriters who now covered them, encouraged by agents who had both a vested interest in their success and a fear of being candid with them, players rarely enjoyed the kind of dispensation granted a superstar like Michael Jordan. Theirs was hardly a popular cause even among those normally accustomed to taking labor's side in salary disputes.

The owners wanted to put some significant limits on the Larry Bird exception in order to keep it within the agreed-upon boundaries of the salary cap. They were not, they said, trying to turn back the clock or move the pay scale downward, nor even trying to stop the ability of players to enjoy considerable freedom of movement. Instead, they were, in the period after Kevin Garnett's signing, trying to limit the ever-escalating madness—not just of the players but of themselves. If accepted, their offer would bring the total payroll to $1.2 billion in four years, roughly a 5 percent annual increase. Under the old shared-revenue agreement, the players were supposed to get 52 percent of gross revenues, but the annual increase in salaries had been so steep—roughly 15 or 16 percent a year—that the league now claimed that the figure had reached 57 percent and was still climbing. As Kevin McHale said when he finished up the Kevin Garnett salary negotiations, "We've got our hand on the goose which has been laying the golden egg, and we're already squeezing too hard."

That Michael Jordan was special because he had helped change the economics of the game, and that his big paydays had come quite late in his career, seemed to be concepts beyond the comprehension of many of the players. A player named Jerry Stackhouse was a good example, although there were many others like him. Stackhouse had come out of Carolina after only two years in the Dean Smith program, and he had seemed at first to have the potential for true greatness—he was a slasher, someone whose drives to the basket were hard to stop because of his power and speed. He had entered the league with a handsome new sneaker contract and all the other accoutrements of the modern celebrity athlete. But he was still an unfinished player, and he did not improve greatly in his first three professional seasons. In part because his outside shot remained suspect, defenses could drop off him, and that cut down on his ability to drive to the basket. In addition, his posse—that is, his group of followers—did not seem to get along with Allen Iverson's posse, and in time, in his third season, he was traded to Detroit. But he was also heard to say that he was thinking in terms of a big contract, at least $10 million a year: If Michael Jordan was worth $30 million, he said, he was at least a third as good a player as Michael. Who would ever know if that were true or not.

What was probably happening was that after a period of truly phenomenal growth in which all sides had benefited across the board beyond anyone's expectations, and the league had enjoyed a rise in popularity and a general growth unparalleled in sports history—in no small part because of profound technological change—and one great player had become the showcase for an entire sport, owners, commissioners, players, and agents were trying to define what the post-Jordan reality was—reality in a world that had no reality because it was driven, in all ways in the end, by fantasy.

No company enriched Michael Jordan more than Nike or benefited more from his career. Jordan had made around $130 million from Nike over his career by 1998. Given his baseball sabbatical, that averaged out to around $10 million a year from just one company. In turn, he not only made Nike literally billions of dollars, he helped it win a series of epic life-or-death battles against Reebok at the height of the great global sneaker wars. Nike had just begun to slip behind Reebok when it signed Jordan, and the Jordan line changed that equation dramatically. In their first year the Air Jordans grossed an unheard-of $130 million, and the Nike comeback had begun. In 1986, because of a number of earlier quite serious miscalculations at Nike, the Reebok share of the domestic sneaker market was far greater than that of Nike: 31.3 percent to 20.7. Four years later, in no small part because of Jordan's presence, Nike regained the lead and widened it steadily. Among the first companies to learn that Michael's presence both on and off-court was special, and not easily repeated, was Reebok. It had placed a huge bet on Shaq but had not prospered. Shaq, eventually cut loose from his five-year $15 million deal, had become, by 1998, something relatively new in American sports, a free agent in the sneaker world. Not every athlete, it was clear, no matter what the level of charm or ability, could replace Jordan either on the court or on the screen.

Not all of Nike's growth was attributable to Jordan's presence, of course, but in 1984 the company had revenues of $919 million and a net income of about $40 million, and by the end of 1997, Nike's revenues were over $9 billion, with a net of around $800 million, stunning annual growth rates.

Michael Jordan had never become very close to Phil Knight, the most iconoclastic and least predictable of American CEOs. Knight was self-evidently a visionary, but he often seemed extremely awkward socially, and he was by no means the kind of person Jordan felt at ease with. Over the years the small talk between them was quite limited. At one point Jordan came very close to leaving Nike to become a full-fledged partner in a new sneaker company that was going to be set up by Rob Strasser and Peter Moore, former Nike men with whom he felt a far greater sense of connection. The showdown meeting between Jordan and Knight had not been a pleasant one: Jordan had kept Knight waiting for several hours, someone involved in the meeting remembered, and arrived in a hostile, angry mood. He had clearly been primed for battle by the ex-Nike renegades, apparently made aware of how small his cut of the giant pie he had helped to create really was. But in the end there had been too much risk involved, particularly for someone whose career could end with injury at any moment, and the prospect of an enraged Phil Knight using all of Nike's not inconsiderable might and muscle to keep a new Jordan-driven company out of the world's biggest sneaker stores was not something Jordan or Falk wanted to take on. One thing that did come out of those negotiations was a far better cut in the revenues for Jordan, and by the early nineties, very quietly, without too much public fuss, he was making around $20 million a year from Nike.

Nike soon found that its success with Jordan was not lightly transferable to other athletes. To be sure, a campaign based around Charles Barkley had charm and wit and intelligence, in no small part because Barkley himself, whatever the egregious aspects of his behavior, was charming, witty, and intelligent. (Danny Ainge, his onetime teammate, once noted that he had been around a lot of players who were essentially bad guys trying to pretend they were good guys, but Charles was the only person he had ever met who was a good guy trying to pretend he was a bad guy.) But a good many other campaigns seemed to fall flat, most notably a campaign to promote a football-baseball player named Deion Sanders as a kind of comparable cultural hero. That Sanders was a gifted athlete was undeniable, but that he was any kind of cultural icon or even particularly likable to a broad spectrum of his fellow citizens was dubious. What was believed to be his charisma reflected all too accurately the aberrant quality of much of contemporary celebrity: It seemed to stem largely from his willingness to do wildly egocentric self-congratulatory dances in the end zone, as if each visit there was his first.

Part of the problem in Nike's larger public relations, in commercials featuring Sanders and a number of other athletes, was that these commercials tended to reflect an important part of the company culture, that of being mavericks and upstarts ready to take on the rest of the world. After all, Knight started the company in his home, using a waffle iron to make sneakers designed by his old track coach, and at first he had gone from track meet to track meet selling his shoes out of his car. That was still the way he saw himself—a little guy taking on the big guys. The Nike guys liked to see themselves as "outlaws with morals," as one consultant who worked with the company said. So when Deion Sanders poured a bucket of ice cold water on an unsuspecting and fully clothed baseball announcer, Tim McCarver, because McCarver had questioned Sanders's athletic loyalty as he jockeyed back and forth between football and baseball in the midst of baseball playoff games (apparently encouraged by Nike, which paid for the helicopters that got him to and from games), no one at Nike seemed at all upset. In their opinion, Sanders was just a Nike guy doing a Nike kind of thing.

But by the late nineties Nike was no longer a little guy taking on big guys; it was a very big guy whose reach and logo seemed to be everywhere, not just a multinational giant, but more like a huge octopus with tentacles that reached everywhere into the sports world. Its swoosh symbol seemed to be omnipresent, and its power—the immense sums it paid college coaches in order to be the sneaker and uniform provider of choice, caused a great deal of uneasiness among traditionalists in sports. Inevitably, because of its own high visibility and the singular visibility of its athletes, it became the ideal target for critics concerned with the broader issue of the labor practices of American multinationals in poor, third world countries. Charges of unacceptably low pay, unsafe working conditions, and exploitation of child labor were aimed against the company in general, and against Jordan in particular as the Nike poster boy. The Nike factories in Vietnam, where wages were said to be under two dollars a day, came under special criticism.

The furor seemed to bewilder Jordan, who, like other celebrities caught in the name brand apparel game, never thought that the easy affluence his endorsements brought him would or should have that kind of a downside, nor that he would become a target of pickets for allegedly exploiting children in some far-off country. A series of cartoons mocking both Jordan and Nike soon appeared in the comic strip "Doonesbury." There was talk in the spring of 1998 that Jordan might visit the Vietnam factories in the summer with a select media entourage, a trip that would produce great television footage and comparable pro-company spin. By the early fall that trip seemed to be postponed indefinitely.

If there was anyone more bewildered than Jordan by the furor it was Knight himself. Asia had long fascinated him. Long ago he had sensed the rising importance of that region not just as a market but, more important, as a challenger to traditional Western economic hegemony. He saw himself as both pioneer and visionary in a new world order in which the importance of Western Europe declined and that of Asia and the Pacific Rim ascended, someone who had seen the future before anyone else, or at least long before most other American CEOs. He did not respond well to charges that he was less a visionary of the future than he was an exploiter of the present. His early responses to these charges were remarkably insensitive, in no small part because he was so sure that Nike was good for these countries. In time, he made the mistake of granting an interview to Michael Moore, the irreverent filmmaker. Perhaps Knight thought they were fellow mavericks, soulmates who wanted the same thing. The segment, in a film called *The Big One,* was a disaster for Knight and Nike. Among other things it featured Moore inviting Knight to open a factory in Flint, Michigan, one of America's most depressed former industrial sites, rather than opening yet another factory in some village in Asia. In May 1998, realizing finally that much of the world did not see his company or his economic practices the way he saw them, he announced significant changes in Nike's overseas production. Its Asian factories would meet American health and safety standards, and the minimum age for new workers would be moved to eighteen from sixteen. He did not mention any increase in pay for workers, a likely future sticking point.

When Michael Jordan hit that final jump shot against Utah in June, many of the people closest to him, like Roy Williams, believed that it was the final act of a brilliant career. The assumption was that the curtain had at last come down on his remarkable tour with the Chicago Bulls, despite the fact that in some ways he was playing as well as ever, and despite the fact that his taste for the game had not declined at all. He remained as hungry as ever. Still, Phil Jackson was gone, and could barely wait to clean out his desk at the Berto Center. Jordan had sworn that he would not play for a different coach, although there was some evidence that he might overcome that particular vow; even more important, it was unlikely that Scottie Pippen, the most critical of the dominoes now, was going to return. Furious at the Bulls organization, apparently burning with a desire to go elsewhere, Pippen appeared almost certain to depart, thus leaving Jordan unusually vulnerable to the assaults of would-be contenders. The 1997–1998 season had been hard enough and there was ample evidence that the Bulls as a team were wearing down. But a full season without Pippen as his alter ego, even with the ability of the Bulls to add other free agents, might expose Jordan as an aging star able to do only so much on the court.

But the lockout changed all equations. Suddenly not only was all player movement limited, but players could not even talk to management. No one, as December 1998 started, knew when the season might start, or whether there would even be a season. Pippen remained frozen in place, seething with rage at the injustice of a world that, when it was finally his chance to have a big payday, had placed yet another obstacle in his way. The possibility of a short season, however, might, some people close to Jordan believed, affect Michael's attitude and might make him more inclined to come back. Perhaps, this thinking went, Michael and a patched-together team might be able to make the playoffs, where, by the power of his will, he would be able to dominate once again.

If the answer by December was not yet in whether or not he would play again, there was plenty of evidence upon which to make an estimation of what his special role had been in American sports. He was not in any classic sense history's man, not one of those men like Jack Johnson, Paul Robeson, Jackie Robinson, Muhammad Ali, or Arthur Ashe whose own complicated lives and painful struggles against long-established prejudices and racial barriers revealed a great deal not merely about sports but about the history of race in America. He was not the *first* as Robinson, Ashe, and Johnson were, for example, nor did he end up by making a broader and on occasion more torturous political challenge to the white establishment as Robeson and Ali did. The timing of his entrance upon the American educational, athletic, and commercial scene was impeccable and precious little had been denied him because of his race. To the degree that his career reflected anything larger than sports in historical racial terms, it was the willingness of corporate America, however reluctantly, to understand that a stunningly gifted and attractive black athlete could be a compelling salesman of a vast variety of rather mundane products. Not that Jordan had not faced prejudice in this area at first. When he had first started out as a pitchman and David Falk had pushed him at a number of large American corporations, a representative of one multinational had suggested Jordan might be perfect to push Beanie Weanies, a sausage and beans product popular with poor blacks in the South, an offer in commercial terms not unlike the Harlem Globetrotters trying to sign him when he left Carolina after being college player of the year. Falk and Jordan had politely declined, and in that first year, to everyone's amazement, the Air Jordan line had broken all existing records for an endorsed product. With that the gap was breached, and he had transcended racial barriers in the world of advertising. In time he became a record holder in this area as well, for it was almost certain that no American salesman of any color had ever entered more homes, here or abroad, or successfully sold more products; in the summer of 1998, *Fortune* magazine undertook a detailed study of Jordan as a figure of modern capitalism, and estimated that he had helped generate $10 *billion* in revenues for the game, its broadcasters, and for his varying corporate partners.

If he was not a figure from the pantheon of athletes as were such historical figures as Ali and Robinson and Johnson, men whose racial travails were at least as compelling as their athletic deeds, then what the average fan was left with was something less than a series of remarkable images of him as an athlete: a human comet who, miraculously enough, did repeat performances, and whom we were privileged to see flash through the night again and again and again, the most charismatic player ever in his sport—brilliant, balletic, and, of course, fierce. He possessed in the highest proportions all the requisite qualities for greatness; in addition, it was as if some geneticist had injected a magical solution for supercompetitiveness into his DNA, and he came to represent, more than any athlete of recent years, the invincible man, someone who simply refused to be defeated.

He seemed sometimes to be as much explorer as athlete, explorer in terms of going beyond previously accepted limits of what was humanly possible, and somehow by dint of physical excellence and unmatched willpower, pushing those limits forward that much more. That, for the millions who watched him over the years, was no small gift.

And then one day he was gone. The strike was over, and the players went back to work in a strike-abbreviated season. Not only was Michael Jordan gone, but the Bulls were a completely different team too. It was time for a new champion to ascend, and for younger players of significant talent to share a spotlight which in recent years had been focused so exclusively on Jordan and his teammates.

Michael Jordan had not merely retired, he seemed to disappear almost completely. There were few sightings, other than hit-and-run appearances at varying American golf courses. He seemed to luxuriate in getting back some control of his life. He avoided almost all media appearances, and turned down a series of high-profile television offers from various television news magazines. There were some appearances at inner-city schools; one in Washington, D.C., drew somewhat negative notices, a hit-and-run visit by Jordan in which he barely had time to meet with the school's teachers, let alone the students, and at which he had his autograph Xeroxed for the students. He remained a commercial icon and even in retirement there were a number of major advertising campaigns featuring him, including one for a telephone company, where he appeared with a group of cartoon figures and which managed to achieve the unthinkable—the commercials managed to make Michael Jordan look unattractive and uncomfortable. A different series showing him going one-on-one in a series of sports with Mia Hamm, the soccer star, done for Gatorade, was charming and attractive, but it seemed in style and texture so much like the Nike

420 David Halberstam

commercials that it probably ended up selling as many sneakers as it did soft drinks.

The Bulls were no longer the Bulls. Scottie Pippin was gone, signed to a big contract in Houston. There, playing alongside Charles Barkley and Hakeem Olajuwon, he endured a difficult season: Pippen, arguably the best and most versatile transition player in the game, seemed out of place in the more structured, slower Houston half-court set. His frustrations were considerable, and at one point he wondered openly why the Rockets had bothered to sign him if they were not going to exploit his singular talents. Dennis Rodman, volatile and egocentric, his drinking problems more severe than ever, was not resigned by Chicago. It appeared at one point that he had gotten married during the summer to an actress named Carmen Electra, and quite possibly divorced within the same week. His long-suffering agent, Dwight Manley, exhausted by years of nursemaiding Rodman through a series of difficult confrontations, was either fired or resigned, depending on the source of the story, making Rodman more vulnerable to the outside world than ever before. He made a cameo appearance with the Lakers (against, it was said, the ever-wise judgment of Jerry West, who thought Rodman's erratic behavior would be unsettling for so young and unfocused a team). There he played a few games, missed a few games, and soon retired, allegedly to pursue his acting career. With Jordan, Pippen, and Rodman gone, other teams feasted off the Bulls, and they ended up with one of the worst records in the league, and won the lottery—and with it the right to choose first in the draft.

Phil Jackson, clearly exhausted by his tour in Chicago, took the season off, lecturing and reading, and awaiting the many handsome offers from troubled franchises that came his way. The job he wanted was the one in Los Angeles, because he thought the players, particularly Shaquille O'Neal, would profit from the triangle offense. Though the New Jersey Net owners, with a group of talented young players under contract, pursued him avidly, he held back for a time because of the Laker job. It was not a sure thing—the Lakers did not like to pay coaches top dollar, nor did they like to go outside their family for coaching talent. But when it became clear after another disappointing playoff round that the team had not improved at all, and the players, despite their considerable talent, were not meshing well (and the tensions between O'Neal and the infinitely talented but unfinished Kobe Bryant had yet to be resolved), Los Angeles called. Jerry Buss, the Laker owner, aware that some form of order and cohesiveness was necessary for these players, made Jackson the offer he wanted—roughly five years at $30 million. Getting what you wished for was always a dangerous thing in life, but once again it appeared as with Chicago that Jackson's timing was blessed; at the very least, he was arriving at a moment when his gifted young superstars, their frustration level high, would be willing to listen.

Life in the NBA went on without Michael, perhaps a bit more mundane, a bit more about basketball than celebrity than in recent years. The league endured the inevitable drop in ratings sure to follow the departure of so galvanizing a superstar as Jordan. Because of the strike, many of the players arrived in their preseason camps in less than perfect shape, and had less time to get ready for the season, none more so than that noted union leader Patrick Ewing. Because the season was so short, there were too many games in too short a time, and many of them were predictably inartistic. Still, the season represented the perfect opportunity for serious fans to admire the talents of some of the league's younger players. Vince Carter, a former North Carolina player with Jordan-like physical ability (obviously a player whose athleticism had also been suppressed by the coaches in Chapel Hill), caused a great deal of commotion, and he became the Rookie of the Year, as well as the star of many a highlight film.

The best player in the league, it soon became clear, was young Tim Duncan, the forward-center for San Antonio playing in his second season. He was clearly the most talented young player to enter the league since Michael Jordan, and the most complete as well, well coached, emotionally balanced, with a refined sense of the sport, and of the tempo of each game. He could play a strong, surprisingly muscular game around the basket, and yet shoot the softest of shots. There was no weakness to his game, and he made few mistakes. He seemed to be the first big man to arrive in the league since the young Bill Walton, who from the very start played like a coach on the court. Watching him play with such fluidity and intelligence, seeing his remarkable footwork—exceptional for any player, let alone a seven-footer—was sheer pleasure for those fans who had tired of the increasing physicality of the league. When Duncan played head-to-head against Shaquille O'Neal, the difference in the level of their games—despite the fact that O'Neal was bigger, stronger, and perhaps faster—was shocking.

In the post-Michael vacuum, as teams jockeyed for a chance to replace the Bulls as champions, the two preseason favorites, based on their performances in 1998, the Indiana Pacers and the Utah Jazz, both fell short. The Pacers did not notably improve the team that had terrified the Bulls during the '98 Conference Finals; against the Bulls in 1998 they had looked young and deep, but against the surprisingly athletic young Knicks in the 1999 Eastern Conference Finals, they seemed to have aged overnight. In the West, much the same thing happened to the Jazz—it was still a very good team, and no team executed its offense with as much discipline and intelligence. But it was also older and perhaps thinner than some opponents. In the playoffs, it lost to a very deep, very athletic Portland team.

Not surprisingly in the end, San Antonio won the championship. It had the best player in the league in Duncan and two of the league's best big men in Duncan and David Robinson. Robinson, often criticized in the past, deftly tailored his game to accommodate to the greater skill level of Duncan, taking on much of the less glamorous heavy lifting around the basket, and freeing Duncan to be what he was meant to be, a far more complete offensive threat. Like the Bulls, each of the Spurs seemed to know what was expected of him, to stay within his limits, and to play exemplary defense. One beneficiary of their championship run was Steve Kerr, the Bulls' talented outside shooter, who had landed in San Antonio with the dismantling of the Chicago team, and who, though he did not play a particularly large role for San Antonio, might have seemed, a year earlier, the most unlikely of the Bulls to get a fourth straight ring.

ACKNOWLEDGMENTS

I am grateful to the beat writers with whom I worked this past year, most notably, in Chicago, Terry Armour, Lacy Banks, John Jackson, Kent McDill, and Skip Myslenski, as well as journalists Sam Smith, Ron Rapoport, and Rick Telander for their friendship and help. Mark Heisler, from the *Los Angeles Times*, and *The Boston Globe* all-stars, Bob Ryan, Dan Shaughnessy, and Peter May were helpful and wonderful companions, as was Mike Wilbon of *The Washington Post*. Steve Jones, a wonderful, funny, shrewd colleague, has been a pal since I did my first basketball book, and we were able to enrich our friendship during the past season. Among those I worked with I want to single out Bob Ryan in particular. We've been pals for almost twenty years now, a friendship that began when I, a faithful reader of his, wrote my earlier basketball book and he reached out to help me and welcome me into his universe. He is an invaluable and cherished colleague. Not only is he a brilliant and flawless instant reference source ("That was in Game Six of the Finals. There was a minute fifty left on the clock. Bird took the inbound pass. He had injured one of the fingers on his left hand on the previous possession, and so the Lakers were trying to push him to his left. But he knew that they were going to do that and . . ."), but he is also a marvelous ethicist: His passion for the game, for what is right and wrong about it, remains unmatched. Those of us who trail along with him are the beneficiaries of that passion.

In 1956, covering the Melbourne Olympics, Red Smith had written that the two great postwar powers were well represented there, Japan and *Sports Illustrated*, and that is much the way anyone covering sports these days has to feel about ESPN. Its people seem omnipresent and many of them are very, very good, and despite the fact that they work for television, they still go out and work like reporters. Bryan Burwell and David Aldridge were very helpful to me. Anyone covering this era in the NBA is particularly grateful for all the hard work of *Sports Illustrated* and its writers, most notably Jack McCallum, Frank Deford, Rick Reilly, Curry Kirkpatrick, Phil Taylor, and Alexander Wolff. Deford, it should be added, sets so high a standard of professionalism—literary and intellectual—that it makes his work constantly stand out as the touchstone to which others aspire.

Those who have gone before always make the work of those who follow easier, and in this case Sam Smith's *The Jordan Rules* and *Second Coming*, Mitchell Krugel's *Michael Jordan*, Rick Telander's *The Year of the Bull*, Melissa Isaacson's *Transition Game*, Bob Greene's *Hang Time* and *Rebound*, and Roland Lazenby's *Blood on the Horns* made my work easier. In addition, Lazenby published several other books that were helpful for any basketball junkie: *And Now Your Chicago Bulls; The Lakers;* and *The NBA Finals, A Fifty-Year Celebration*.

Phil Jackson's two books, *Maverick* (with the ever insightful Charley Rosen) and *Sacred Hoops*, were valuable. Two books helped me with the Carolina part of the book: Art Chansky's *The Dean's List* and John Feinstein's *A March to Madness*. Dan Bickley's *The Unauthorized Biography of Dennis Rodman* (as well as Rodman's own best-seller, *Bad as I Wanna Be*) helped me with that most unusual young man. Two books on Nike, one by Donald Katz, *Just Do It*, the other by J. B. Strasser and Laurie Becklund, *Swoosh*, were helpful for the Nike section.

For the sections on the Celtics, Peter May's *The Last Banner*, Dan Shaughnessy's *Ever Green*, and Bob Ryan's book done with Larry Bird, *Drive*, were invaluable. Isiah Thomas and Matt Dobek combined on *Bad Boys!*, which helped with the Pistons section; Pat Riley's *Show Time* and Mark Heisler's *The Lives of Pat Riley* were invaluable for understanding the Laker years, as was Magic Johnson's autobiography, *My Life*, and Spike Lee's *Best Seat in the House*, which helped me with Spike Lee.

Finally, Arthur Ashe's three-volume *A Hard Road to Glory: A History of the African-American Athlete* remains an invaluable reference for anyone writing about race and sports in America.

I am indebted to many people. In the Bulls' organization they are Tim Hallam, Tom Smithburg, and Darryl Arata, all of whom were wonderful and very good at what they do. Given the divisions within the organization, they were constantly walking in a minefield and I think they are among the most professional people I've ever dealt with. I've never dealt with a better press officer than Tim Hallam. In David Stern's office I am grateful to Linda Tosi, Marie Sailler, Carolyn Blitz, Russ Granik, Zelda Spoelstra, and Erin O'Brien; in David Falk's office, Mary Ellen Nunes; in Jimmy Sexton's office, Amy Wilson. They all made my life easier. Grace Gallo in John Walsh's office at ESPN helped me again and again as did Chris LaPlaca. The sports information director at Chapel Hill, Steve Kirschner, was very helpful, as was Mike Cragg at Duke.

At my end, my friend Elizabeth Arlen helped me early on with a great deal of research material, as did her friend Nick Dolin; late in the book Brian Farnham proved invaluable in checking out factual material. Bill Vourvoulias at *The New Yorker* saved me from a considerable mistake with his fact checking. My friend Bruce Schnitzer made sure I did not miss Game Seven of the Eastern Conference Finals despite a party given for my daughter's prep school graduation. The Reverend Jack Smith was very helpful in checking any and all theological references and biblical quotations. Over the years Graydon Carter has been the most supportive and sensitive of magazine editors, a genuine friend to a vast number of writers. I count myself lucky that he is both friend and colleague. Philip Roome, in a year filled with crunching deadlines, and the publication of another book of mine in the very middle of the season, got me to the games on time.

At Random House the gifted young Scott Moyers edited this complicated book with enthusiasm and grace under the most intense deadline pressure I can remember, and I am grateful as well for the help of Wanda Chappell, Kate Niedzwiecki, Tom Perry, and Liz Fogarty, as well as Amy Edelman, Andy Carpenter, and Sybil Pincus. My lawyer Marty Garbus, his sidekick Bob Solomon, as well as Fredda Tourin in their office, helped negotiate the ever more difficult professional world for me, and Carolyn Parqueth did a marvelous job of typing my interview notes, thereby making my life infinitely more pleasant.

The idea for this book came from my friend Doug Stumpf, once my editor at Morrow, then at Random House, and now at *Vanity Fair*. At first I was wary of taking it on for a variety of reasons: I had already done one book on basketball; I was wary of writing about someone about whom so much had already been written; I was hardly eager to enter a world where there were so many other journalists working (writers of books, I believe, work best when they are out there essentially alone, and away from the media crowd); and I was even warier of entering a world of such high celebrity where access was likely to be so tightly controlled. In the end I decided to go ahead, as much to write about how the world of basketball had changed in the eighteen years since I wrote a book about the NBA called *The Breaks of the Game* as anything else.

It was a world I liked very much in the past. When I wrote *The Breaks of the Game*, during the 1979–80 season, players still traveled on commercial airlines, and the tiny handful of beat writers flew with them and rode back and forth from the airport to the hotel on the same chartered bus. Over a long season, writers and players could get to know one another at a series of hotel coffee shops, and because of that a great many normal barriers fell along the way. I liked the world of basketball in those days and many of the professionals in it. There seemed to me to be an exceptionally high level of both humanity and intelligence, and many of the better coaches and assistant coaches reminded me of the people I had known when I wrote about politics, back in an era, before television, when politics was a great deal more fun to cover. Out of that book came lasting friendships or at least connections with a number of people I wrote about: Jack Ramsay, Bucky Buckwalter, Kermit Washington, Bill Walton, Lionel Hollins, Maurice Lucas, Steve Jones, and Mychal Thompson.

That world, in such a short time, is largely gone. The separation caused by huge no-cut contracts, and charter flights (no journalists need apply), is almost complete. The players certainly no longer need to talk to reporters; their idea of dealing with the media is about being seen on a brief ESPN video clip slam-dunking the ball. Their agents, comparatively powerless eighteen years ago, and therefore always eager to talk to writers, are far less accessible now; they exist now in an age of virtually complete free agency and have become in many cases more powerful than some of the owners.

The media, too, has changed. Twenty years ago it was a relatively small handful of writers, all of whom cared about basketball and wrote about basketball and made a fair-minded separation about people's private lives and public activities. In today's media, particularly with a celebrity team like the Bulls, the still relatively small number of beat writers who observe the old-fashioned (and often now discarded) codes is vastly outnumbered by people who come and go at will, and work for the new celebrity-driven media—particularly cable shows that are part of the new around-the-clock televised news organizations. These new media people are rarely known to the players, and the players, not without some degree of shrewdness, have come to believe that these people exist, as happens too often now in the world of modern celebrity, to illuminate their rise as they first begin to ascend, but far more important, to chew on their bones when they make a slip or when they eventually begin their inevitable descent. Naturally the players make little distinction between them and the more serious beat writers. None of this is unique to basketball, or for that matter sports, but none of it makes working in any crowded venue like the NBA particularly pleasant. The result is an NBA where there is seemingly more access, but in reality a great deal less, and even worse, a great deal less humanity. While I went faithfully to the locker room before and after the forty or so games I saw, I have not counted what I listened to there as interviews because they did not seem to be interviews to me. In truth, I managed to go the entire season without asking a question in a locker room. Perhaps that is a journalistic first.

In the end, I decided to go ahead with the book as much to write about the changes in the world of sports and what caused them as anything else. What interested me was not just Michael Jordan—the obvious journalistic question of what made him so great an athlete—but equally important, the phenomenon of him. The question I set out to answer was a simple one: When I was a young boy growing up in the forties, the signature figures of American athletics were all white baseball players—Williams, DiMaggio, Musial, Feller—and the NBA did not even exist. How, then, in my lifetime, had it happened that the most famous athlete in the world was a young black man playing professional basketball, who had graduated from a southern school he would not even have been able to attend when I was a young foreign correspondent?

I had dealt with Michael Jordan once before. In January 1992, *Sports Illustrated* had put him on the cover as its Sportsman of the Year, and it asked me to write one of the pieces about him. I had readily agreed; after all, I had watched him over the years with mounting pleasure and admiration. My time with him that day was extremely pleasant, several hours with a bright, articulate, interesting, and interested young man who was very much at ease with himself. What I came away with was his personal elegance, the immensity of his personal comfort zone, and his high off-the-court intelligence. I also thought he dealt with a level of celebrity and scrutiny the likes of which I had never seen before with exceptional grace, treating those around him with singular courtesy. After the article came out, David Falk, his agent, called to say that Michael was thinking of writing a book, had liked dealing with me very much, and was interested in whether I might be a potential collaborator. I answered first that he ought to wait a good long while until he wrote a book, until long after his career was over, that so far I had not collaborated with anyone on a book despite a number of very profitable offers and that therefore I was an unlikely collaborator. But I did not close the door completely; I said I had no idea what I would think in ten years' time.

In the late summer of 1997, when I finally decided to do this book, I called David Falk. I could immediately feel his resistance, and in time that of Michael Jordan. Michael, he said, was absolutely overloaded in terms of his obligations, and too much was being written about him anyway. I could certainly understand that. Clearly cooperation would be minimal. Eventually a deal was worked out between Falk and me: Michael would not see me during the season, but when the season was over, he would see me and give me a fair chance to ask questions. I had a sense that we were talking about two or three sessions of roughly two hours each. That was fine with me. What was far more important was that while I was working on the book Michael never tried to block my access to important people who were close to him and who checked with him as to whether it was okay to go ahead and talk. As such I had exceptional access to a number of uncommon people who were very close to him and who were very helpful to me, for example Roy Williams, Harvest Leroy Smith, Buzz Peterson, Tim Grover, Howard White, Fred Whitfield, and Dean Smith. That kind of access is the lifeblood of any working reporter.

When the season was over it became increasingly clear to me that Michael was going to renege on our unofficial agreement. Somehow I was not surprised. Why he did not see me is intriguing: Perhaps it was combat fatigue for someone utterly depleted after an unusually draining season who was completely media-ed out and commercial-ed out? Perhaps he was competitive as ever and wanted to save his best stuff for his own book? There was that suggestion from Falk, which would certainly not be out of character: Michael competes at everything all the time. Who knows? So I did what real reporters have always done—I worked harder. Although at that point, mid-June, the season was over, and ostensibly my interviewing over as well, I made a point to do one additional interview each day for the next three months even as I was writing, just to strengthen the book. In the end, while I wish we had been able to do the two long semi-promised interviews, I am pleased that Michael Jordan allowed me such easy entrée into his professional world, and as a writer I remain particularly grateful for the last chapter he wrote for this book during Game Six in Utah.

One final word: The world of basketball is very different in the late nineties. It is richer and more brittle. The stakes are far far bigger, the pressures greater, and the daily humanity (predictably) smaller. The rewards are bigger for everyone and that includes coaches—the tailoring is better, the haircuts are better, and the quality of spin in this business as in so many others has gone up dramatically. If there is, for a writer like me, any redeeming part of a landscape that is changing so quickly, it remains the lifers, the assistant coaches, scouts, trainers, and writers who love the game and commit their lives to it because they can't conceive of doing anything else. Almost as much as playing or watching the game, they love talking about it. And while the chance to watch Michael Jordan play night after night at so remarkable a level gave me no small amount of pleasure, in the end it was spending time with the lifers, going out to dinner and talking basketball with them well into the night, that made the past year truly enjoyable.

This is a partial list of interviews. A number of other people I interviewed were unwilling to have their names listed because they continued to do business with some of the principals in the book, and were wary of their names being used.

Mike Abdenour, Danny Ainge, Stan Albeck, Mitch Albom, David Aldridge, Cliff Alexander, Terry Armour, B. J. Armstrong, John Bach, Lacy Banks, Dave Blackwell, Tom Boswell, Bill Bradley, Dean Buchan, Bucky Buckwalter, Bryan Burwell, P. J. Carlesimo, Rick Carlisle, Jimmy Cleamons, Gary Cole, Ron Coley, Doug Collins, Dave Corzine, Bob Costas, Billy Cunningham, Chuck Daly, Frank Deford, Matt Dobek, Matt Doherty, Mike Dunleavy, Don Dyer, Dick Ebersol, David Falk, Lee Fentress, Bob Ferry, Bill Fitch, Chris Ford, Barry Frank, Mike Fratello, Peter Gammons, Howard Garfinkel, Bob Geoghan, Tim Grover, Steve Hale, Tim Hallam, David Hart, Dick Harter, Tinker Hatfeld, Dr. John Hefferon, Mark Heisler, Dick Holbrooke, Lionel Hollins, Red Holzman, Jan Hubbard, Rod Hundley, Ben Jackson, Chuck Jackson, Joe Jackson, John Jackson, June Jackson, Phil Jackson, Rodney Johnson, Arch Jones, Steve Jones, David Kahn, George Karl, Tom Kearns, Steve Kelley, Johnny (Red) Kerr, Steve Kerr, Bob Knight, Phil Knight, Tom Knight, Dave Konchalski, Jon Kovler, Jerry Krause, Arthur Kretchmer, Dave Krider, Mike Krzyzewski, Mitch Kupchak, Frank Layden, Roland Lazenby, Spike Lee, Dr. Michael Lewis, Bob Ley, Luc Longley, Kevin Loughery, Maurice Lucas, Mike Lupica, Brendan Malone, Kent McDill, Jack McCloskey, Kevin McHale, Brian McIntyre, Ray Melchiore, Fred Mitchell, Doug Moe, Mike Monroe, David Moore, Peter Moore, Lester Munson, Todd Musburger, Skip Myslenski, Billy Packer, John Paxson, Paul Pederson, Buzz Peterson, Mark Pfeil, Pat O'Brien, Dan O'Neal, Jack Ramsay, Ron Rapoport, Ahmad Rashad, Bill Rasmussen, Jerry Reinsdorf, Pat Riley, Jim Riswold, Doc Rivers, Jimmy Rodgers, Charley Rosen, Josh Rosenfeld, Phil Rosenthal, Bob Ryan, John Sally, Chip Schaefer, Bill Schmidt, John Seigenthaler, Jimmy Sexton, Dan Shaughnessy, Randy Shepherd, Gene Shue, Joe Silverberg, Howard Slusher, Harvest Leroy Smith, Tom Smithburg, Zelda Spoelstra, David Stern, Dick Stockton, Rick Telander, Mike Thibault, Isiah Thomas, Rod Thorn, Sonny Vaccaro, Mark Vancil, Peter Vecsey, Al Vermeil, Ailene Voisin, Donnie Walsh, John Walsh, Bill Walton, Kermit Washington, Donald Wayne, Tom Weinberg, Rick Welts, Bill Wennington, Jerry West, Howard White, Fred Whitfield, Michael Wilbon, Lenny Wilkens, Pat Williams, Roy Williams, Tex Winter, James Worthy.

ABOUT THE AUTHOR

DAVID HALBERSTAM is the author of sixteen books, including *The Best and the Brightest*, *The Powers That Be*, *The Reckoning*, *The Breaks of the Game*, *Summer of '49*, *October 1964*, and *The Amateurs*. He has received every major journalistic award, including the Pulitzer Prize, and is a member of the Society of American Historians.